THE
SCOTT
STAMP
ATLAS

THE SCOTT STAMP ATLAS

Ludvik Mucha and Bohuslav Hlinka

© Geodetic and Cartographic Enterprise in Prague, 1987
First published in Great Britain by Orbis Book Publishing Corporation Ltd, 1987
First published in the United States by Scott Publishing Company, 1987

Printed in Czechoslovakia

ISBN 0-89487-076-9

CONTENTS

Maps

Text

MAPS

EXPLANATORY NOTES

● Napoli	capitals of states or stamp-issuing countries
● KOTOR	stamp-issuing towns
C U B A	stamp-issuing countries
W a l e s	other territories
——————	frontiers of stamp-issuing countries on land
- — —	frontiers of stamp-issuing countries at sea
....	other frontiers

All maps in this atlas are drawn to illustrate stamp-issuing countries so that they often differ from political maps of territorial units. The maps and descriptions refer in particular to all contemporary stamp-issuing countries given in stamp catalogues and journals irrespective of their international standing and social system. This should be borne in mind when working with this atlas.

U.S.A.

CANADA

U.S.A.

MEXICO

Greenland

ICELAND

CUBA
BAHAMAS

78 74
85 81
82
84
80 76
83

NORW
6 21 5
2 72
18
FRANCE 20
14   19

MOROCCO

PANAMA

VENEZUELA
COLOMBIA
ECUADOR

72
87 75
77 88
73
89
9
86
Fr.Guiana

ALGERIA

63
MAURITANIA   NIGER
48   55
64a
47 46 41a
56 50 52 45
60 NIGERIA
58 CAMERO
44

PERU

BRAZIL

BOLIVIA
PARAGUAY

ARGENTINA

90

PITCAIRN I.

P   A   C   I   F   I   C   O   C   E   A   N

A   T   L   A   N   T   I   C   O   C   E   A   N

ASCENSION

ST. HELENA

TRISTAN DA CUNHA

FALKLAND IS.

SOUTH GEORGIA

BRITISH ANTARCTIC
TERRITORY

A   N   T   A

A

EUROPE

1 ALBANIA
2 BELGIUM
3 BULGARIA
4 CZECHOSLOVAKIA
5 DENMARK
6 IRELAND
7 ITALY
8 YUGOSLAVIA
9 HUNGARY
10 MALTA
11 GERMAN DEMOCRATIC REP.
12 NETHERLANDS
13 POLAND
14 PORTUGAL
15 AUSTRIA
16 RUMANIA
17 GREECE
18 FEDERAL REP. OF GERMANY
19 SPAIN
20 SWITZERLAND
21 GREAT BRITAIN

ASIA

22 AFGHANISTAN
23 BAHRAIN
24 BANGLADESH
25 BHUTAN
26 ISRAEL
27 SOUTH YEMEN
28 REP. OF KOREA
29 JORDAN
30 KAMPUCHEA
31 QATAR
32 DEMOCRATIC PEOPLE'S REP. OF KOREA
33 KUWAIT
34 CYPRUS
35 LEBANON
36 SINGAPORE
37 UNITED ARAB EMIRATES
38 SRI LANKA
39 SYRIA

AFRICA

40 BENIN
41 BOTSWANA
41a BURKINA FASO
42 BURUNDI
43 DJIBOUTI
44 GABON

45 GHANA
46 GUINEA
47 GUINEA - BISSAU
48 CAPE VERDE IS.
49 LESOTHO
50 LIBERIA
51 MALAWI
52 IVORY COAST
53 EQUATORIAL GUINEA
54 RWANDA
55 SENEGAL
56 SIERRA LEONE
57 CENTRAL AFRICAN REP.
58 SÃO TOMÉ E PRÍNCIPE
59 SWAZILAND
60 TOGO
61 TUNISIA
62 UGANDA
63 Western Sahara
64 ZIMBABWE
64a GAMBIA

OCEANIA

65 FIJI
66 KIRIBATI
67 NAURU
68 TONGA
69 TUVALU
70 VANUATU
71 WESTERN SAMOA

AMERICA

72 ANTIGUA AND BARBUDA
73 BARBADOS
74 BELIZE
75 DOMINICA
76 DOMINICAN REPUBLIC
77 GRENADA
78 GUATEMALA
79 GUAYANA
80 HAITI
81 HONDURAS
82 JAMAICA
83 COSTA RICA
84 NICARAGUA
85 EL SALVADOR
86 SURINAME
87 ST. LUCIA
88 ST. VINCENT AND THE GRENADINES
89 TRINIDAD AND TOBAGO
90 URUGUAY

LIST OF MAPS

34

In Europe:
1 GREAT BRITAIN (6.5.1840)
2 ZÜRICH (1.3.1843)
3 GENEVA (1.10.1843)
4 BASLE (1.7.1845)
5 FRANCE (1.1.1849)
6 BELGIUM (1.7.1849)
7 BAVARIA (1.11.1849)
8 SPAIN (1.1.1850)
9 SWITZERLAND (5.4.1850)
10 AUSTRIA (1.6.1850)
11 SAXONY (29.6.1850)
12 PRUSSIA (15.11.1850)
13 SCHLESWIG - HOLSTEIN (15.11.1850)
14 HANNOVER (1.12.1850)

1   Stamp-issuing countries before 1850

14

EUROPE

List of present-day stamp-issuing countries and their currencies

Åland Islands	Finnish currency
Albania	Lek (100 qindarka)
Alderney	British currency
Andorra	French and Spanish currency
Austria	Austrian Shilling (100 groschen)
Belgium	Belgian Franc (100 centimes)
Bulgaria	Lev (100 stotinki)
Czechoslovakia	Czechoslovak Koruna (100 hellers)
Denmark	Danish Krone (100 øre)
Faeroe Islands	Faeroese Krone (100 øre)
Federal Republic of Germany	Deutsche Mark (100 pfennige)
Finland	Markka (100 penniä)
France	French Franc (100 centimes)
German Democratic Republic	Mark (100 pfennige)
Gibraltar	Gibraltar £ (100 pence)
Great Britain and Northern Ireland	£ Sterling (100 pence)
Greece	Drachma (100 lepta)
Guernsey	British currency
Hungary	Forint (100 filler)
Iceland	Icelandic Krona (100 aurar)
Ireland	Irish £ (100 pence)
Isle of Man	British currency
Italy	Italian Lira (100 centesimi)
Jersey	British currency
Liechtenstein	Swiss currency
Luxembourg	Luxembourg Franc (100 centimes)
Malta	Maltese Lira/£ (100 cents/1000 mils)
Monaco	French currency and Monacan Franc (100 centimes)
Netherlands	Netherlands Gulden (100 cents)
Norway	Norwegian Krone (100 øre)
Poland	Zloty (100 groszy)
Portugal	Escudo (100 centavos)
Romania	Leu (100 bani)
San Marino	Italian currency and San Marino Lira (100 centesimi)
Soviet Union	Rouble (100 kopeks)
Spain	Peseta (100 centimos)
Sweden	Swedish Krona (100 öre)
Switzerland	Swiss Franc (100 rappen)
Vatican City	Italian currency and Vatican Lira (100 centesimi)
West Berlin	West German currency
Yugoslavia	Yugoslav Dinar (100 para)

②

2 EUROPE 1985

FINLAND

Onežskoje Oz.
(Lake Onega)

Ladožskoje Oz.
(Lake Ladoga)

• Helsinki

S O V I E T   U N I O N

Volga

• Moskva
(Moscow)

Dnepr

Don

Volga

Warszawa
(Warsaw)

N D

Dnepr

C A S P I A N   S E A

KIA

est

GARY

ROMANIA

Dunav

Bucureşti
(Bucharest)

Beograd
(Belgrade)

Dunav (Danube)

Sofija
(Sofia)

AZOVSKOJE MORE
(SEA OF AZOV)

B U L G A R I A

AVIA

ALBANIA

B L A C K   S E A

GREECE

• Ankara

T U R K E Y

• Athínai
(Athens)

N   S E A

IS.

SEA

sła

1 WEST BERLIN
2 LUXEMBOURG
3 LIECHTENSTEIN
4 ANDORRA
5 MONACO
6 SAN MARINO
7 VATICAN CITY

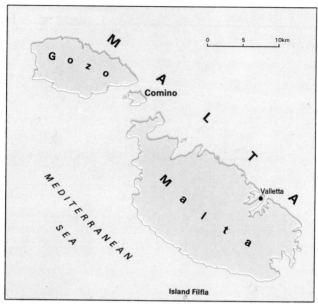

3 Malta

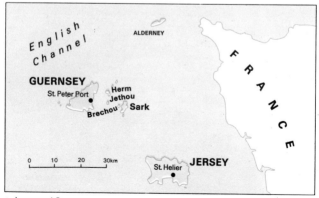

4 Jersey and Guernsey

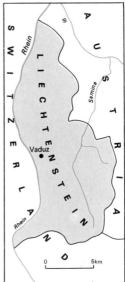

5 San Marino

6 Liechtenstein

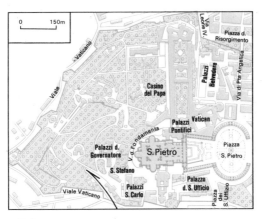

7 Vatican

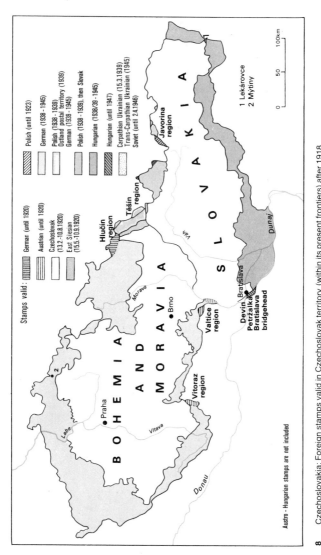

Stamps valid:

‖‖‖	German (until 1920)
‖‖‖	Austrian (until 1920)
☐	Czechoslovak (13.2.-10.8.1920)
▨	East Silesian (15.5.-10.9.1920)

▨	Polish (until 1923)
☐	German (1938 - 1945)
☐	Polish (1938 - 1939) Ostland postal territory (1939) German (1939 - 1945)
▨	Polish (1938 - 1939), then Slovak
▨	Hungarian (1938/39 - 1945)
▨	Hungarian (until 1947)
▨	Carpathian Ukrainian (15.3.1939) Trans-Carpathian Ukrainian (1945) Soviet (until 24.1946)

1 Lekárovce
2 Mýtiny

Austro - Hungarian stamps are not included

8 Czechoslovakia: Foreign stamps valid in Czechoslovak territory (within its present frontiers) after 1918

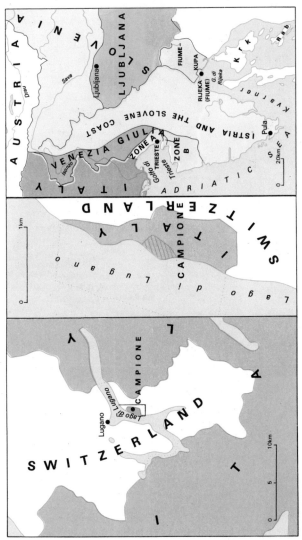

10 Trieste and Istria

9 Campione

11 Germany after the Second World War (until 1949)

12 Germany: Local issues in 1945

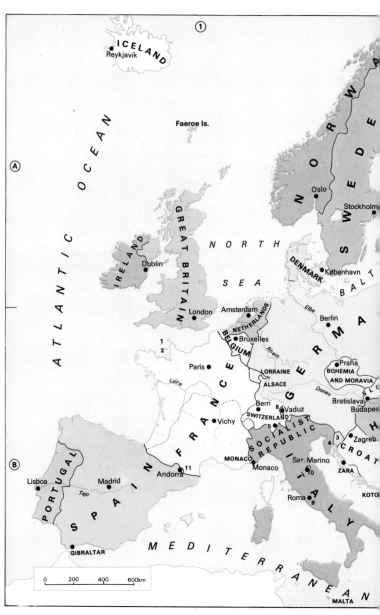

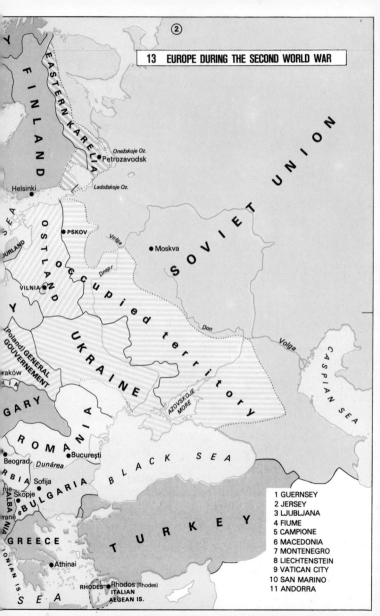

13 EUROPE DURING THE SECOND WORLD WAR

FINLAND

EASTERN KARELA

Onežskoje Oz.
Petrozavodsk

Helsinki

Ladožskoje Oz.

CURLAND

OSTLAND

PSKOV

SOVIET UNION

VILNIA

Volga

Moskva

Dnepr

(Poland) GENERAL GOUVERNEMENT

Occupied territory

UKRAINE

Don

Volga

CASPIAN SEA

kraków

AZOVSKOJE MORE

GARY

ROMÂNIA

Bucureşti

Beograd

Dunărea

BLACK SEA

RBIA

Sofija

Skopje

nje

ALBA

BULGARIA

rane

NIA

TURKEY

GREECE

Athinai

ONIAN IS.

SEA

RHODES

Rhodos (Rhodes)
ITALIAN
AEGEAN IS.

1 GUERNSEY
2 JERSEY
3 LJUBLJANA
4 FIUME
5 CAMPIONE
6 MACEDONIA
7 MONTENEGRO
8 LIECHTENSTEIN
9 VATICAN CITY
10 SAN MARINO
11 ANDORRA

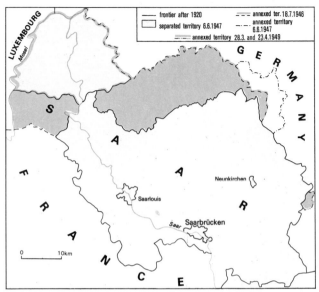

14 Saar

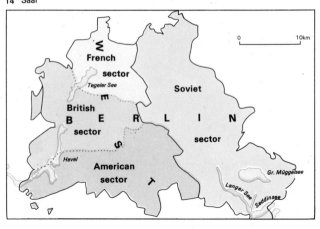

15 Berlin 1945 - 1949

16 The Balkan Peninsula during the Second World War

17 EUROPE AFTER THE FIRST WORLD WAR

17a North Ingermanland

RSFSR

Rautu
Maanselkä
Lipola
Kurjasalo
Raasuli
FINLAND

0   5   10 km

KARELIA

FINLAND

Petrozavodsk

Onežskoje Oz.

AUNUS

Helsinki

Ladožskoje Oz.

1

Tallinn
(Reval)

ESTONIA

RUSSIAN

Volga

S F S R

Rīga

LATVIA

Volga

Moskva

apāja

LITHUANIA
Kaunas

RMANY
ENSTEIN

Vilnius

CENTRAL
LITHUANIA

ARWISZKI

P O L A N D

Dnepr

Warszawa

Wisła

Don

Volga

Kijev
(Kiev)

UKRAINE

L'vov
WEST.
UKRAINE

CASPIAN SEA

KIA

dapest

AZOVSKOJE MORE

GARY

R O M A N I A

București

Bucurest

Dunărea

SKA
BANAT

BLACK   SEA

eograd

16

Sofija

CUTARI

BULGARIA

Tiranë

KORYTZA

15

Komotini

CONSTANTINOPLE

Kerkyra

RFU

GREECE

T U R K E Y

Athínai

SEA

RHODES
ITALIAN
AEGEAN IS.

1 NORTH INGERMANLAND
2 DANZIG (GDAŃSK)
3 MARIENWERDER
4 UPPER SILESIA
5 EASTERN SILESIA
6 LUXEMBOURG
7 SAAR
8 LIECHTENSTEIN
9 ANDORRA
10 VENEZIA GIULIA
11 BARANYA
12 VATICAN CITY
13 KVARNER, ARBE, VEGLIA   see map No. 20
14 CARINTHIA
15 WESTERN THRACE
16 KINGDOM OF THE SERBS,
   CROATS AND SLOVENES

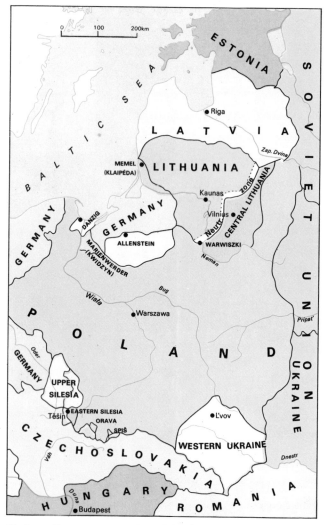

18 Eastern Europe after the First World War (early 1920s)

19 Eupen, Malmédy and Saar in 1920

20 Venezia Giulia in the years 1918-1920

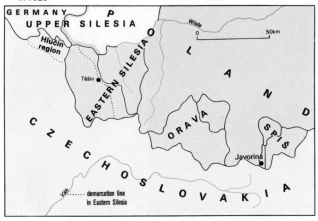

21 Eastern Silesia, Spiš and Orava in 1920

border of the Czechoslovak Republic

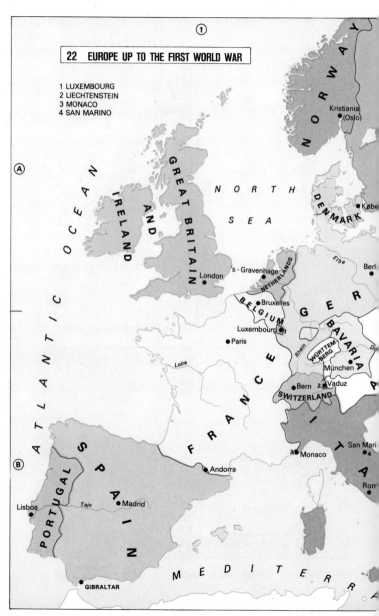

22 EUROPE UP TO THE FIRST WORLD WAR

1 LUXEMBOURG
2 LIECHTENSTEIN
3 MONACO
4 SAN MARINO

②

FINLAND

Gel'singfors
(Helsinki) •

Ladožskoje Oz.

S. Peterburg

Onežskoje Oz.

ckholm

Volga

R U S S I A

Dnepr

Don

A U S T R I A

Dnepr

Wien •

Budapest

AZOVSKOJE
MORE

H U N G A R Y

R O M A N I A

București •

Dunărea

B L A C K   S E A

BOSNIA AND
HERZEGOVINA

Beograd •

Sarajevo •

MONTE-
NEGRO

S E R B I A

B U L G A R I A

Sofija •
Plovdiv •

EAST. RUMELIA

Istanbul •

O T T O M A N
E M P I R E

Cetinje •

A L B A N I A

Tiranë •

PORT LAGOS
CAVALLA •

SALONICA

DEDEAGATZ •

0   200   400   600km

G R E E C E

ATHOS •

Athinai •

Rhodos •
RHODES

V E A N   S E A

CRETE

Iráklion •

ITALIAN AEGEAN ISLANDS

SCUTARI •

DURAZZO •   • TIRANA

CENTRAL
ALBANIA

VALONA •

KORYTZA •

HIMARA •

NORTH. EPIRUS

GJIROKASTËR •

22a   Albania

0   100 km

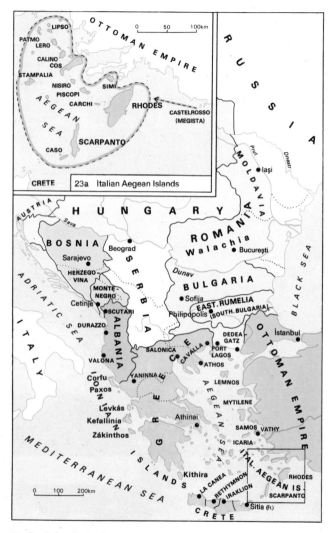

23 The Balkan Peninsula up to 1914

Inset map labels:

OTTOMAN EMPIRE

0   50   100km

LIPSO
PATMO
LERO
CALINO
COS
STAMPALIA
NISIRO
PISCOPI
CARCHI
SIMI
RHODES
CASTELROSSO (MEGISTA)

A E G E A N   S E A

SCARPANTO

CASO

CRETE

23a Italian Aegean Islands

R U S S I A

Main map labels:

Prut   Dnestr

MOLDAVIA   Iaşi

AUSTRIA

H U N G A R Y

Sava

B O S N I A   Beograd

Sarajevo

HERZEGO-VINA

MONTE-NEGRO

Cetinje   SCUTARI

S E R B I A

R O M A N I A

Walachia   Bucureşti

Dunav

B U L G A R I A

Sofija

EAST. RUMELIA
(SOUTH. BULGARIA)

Philipopolis

BLACK SEA

İstanbul

OTTOMAN EMPIRE

A D R I A T I C   S E A

DURAZZO

A L B A N I A

VALONA

YANINNA

Corfu
Paxos

Levkás

Kefallinía

Zákinthos

I T A L Y

M E D I T E R R A N E A N   S E A

0   100   200km

SALONICA
CAVÁLLA
ATHOS
PORT LAGOS
DEDEA GATZ

LEMNOS

MYTILENE

A E G E A N   S E A

SAMOS   VATHY

ICARIA

Athinai

G R E E C E

I S L A N D S

Kithira

ITAL. AEGEAN IS.

RHODES

SCARPANTO

LA CANEA   RETHYMNON   IRAKLION

C R E T E   Sitia (Fr.)

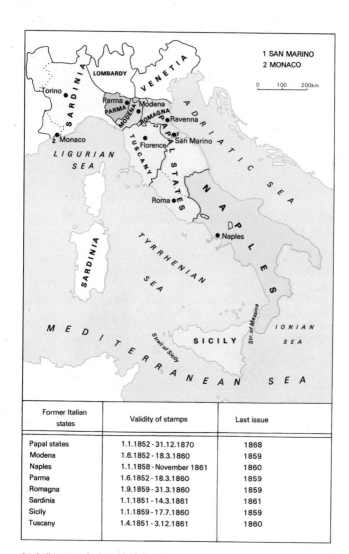

Former Italian states	Validity of stamps	Last issue
Papal states	1.1.1852 - 31.12.1870	1868
Modena	1.6.1852 - 18.3.1860	1859
Naples	1.1.1858 - November 1861	1860
Parma	1.6.1852 - 18.3.1860	1859
Romagna	1.9.1859 - 31.3.1860	1859
Sardinia	1.1.1851 - 14.3.1861	1861
Sicily	1.1.1859 - 17.7.1860	1859
Tuscany	1.4.1851 - 3.12.1861	1860

24 Italian states in the mid-19th century

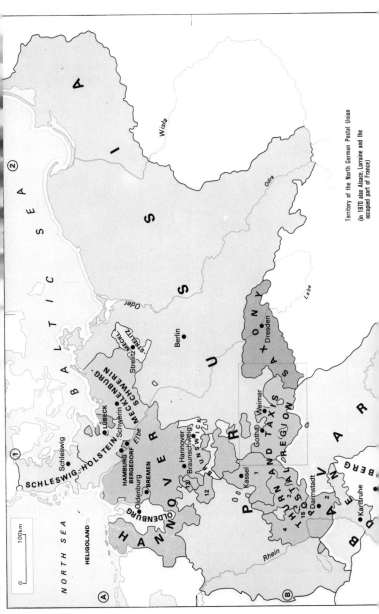

Territory of the North German Postal Union
(in 1870 also Alsace, Lorraine and the
occupied part of France)

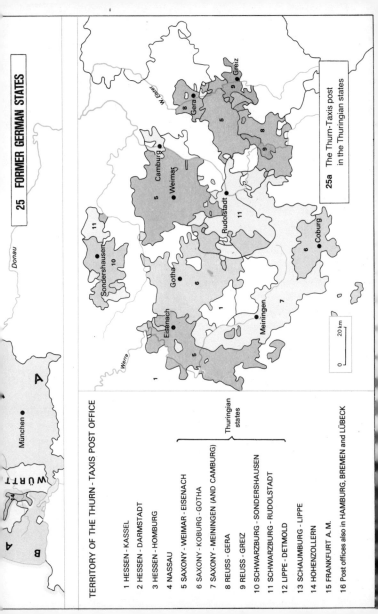

25 FORMER GERMAN STATES

25a The Thurn-Taxis post in the Thuringian states

TERRITORY OF THE THURN-TAXIS POST OFFICE

1 HESSEN - KASSEL
2 HESSEN - DARMSTADT
3 HESSEN - HOMBURG
4 NASSAU
5 SAXONY - WEIMAR - EISENACH
6 SAXONY - KOBURG - GOTHA
7 SAXONY - MEININGEN (AND CAMBURG)
8 REUSS - GERA
9 REUSS - GREIZ
10 SCHWARZBURG - SONDERSHAUSEN
11 SCHWARZBURG - RUDOLSTADT
12 LIPPE - DETMOLD
13 SCHAUMBURG - LIPPE
14 HOHENZOLLERN
15 FRANKFURT A.M.
16 Post offices also in HAMBURG, BREMEN and LÜBECK

Thuringian states

0   20 km

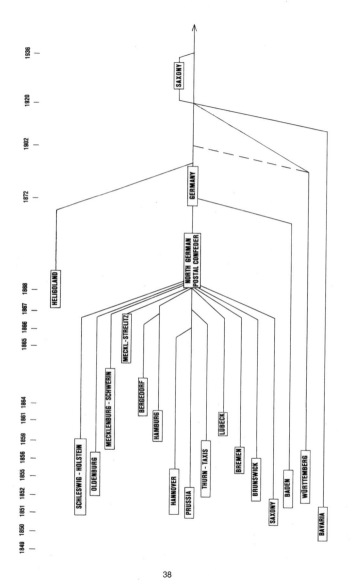

38

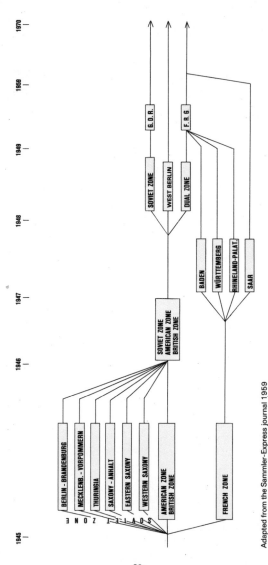

Adapted from the Sammler-Express journal 1959
Territories annexed or occupied during the Second World War have not been included

26 Chart showing the unification and division of German stamp-issuing territories since 1849

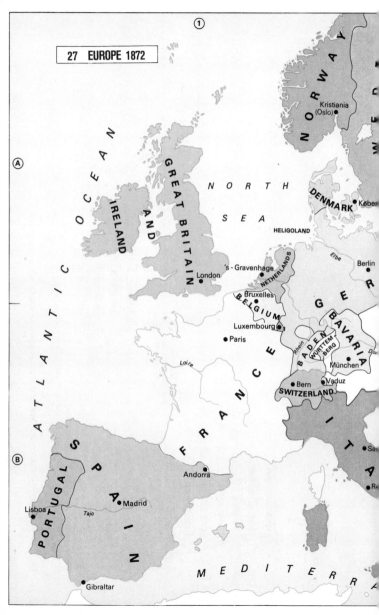

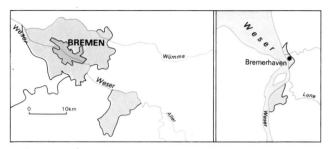

28 Bremen

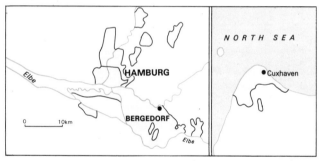

29 Hamburg - Bergedorf

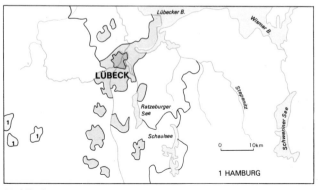

30 Lübeck

42

ASIA

List of present-day stamp-issuing countries and their currencies

Afghanistan	Afghani (100 puls)
Bahrain	Bahrain Dinar (1000 fils)
Bangladesh	Taka (100 poisha)
Bhutan	Ngultrum (100 chetrum)
Brunei	Brunei $ (100 cents)
Burma	Kyat (100 pyas)
China	Chinese Yuan (10 jiao = 100 fen)
Christmas Island	Australian currency
Cocos Islands	Australian currency
Cyprus	Cyprus £ (100 cents)
Cyprus, Northern	Turkish currency
Hong Kong	Hong Kong $ (100 cents)
India	Indian Rupee (100 paisa)
Indonesia	Rupiah (100 sen)
Iran	Iranian Rial (100 dinars)
Iraq	Iraqui Dinar (1000 fils)
Israel	Shekel (100 agorots)
Japan	Yen (100 sen)
Johore	Malaysian currency
Jordan	Jordanian Dinar (1000 fils)
Kampuchea	Riel (100 sen)
Kedah	Malaysian currency
Kelantan	Malaysian currency
Korea, North	North Korean Won (100 chon)
Korea, South	South Korean Won (100 chon)
Kuwait	Kuwaiti Dinar (1000 fils)
Laos	Kip (100 at)
Lebanon	Lebanese £ (100 piastres)
Macau	Pataca (100 avos)
Malacca	Malaysian currency
Malaysia	Ringgit (100 sen)
Maldive Islands	Rufiyaa or Maldivian Rupee (100 laaris)
Mongolia	Toğrög (100 möngö)
Negri Sembilan	Malaysian currency
Nepal	Nepalese Rupee (100 paisa)
Oman	Rial Omani (100 baiza)
Pahang	Malaysian currency
Pakistan	Pakistani Rupee (100 paisa)
Penang	Malaysian currency
Perak	Malaysian currency
Perlis	Malaysian currency
Philippines	Philippine Peso (100 centavos)
Qatar	Qatar Riyal (100 dirhams)
Sabah	Malaysian currency
Sarawak	Malaysian currency
Saudi Arabia	Saudi Riyal (100 halala)
Selangor	Malaysian currency
Singapore	Singapore $ (100 cents)
South Yemen	Yemen Dem. Rep. Dinar (1000 fils)
Sri Lanka	Sri Lanka Rupee (100 cents)
Syria	Syrian £ (100 piastres)
Taiwan	New Taiwan $ (100 cents)
Thailand	Baht (100 satanga)
Trengganu	Malaysian currency
Turkey	Turkish Lira (100 kurus)
United Arab Emirates	UAE Dirham (100 fils)
Vietnam	Dong (10 hao = 100 xu)
Yemen	Yemeni Riyal (100 fils)

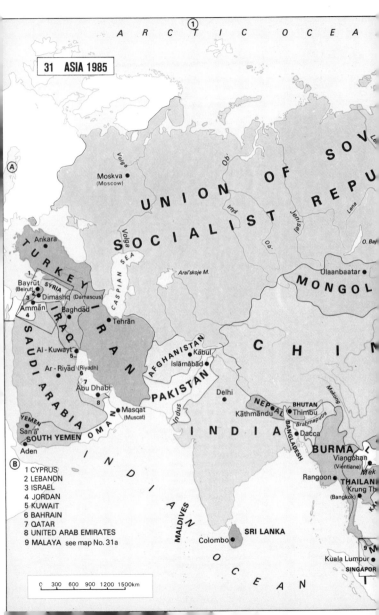

31 ASIA 1985

Ⓐ

Ⓑ

1 CYPRUS
2 LEBANON
3 ISRAEL
4 JORDAN
5 KUWAIT
6 BAHRAIN
7 QATAR
8 UNITED ARAB EMIRATES
9 MALAYA see map No. 31a

0 300 600 900 1200 1500km

ARCTIC OCEAN

Moskva ● (Moscow)

Volga

UNION OF SOV...

SOCIALIST REPU...

Ob'

Irtyš

Jenisej

Lena

O. Baj...

Ulaanbaatar ●

MONGOL...

C H I N...

Ankara ●

TURKEY

Bayrūt (Beirut)
SYRIA
Dimashq (Damascus)
Ammān ●

IRAQ
Baghdād ●
Tehrān ●

IRAN

SAUDI ARABIA
Al-Kuwayt ●
Ar-Riyād ● (Riyadh)
Abu Dhabi ●
Masqat ● (Muscat)
OMAN

YEMEN
San'a'
SOUTH YEMEN
Aden ●

CASPIAN SEA

Aral'skoje M.

AFGHANISTAN
Kābul ●
Islāmābād ●

PAKISTAN
Indus

Delhi ●

NEP...
Kāthmāndu ●
Thimbu ●
BHUTAN

I N D I A

Brahmaputra
BANGLADESH
Dacca ●

BURMA
Viangchan (Vientiane)
Rangoon ●
THAILAN...
Krung Th... (Bangkòk)
Mekong
Mek...

MALDIVES

SRI LANKA
Colombo ●

INDIAN OCEAN

Kuala Lumpur ●
SINGAPOR...

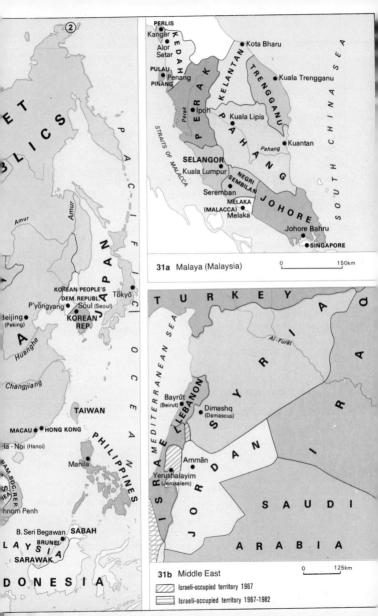

31a Malaya (Malaysia)

0   150km

31b Middle East

Israeli-occupied territory 1967

Israeli-occupied territory 1967-1982

0   125km

32 Cyprus including Northern Cyprus (Turkish administration)

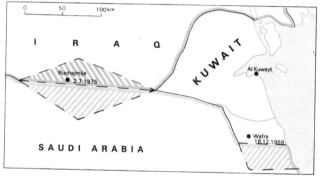

33 Division of neutral zones on the Arabian peninsula

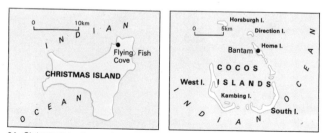

34 Christmas Island

35 Cocos Islands

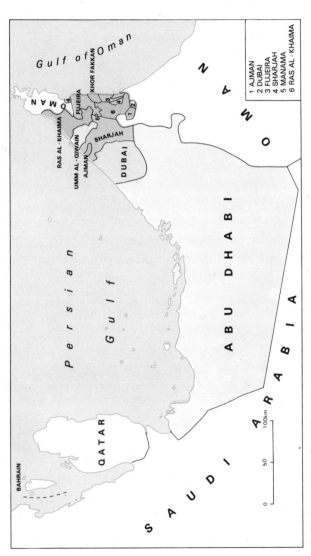

Gulf of Oman

1	AJMAN
2	DUBAI
3	FUJEIRA
4	SHARJAH
5	MANAMA
6	RAS AL - KHAIMA

KHOR FAKKAN

OMAN

FUJEIRA

OMAN

RAS AL - KHAIMA

UMM AL - QIWAIN

AJMAN

SHARJAH

DUBAI

ABU DHABI

Persian Gulf

BAHRAIN

QATAR

SAUDI ARABIA

0   50   100km

36 Trucial States (United Arab Emirates)

47

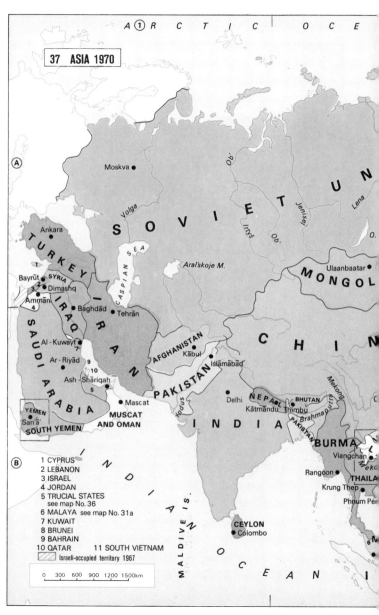

ARCTIC OCE

37 ASIA 1970

A

Moskva ●

SOVIET UN

MONGOL

CHIN

Ulaanbaatar ●

TURKEY

Ankara ●

Bayrūt
SYRIA
Dimashq ●
Ammān ●
Baghdād ●
IRAQ
Tehrān ●

SAUDI ARABIA

Al-Kuwayt ●

Ar-Riyād ●

Ash-Shāriqah

Mascat ●

IRAN

AFGHANISTAN

Kābul ●

Islāmābād ●

PAKISTAN

MUSCAT AND OMAN

YEMEN
San'a ●
SOUTH YEMEN

Delhi ●

NEPAL
Kātmāndu ●
Thimbu
BHUTAN

INDIA

PAKISTAN

BURMA

Viangchan ●

Rangoon ●

THAILA

Krung Thep ●

Phnum Pén

B

1 CYPRUS
2 LEBANON
3 ISRAEL
4 JORDAN
5 TRUCIAL STATES
  see map No. 36
6 MALAYA see map No. 31a
7 KUWAIT
8 BRUNEI
9 BAHRAIN
10 QATAR   11 SOUTH VIETNAM

▧ Israeli-occupied territory 1967

CEYLON
Colombo ●

MALDIVE IS.

INDIAN OCEAN

0 300 600 900 1200 1500km

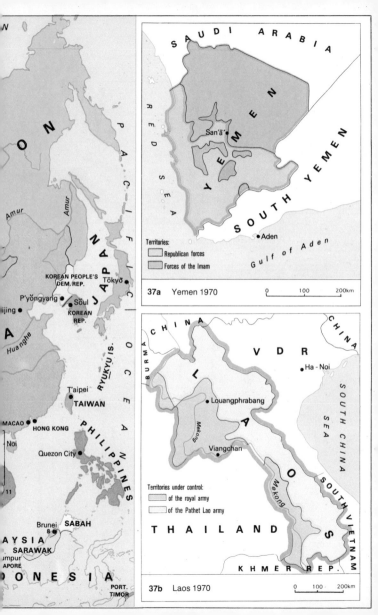

37a Yemen 1970

Territories:
- Republican forces
- Forces of the Imam

0   100   200km

37b Laos 1970

Territories under control:
- of the royal army
- of the Pathet Lao army

0   100   200km

KOREAN PEOPLE'S DEM. REP.
P'yŏngyang
Sŏul
KOREAN REP.
Tōkyō
Beijing
Huanghe
Amur
Amur
T'aipei
TAIWAN
RYUKYU IS.
MACAO
HONG KONG
PHILIPPINES
Quezon City
Brunei
SABAH
SARAWAK
AYSIA
umpur
APORE
DONESIA
PORT. TIMOR

SAUDI ARABIA
YEMEN
San'ā
RED SEA
SOUTH YEMEN
Aden
Gulf of Aden

CHINA
V D R
Ha-Noi
BURMA
CHINA
L
Louangphrabang
A
Viangchan
Mekong
Mekong
O
SOUTH CHINA SEA
SOUTH VIETNAM
S
THAILAND
KHMER REP.

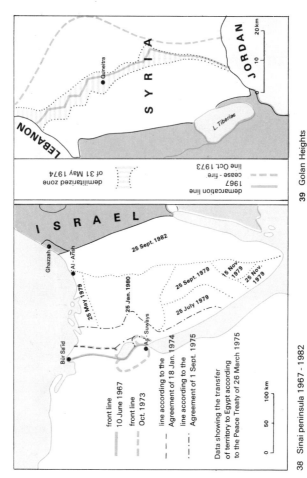

39 Golan Heights

demarcation line 1967

cease-fire line Oct. 1973

demilitarized zone of 31 May 1974

QUneitra

SYRIA

LEBANON

JORDAN

L. Tiberias

10   20 km

front line 10 June 1967

front line Oct. 1973

line according to the Agreement of 18 Jan. 1974

line according to the Agreement of 1 Sept. 1975

Data showing the transfer of territory to Egypt according to the Peace Treaty of 26 March 1975

0   50   100 km

ISRAEL

Ghazzah

Al-Arīsh

Būr Saʿīd

Aṣ-Suways

25 May 1979

25 Jan. 1980

25 Sept. 1982

25 Sept. 1979

25 July 1979

15 Nov. 1979

25 Nov. 1979

38 Sinai peninsula 1967 - 1982

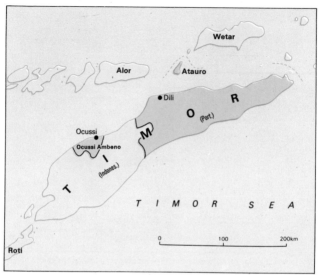

40 Timor

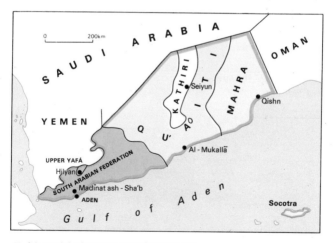

41 Aden and the former states of South Yemen

42 China: Foreign post offices and other provincial stamp-issuing territories

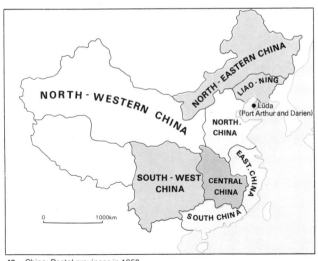

43 China: Postal provinces in 1950

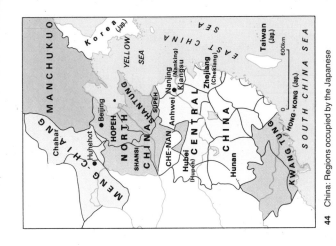

44 China: Regions occupied by the Japanese

45 The Levant

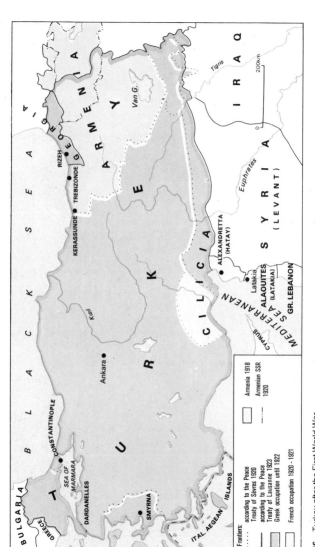

Frontiers:

- `·····` according to the Peace Treaty of Sèvres 1920
- `———` according to the Peace Treaty of Lausanne 1923
- (grey) Greek occupation until 1922
- (white) French occupation 1920–1921

- `□` Armenia 1918
- `—·—·—` Armenian SSR 1920

46 Turkey after the First World War

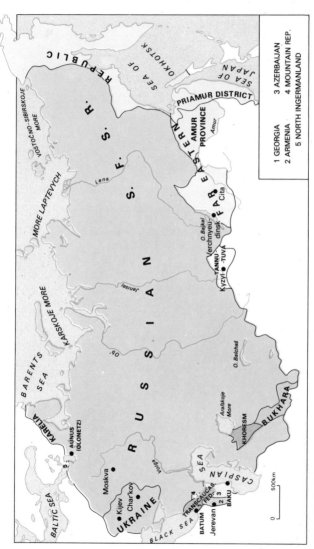

47 The Soviet Union at the time of its foundation

1 GEORGIA   3 AZERBAIJAN
2 ARMENIA   4 MOUNTAIN REP.
      5 NORTH INGERMANLAND

R. S. F. S. R.

EASTERN SIBERIAN REPUBLIC

SEA OF OKHOTSK

SEA OF JAPAN

PRIAMUR DISTRICT

AMUR PROVINCE

Amur

FAR EASTERN REPUBLIC

Cita

Verchnyeu-dinsk

O. Bajkal

TANNU-TUVA

Kyzyl

VOSTOČNO-SIBIRSKOJE MORE

Lena

MORE LAPTEVYCH

Jenisej

Ob'

O. Balchaš

KARSKOJE MORE

BARENTS SEA

Aralskoje More

KHORESM

BUKHARA

KARELIA

AUNUS (OLONETZ)

BALTIC SEA

Moskva

Kijev

Char'kov

UKRAINE

Volga

CASPIAN SEA

BAKU

TRANSCAUCAS. FED.

BATUM

Jerevan

BLACK SEA

0   500km

55

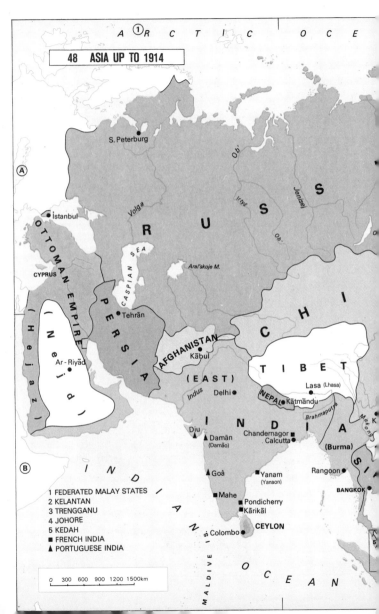

48 ASIA UP TO 1914

A R C T I C   O C E

S. Peterburg

RUSS

Volga

Ob'

Irgš

Jenisej

Ob'

CASPIAN SEA

Aral'skoje M.

İstanbul

OTTOMAN EMPIRE

CYPRUS

(Hejaz)

(Nejd)

Ar - Riyād

PERSIA

Tehrān

AFGHANISTAN

Kābul

(EAST)

Indus

Delhi

CHI

TIBET

Lasa (Lhasa)

NEPAL Kātmāndu

INDIA

Brahmaputra

Mekong

Diu

Damān
(Damão)

Chandernagor

Calcutta

(Burma)

Goâ

Yanam
(Yanaon)

Rangoon

SIA

Mahe

Pondicherry

Kārikāl

CEYLON

BANGKOK

Colombo

INDIAN

1 FEDERATED MALAY STATES
2 KELANTAN
3 TRENGGANU
4 JOHORE
5 KEDAH
■ FRENCH INDIA
▲ PORTUGUESE INDIA

MALDIVE IS.

OCEAN

0 300 600 900 1200 1500km

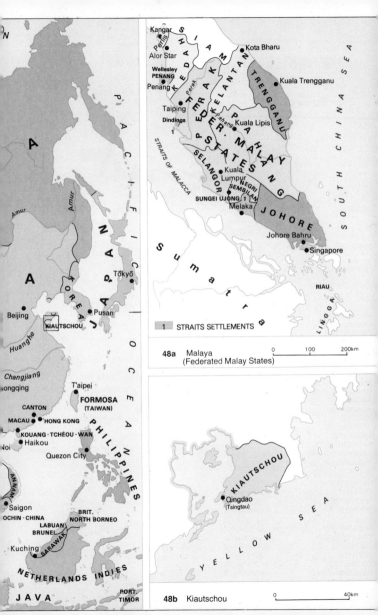

Kangar
Alor Star
Kota Bharu
KEDAH
PERLIS
S
H
I
A
M
Kuala Trengganu
Wellesley PENANG
Penang
Parak
PERAK
TRENGGANU
KELANTAN
Taiping
Dindings
1
FEDER.
MALAY
Kuala Lipis
Pahang
STATES
PAHANG
SELANGOR
Kuala Lumpur
NEGRI
SEMBILAN
STRAITS OF MALACCA
SUNGEI UJONG
1
Melaka
JOHORE
Johore Bahru
Singapore
RIAU
Sumatra
SOUTH CHINA SEA
LINGGA

1   STRAITS SETTLEMENTS

48a   Malaya
(Federated Malay States)

0   100   200km

N
A
A
Amur
Amur
PACIFIC
KOREA
JAPAN
Tōkyō
Beijing
Pusan
KIAUTSCHOU
Huanghe
OCEAN
Changjiang
ongqing
T'aipei
FORMOSA
(TAIWAN)
CANTON
MACAU   HONG KONG
KOUANG-TCHÉOU-WAN
loi   Haikou
PHILIPPINES
Quezon City
AN-NAM
Saigon
OCHIN-CHINA
BRIT.
NORTH BORNEO
LABUAN
BRUNEI
Kuching
SARAWAK
NETHERLANDS INDIES
JAVA
PORT.
TIMOR

KIAUTSCHOU
Qingdao
(Tsingtau)
YELLOW SEA

48b   Kiautschou

0   40km

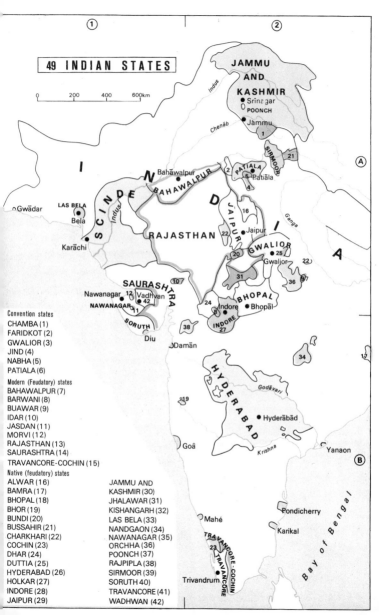

49 INDIAN STATES

0   200   400   600km

JAMMU AND KASHMIR

Srinagar
POONCH
Jammu
SIRMOOR

I N D E

SCINDE

LAS BELA
Bela
Gwādar

Indus
Bahāwalpur
BAHAWALPUR

PATIALA
Patiāla

Karāchi

RAJASTHAN

JAIPUR
Jaipur

Ganga

GWALIOR
Gwalior

A

SAURASHTRA
Nawanagar Vadhvan
NAWANAGAR
SORUTH
Diu

BHOPAL
Indore Bhopāl
INDORE

Damān

HYDERABAD

Godāvari

Goâ
Krishna
Hyderābad

Yanaon

B

Mahé
TRAVANCORE-COCHIN
TRAVANCORE
Trivandrum

Pondicherry
Karikal

Bay of Bengal

Convention states
CHAMBA (1)
FARIDKOT (2)
GWALIOR (3)
JIND (4)
NABHA (5)
PATIALA (6)

Modern (Feudatory) states
BAHAWALPUR (7)
BARWANI (8)
BUAWAR (9)
IDAR (10)
JASDAN (11)
MORVI (12)
RAJASTHAN (13)
SAURASHTRA (14)
TRAVANCORE-COCHIN (15)

Native (feudatory) states
ALWAR (16)
BAMRA (17)
BHOPAL (18)
BHOR (19)
BUNDI (20)
BUSSAHIR (21)
CHARKHARI (22)
COCHIN (23)
DHAR (24)
DUTTIA (25)
HYDERABAD (26)
HOLKAR (27)
INDORE (28)
JAIPUR (29)

JAMMU AND
KASHMIR (30)
JHALAWAR (31)
KISHANGARH (32)
LAS BELA (33)
NANDGAON (34)
NAWANAGAR (35)
ORCHHA (36)
POONCH (37)
RAJPIPLA (38)
SIRMOOR (39)
SORUTH 40)
TRAVANCORE (41)
WADHWAN (42)

AFRICA

List of present-day stamp-issuing countries and their currencies

Algeria	Algerian Dinar (100 centimes)
Angola	Kwanza (100 lwei)
Ascension	British currency
Azores	Portuguese currency
Benin	West African Franc CFA (100 centimes)
Bophuthatswana	South African currency
Botswana	Pula (100 thebe)
Burkina Faso	West African Franc CFA (100 centimes)
Burundi	Burundi Franc (100 centimes)
Cameroon	Central African Franc CFA (100 centimes)
Cape Verde Islands	Cape Verde Escudo (100 centavos)
Central African Republic	Central African Franc CFA (100 centimes)
Chad	Central African Franc CFA (100 centimes)
Ciskei	South African currency
Comoro Islands	Comoro Franc (100 centimes)
Congo	Central African Franc CFA (100 centimes)
Djibouti	Djibouti Franc (100 centimes)
Egypt	Egyptian £ (100 piastres = 1000 milliemes)
Equatorial Guinea	Ekuele (100 centimes)
Ethiopia	Birr (100 cents)
Gabon	Central African Franc CFA (100 centimes)
Gambia	Dalasi (100 butut)
Ghana	Cedi (100 pesewas)
Guinea	Syli (100 cauris)
Guinea-Bissau	Guinea-Bissau Peso (100 centavos)
Ivory Coast	West African Franc CFA (100 centimes)
Kenya	Kenyan Shilling (100 cents)
Lesotho	Loti (100 lisente)
Liberia	American currency and Liberian $ (100 cents)
Libya	Libyan Dinar (1000 dirhams)
Madeira	Portuguese currency
Malagasy Republic	Malagasy Franc (100 centimes)
Malawi	Malawi Kwacha (100 tambala)
Mali	Mali Franc (100 centimes)
Mauritania	Ouguiya (5 khoums)
Mauritius	Mauritian Rupee (100 cents)
Morocco	Moroccan Dirham (100 centimes)
Mozambique	Metical (100 centavos)
Namibia	see SW Africa
Niger	West African Franc CFA (100 centimes)
Nigeria	Naira (100 kobo)
Outer Seychelles	Seychelles currency
Rwanda	Rwanda Franc (100 centimes)
St. Helena	St. Helena £ (100 pence)
São Tomé e Príncipe	Dobra (100 centavos)
Senegal	West African Franc CFA (100 centimes)
Seychelles	Seychelles Rupee (100 cents)
Sierra Leone	Leone (100 cents)
Somalia	Somali Shilling (100 cents)
South Africa	Rand (100 cents)
South West Africa	South African currency
Sudan	Sudanese £ (100 piastres)
Swaziland	Lilangeni (100 cents)
Tanzania	Tanzanian Shilling (100 cents)
Togo	West African Franc CFA (100 centimes)
Transkei	South African currency
Tristan da Cunha	British currency
Tunisia	Tunisian Dinar (1000 millimes)
Uganda	Ugandan Shilling (100 cents)
Upper Volta	see Burkina Faso
Venda	South African currency
Zaïre	Zaïre (100 makuta = 10000 sengi)
Zambia	Zambian Kwacha (100 ngwee)
Zimbabwe	Zimbabwe $ (100 cents)

Note: CFA = Communauté Financière Africaine

RRANEAN SEA

Al - Qāhirah
(Cairo)

EGYPT

Nile

RED SEA

CHAD

SUDAN

Al - Khurtûm
(Khartoum)

White Nile

Blue Nile

ETHIOPIA

DJIBOUTI
Djibouti

Addis Ababa

CENTRAL
FRICAN REPUBLIC
Bangui

Congo (Zaïre)

S O M A L I A

UGANDA
Kampala

Kigali
RWANDA
BURUNDI
Bujumbura

KENYA
Nairobi

L. Victoria

Mogadiscio

ZAÏRE

Kasai

TANZANIA

L. Tanganyika

Zanzibar
Dar es - Salaam

SEYCHELLES
Victoria

I N D I A N

C O M O R O S

Mayotte

OLA

ZAMBIA

Zambezi

Lusaka

MALAWI

L. Malawi

Lilongwe

Zambezi

MOZAMBIQUE

Harare

ZIMBABWE

Antananarivo

MALAGASY REPUBLIC

O C E A N

Port Louis
St.-Denis
MAURITIUS
Réunion
(Fr.)

Windhoek

BOTSWANA

VENDA

Gaborone
Mmabatho

BOPHUTHATSWANA

RICA

OUTH AFRICA

SWAZILAND

Maputo
Mbabane
Pretoria

Maseru
LESOTHO

CISKEI

TRANSKEI

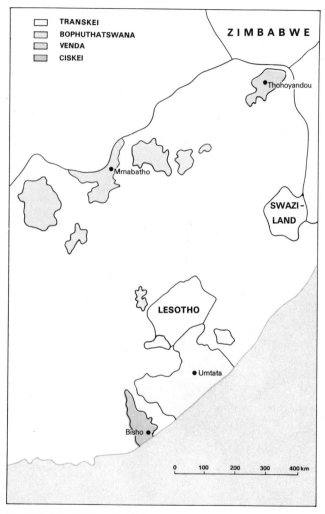

51 South African Bantustans which issue their own stamps

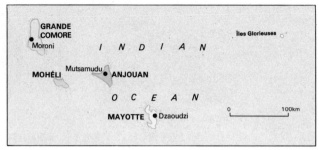

52 Comoro Islands

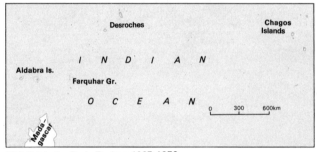

53 British Indian Ocean Territory 1967-1976

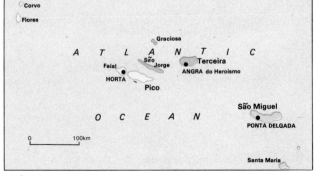

54 Azores

63

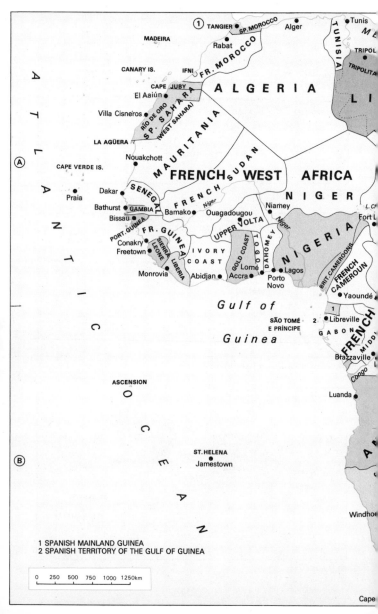

① TANGIER
MADEIRA
SP.MOROCCO
Alger
Tunis
Rabat
TUNISIA
TRIPOL
CANARY IS.
IFNI
FR. MOROCCO
TRIPOLITA
CAPE JUBY
El Aaiún
ALGERIA
LI
Villa Cisneros
RÍO DE ORO
SP. SAHARA
(WEST SAHARA)
LA AGÜERA
MAURITANIA
Nouakchott
CAPE VERDE IS.
FRENCH WEST AFRICA
SUDAN
A
Praia
Dakar
SENEGAL
Niger
NIGER
FRENCH
Niamey
L.C
Bathurst GAMBIA
Bamako
Ouagadougou
Fort L
Bissau
PORT.GUINEA
FR. GUINEA
UPPER VOLTA
Niger
NIGERIA
Conakry
SIERRA
LEONE
IVORY
COAST
GOLD COAST
TOGO
DAHOMEY
BRIT CAMEROONS
FRENCH
CAMEROUN
Freetown
LIBERIA
Monrovia
Abidjan
Accra
Lomé
Porto
Novo
Lagos
Yaoundé

Gulf of
SÃO TOMÉ
E PRÍNCIPE
1
2 Libreville
GABON
FRENCH

Guinea
Brazzaville
Congo
MIDD

Luanda

ASCENSION
O
C
E
A
N

ST.HELENA
Jamestown

A

Windhoe

1 SPANISH MAINLAND GUINEA
2 SPANISH TERRITORY OF THE GULF OF GUINEA

0   250   500   750   1000 1250km

Cape

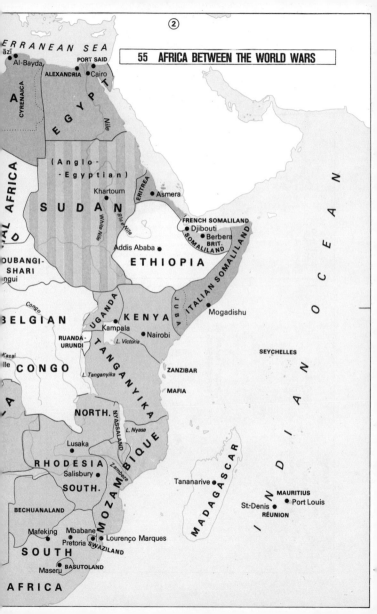

55 AFRICA BETWEEN THE WORLD WARS

ERRANEAN SEA

azi

Al-Bayda

PORT SAID

A

ALEXANDRIA • Cairo

CYRENAICA

E G Y P T

Nile

AL AFRICA

(Anglo-
-Egyptian)

Khartoum

ERITREA

Asmera

FRENCH SOMALILAND

Djibouti

Berbera

BRIT.

SOMALILAND

S U D A N

White Nile

Blue Nile

OUBANGI-
SHARI

ngui

Addis Ababa •

E T H I O P I A

ITALIAN SOMALILAND

JUBA

Mogadishu

BELGIAN

UGANDA

K E N Y A

Kampala

Nairobi •

Congo

RUANDA-
URUNDI

L. Victoria

Kasai

lle

C O N G O

TANGANYIKA

L. Tanganyika

ZANZIBAR

MAFIA

SEYCHELLES

I
N
D
I
A
N

O
C
E
A
N

NORTH.

NYASSALAND

L. Nyasa

M
O
Z
A
M
B
I
Q
U
E

Lusaka

Zambeze

R H O D E S I A

Salisbury •

SOUTH.

Tananarive •

M
A
D
A
G
A
S
C
A
R

MAURITIUS

St-Denis •

• Port Louis

RÉUNION

BECHUANALAND

Mafeking •

Mbabane •

Lourenço Marques

Pretoria • SWAZILAND

S O U T H

Maseru •

BASUTOLAND

A F R I C A

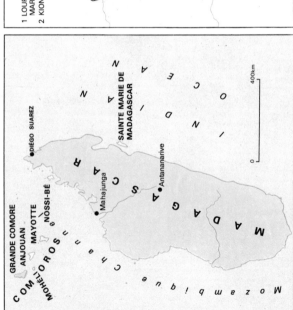

56 Madagascar and the Comoro Islands

57 Mozambique

56 Madagascar and the Comoro Islands

GRANDE COMORE
ANJOUAN
MAYOTTE
MOHÉLI
NOSSI-BÉ
C O M O R O S

M A D A G A S C A R

•DIÉGO SUAREZ

Mahajunga

SAINTE MARIE DE MADAGASCAR

•Antananarive

Mozambique Channel

I N D I A N   O C E A N

0   400km

57 Mozambique

1 LOURENÇO MARQUES
2 KIONGA

N Y A S S A
MOZAMBIQUE
•Moçambique
Vila Cabral

L. Nyassa

Z A M B E Z I A
QUELIMANE
Quelimane

T E T E
•Tete
Zambezi

MOZAMBIQUE COMPANY

INHAMBANE
•Inhambane

Limpopo

•Lourenço Marques
1

Ruvuma
2

I N D I A N   O C E A N

0   400km

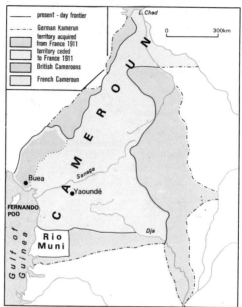

58 The Cameroons after 1884

Legend:
- present - day frontier
- German Kamerun
- territory acquired from France 1911
- territory ceded to France 1911
- British Cameroons
- French Cameroun

L. Chad

0   300km

C A M E R O U N

Buea

Yaoundé

Sanaga

FERNANDO POO

Gulf of Guinea

Rio Muni

Dja

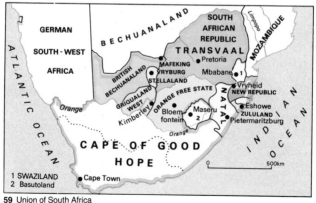

59 Union of South Africa

GERMAN SOUTH - WEST AFRICA

BECHUANALAND

SOUTH AFRICAN REPUBLIC

TRANSVAAL

MOZAMBIQUE

Limpopo

MAFEKING
VRYBURG
STELLALAND

Pretoria

BRITISH BECHUANALAND

Mbabane

GRIQUALAND WEST

ORANGE FREE STATE

Vryheid
NEW REPUBLIC

ATLANTIC OCEAN

Orange

Kimberley

Bloemfontein

Maseru
2

NATAL

Eshowe
ZULULAND
Pietermaritzburg

INDIAN OCEAN

Orange

CAPE OF GOOD HOPE

1 SWAZILAND
2 Basutoland

Cape Town

0   500km

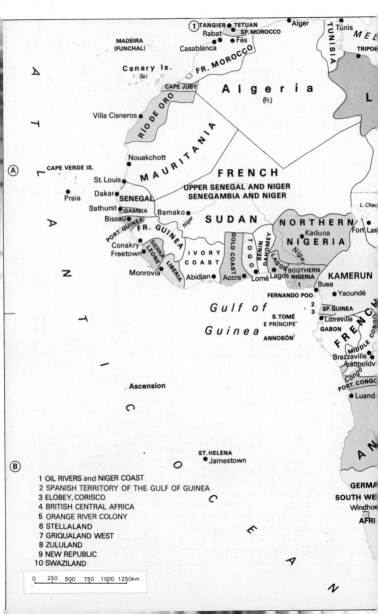

① TANGIER ● TETUAN   ● Alger   TÚNIS
MADEIRA   ● SP.MOROCCO   TRIPO
(FUNCHAL)   Rabat ● Fès
Casablanca
Canary Is.   FR. MOROCCO
(Sp)   CAPE JUBY   A l g e r i a
(Fr.)

Villa Cisneros   RÍO DE ORO

Nouakchott
MAURITANIA   FRENCH
St. Louis   UPPER SENEGAL AND NIGER
Dakar   SENEGAL   SENEGAMBIA AND NIGER
Bathurst ● GAMBIA   Bamako ●
Bissau   PORT. GUINEA   SUDAN   NORTHERN   L. Chad
FR. GUINEA   Niger   Kaduna   Fort Lai
Conakry   SIERRA   IVORY   GOLD COAST   TOGO   BENIN   NIGERIA
Freetown   LEONE   LIBERIA   COAST   DAHOMEY   Niger
Monrovia   Abidjan ●   Accra ●   Lomé   Lagos   SOUTHERN
                                        Lagos   NIGERIA   KAMERUN
                        FERNANDO POO   Buea   ● Yaoundé
Gulf of   2   SP.GUINEA
3   ● Libreville
Guinea   S. TOMÉ   GABON   F
E PRÍNCIPE   MIDDLE CONGO
ANNOBÓN   Brazzaville ●
Léopoldv
Congo
PORT. CONGO
Ascension   ● Luand

ST. HELENA
● Jamestown

1 OIL RIVERS and NIGER COAST   A N
2 SPANISH TERRITORY OF THE GULF OF GUINEA
3 ELOBEY, CORISCO   GERMA
4 BRITISH CENTRAL AFRICA   SOUTH WE
5 ORANGE RIVER COLONY   Windho
6 STELLALAND   AFRI
7 GRIQUALAND WEST
8 ZULULAND
9 NEW REPUBLIC
10 SWAZILAND

0   250   500   750   1000   1250km

60   AFRICA UP TO 1914

ERRANEAN SEA

BENGASI   ALEXANDRIA
PORT SAID
Suez
SUEZ CANAL
Cairo

YA

EGYPT

Nile

Wādi Halfā

Dongola   Port Sudan

Omdurman   Mitsiwa

ERITREA

Khartoum

White Nile
Blue Nile

OBOCK
DJIBOUTI

Fashoda   Berbera   BRITISH
Addis Ababa   Harer   SOMALILAND

CONGO

SUDAN

ETHIOPIA

ongo

BELGIAN
CONGO

UGANDA

BENADIR
ITALIAN SOMALILAND

Entebbe   BRITISH
EAST
AFRICA   Mogadishu

L. Victoria   Nairobi

WITU

L. Tanganyika

GERMAN   Mombasa

EAST   ZANZIBAR

AFRICA   Dar es - Salaam

SEYCHELLES

Kionga

LA

NYASSA

NYASALAND   L. Nyassa

BRITISH SOUTH AFRICA
COMPANY
(Rhodesia)   TETE

DIÉGO SUAREZ

NOSSI-BÉ

Zambezi

Salisbury

Zambezi

MOZAMBIQUE

QUELIMANE

MOZAMBIQUE
COMPANY

Tananarive

MADAGASCAR

STE. MARIE
DE MADAGASCAR

MAURITIUS

RÉUNION   Port Louis
St.- Denis

BECHUANALAND

MAFEKING

TRANSVAAL
SOUTH AFR. REP.

INHAMBANE

BRITISH   Pretoria   LOURENÇO MARQUES

BECHUANALAND   SOUTH   10

PE OF GOOD   AFRICA   5   7   9

HOPE   NATAL   8

Cape Town

61 Spanish territories in the Gulf of Guinea

62 French Somaliland

63 Portuguese Congo

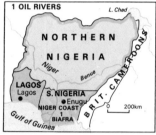

64 Nigeria

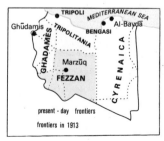

65 Libya

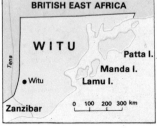

66 Witu

67 Italian East Africa

68 Zululand and New Republic

69 Ruanda - Urundi

70 Togo and Dahomey

71 Belgian Congo

72 Zanzibar

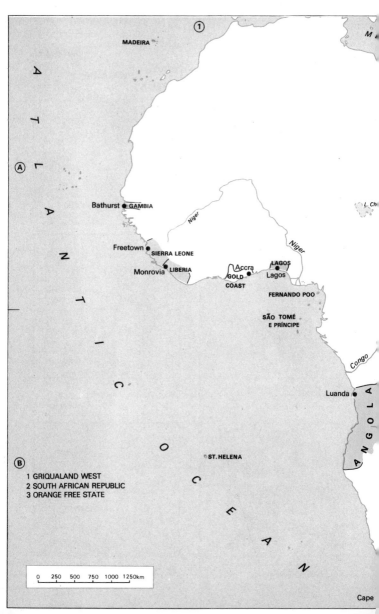

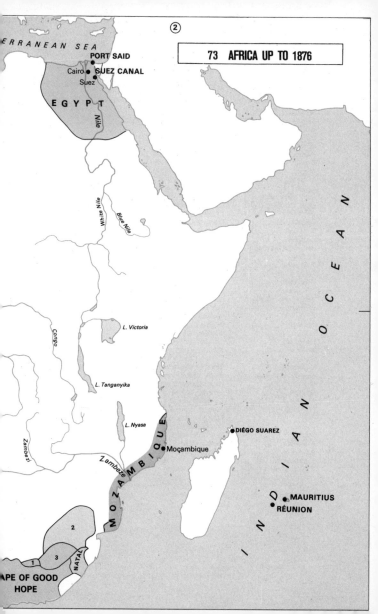

② 73 AFRICA UP TO 1876

MEDITERRANEAN SEA

PORT SAID
Cairo ● SUEZ CANAL
Suez ●
EGYPT
Nile

White Nile
Blue Nile

Congo

L. Victoria

L. Tanganyika

Zambezi

L. Nyasa

MOZAMBIQUE
Zambeze
Moçambique

● DIÉGO SUAREZ

INDIAN OCEAN

● MAURITIUS
● RÉUNION

2

3

NATAL

CAPE OF GOOD HOPE

1

THE AMERICAS

List of present-day stamp-issuing countries and their currencies

Anguilla	East Caribbean $ (100 cents)
Antigua and Barbuda	East Caribbean $ (100 cents)
Argentina	Argentine Peso (100 centavos)
Bahamas	Bahamian $ (100 cents)
Barbados	Barbados $ (100 cents)
Belize	Belize $ (100 cents)
Bermuda	Bermudan $ (100 cents)
Bolivia	Bolivian Peso (100 centavos)
Brazil	Cruzeiro (100 centavos)
British Virgin Islands	American currency
Canada	Canadian $ (100 cents)
Cayman Islands	Cayman $ (100 cents)
Chile	Chilean Peso (100 centavos)
Colombia	Colombian Peso (100 centavos)
Costa Rica	Costa Rican Colon (100 centimos)
Cuba	Cuban Peso (100 centavos)
Dominica	East Caribbean $ (100 cents)
Dominican Republic	Dominican Peso (100 centavos)
Ecuador	Sucre (100 centavos)
El Salvador	El Salvador Colón (100 centavos)
Falkland Islands	Falkland £ (100 pence)
Greenland	Danish currency
Grenada	East Caribbean $ (100 cents)
Grenadines of Grenada	East Caribbean $ (100 cents)
Grenadines of St Vincent	East Caribbean $ (100 cents)
Guatemala	Quetzal (100 centavos)
Guyana	Guyana $ (100 cents)
Haiti	Gourde (100 centimes)
Honduras	Lempira (100 centavos)
Jamaica	Jamaican $ (100 cents)
Mexico	Mexican Peso (100 centavos)
Montserrat	East Caribbean $ (100 cents)
Netherlands Antilles	Netherlands Antilles Gulden (100 cents)
Nevis	East Caribbean $ (100 cents)
Nicaragua	Córdoba (100 centavos)
Panama	American currency and Balboa (100 centesimos)
Paraguay	Guarani (100 centimos)
Peru	Sol (100 centavos)
St Kitts	East Caribbean $ (100 cents)
St Lucia	East Caribbean $(100 cents)
St Vincent	East Caribbean $ (100 cents)
Suriname	Suriname Gulden (100 cents)
Trinidad and Tobago	Trinidad and Tobago $(100 cents)
Turks and Caicos Islands	Bahamian currency
United States of America	American $ (100 cents)
Uruguay	Uruguayan Peso (100 centesimos)
Venezuela	Bolivar (100 centimos)

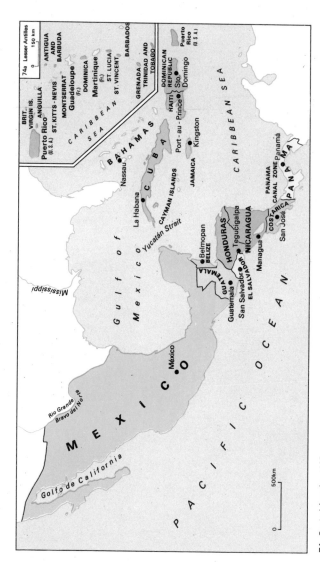

74a Lesser Antilles
0   150 km

BRIT.
VIRGIN IS.
ANGUILLA
Puerto Rico
(U.S.A)
ST. KITTS – NEVIS
MONTSERRAT
Guadeloupe
(Fr.)
DOMINICA
Martinique
(Fr.)
ST. LUCIA
ST. VINCENT
GRENADA
TRINIDAD AND
TOBAGO
BARBADOS
ANTIGUA
AND
BARBUDA

*CARIBBEAN
SEA*

DOMINICAN
REPUBLIC
HAITI
Port - au - Prince
Sto.
Domingo
Puerto
Rico
(U.S.A)

BAHAMAS

Nassau

C U B A

La Habana

CAYMAN ISLANDS

Yucatán Strait

*Gulf
of
Mexico*

Kingston

JAMAICA

C A R I B B E A N   S E A

Belmopan
BELIZE

Tegucigalpa
HONDURAS

GUATEMALA

Guatemala

San Salvador
EL SALVADOR

Managua

NICARAGUA

PANAMA

COSTA RICA

San José

CANAL ZONE
Panamá

P A N A M A

Mississippi

M E X I C *O*

México

Rio Grande
Bravo del Norte

P A C I F I C   O C E A N

Golfo de California

500km
0

74 Central America 1985

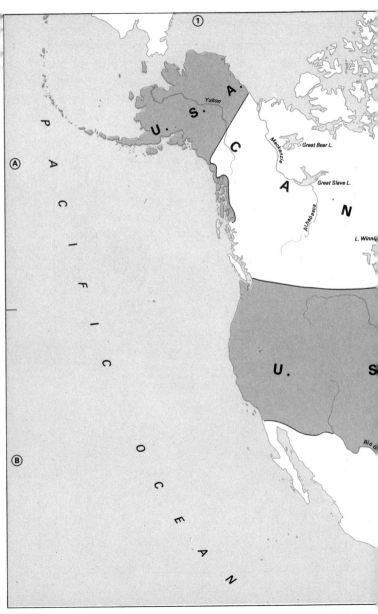

GREENLAND

②

75 NORTH AMERICA 1985

ATLANTIC

• Godthåb

A   D   A

L. Superior   • Ottawa

Mississippi

L. Huron

L. Michigan

Washington •

OCEAN

A.

BERMUDA
• Hamilton

Mississippi

0 250 500 750 1000 1250km

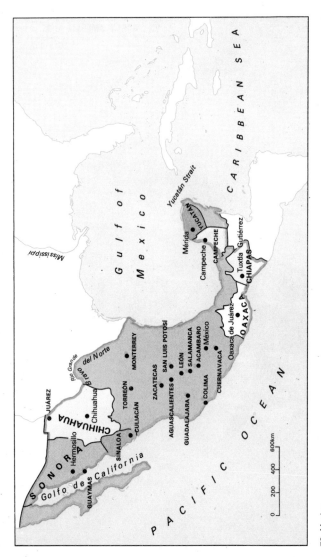

76 Mexico

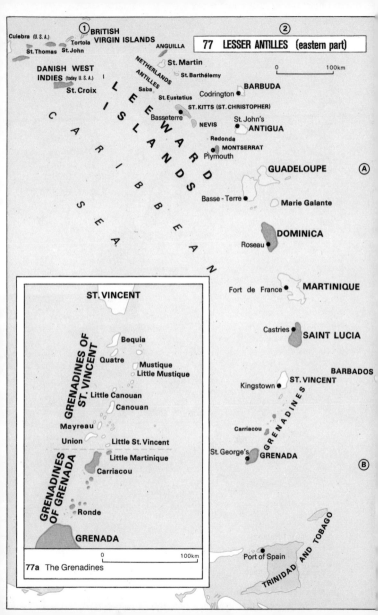

① BRITISH VIRGIN ISLANDS
② 77 LESSER ANTILLES (eastern part)

Culebra (U.S.A.)
Tortola
St. Thomas   St. John
ANGUILLA
St. Martin
NETHERLANDS ANTILLES
St. Barthélemy
Saba
DANISH WEST INDIES (today U.S.A.)
St. Croix
St. Eustatius
Codrington   BARBUDA
ST. KITTS (ST. CHRISTOPHER)
Basseterre
NEVIS
St. John's   ANTIGUA
LEEWARD ISLANDS
Redonda
MONTSERRAT
Plymouth
GUADELOUPE   (A)
Basse-Terre   Marie Galante

C A R I B B E A N   S E A

DOMINICA
Roseau

Fort de France   MARTINIQUE

Castries   SAINT LUCIA

BARBADOS
Kingstown   ST. VINCENT
Carriacou   GRENADINES
St. George's   GRENADA   (B)

TRINIDAD AND TOBAGO
Port of Spain

0   100km

77a The Grenadines

ST. VINCENT

GRENADINES OF ST. VINCENT

Bequia
Quatre
Mustique
Little Mustique
Little Canouan
Canouan
Mayreau
Union   Little St. Vincent
Little Martinique
Carriacou

GRENADINES OF GRENADA

Ronde

GRENADA

0   100km

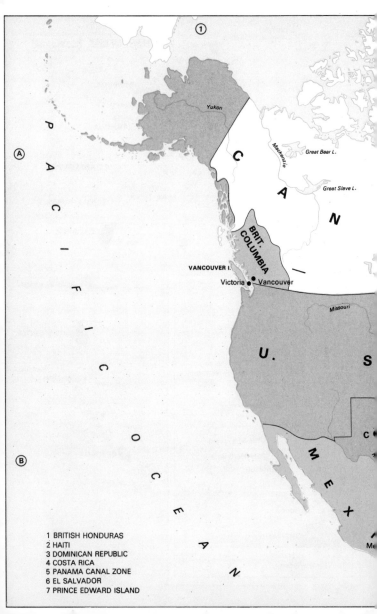

Yukon

C

Mackenzie

Great Bear L.

Great Slave L.

A

N

P
A
C
I
F
I
C

BRIT.
COLUMBIA

VANCOUVER I.

Victoria • • Vancouver

U.

S

Missouri

O
C
E
A
N

C

M
E
X

Me

1 BRITISH HONDURAS
2 HAITI
3 DOMINICAN REPUBLIC
4 COSTA RICA
5 PANAMA CANAL ZONE
6 EL SALVADOR
7 PRINCE EDWARD ISLAND

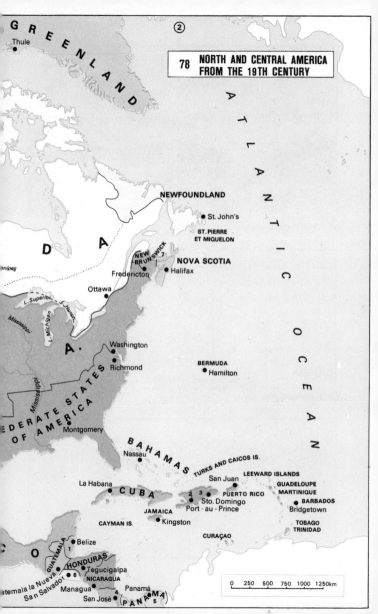

②

78 NORTH AND CENTRAL AMERICA FROM THE 19TH CENTURY

Thule

G R E E N L A N D

A T L A N T I C   O C E A N

NEWFOUNDLAND

St. John's

ST. PIERRE ET MIQUELON

NEW BRUNSWICK 7 **NOVA SCOTIA**

Fredericton Halifax

D   A

anipeg

Ottawa

L. Superior L. Huron

L. Michigan

Mississippi

A.

Washington

Richmond

BERMUDA
Hamilton

Mississippi

EDERATE STATES OF AMERICA

Montgomery

B A H A M A S

Nassau

TURKS AND CAICOS IS.

San Juan **LEEWARD ISLANDS**

La Habana **CUBA** 2 **PUERTO RICO** **GUADELOUPE**
                3 Sto. Domingo **MARTINIQUE**
           JAMAICA Port - au - Prince **BARBADOS**
CAYMAN IS.   Bridgetown

Kingston **TOBAGO**
TRINIDAD

CURAÇAO

Belize

O

1

GUATEMALA **HONDURAS**
                Tegucigalpa
           6 **NICARAGUA**
atemala la Nueva
San Salvador Managua Panamá M A
San José 4   5
            (P A N A)

0   250   500   750   1000 1250km

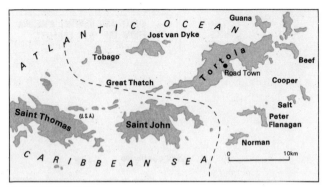

79 British Virgin Islands

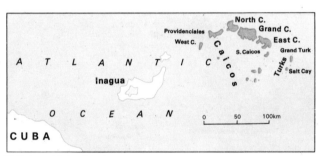

80 Turks and Caicos Islands

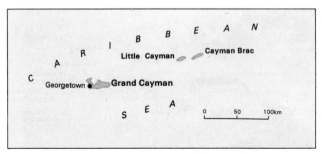

81 Cayman Islands

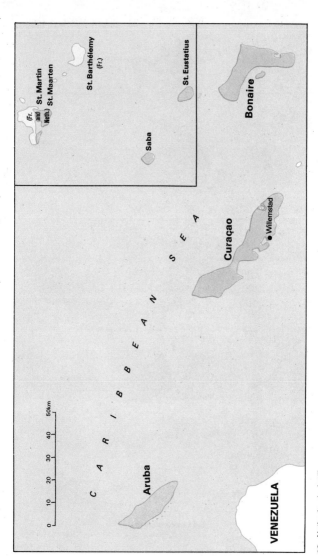

St. Martin (Fr.) and St. Maarten (Neth.)

St. Barthélemy (Fr.)

Saba

St. Eustatius

Bonaire

Curaçao

● Willemstad

C A R I B B E A N   S E A

Aruba

0   10   20   30   40   50km

VENEZUELA

82 Netherlands Antilles

83

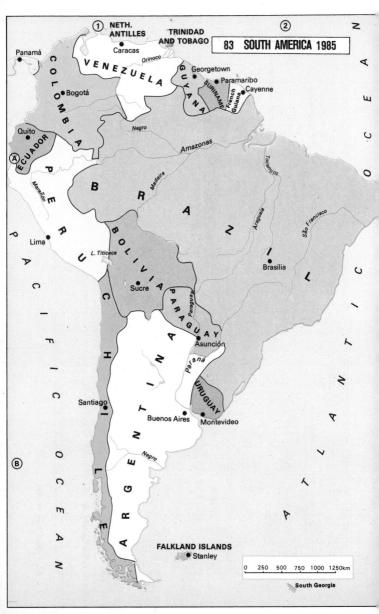

83 SOUTH AMERICA 1985

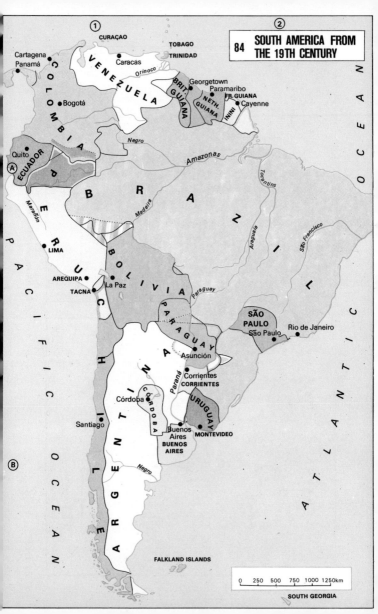

84 SOUTH AMERICA FROM THE 19TH CENTURY

① CURAÇAO

Cartagena
Panamá

COLOMBIA

Bogotá

TOBAGO
TRINIDAD

Caracas

VENEZUELA

Orinoco

BRIT. GUIANA

② SOUTH AMERICA FROM THE 19TH CENTURY

Georgetown
Paramaribo FR. GUIANA
NETH. Cayenne
GUIANA ININI

Ⓐ ECUADOR

Quito

Negro

Amazonas

P

E

R

Marañón

LIMA

U

AREQUIPA

TACNA

La Paz

BOLIVIA

BRAZIL

Madeira

Tocantins

Araguaia

São Francisco

Paraguay

SÃO PAULO

São Paulo

Rio de Janeiro

PARAGUAY

Asunción

C

H

Santiago

I

Córdoba

CÓRDOBA

ARGENTINA

Corrientes
CORRIENTES

Paraná

URUGUAY

Buenos
Aires
BUENOS
AIRES

MONTEVIDEO

L

Negro

E

Ⓑ

P A C I F I C   O C E A N

A T L A N T I C   O C E A N

FALKLAND ISLANDS

0   250 500 750 1000 1250km

SOUTH GEORGIA

O C E A N

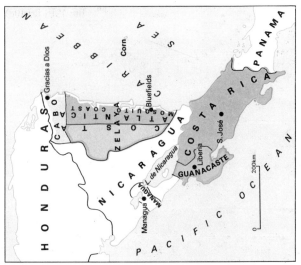

85 Peru

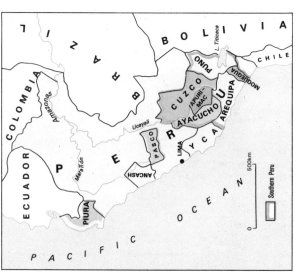

86 Nicaragua and Costa Rica

86

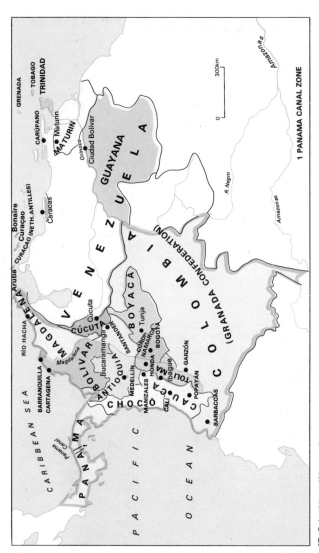

87 Colombia and Venezuela

GRENADA
TOBAGO
TRINIDAD
CARÚPANO
Maturin
MATURIN
Orinoco
Ciudad Bolívar
GUAYANA
Amazonas
V E N E Z U E L A
Bonaire
Aruba CURAÇAO (NETH. ANTILLES)
Curaçao
Caracas
R. Negro
Amazonas
RIO HACHA
Cúcuta
CÚCUTA
BOYACA
Tunja
SANTANDER
Bucaramanga
Cúñora
Namarca
BOGOTÁ
COLOMBIA
(GRANADA CONFEDERATION)
MAGDALENA
BARRANQUILLA
CARTAGENA
Magdalena
BOLIVAR
ANTIOQUIA
MEDELLÍN
MANIZALES
HONDA
Ibagué
CALI
CAUCA
GARZÓN
TOLIMA
POPAYÁN
BARBACOAS
CHOCÓ
PANAMA
Panama Canal
CARIBBEAN SEA
PACIFIC
OCEAN
300 km
0
1 PANAMA CANAL ZONE

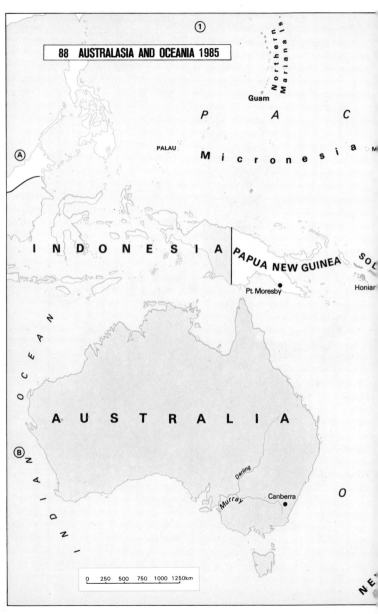

88 AUSTRALASIA AND OCEANIA 1985

Northern Mariana Is.

Guam

PALAU

Micronesia

INDONESIA

PAPUA NEW GUINEA

SOL

Pt. Moresby

Honiar

AUSTRALIA

Darling

Murray

Canberra

INDIAN OCEAN

PACIFIC OCEAN

0 250 500 750 1000 1250km

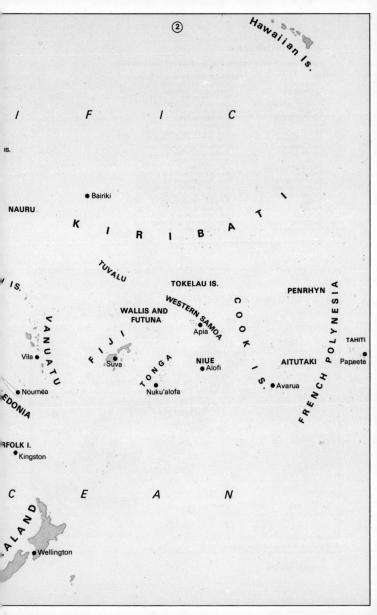

Hawaiian Is.

I   F   I   C

IS.

● Bairiki

NAURU

K   I   R   I   B   A   T   I

TUVALU

TOKELAU IS.

WESTERN SAMOA

**WALLIS AND
FUTUNA**

Apia ●

PENRHYN

C
O
O
K

I
S
.

F
R
E
N
C
H

P
O
L
Y
N
E
S
I
A

IS.

V
A
N
U
A
T
U

F
I
J
I

Vila ●

Suva ●

T
O
N
G
A

Nuku'alofa ●

NIUE
● Alofi

AITUTAKI

Avarua ●

TAHITI

Papeete ●

● Nouméa

EDONIA

RFOLK I.
● Kingston

C   E   A   N

ALAND

✦ Wellington

AUSTRALASIA AND OCEANIA

List of present-day stamp-issuing countries and their currencies

Aitutaki	New Zealand currency
Australia	Australian $ (100 cents)
Cook Islands	New Zealand currency
Fiji	Fiji $ (100 cents)
French Polynesia	Franc CFP (100 centimes)
Kiribati	Kiribati $ (100 cents)
Marshall Islands	American currency
Nauru	Australian currency
Niue	New Zealand currency
New Caledonia	Franc CFP (100 centimes)
New Zealand	New Zealand $ (100 cents)
Norfolk Island	Australian currency
Palau	American currency
Papua-New Guinea	Kina (100 toea)
Penrhyn	New Zealand currency
Pitcairn Islands	New Zealand currency
Solomon Islands	Solomon Islands $ (100 cents)
Tokelau Islands	New Zealand currency
Tonga	Pa'anga (100 seniti)
Tuvalu	Australian currency
Vanuatu	Vatu (100 centimes)
Wallis and Futuna	Franc CFP (100 centimes)
Western Samoa	Tala (100 sene)

Note: CFP = Communauté Financière du Pacifique

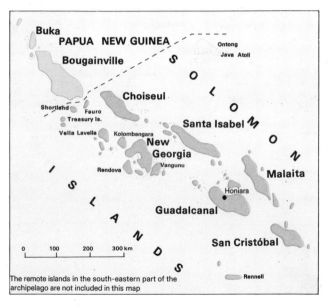

The remote islands in the south-eastern part of the archipelago are not included in this map

89 Solomon Islands

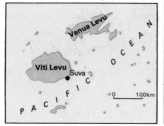

90 Fiji

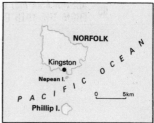

91 Norfolk Island

92 New Caledonia

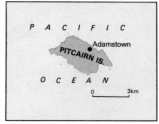

93 Pitcairn Islands

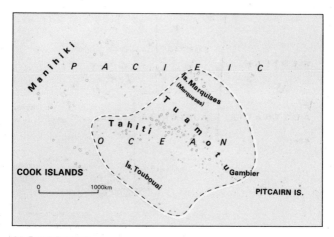

94 French Polynesia

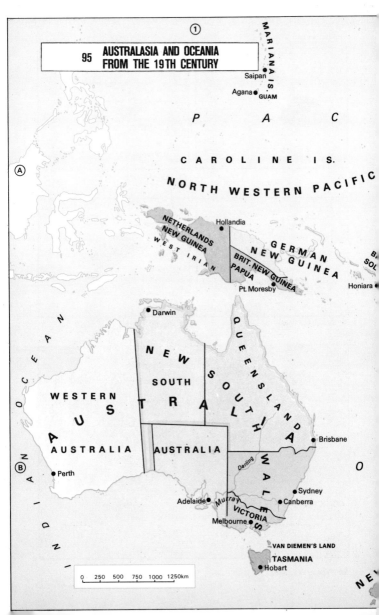

95 **AUSTRALASIA AND OCEANIA FROM THE 19TH CENTURY**

MARIANA IS.

Saipan

Agana • GUAM

P A C

C A R O L I N E   I S.

NORTH WESTERN PACIFIC

Ⓐ

NETHERLANDS NEW GUINEA

Hollandia

WEST IRIAN

GERMAN NEW GUINEA

BRIT. NEW GUINEA

PAPUA

Pt. Moresby

B. SOL

Honiara •

• Darwin

NEW SOUTH

SOUTH

QUEENSLAND

WESTERN AUSTRALIA

AUS TRA WAL S

SOUTH AUSTRALIA

I N D I A N

Ⓑ Perth •

O C E A N

Darling

• Brisbane

O

Adelaide •

Murray

• Sydney

• Canberra

VICTORIA

Melbourne •

VAN DIEMEN'S LAND

TASMANIA

• Hobart

0   250   500   750   1000   1250km

NE

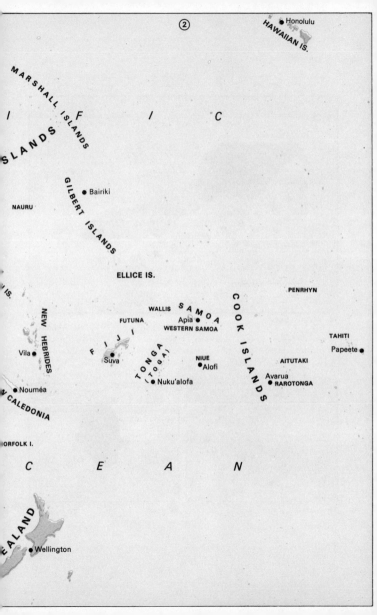

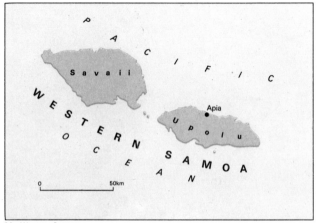

96 Western Samoa

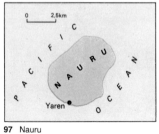

97 Nauru

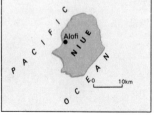

98 Niue

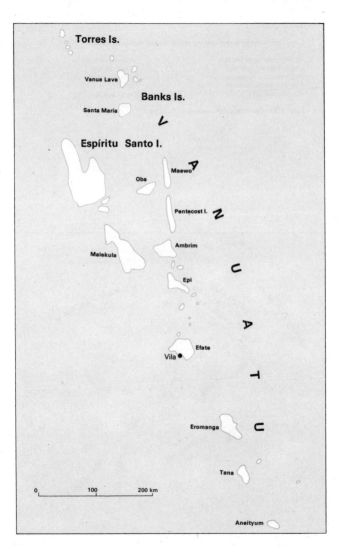

Torres Is.

Vanua Lava

Banks Is.

Santa Maria

V

Espíritu Santo I.

Maewo

Oba

A

Pentecost I.

N

Ambrim

Malekula

Epi

U

A

Efate

Vila ●

T

Eromanga

U

Tana

0   100   200 km

Aneityum

99 Vanuatu

ANTARCTICA

List of present-day stamp-issuing countries and their currencies

Australian Antarctic Territory	Australian currency
British Antarctic Territory	British currency
Falkland Islands Dependencies	Falkland currency
French Antarctic Territory	Franc CFP
Ross Dependency	New Zealand currency

Note: CFP = Communauté Financière du Pacifique

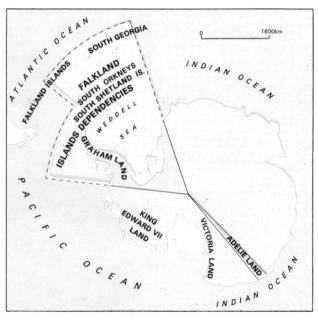

100 The Antarctic before 1955

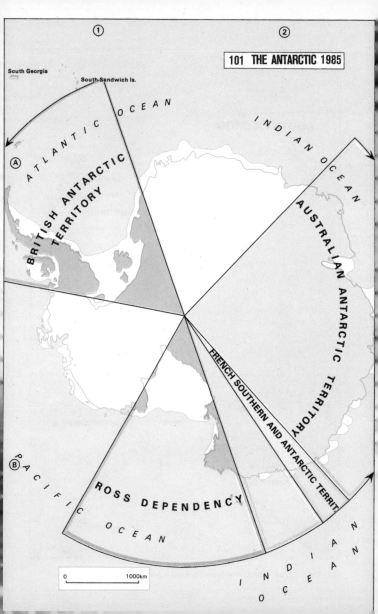

South Georgia

South Sandwich Is.

101 THE ANTARCTIC 1985

① ②

Ⓐ

A T L A N T I C   O C E A N

I N D I A N   O C E A N

BRITISH ANTARCTIC TERRITORY

AUSTRALIAN ANTARCTIC TERRITORY

FRENCH SOUTHERN AND ANTARCTIC TERRIT

Ⓑ

P A C I F I C   O C E A N

ROSS DEPENDENCY

I N D I A N   O C E A N

0   1000km

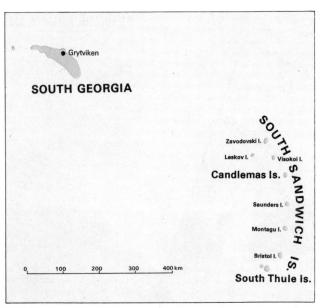

102 Falkland Islands Dependencies

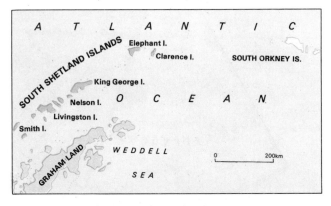

103 South Orkney Islands and South Shetland Islands

TEXT

INTRODUCTION

Nearly all stamps that are collected bear the name of an issuing country, but in terms of geography this name often means very little, because unless the stamp is a contemporary one it can be quite difficult to find out the precise whereabouts of the country or territory. Theoretically it should be possible to look it up in an atlas, but this is seldom helpful: current atlases have no reason to pay particular attention to territories where stamps are, or were once, issued, since these were often quite small, or existed only briefly. Historical atlases might be thought to provide the answer, but they seldom do so, since it is unlikely that any historical atlas will record all the changes in names, states and boundaries over the entire period of issuing postage stamps. Also, postal systems did not always coincide with political frontiers, as in the case of the long-lived Thurn and Taxis post (see p.316).

The total number of stamp-issuing countries far exceeds the number of present-day stamp-issuing countries. This survey, which begins with the issue of the world's first postage stamp in 1840, lists some 740 stamp-issuing territories, only about one-third of which still exist. The book has been devised, not only to fill the geographical gaps left by conventional atlases, but also to provide further information which a stamp collector will find helpful and interesting. It presents a complete survey of every stamp-issuing authority ever to have existed, showing by means of the maps at the front precisely where these authorities, and the countries involved, were located. The maps themselves have been specially drawn to relate to the text. The text lists the names of each individual stamp-issuing country, providing data on the historical and political background, and discusses the actual production of stamps in considerable detail: the number of stamps printed in each issue, the design, the methods of printing and the relative rarity. The entire world stamp production, of about 230,000 stamps, is represented.

Some definitions

Stamp collecting gains in popularity all the time, and postage stamps are issued in ever greater numbers, showing more and more variety and invention. Since many of these stamps, often printed with collectors, rather than postage, in mind, seem to have little to do with the obvious function of the stamp, we may wonder whether they are really postage stamps at all. It is thus necessary to try to define the twin terms 'postage stamp' and 'stamp-issuing country'.

The latter term, an accepted one among collectors, is reasonably simply defined, although, as will be seen, there are some discrepancies within the broad definition. A stamp-issuing country means a country or territory, regardless of size or form of government or whether legally independent or dependent, which has its own postal authorities and uses its own stamps. Such a country has a sovereign post office with the capacity and authority to provide postal services in that territory, and postage stamps are issued by the postal authorities for public use. The postal services must also be linked to the international postal network, which involves membership of the Universal Postal Union (UPU). The constitution of the UPU states that the member countries represent a unified postal territory, designated the Universal Postal Union, for the mutual exchange of mail. Freedom of transit is guaranteed throughout the entire territory of the UPU, and its purpose is to provide for the organization and continued improvement of worldwide postal services and to encourage the development of international co-operation in this respect. Membership of the UPU is no mere formality; each postal authority must be able to participate in postal services, observe the relevant international regulations and, last but not least, share in the cost of maintaining the carriage of mail.

Membership of the UPU is open to every member of the United Nations Organization, but sovereign countries that are not members of the UN can still apply for membership of the UPU. The constitution further lays down that the territorial scope of the UPU comprises: a) the territory of member countries; b) post offices set up by member countries on territory not included in the UPU; c) territory that is not part of the UPU but is included since its postal relations are dependent on a member country. The Universal Postal Union records having registered a total of 168 member countries in August 1985, which is more than the number of members of the United Nations, a clear indication of the universality of the UPU. However, this is still a far smaller number than the total of present-day stamp-issuing countries in existence, because the label 'member country' often includes dependent territories, many of which issue their own stamps. For instance, overseas territories of Great Britain and Northern Ireland comprise no fewer than nineteen territories whose participation in UPU membership is through Great Britain's membership.

To add even further to the number of 'stamp-issuing countries' several member countries contractually hand over certain rights and duties to another postal authority within the framework of their own postal sovereignty. For instance, there is the postal authority of the United Nations Organization in its headquarters in New York, which has the right to issue its own stamps on the basis of an agreement with the postal authorities of the USA. Similarly, stamps are issued by other bodies of the UN in Switzerland and Austria on the basis of an agreement with the respective postal authorities. Here, of course, the use of the term 'stamp-issuing country' is imprecise, since in the case of the UN there is no 'country' to issue the stamps. But, in spite of a few exceptions, membership of the UPU is vital, and in nearly all cases a stamp-issuing country cannot be defined as such without either membership or an agreement approved by the member countries that mail with valid postage stamps will be delivered throughout the entire UPU territory, in other words, anywhere in the world.

The first and most important definition of the postage stamp itself is that it fulfils postal functions; a stamp that does not do so is not a true postage stamp, but a label. There are many examples, past and present, of postage stamps being issued when either there was no competent postal authority to provide the required services, or there was another postal authority using its own stamps in the same territory. An important regulation in the UPU constitution and its standing orders states that postage stamps intended to frank mail can only be issued by one postal authority within the member country.

Scope of this book

Philatelic atlases have a certain tradition and were preceded by philatelic maps. The first map was published in 1895 at St Louis in the USA (*Mekeel's Stamp Collector's Map of the World*). A second map appeared in 1906 in Berlin (*Philatelistische Weltkarte* by F. von Eynanten) with a commentary that contained an alphabetical list of all stamp-issuing countries of the time, with a brief description of the main features, and an index that marked the position on the map. It was an excellent aid and rivalled *Lücker's Atlas der Briefmarken-Geographie*, despite the latter's more pretentious name. This was written by C. Opitz and P. Lederer and was first published in Leipzig in 1917 by the house who produce the well-known Schaubek albums of postage stamps. The main content of the book was small maps of individual stamp-issuing countries that could be cut out and glued onto the sheets of the albums.

The twenties saw small and large editions of the Italian *Atlante filatelice*; both contained identical maps mainly of a contemporary political nature but were given a 'philatelic' character by the presence of grey pictures of various stamps in the margins.

In 1933 R. A. Kimble published the *Stamp Collector's Atlas and Dictionary*, printed in Chicago. Later publications include *Politischer Atlas für Briefmarkenkunde und Weltverkehr* by R. Bayer and R. Sauer, issued in Vienna, and an unfinished wartime publication *Deutschland-Atlas* by Schaubek, the first six maps of which were issued in Leipzig in 1941. Other similar publications are *Lücker's Länder und Weltverkehrskarte für Postwertzeichen-Sammler* by C. Opitz and P. Lederer (Leipzig, 1921 and 1923), and more recently *Image Deutschland-Karte für Briefmarkenfreunde* by H. Munsch (Hamburg, 1949) and *Európa bélyegtérképei* by D. Sóky (Budapest, 1974), and finally the West German *Weltatlas für Philatelie* (Braunschweig, 1980) by H. H. Gulach. Schematic maps of stamp-issuing countries (outside the USSR) are included in L. L. Lepeshinski's *Filatelisticheskaya geografiya* (Moscow, 1967), and basic information on stamp- issuing countries is to be found in R. J. Sutton's *The*

Stamp Collector's Encyclopaedia (London, 1951; 8th edition, 1966), U. Häger's *Grosses Lexikon der Philatelie* (Gütersleh, 1973), Vladinec's *Filatelisticheskaya geografiya, Yeuropeyskiye sarubezhnye strany* (Moscow, 1981), *USSR* (Moscow, 1982) and *Aziya* (Moscow, 1984), and K. Wood's *Where in the World? An Atlas for Stamp Collectors* (USA, 1985).

The present philatelic atlas has been compiled by two Czech authors known for their philatelic publications: B. Hlinka (who has written many other books on stamps); and Dr L. Mucha of the Department of Cartography at Charles University in Prague. It was first published in Czech under the title *Filatelistický atlas známkových zemí* (Prague, 1971). A second edition was issued in 1978 and a third in 1986. This edition was translated into English by Dr T. Gottheinerova, and was adapted for an English-speaking readership by K. F. Chapman.

The reference sources for this book were the catalogues of Gibbons, Lipsia, Michel, Minkus, Scott, Yvert and Zumstein and other publications both of a philatelic and non-philatelic character, dealing with geography, history and postal history. Publications of the Universal Postal Union also proved extremely helpful.

It is interesting to note that these publications often demonstrate deviating, sometimes dramatically opposed, viewpoints in recording stamp-issuing countries. In this book, however, we take as the basic assumption that the name on the postage stamp is that of the stamp-issuing country, as stipulated by the UPU.

Before the establishment of the UPU in 1874, a number of countries did not include the name on the stamp, but these must, of course, be regarded as stamp-issuing countries. Examples are the Papal States, Moldavia, Sardinia and others. Even Russia did not include the country's name on its stamps until 1917.

In some cases the name of the country is given in a script other than Latin despite the attempts of the UPU to enforce its rules. One such present-day issue is the Chinese People's Republic. Among older stamps which broke the rule were issues of Hejaz and Nejd (see p. 178) from 1916 to 1929.

It should be mentioned that there are a number of stamp-issuing countries that give their name on the postage stamp in abbreviated form, for instance USSR, USA, DDR (East Germany), R.F. (République Française), B.C.A. (British Central Africa), B.I.O.T. (British Indian Ocean Territory), S.W.A. (South West Africa). In addition, there are a number of countries that do not use the Latin script and simply give the abbreviations in Latin script on their stamps. Examples are UAR (Egypt), D.P.R.K. (Democratic People's Republic of Korea, i.e. North Korea). There are also many abbreviations of various military and occupation issues, local issues and field posts, which are not included here among the stamp-issuing countries. As exceptions, we have accepted certain plebiscite territories and other emergency issues, for example S.O. = Eastern Silesia, R.O. = Eastern Rumelia, K.G.C.A. = Carinthia, and A.M.G.-F.T.T. = Trieste. These are shown in this atlas as independent stamp-issuing 'countries', although the term is not precise in such cases.

Straightforward surcharges or other indications of altered value do not normally involve a change of name as far as the stamp-issuing country is concerned. For instance, French stamps were valid in Réunion with a surcharge of 'CFA' francs, but they were still French stamps. Similarly, German stamps with face value given in piastres for use in the Levant remain German stamps, as do Austrian stamps issued in kreuzer and soldi for use in Lombardy and Venetia, since no name is given on the stamps. In general, the fact that a stamp is limited to use in a certain territory is not a decisive factor in determining the country of issue, unless that territory is specifically mentioned in the inscription on the stamp.

The system of government and/or political changes do not affect the inclusion in this book of a stamp-issuing country, as long as the name, particularly the geographical name, remains the same. For example, Selangor is only one stamp-issuing country, even though its existence has been sporadic, from 1878 to 1900, from 1935 to 1942, and from 1948 until the present, because the name on the stamps has remained unchanged. Similarly Gabon comprises the period of the former French colony and the present republic despite the time gap in between, and all Bulgarian stamps bear the name 'Bulgaria' despite the fact that the country has undergone changes in the social system. On the other hand, the Gold Coast and Ghana, although geographically the same, are two different stamp-issuing countries since, on acquiring independence, the state changed its name and the new name appeared on its stamps. Similarly, we distinguish Persia and Iran, the Ottoman Empire and Turkey, the Kingdom of the Serbs, Croats and Slovenes and Yugoslavia, since these differing names are given on the stamps. Mere changes in spelling, of course, such as Mejico to the later Mexico, does not make the territory a different stamp-issuing country.

In this book we have on principle excluded 'stamp-issuing countries' that are not included in the standard catalogues, since many of them are obvious frauds (for example, the 'Kingdom of Sedang'). Also excluded are issues of various governments in exile or agencies which are engaged in issuing stamps with the names of small islands or uninhabited territories which do not require, and usually do not have, a postal service in operation. In such cases, where the catalogues themselves draw attention to the fact that no postal function exists (examples are the Galápagos Islands, Maluku Selatan, Jethou and Redonda), a list is given at the end of the book.

Since the starting point for this atlas is the geographical existence of the stamp-issuing country, we cannot logically include stamps issued by shipping companies and airlines — for example, the David Brice issue for S.S. *Lady McLeod,* the Danube Steam Navigation Company and SCADTA, and various military or occupation army issues such as TEO, EAF and Deniken Army issue. Most of these issues are in the form of overprinted provisional stamps without the name of a country and with no precise geographical location; furthermore, the general postal function is disputable (some are merely issues of army field posts). Many local issues, likewise, could not be included as independent stamp-issuing countries; some of them are simply mentioned within the framework of a broader region, as in the cases of Sonora, Colima, Juarez and others which are included under Mexico.

Generally, however, exclusions are the exception; indeed, we have tended to include more stamp-issuing countries than would stand up to a strict test, especially with regard to the stamps' real postal function, as for example in the cases of Western Hungary, Manama and Mahra. A major problem has been to assess the postal function, owing to a lack of reliable specialist literature containing data of comparable international standard. Stamp catalogues are intended for collectors and sometimes include other items besides postage stamps. It is up to the collector to decide what to include in his collection, whether exclusively postage stamps or other objects as well, such as labels, drawings or graphs. If he is interested in postage stamps, the criterion must be their postal validity. If a given territory issues its own stamps but has no post office (as in Upper Yaffa), then serious doubts are cast on the postal function of such an issue. Stamps must be valid for franking mail of the issuing postal authority, which also must be able to provide postal services linked to the international postal network.

Numerous stamps and labels that never were, nor could be, used for postage are in circulation among collectors. These seem only to show that some person or persons played at being the post office; proving that the stamps had a postal function would be very difficult. To do so we would need sufficient data on the scope of the postal services, the network of post offices, the range of postal facilities (including a statement of the number of mail items transported per annum), the size of issues of stamps and their distribution, and the year-round requirement for stamps. Similarly, we would need to know what circumstances permitted the issue of stamps by a non-member country of the UPU.

It is surprising how little notice the philatelic world in general takes of so decisive a feature as the postal function of the stamp, even though this is the logical defence against the output of 'stamps', which cannot be postage stamps. There are several new 'stamp-issuing countries', which cannot merit that title since they lack this basic postal justification. Most of them are small off-shore islands, some are even uninhabited.

Notes on the text

In this philatelic atlas the stamp-issuing countries are arranged alphabetically within six geographical divisions corresponding to the six continents. Thus, in accordance with this geographical standpoint, Cyprus is included in Asia, although most philatelic works would count it as part of Europe. Further sections cover postal areas in which several countries are associated (e.g. Levant and the Thurn and Taxis postal system and Ostland) as well as stamp issues of international institutions (UNO, UNESCO, WHO). The final section deals with the publishers of fake stamps. The names of the present-day stamp-issuing countries are printed in spaced capital letters (**P O L A N D**), to differentiate them from the stamp-issuing countries that are no longer postally in existence (**GRIQUALAND WEST**). However, it should be borne in mind that there are some borderline cases, the existence and disappearance of individual stamp-issuing countries being a reflection of changes in legal status, political and military events and, naturally, postal matters. Thus a certain tolerance has to be adopted when circumstances do not quite fit into the general pattern. Cross-references in the text to other stamp-issuing territories are indicated in italics.

The text covering each individual stamp-issuing country gives the following information:

The name of the stamp-issuing country in English.

A geographical, historical and political survey including brief geographical characteristics; data on the size of the country; the number of inhabitants; the name of the capital city; historical and political development at the time when the stamps were issued and the present-day political status. If the country is no longer in existence, the number of inhabitants and geographical features are usually omitted. The statistical data on the size and population of existing countries comes from standard reference works, information on the historical development of individual countries has been taken from various encyclopaedias and historical books, and stamp catalogues provided certain philatelic facts. It should be pointed out that information from different sources can sometimes vary, and thus a few minor inconsistencies may occur in the text.

Membership of the Universal Postal Union. In the case of each existing stamp-issuing country, the text records whether UPU membership is as specified by the *Rapport sur les activités de l'Union 1979* (Bern 1980) and by the complementary official *Liste des Pays-membres de l'Union postale universelle* (Bern 1981). We cite as direct members, so called by the UPU, those member countries that are normally independent states, and we cite as indirect members various territories, also named by the UPU, which are to some extent dependent on member countries. The date of enrolment in the UPU is also given, and this is important, as it is on becoming a member that stamps issued by a country have an unquestioned international validity. We can thus recognize, for instance, that Maltese stamps in the years 1860–75 were valid only inside the country, while for mail abroad British stamps had to be used; only after taking up membership in the UPU in 1885 could mail be franked with Maltese stamps when sent abroad. Similarly, in the case of Afghanistan there were only local stamps until the country took up UPU membership in 1929; before that date, mail for abroad had to be franked with Indian stamps.

Postal conditions in the country before the issue of its own stamps. This explains who administered the post and whose stamps, if any, were used before the country joined the UPU. Sometimes there are instances of complicated legal status or postal development, which have stimulated philatelic research into the issues made in those countries.

The year issues were first brought out. This is not necessarily the date when the issue assumed the full postal function as decreed by the UPU. It should also be stressed that different catalogues and publications cite differing years for the issue of the first stamps.

The manner of issue. Definitive stamps, local provisional issues, or overprinted provisional stamps reveal the postal and legal status of the country of issue. Definitive stamps require a longer span of time from their design to printing and dispatch. The issuing of definitive stamps after an announcement of their impending release means that the issue has been in the planning programme. Provisional overprints at the beginning of stamp issuing suggest the need for a quick adjustment to a new situation caused either by changes in postal authorities, legal status, war or some other unexpected event; or simply that the importance of the newly established postal authorities was not fully appreciated.

The name of the country of issue. Quotations from the stamp's text are given, indicating as far as possible whether the text is in capital letters or capital and small letters. Since we are primarily interested in the name of the country, we have omitted all other texts on stamps (for instance, 'CORREOS', 'POSTAGE', 'TO PAY', 'POSTE', 'OFFICIAL', 'AEREO' and many others). The names given on the stamps are usually the names of the countries themselves, but sometimes they represent the type of state ('RÉPUBLIQUE RWANDAISE', 'RÉPUBLIQUE ISLAMIQUE DE MAURITANIE', 'COMMONWEALTH OF THE PHILIPPINES'), a closer geographical definition ('ARCHIPEL DES COMORES', 'FALKLAND ISLANDS') or adherence to another state ('RIO MUNI/ESPANA', 'SELANGOR/MALAYA').

The total number of stamps issued by countries no longer in existence. Thus, for Labuan, 123 + 9 stamps indicates the overall scope of that country's stamp-issuing activity. The first figure gives the number of different stamps used by the general public (commercial sales, stamps issued for collectors, airmail stamps, etc.) and the second figure gives the number of stamps that could not be used by the general public (official stamps, postage-due stamps used only by the postal authorities, etc.). A large number of stamps in the second category would suggest certain specific trends in stamp production. The data is taken from stamp catalogues, but anyone who uses these knows how data differs from catalogue to catalogue, so the total number should only be regarded as a general guide. In the case of current stamp-issuing countries there are even greater problems in stipulating the exact number of stamps issued to date since new ones are constantly being brought out. For that reason no figures are given on the total issue.

The characterization of stamp production is based on four basic functions of the postage stamp, which greatly influence content and form. The stamp is issued for a postal function to serve postal purposes, to frank mail. For that reason it is issued in a large edition, with a relatively small number of titles, is valid over a long period, is sold at all post offices, and the picture on the stamp is generally subsidiary to the fulfilment of its postal purpose and given in symbols, text or numerals.

Similar features are found if the stamp fulfils a function of publicity for the country. However, the pictures on such stamps deal with a broader range of subjects, according to publicity requirements, stressing legal status and social phenomena as well as other aspects pertaining to the stamp-issuing country.

The commercial and philatelic function presents the stamp as a commodity designed primarily for the collectors' market, taking into account its requirements and laws. Such stamps usually appear in small, often insignificant editions (the smaller, the 'more precious') with a large number of titles, are sold only sporadically at post offices, and often go straight from printing house or agency to wholesale trade and from there into collections. The pictures on the stamps cover an exceptionally broad range of subject matter. They are attractive pictorial stamps with increasingly more curious topics (pictures of snakes, shells, bones, film stars, popular scenes, etc.), and are made on ever more unusual materials (printed on gold foil, artificial silk, aluminium foil, etc.) or of strange shapes (circular, pear-shaped, in the form of a map of the country or entirely irregular) in order to attract the interest of purchasers. The artistic function shows the quality of the stamp picture, stressing its content and artistic execution.

Collectors are also interested in knowing where, and how, stamps are printed. For instance, Senegalese stamps are of French origin, having been printed by a French printing house and, in most cases, designed by French artists. This can greatly influence the style of the stamp. Identity of style was sometimes so widespread, especially in the earlier period, that the printers made a prototype pattern of the design on the stamp, called the key-type, which was then used for a larger number of stamps differing only in the name of the country and the currency denomination inscribed on them. This applies, in particular, to the 'key-and-duty' designs of stamps issued throughout the former British Empire, and to the German 'colonial key-type yacht' stamps, which used a picture of the yacht *Hohenzollern* as the basic design.

Stamp printing is so specialized a business that comparatively few countries can undertake the work, and thus some countries will print stamps for a number of others as well as their own. Among the most renowned of such printing houses at present are Harrison & Sons Ltd in Great Britain; Enschedé in the Netherlands; the Austrian State Printing House in Vienna; Courvoisier in Switzerland and the French State Printing House. Printing technology, of course, changes with the course of time, even within one printing house, and this too has a bearing on the nature of the finished design. Artists are told the printing method which will be used and they design their artwork to suit it. The designs can vary from the purely functional for definitive issues to the deliberately appealing designs and bolder colours (not necessarily good art) for issues virtually planned for the collector's market.

A modern trend is for 'omnibus' issues, when a number of countries bring out stamps with identical subject matter. In varying or unified designs, they are issued for special anniversaries, such as '20 Years of UNESCO', the '75th Anniversary of UPU', the 'Freedom from Hunger Campaign' and similar internationally organized occasions. The aim of publicity for the organizations is often linked with even more powerful philatelic motives, since such stamps are mainly aimed at the collector's market.

Some stamp-issuing countries produce classes of stamps for special postal purposes, like the railway parcel stamps in Belgium. There are other kinds, too, with interesting features, eccentric shapes and curious or doubtful postal functions. Such stamps are mentioned in this book, as are rare and highly valuable stamps in individual cases.

The year when stamp issuing ceased in any particular country is not necessarily the year in which the country, as such, ceased to exist. In the case of older stamp-issuing countries, or countries where the production of stamps is on a small scale (not even, necessarily, every year) it is quite possible for issued stamps to remain postally valid for several years longer than the existence of the country as such, or than the activity of the appropriate postal authorities. For instance, the last issue for Funchal appeared in 1897–1905, but Funchal did not become part of the postal territory of Portugal until 1910. Often, the successors to postal and state authorities are given for stamp-issuing countries no longer in existence.

The commercial aspects of stamp production are important to many postal authorities, who may issue stamps with an eye to the local and foreign philatelic market, a useful source of foreign currrency. This is carried out in a number of ways. Sometimes marketing is undertaken by the postal authorities themselves (usually through an official philatelic bureau); in other cases, it is carried out by private wholesale firms, nationalized foreign trade corporations or agents and agencies, providing for a highly complex, influential and changing network of commercial relations. The commercial success of any issue provides feedback for the choice of subject matter for future stamps, and for their artistic and technical execution. In extreme cases, foreign agencies see to the entire production of stamp issues including their sale on foreign markets, and the 'issuing' authority only receives an agreed sum in foreign currency, perhaps 60 per cent of the face value of stamps sold. These stamps do not have to serve postal requirements in the relevant 'issuing' country. When such a stamp-producing agency is taken over by the client postal authority or substituted by another agency, it often involves a striking change in stamp production, evident in the form, content and quantity of stamps issued in the country concerned.

In the text of this atlas, we have given the names (as used in foreign trade) of official institutions involved in commercial stamp transactions. Of the related agencies mention is only made of the largest and best known. If more than one agency is involved, they are usually territorially limited in their transactions. Then, as a rule, each agency is restricted to a given area, such as Canada and the USA, the Scandinavian countries or some similar grouping. The location of three agencies whose names appear frequently in the text has not been supplied on each occasion — they are the Crown Agents' Stamp Bureau, Sutton, England; the Inter-Governmental Philatelic Corporation, New York, NY, USA; and the Agence des Timbres-Poste d'Outre Mer, Paris, France.

ÅLAND ISLANDS
Area 1,527 sq.km, **population** 23,251 (1982), **capital** Mariehamn.

An archipelago of approximately 6,500 small islands (of which about a hundred are inhabited) lying across the Gulf of Bothnia between Finland and Sweden. Originally part of the Swedish empire in the Baltic from the 12th century, the islands, together with Finland, were ceded to Russia in 1809, during the Napoleonic Wars. When Finland gained political independence from Russia in 1917 the Åland Islands remained under Finnish control but with internal self-government by thirty members of the elected *Landstinget*. Autonomy under Finnish administration was granted on 5 February 1982. Despite the long Russian and Finnish periods of government, Swedish cultural influences still prevail.

The first independent stamp issue appeared in March 1984, simply inscribed 'ÅLAND', and was valid for international postage.

Philatelic bureau Post Office, Mariehamn, Åland, Finland.

ALBANIA
Area 28,748 sq.km, **population** 2.75m (1981), **capital** Tirana.

People's Socialist Republic since 1976. After the defeat of the Ottoman Empire in the first Balkan War the independence of the country was proclaimed in Valona on 28 November 1912 and was internationally recognized at a Conference of Ambassadors in London on 20 December 1912. However, in the following year the Great Powers declared it a protectorate, and in 1914 the German Prince Wilhelm of Wied was established as ruler. He was soon overthrown (ruling only from 7 March to 4 September 1914). A republic was proclaimed with Essad Pasha as President until 1916, but Albania was not united, and interested powers were thus able to send in their armies during the First World War. Various parts of the country were at times occupied by the Serbs, Greeks, Italians, Bulgarians, Austrians and French. In 1917 there was a new declaration of independence, but in the years 1919–20 Italy was given mandatory power over the country. It was not until 9 November 1920 that the Conference of Ambassadors in London once again acknowledged the independence of Albania. The country was proclaimed a republic in 1925, and became a kingdom in 1928. In 1939 it was occupied by the Italian army and linked to Italy formally in a personal union; in fact, its dependence was almost colonial in character. In 1941 (after the preceding invasion of Greece by the Italian army) the south of Albania was occupied by the Greek army. In the years 1941–4 the territory of Albania was enlarged by the addition of part of Yugoslavia. After the capitulation of Italy the German army occupied Albania in 1943 and established a country under German protection (10 September 1943 to 20 November 1944). Part of the territory was liberated by the partisans and an interim government was formed during the struggle. The People's Republic was proclaimed on 11 January 1946. The Albanians call themselves Shqipetars, and the official name of their country, 'Shqiperia', derives from this. Indirect UPU membership from 1 July 1875 (Turkey), direct from 1 July 1879.

Until the declaration of independence in 1912 the territory of Albania was under Turkish domination, and the stamps of the Ottoman Empire were used. But during this period there were also other post offices, the Austrian, the Greek and the Italian, the latter being the only one to use stamps with the name Albania. From 1902 onwards a total of 6 overprinted provisionals appeared — with the overprint 'ALBANIA' on Italian stamps. These were issued until 1916, when the last overprinted issue appeared. After the first issue in 1909 separate stamps appeared for individual Italian post offices (see also *Durazzo, Scutari, Valona*). The Italian post offices were closed in October 1911, re-opened in October 1912, and most of them were finally closed in 1916.

In 1913, a year after the declaration of independence in 1912, the first Albanian stamps of the new country appeared, first mainly just postmarks and overprinted provisionals on issues of the Ottoman Empire, and then definitives with the name 'SHQIPËNIA'. 46 + 9 stamps were issued until the First World War. During the years 1914–19 a number of local issues appeared in the territory of Albania. In 1914 there was an issue of the Muslim rebels in Valona, a primitive issue printed with a hand-made postmark bearing the text 'POSTE D'ALBANIE'. There were further issues (see also *Koritza, Scutari* and *Central Albania*), not to speak of other local issues, whose true postal function is rather dubious. At that time the postal country, *Northern Epirus,* existed in part of Albania, and the Italian postal authorities were also active in Albania together with other countries whose armies were operating there.

After 1919 came overprinted provisionals, and the first definitive issue with the name of the country appeared three years later. However, the name changed so often that the resulting inscriptions on its stamps were unique in world stamp production: SHQIPËNIA, SHQI-PËNIE, SHQYPNIS, REPUBLIKA SHQIPTARE, POSTA SHQYPTARE, MBRETNIA SHQYPTARE, SHQIPNI, MBRETNIJA SHQIPTARE, SHQIPTARE, SHQIPNIJA, QEVERI-JA DEMOKRATIKË E SHQIPERISE, REPUBLIKA POPULORE E SHQIPERISË, R. P. E SHQIPERISË, SHQIPERIA. From 1977 the name appears as REPUBLIKA POPULLORE SOCIALISTE E SHQIPERISË, abbreviated also as R.P.S. E SHQIPERISË.

Albanian stamps were first produced in various foreign printing houses, mainly in Vienna, Berlin, Paris and Athens; in the 1930s in Italy, and after the Second World War in Belgrade, Budapest and Prague. More recently printing has been by the offset-litho process in Tirana, which has had an influence on the designs of Albanian stamps, which for a long time served almost exclusively the purpose of publicising the state. Since the 1960s, with the issue of thematic stamps on general topics such as animals, flowers, historical vehicles, football and hunting, attention has been paid also to the philatelic market. These stamps have appeared perforated and imperforate in small printings, sometimes no more than 10,000. The annual output at present amounts to roughly 50 stamps.

Philatelic bureau Albimpeks, Tirana.

ALDERNEY

Area 7.9 sq.km, **population** about 2,000, **principal town** St Anne's.

Island forming part of the Bailiwick of Guernsey. Stamps inscribed 'Alderney, Bailiwick of Guernsey' were first issued in 1983 under the authority of the Guernsey post office. There was one annual issue of British provenance. The pictorial stamps that were issued depicted various aspects of life on the island.

Philatelic bureau as Guernsey.

ALLENSTEIN

The East Prussian territories of Allenstein, Ortelsburg, Osterode, Sensburg, Johannisburg, Lotzen, Lyck and Neidenburg (11,520 sq.km) were occupied by an Allied Commission of the Treaty of Versailles, and a plebiscite was held on 11 July 1920, which resulted in the return of the area to Germany.

In 1920 German stamps were overprinted 'PLÉBISCITE OLSZTYN ALLENSTEIN' and also with a self-explanatory overprint referring to the Treaty of Versailles: a total of 28 overprinted provisionals, which were valid from April 1920, and after the departure of the International Commission could be used until October of that year.

ALSACE

Alsace became part of France in 1648 (**area** 8,924 sq.km, **capital** Strasbourg). During the Franco-Prussian War, in 1870, it was occupied together with Lorraine, and became part of the German Empire in 1871. In 1919 under the Treaty of Versailles it was returned to France. During the Second World War, in 1940, it was once again occupied by the German army, but since 1945 Alsace has been French territory.

During the first occupation in 1870 Germany issued stamps which did not bear the name of the country and which were valid also in Lorraine and throughout occupied France. In 1940 an issue of 16 German stamps appeared with the overprint 'Elsass' in Gothic characters. After the truce with France in 1940 French stamps remained valid in Alsace until 14 August 1940, then the overprinted issue was used, while German stamps were equally valid. From 1 January 1942, only German stamps were valid.

ANDORRA

Area 467 sq.km, **population** 39,940 (1982), **capital** Andorra la Vella.

Agricultural and cattle-breeding country high in the Pyrenees between France and Spain. It is under the protection of the President of France (legal representative of the former Counts of Foix) and the Spanish Bishop of Seo de Urgel. Andorra has a customs and currency union with both countries. Tourism plays a major role in the economy. UPU membership represented by the French and Spanish administrations.

Internal mail is handled free of postage charge. Before the issue of Andorran stamps, mail abroad was franked either with Spanish or French stamps according to whichever post carried the mail. Until the end of 1927 foreign mail was taken to the neighbouring Spanish or French post offices, but on 1 January 1928 the first Spanish post office was opened in Andorra, and originally used Spanish stamps.

In March 1928 Spanish stamps were issued bearing the overprint 'ANDORRA'. Definitive stamps of Spanish status appeared in 1929. The stamp production, mostly pictorial, with motifs to publicize the country, features local landscapes. Subjects are taken from Spanish stamp designs, and are printed in Madrid by the same method as the Spanish stamps. They are limited issues not exceeding, in recent years, 2 to 4 issues annually.

Philatelic bureau Postes Espagnol d'Andorra, Servei d'Emissiens, Andorra la Vella.

In 1931 the French postal authorities began issuing stamps. The first French stamps had the overprint 'ANDORRE'; then in 1932 came definitives, all of French origin and inscribed 'VALLEES D'ANDORRE', and from 1944, 'ANDORRE'. Since 1975 the bilingual French-Catalan name 'ANDORRE/ANDORRA' has been used but after 1978 only the Catalan name 'PRINCIPAT D'ANDORRA'. The stamps — particularly those of the present period — are pictorial in character, some being identical with designs used in French issues. Most of the designs relate to the territory of Andorra, but at present there are a number of joint issues with the French posts on other themes. Most stamps are printed by the recess-printing method and designed by French artists. At the present time there are fewer than 10 stamps annually.

Philatelic bureau Service Philatélique, Administration des PTT, Andorra la Vella, or Service Philatélique des Postes et Telecommunications, Paris, France.

ARBE (RAB)

Yugoslav island lying in Kvarner Bay (Arbe is the Italian name). It was for a time occupied by the Italian d'Annunzio volunteers (13 November 1920–5 January 1921), but the island remained Yugoslav. (See also *Fiume, Kvarner, Veglia.*)

After issues for the whole Kvarner region 8 Fiume stamps were given the provisional overprint 'ARBE' in November 1920. Their true postal function has never been reliably clarified.

ATHOS (AFON, AGION OROS)

Autonomous monastrial republic on the Khalkidhiki peninsula in Greece, until 1912 under Ottoman, then under Greek, suzerainty. In the years 1909–14 the Russian postal authorities used Russian stamps with the overprint 'Mont-Athos' (in Latin script) or 'S. Afon' (in Russian Cyrillic script): a total of 16 overprinted provisionals. (See also *Levant.*)

AUNUS (OLONETZ)

Aunus is the Finnish name of the Russian town and province Olonetz, lying on a river of the same name near Lake Ladoga, which was occupied by the Finns for a time in 1919.

In 1919 one issue of 8 stamps appeared. They are Finnish stamps with the overprint 'Aunus'. In view of the limited printing of only 1,100 sets this issue is a dubious one with regard to postal usage, even if 40,000 of each of the first four values were released.

AUSTRIA

Area 83,855 sq.km, **population** 7,57 m (1982), **capital** Vienna.

Country with developed industry and agriculture, republic since 1918. In 1156 Austria split off from Bavaria and became an independent duchy, which from 1282 was under the rule of the Hapsburgs, becoming an empire after 1804. In 1859 the empire lost Lombardy; in 1864

Holstein temporarily became a part of Austria; in 1866 Venice was lost; in 1867 Hungary was acknowledged as an equal partner and the dual Austro-Hungarian monarchy was established. The Kingdom of Hungary had its own stamps (see *Hungary*). In 1878 Austria occupied Bosnia and Herzegovina, and in 1908 annexed them. Then in 1914 the First World War started when Austria attacked Serbia. During this war the Austro-Hungarian army for a time penetrated to Russia, Rumania, Serbia, Montenegro, Albania and Italy. After the capitulation, the monarchy disintegrated into a number of new countries. Austria adopted the name Deutsch-Österreich, but under the peace treaty of Saint Germain this name was prohibited and the official name of Österreich (Austria) was used. Austria lost the territory of the southern Tyrol, southern Styria, and acquired Burgenland (without Sopron), while a plebiscite in Carinthia decided that this region should remain part of Austria. In 1938–45 the country was occupied by Germany, when it was called Ostmark, and in 1945–55 it was divided into four zones of occupation — Soviet, American, British and French. Since 1955 Austria has been a neutral country. UPU membership from 1 July 1875.

The first Austrian stamps were issued in 1850 and did not bear the name of the country, but were inscribed 'K.K. POST STEMPEL'. Some later issues were without any country designation, merely having a figure of value in kreutzer. Next followed stamps inscribed 'KAISERLICHE KÖNIGLICHE ÖSTERREICHISCHE POST' or an abbreviation of this. On the declaration of a republic in 1918 'Deutschösterreich' was used, and from 1922 only 'ÖSTERREICH'. After the Second World War the name 'REPUBLIK ÖSTERREICH' came into use. Since silver currency was valid in Lombardy (ceded to Sardinia in 1859) and in Venice (ceded to Italy in 1866), while on the rest of the Austrian territory only paper currency was in use, Austrian stamps appeared from 1850 onwards in an identical design but in varying currency values, such as kreutzer, centesimi and, later, kreutzer and soldi. While the stamps with values in kreutzer were not valid in the territory of Lombardy and Venice, the issues with nominal value in centesimi and soldi, which were intended for Lombardy and Venice, were valid in the whole of Austria, and from 1863–9 they were used also by the Austrian post offices in the Levant.

After the Second World War — in contrast to Germany — no new stamp countries were established in the territory of Austria as part of the individual zones of occupation. Overprinted provisionals on German stamps and definitive issues were released in the Soviet Zone of Occupation until November 1945, and definitive issues of American origin were issued in the American, British and French Zones, these not being valid in the Soviet Zone. Following the establishment of the second republic in 1945 the usual inscription became 'REPUBLIK ÖSTERREICH' on stamps issued throughout Austria.

Austrian stamps are of a high artistic level, represented before the First World War by the work of K. Moser, and after the war by designers such as Renner, Dachauer (Art Nouveau ornaments), Junk and others. After the Second World War there were numerous designers, all for a long time influenced by Pilch. Successful stamp designers numbered among them the Austrian President, Jonas. The traditional detail in execution of stamp designs is underlined by the achievements of the Austrian State Printing House, using line engraving, which is characteristic of Austrian production. This is dependent on the skill of the engravers themselves, Schirnböck in the earlier days and, later, Lorber, Toth and many others. Subjects of tourist publicity for the country alternate with general motifs and have proved popular with collectors. As the stamps appear in printings of several millions they fulfil their postal purpose and adequately provide propaganda for the country. Commercial ability is revealed in the charming and precise treatment of the designs. Annual output is now some 30 stamps.

The most famous of the classic Austrian stamps are newspaper stamps — the scarlet, rose and yellow 'Mercury' design of 1851 are world rarities. Modern Austrian rarities include the 1933 W.I.P.A. miniature sheet (issued for the Vienna International Philatelic Exhibition), a 10 schilling stamp (1936) with the portrait of the assassinated Chancellor Dollfuss, and the four miniature sheets of the Dr Karl Renner commemoratives (1946). Since 1979 United Nations stamps in Austrian currency and with German texts have been issued and used by the United Nations Headquarters in Vienna.

Philatelic bureau Österreichische Post, Briefmarkenversandstelle, Vienna.

BADEN

Grand Duchy (**area** 15,070 sq.km, **capital** Karlsruhe). Since 1871 a federal state in the German Empire. In 1945 the southern part of the *Land* (capital Freiburg) was part of the French Occupation Zone, while the north formed part of Württemberg-Baden in the American Zone. Today, Baden is part of the federal *Land* of Baden-Württemberg in the Federal Republic of Germany.

After 1851, there was a definitive issue with the name 'BADEN'. Until it was incorporated into the German Imperial Post on 1 January 1872 a total of 28 stamps were issued, intended for normal postal use. The stamp design is numerical in conception and the issues were printed locally by W. Hasper of Karlsruhe. Philatelically, these stamps are among the popular classical issues.

Baden appeared as a stamp-issuing country once again after the Second World War. After the joint issue for the French Zone, a definitive stamp with the name 'BADEN' appeared in the year 1947. A total of 57 stamps with publicity themes for the *Land* appeared until 1949; the designs show the influence of contemporary French stamps. The printing was carried out locally by F. Burda of Offenburg. Since the same artist (V. K. Jonynas) designed stamps also for other *Länder* in the French Occupation Zone of Germany, they are similar in appearance and subject matter. After the proclamation of the Federal Republic of Germany the Baden stamps were valid also in other parts of the Republic (after 3 October 1949), in conjunction with the stamps of the Federal Republic, which took their place. The validity of Baden stamps came to an end on 31 March 1950.

BANAT-BACSKA

Formerly a district of Hungary which was occupied by Serbia in 1919 and, with the exception of a small corner near Szeged, was then divided between Yugoslavia (western part) and Rumania (eastern part). In the interim period of a few days between the evacuation of Serbia and the Rumanian occupation, the postal authorities in Temesvar issued Hungarian stamps with the overprint 'Bánát Bácska'; the same wording is on the overprints of Hungarian stamps issued during the Serbian occupation. A total of 52 stamps, all overprinted provisionals, whose real postal function remains dubious; it is alleged that the postal authorities issued the stamps to cover the wages of postal employees.

BARANYA

District in southern Hungary (**area** 1,214 sq.km, **capital** Pecs).

After the withdrawal of German and Hungarian troops from Rumania and Serbia the district was occupied in 1919 by the Serbian army, which supported the establishment of the Republic of Baranya. When the situation clarified, the northern part of this territory was returned to Hungary (on 20 August 1920) and the southern part became part of Yugoslavia.

In 1919 Hungarian stamps with the overprint 'Baranya 1919'. A total of 64 stamps, all overprinted provisionals.

BASLE (BÂLE, BASEL)

Swiss city and semi-canton (37 sq.km) with its own city postal authorities.

In 1845 definitive stamps were issued with the inscription 'STADT POST BASEL'. A single stamp with the picture of a dove — known among philatelists as the 'Basle Dove' — is a rare classic issue which fulfilled a local postal function. It was the first postage stamp in the world to include embossing in its printing. Basle is the fifth oldest stamp-issuing territory in the world. On 1 January 1849 the Swiss federal postal authorities took over the canton posts and their stamps replaced them from 1850. The Basle stamp remained valid until 30 September 1854.

BAVARIA (BAYERN)

From 1806 a kingdom (**area** 75,863 sq.km, **capital** Munich), after 1871 part of the German Empire. It was proclaimed a republic in 1918; the Rhineland-Palatinate split off after the Second World War.

Definitive issues with the name 'BAYERN' from 1849. These were the first stamps to be issued in the territory of Germany. The first stamp, of a 1 kreutzer denomination, appeared on 1 November 1849 and is one of the most sought-after classic stamps. Stamps of 3 kreutzer and 6 kreutzer denominations quickly followed and were notable for a red silk thread in the paper as a security device. A total of 195 + 74 stamps were issued. The stamp designs were at first symbolic (numerals) in character, but portraits and other symbols were also used, apart from a series of overprinted provisionals, particularly from the period when the republic was proclaimed. At this time Bavarian and German stamps were in simultaneous use with an overprint reading either 'Freistaat Bayern' or 'Volksstaat Bayern' in Gothic script. The printing was carried out locally. An issue of official stamps (Dienstmarke) was used by travelling post offices from 1916 to 1920. Bavarian postage due stamps are interesting for their inscription, 'Vom Empfänger zahlbar' ('payable by the recipient'), either in the design (1862) or as an overprint on normal definitive stamps (1876 and 1888). The Bavarian postal authorities transferred their postal rights to the German Reichspost in 1920, when Bavarian stamps became invalid. Since then Bavaria has used stamps of Germany. It is said that Bavaria sold its postal rights for the sum of 620 million marks.

BELGIUM

Area 30,519 sq.km, **population** 9.86 m (1982), **capital** Brussels (Bruxelles).

A developed industrial country with a stress on heavy industry. Independent kingdom since 1830, occupied almost entirely by the German army from 1914 to 1918 and completely from 1940 to 1944. The territory of Eupen-Malmédy was joined to the country in 1920 (postally in 1925) and temporarily separated from it from 1940 to 1945. In Africa, Belgium owned the colonies of the Congo (until 1960) and Ruanda-Urundi (until 1962). Since 1948 the country has formed part of the customs union of Benelux. Direct UPU membership from 1 July 1875.

In 1849 Belgium was one of the first European countries to introduce stamps (after Great Britain, the Swiss cantons and France). At first they did not bear the name of the issuing country. The name 'BELGIQUE' began to appear in 1869, and from 1891 the bilingual inscription, 'BELGIQUE BELGIË', was used. From 1937 the order of the languages in the bilingual inscription has alternated issue by issue. Since the end of the 1970s some issues have additionally carried the German name 'BELGIEN' in deference to the small minority of Germans (0.6 % of the population) in the Eupen-Malmédy region. The earlier stamps mostly bear portraits or symbolic designs, but post-1930 issues include many typical pictorial stamps. The relatively unified style of Belgian stamps is due to the small number of artists producing stamp designs (including J. van Noten, J. de Bast, M. Severin and J. Malvaux) and to the characteristic photogravure printing by Belgian printers. This is also evident in those issues produced by recess printing. Belgium became notorious in the 1930s for charity stamps which were sold at high premiums over the postal face value, some being exceptionally high and reaching up to thirty times the face value (e.g. 1fr + 30 fr). Regard for the collectors' market is reflected in the use of large formats (already by the 1920s), the production of miniature sheets and other philatelic devices. An unusual feature is the issue of a large number of railway parcel post stamps (since 1879 a total of 432), which is unique. Equally remarkable are Belgian telegraph stamps of the last century, which are hexagonal in shape. Another peculiarity was the inclusion of detachable coupons on the stamps issued in the years 1893–1914, giving instructions for the non-delivery of mail on Sundays. If the sender used the stamp without the coupon, the mail would qualify for delivery even on Sundays. During the First World War Belgian territory occupied by the German army used German stamps with the overprint 'Belgien' in Gothic script. A total of 25 stamps, all overprinted provisionals. The present-day annual production amounts to 40 different stamps.

Philatelic bureau Régie des Postes Belges, Bureau des Collectionneurs, Brussels.

BERGEDORF

Town in northern Germany, originally one of the free Hanseatic cities jointly with Hamburg and Lübeck (1420–1867), and which later became incorporated into Hamburg.

In 1861 a definitive issue with the inscription 'BERGEDORF'. Until 1867 a total of 5 values appeared, symbolic in character, which are considered popular classic stamps. The initials 'LHPA' in the corners of the inner frame mean 'Lübeck-Hamburgisches Post-Amt'. At the Bergedorf post offices, stamps of Denmark and Schleswig-Holstein were also sold to frank correspondence to those countries. In 1867, Hamburg secured jurisdiction over Bergedorf and stamps of Hamburg were put into use until the latter town joined the *North German Postal District* in 1868.

BERLIN

Capital city of pre-war Germany, which was occupied by the Soviet army at the end of the Second World War and divided into four Occupation Sectors, Russian, American, British and French. The American and British entered on 3 July 1945 and the French on 12 August 1945. Of the twenty urban districts of Berlin the Americans administered six, the British four, the French two and the remaining eight came under Soviet administration. With the sharpening of political tension, the joint occupation authorities of the whole of Berlin reached a state of crisis and the three Western Occupation Sectors (American, British and French) separated from the Soviet in June 1948. West Berlin established its own authorities and issued its own postage stamps. Since 1949 East Berlin has been the capital city of the German Democratic Republic.

In June 1945, 7 definitive stamps were issued in the Soviet zone of occupation of Germany with the name 'STADT BERLIN', which were valid in the entire territory of Brandenburg (one part of the Soviet Occupation Zone, 26,976 sq.km in area) until 31 October 1946. The stamps of the Soviet Occupation Zone were valid in the whole territory of Berlin (including West Berlin until 31 March 1949, although they were not on sale there). In the years 1945–8 German stamps of the American-British and Soviet Zone, and the joint issues of these Zones were in circulation in West Berlin. After the currency reform in the Western-occupied Zones of Germany on 24 June 1946 the joint issues for the American, British and Soviet Zones were given overprints of individual postal districts including 'BERLIN' for use in the Soviet Zone of Germany.

BOHEMIA AND MORAVIA

When the German army occupied Czech territory on 15 March 1939, separating it from Slovakia, a Protectorate of the German Reich was established on 16 March 1939 (**area** 49,363 sq.km, **capital** Prague or Praha). This came to an end in May 1945.

Two Czechoslovak stamps bearing the name 'ČESKO-SLOVENSKO' appeared after the establishment of the Protectorate of Bohemia and Moravia. From 15 July 1939 Czechoslovak stamps were used with the overprint 'BÖHMEN u. MÄHREN', 'ČECHY A MORAVA', followed soon after by definitives with the same inscription. In 1942 the heading 'DEUTSCHES REICH' was added and in 1943 'GROSSDEUTSCHES REICH'. A total of 124 + 57 stamps of local origin were produced by the Bohemian Graphic Union, Prague, either in photogravure or recess printing. The stamp designs are of two different types: one is a direct continuation or adaptation of the preceding Czechoslovak stamp production (landscape issues and newspaper stamps); the other shows the influence of German stamp design. The majority of the stamps have landscapes, portraits or other naturalistic compositions.

BOSNIA AND HERZEGOVINA

Part of the Ottoman Empire, occupied by Austria-Hungary in 1878 and annexed in 1908 (**area** 51,850 sq.km, **capital** Sarajevo). The area formed part of Yugoslavia in 1918–41 and after its occupation by the German army in the Second World War became part of Croatia. Since 1945 it has been a federal republic of Yugoslavia.

Stamps of the Ottoman Empire were followed by definitive issues from 1879 to 1906 with the Austrian Imperial Arms as the design, but without a name. From 1906 stamps bore the name 'BOSNIEN HERZEGOWINA'. In 1912 the spelling changed to 'BOSNIEN HERCEGO-VINA', to which 'K.U.K. MILITÄRPOST' was added. Subsequent issues retained the 'MILI-TÄRPOST' but omitted the territory name. These stamps were not valid abroad at first, thus avoiding disputes as to the language of the wording. A total of 148 + 26 stamps were issued, mostly symbolic or portraits. A landscape series of the years 1906–12 was designed by Kolo Moser and engraved by F. Schirnböck. In their time these were leading examples of pictorials, representing a stage in European stamp production that was only reached much later by other countries.

In 1918 Bosnia and Herzegovina became part of Yugoslavia, and the remaining Bosnian stamps were overprinted in Latin and Cyrillic script with 'BOSNA I HERCEGOVINA', with the additional words 'DRŽAVA S.H.S.'. A total of 35 stamps, all overprinted provisionals.

BREMEN

Free Hanseatic city with the oldest German port (256 sq.km with the enclaves Vegesack and Bremerhaven), member of the German and North German Confederation from 1868 to 1871, when the German Empire was founded. From 1855 there was a definitive issue with the inscription 'BREMEN'. A total of 15 stamps symbolic in character and of local manufacture were issued, which are regarded philatelically as sought-after classic stamps. They remained valid until 1867. Apart from the Bremen post, the posts of Hanover, Thurn and Taxis, Prussia and Oldenburg were in operation in Bremen, and their stamps were sold at Bremen post offices. They were replaced by the stamps of the *North German Postal District* in 1868.

BRUNSWICK (BRAUNSCHWEIG)

German Duchy (**area** 3,690 sq.km, **capital** Braunschweig) which joined the North German Confederation in 1867 and, after 1871, the German Empire (proclaimed a republic in 1918).

Definitive stamps with the text 'BRAUNSCHWEIG' from 1852: total of 20 locally produced stamps, symbolic in character. These are classic stamps of which, in particular, the first issue ranks as rare. Their validity came to an end in 1867. From 1868 the stamps of the *North German Postal District* came into use. The 1857 issue was made in blocks of four on each sheet, each of the stamps having the face value of one quarter of a gutergroschen and being, in size, one of the smallest stamps in the world.

BULGARIA

Area 110,912 sq.km, **population** 8.93m (1982), **capital** Sofia.

People's Republic; economy — industry and agriculture. Bulgaria freed itself from Turkish domination after the defeat of the Ottoman Empire in 1878, but until 1908 it remained a vassal princedom. Only then did the country gain full independence and proclaimed itself a kingdom (the Bulgarian Tsardom). In 1885 *Eastern Rumelia*, or South Bulgaria, was annexed. In the Balkan Wars, Bulgaria acquired the Aegean coast, but lost Southern Dobrudža and many territories that it had previously conquered. In the First World War, Bulgaria was an ally of the Ottoman Empire and Germany and thus lost Western Thrace, which became Greek, as well as 3,000 square kilometres of further territory, which went to Yugoslavia. In the Second World War Bulgaria, again a German ally, occupied Southern Dobrudža, part of Yugoslavia and Greek Macedonia and Western Thrace, so that its size increased to almost 166,000 square kilometres. In the post-war settlement, however, it again lost these newly acquired territories, with the exception of Southern Dobrudža. In the course of 1944, as the Soviet army advanced, there was an uprising in Bulgaria and the country declared war on Germany. In 1946 the monarchy was abolished and a People's Republic was proclaimed. Indirect UPU Membership from 1 July 1875 (Turkey), direct from 1 July 1879.

Until 1879 stamps of the Ottoman Empire were in use; except for French stamps issued at a French post office operating in Varna. During the Russo-Turkish war of 1877–8 mail was paid for in cash in the occupied Bulgarian territory; later, Russian stamps came into use. Even after the issue of specifically Bulgarian stamps, the Austrian postal authorities played a significant role in conveying mail abroad. Definitive stamps were issued from 1879 on. These bore a Cyrillic inscription meaning 'Bulgarian Post', and from 1911 the name 'BULGA-RIYA' began to appear in Cyrillics, and was used simultaneously with the surviving inscriptions of 'Bulgarian Post' or 'Bulgarian Tsardom'. Before the Second World War, the name 'POSTE BULGARE' or 'BULGARIE' occasionally appeared printed in Latin script, and after the war, in almost every issue, some of the stamps bore the name 'BULGARIA', 'REPUBLI-KA BULGARIA', NARODNA REPUBLIKA BULGARIA' or only 'N.R. BULGARIA' in Latin script. Since 1968 the name has been given exclusively in Cyrillic characters.

The strong Russian political influence was first reflected even in the earliest Bulgarian stamps, which were influenced by Russian stamp designs and were printed in St Petersburg. Later the stamps were also printed in Berlin, Vienna and London. From 1923 printing was by the State Printing House in Sofia in photogravure or offset-lithography. The designs overall are pictorial and publicize national activities as well as general themes. A number of top designers have contributed to stamp production in Bulgaria, especially Kančev, Geristonovova, Rusinev, Koronev and Kosturkovova, whose graphic work has unique characteristics. Certain issues appear in small printings for stamp collectors (300,000 down to 100,000 a series and even fewer), perforated and unperforated stamps or sheets. The present-day annual production runs to 70–80 different stamps.

Philatelic bureau Hemus, Sofia.

CALINO (KALIMNOS)
One of the Italian Aegean islands in the Dodecanese group, held by Italy 1912–47 (**area** 109 sq.km, **capital** Calino).

In the years 1912–32 overprints on Italian stamps 'Calimno' or 'CALINO'. Total issue 26 stamps, all overprinted provisionals. Issues considered to be designed for collectors (with small printings of 10,000 to 12,000 stamps) and of doubtful postal validity. (See also *Rhodes and the Dodecanese Islands*.)

CAMPIONE
A small Italian village lying within Swiss territory in an Italian enclave on the shore of Lake Lugano.

From May 1944 to 1952 a total of 12 stamps were issued bearing the inscription 'COMU-NE DI CAMPIONE' with the heading 'R.R. POSTE ITALIANE' and values in Swiss currency for mail to Switzerland. The first issue depicted the Arms of Campione and the Cross of Savoy and was printed in Zürich. A pictorial issue, in photogravure by Courvoisier, followed, showing scenes from Campione, Modena, Verona and elsewhere in Italy. Campione stamps ceased to have validity in 1952 and Swiss or Italian stamps are used in their place, either issue being internationally valid. Swiss stamps cannot now be cancelled at Campione, but at the post office in Lugano.

CARCHI (KHALKI)
One of the Italian Aegean Islands, Italian 1912–47 (**area** 66 sq.km, **capital** Ofri).

From 1912 to 1932 Italian stamps overprinted 'Karki', 'CARCHI' or 'CALCHI'. A total of 26 stamps, overprinted provisionals considered to have been issued for the collectors' market (total 10,000–12,000 stamps) and of doubtful postal purpose. (See also *Rhodes and the Dodecanese Islands*.)

CARINTHIA
The southernmost Austrian province (**area** 5,922 sq.km, **capital** Klagenfurt), bordering on Italy and Yugoslavia, and with a large Slovene population. In 1919 nationality was decided by plebiscite and the territory was divided into zone A and zone B, zone B voting only in the event that the plebiscite in zone A came out in favour of Yugoslavia. Voting in the southern zone A (the Klagenfurt region) took place on 10 October 1920 and was in favour of Austria.

In 1920 Austrian stamps with the Gothic-character overprint 'Kärnten Abstimmung', total of 19 overprinted provisionals resulting. There were also stamps of the *Kingdom of the Serbs, Croats and Slovenes* (Yugoslavia), with interesting Art Nouveau overprints 'KGCA' (Koroska Glasovalna Cona A), a total of 6 overprinted and surcharged provisionals. Both issues were sold at post offices at three times the face value.

CARPATHIAN UKRAINE

The most easternly part of Czechoslovakia, called Ruthenia, which proclaimed independence on 14 March 1939 as Carpathian-Ukraine (**area** 11,094 sq.km, **capital** Khust). However, the following day Khust was occupied by the Hungarian army and the entire country was occupied by 18 March. (See also *Transcarpathian Ukraine*.)

The first and only issue in 1939 (a 3 koruny Czechoslovak pictorial of Jasina) with the name Carpatho-Ukraine (in Cyrillic script) as an addition to Česko-Slovensko. The stamp was issued on the occasion of the inauguration of the Carpatho-Ukrainian Parliament. Issued in Prague and Khust 15 March (on the declaration of independence of Carpatho-Ukraine). Used for postal purposes only in Khust until the arrival of the Hungarian army on 16 March, so that it was in circulation for only a few hours.

CASO (KASOS)

One of the Italian Aegean Islands, Italian 1912-47 (**area** 66 sq.km, **capital** Ofri).

In the years 1912–32 overprints on Italian stamps reading 'Caso' or 'CASO'. A total of 26 stamps, all overprinted provisionals. Considered to be issued for the collectors' market with printings ranging from 10,000 to 12,000 for different values. The postal need for these stamps was questionable. (See also *Rhodes and the Dodecanese Islands*.)

CASTELROSSO or CASTELLORIZO (MEGISTA)

Island (11 sq.km) off the Asia Minor coast of Turkey in the eastern Mediterranean. It was occupied by French naval units from 24 December 1915 to 21 August 1921, ceded to Italy under the peace treaties of Sèvres and Lausanne and incorporated in the Italian Aegean Islands (Dodecanese). In 1942-5 the island was occupied by the British, then ceded to Greece. In 1976 the name was changed to the Greek name of Megista.

From 1915 stamps of the French postal authorities in the Levant with the overprint 'BNF CASTELLORIZO' (BNF = Base Navale Française) or 'ONF CASTELLORIZO' (ONF = Occupation Navale Française). Later, French stamps with the overprint 'OF CASTELLORISO' (OF = Occupation Française). A total of 34 stamps, all overprinted provisionals.

After the withdrawal of the French army in 1921, stamps of the Italian Aegean Islands (Dodecanese) were used (see *Rhodes and the Dodecanese Islands*), followed in 1922 by Italian stamps with the overprint 'CASTELROSSO': a total of 39 stamps, mostly overprinted provisionals. There was one definitive issue in 1923 on the occasion of the second anniversary of the Italian occupation of the island (a map of the island and the Italian flag), the printing being 100,000 sets, obviously designed as propaganda. Other issues had printings of only 10,000 to 12,000 stamps and were aimed at the collector's market, their postal function being minimal. In the years 1932–41 issues of the Italian Aegean Islands were in use; in 1942–43 a British occupation issue with overprint 'MEF' (Middle East Forces). After cession to Greece, Greek stamps came into use.

CAVALLA

Port in eastern Macedonia, Turkish until 1912, occupied by Bulgaria 1913, and that same year by Greece, on whose territory it lies to this day.

From 1893 the French postal authorities used their own stamps – the French Peace and Commerce and later definitives with an overprint, or the inscription, 'CAVALLE': a total of 16 stamps. The French post was abolished in 1914. During the Greek occupation in 1913 Bulgarian stamps were used with an overprint referring to the Greek administration. (See also *Levant*.)

CENTRAL ALBANIA

After the overthrow in September 1914 of the Albanian monarch (the German Prince Wilhelm of Wied) installed by the Great Powers, Albania was proclaimed a republic with an appointed President, General Essad Pasha, who was supported by Italy. He used his army to control the territory of Central Albania until 1916. The local post office used Albanian Skanderberg stamps of 1913 and a non-issued series of the same year with the inscription, 'QEVERRIA

E SQPNIS/ALBANIE CENTRALE', which had control overprints in Turkish. A total of 21 + 7 values appeared. Their true postal function has never been reliably confirmed and forgeries are known.

CENTRAL LITHUANIA
Territory covering four districts on the frontier of Lithuania (**area** 13,014 sq.km, **capital** Vilnius), which Russia ceded to Lithuania and which was occupied in 1919 by Poland. A second occupation occurred on 9 October 1920 by the Polish General Zeligowski, when the territory became Central Lithuania. In March 1922 the entire territory was incorporated into Poland, and on 10 October 1939 again became part of Lithuania under a treaty between the U.S.S.R. and Lithuania.

In 1920 Lithuania issued stamps with overprints and definitive stamps, all bearing the Polish text 'SRODKOWA LITWA', a total of 47 + 6 stamps of Lithuanian and Polish origin. The overprinted issue appeared in a small printing of 360 sets, otherwise the printings were often as high as 600,000 and even a million in some cases. From April 1922 Polish stamps became valid.

CONSTANTINOPLE
Capital city of the Ottoman Empire (now Istanbul), where a number of foreign post offices operated.

In the years 1896 to 1919 the Rumanian post office was in operation here, and in 1919 6 overprinted provisionals were issued consisting of Rumanian stamps overprinted 'POSTA ROMANA CONSTANTINOPOL' and the date '1919'. From 1909 to 1914 the Russian post office used Russian stamps with the overprint 'Constantinople', a total of 9 overprinted provisionals. The Italian postal authorities (1909–23) issued a total of 27 + 6 stamps with the overprint 'Constantinopoli' and a local currency surcharge. (See also *Levant*).

CORFU (KERKYRA)
Greek island in the Ionian Sea (593.5 sq.km) occupied by Italy at the end of August 1923 as reprisal for members of an Italian commission who were killed in northern Greece. The Serbian government in exile (see *Serbia*) had its seat on the island after 1916. The Italian occupation continued until the end of September 1923. A second Italian occupation took place in 1941, and was superseded in 1943 by the German one. In 1923 a total of 11 overprinted provisionals appeared. They were Italian stamps with the overprint 'CORFU' in insignificant printings of 5,000 to 10,000 stamps. In 1941, during the second Italian occupation, Greek stamps were also overprinted 'CORFU' (a total of 31 + 14). In view of certain very small printings (only 62 stamps in some cases) it is doubtful if they ever fulfilled a postal function. During the German occupation in 1943 Greek stamps were reintroduced. (See also *Ionian Islands*).

COS (COO)
One of the Italian Aegean Islands, Italian 1912–47 (**area** 283 sq.km, **capital** Cos).

In 1912–32 overprints on Italian stamps with the word 'Cos' or 'COO'. A total of 26 stamps, all overprinted provisionals. These issues were designed mainly for the collector market, with printings of 10,000 to 12,000, so that their postal function is dubious.

COURLAND
Latvian territory between the Bay of Riga and the Baltic Sea. The part with a German garrison was cut off from the main territory by the Soviet offensive in January 1945. On 20 April 1945, 4 German stamps were issued with the overprint 'KURLAND' (total printings 45,000 to 125,000) for civilian use.

CRETE
The largest of the Greek islands in the Sea of Crete (**area** 8,335 sq.km, **capital** Herakleion, Iraklion or Candia).

Crete was Turkish after 1669, gained independence in 1878, but was controlled by the Turks from 1889. In 1897 an uprising of the local population took place with Greek aid (causing the Greco-Turkish war), and the Turks appealed to the European powers to intervene. Great Britain, France, Italy and Russia sent ships in 1898 (Germany and Austria did not participate) and occupied the island until 1909. Italy occupied the west (Chania, Khanea or La Canea), France the east (Sitia, Lasithion), Great Britain the centre (Iraklion, Herakleion or Candia) and Russia the territory between the British and the Italian part (Retymnon or Rethymno). Turkey was then requested to withdraw its troops from Crete in 1898. The Greek prince became governor, and in 1908 the Cretan Parliament proclaimed union with Greece, which was achieved after the Balkan wars in 1913, when Crete became a Greek province.

At various times there were Turkish, Greek, Austrian, French and Italian post offices on Cretan territory. The 1898 uprising resulted in stamps for the occupied areas (see *Iraklion*, British P.O., *La Canea*, Italian P.O., and *Rethymnon*, Russian P.O.)

After 1900 the independent Cretan postal authorities issued their own stamps, beginning with definitives bearing the name Crete in Greek lettering. Some of these stamps were given Greek overprints meaning 'Provisional'. This issue was used for mail for abroad until Crete joined the UPU in 1902. A total of 34 + 11 stamps, mostly recess-printed in London, apart from numerous overprinted provisionals. After 1908 Greek stamps were used, the first Greek issues being Cretan stamps with the Greek overprint 'ELLAS'. Remainders of Cretan stamps were used in Greece in 1923 with a Greek overprint meaning 'Revolution'. The French post office on Crete used French issues with the word 'CRÈTE' from 1902 on. A total of 20 stamps, all overprints on contemporary French definitive issues. The French post office on Crete was closed in 1914.

CROATIA

On 29 October 1918 the Croatian National Council announced the formation of a state that comprised all the Yugoslav territory that had formerly belonged to the Austro-Hungarian Empire. In November of that year they agreed with the government of Serbia and the Yugoslav Commission to form a Kingdom of the Serbs, Croats and Slovenes (S.H.S.). During the Second World War, after the occupation of Yugoslavia by Germany and Italy, a Croatian state was established on 10 April 1941, which remained formally a kingdom until 1943. (Independent enclave of Croatia, **area** 102,724 sq.km including Bosnia and Herzegovina, **capital** Zagreb.) The puppet state of Croatia ended in 1945. After the capitulation of Italy in 1943 its territory was enlarged by parts of Dalmatia, which the Italians occupied in 1941.

In 1918 the first definitives were issued with the name 'HRVATSKA' and the date of the declaration of independence (29 October) and were contemporary with overprints on Hungarian stamps with the name as 'HRVATSKA SHS'. These and a further definitive issue (January 1919) were followed by stamps of the *Kingdom of the Serbs, Croats and Slovenes* in 1921. A total of 48 stamps, the definitives of local provenance, the majority with symbols of liberation.

After 1941 came Yugoslav stamps overprinted 'NEZAVISNA DRŽAVA HRVATSKA', followed by definitives with the same wording, or the abbreviation 'N.Z. HRVATSKA'. A total of 230 stamps, mostly pictorials of topical and political themes concerning Croatia. Printings were limited with an eye to the collectors' market — for instance, of the second overprinted issue there were only 5,000 stamps, and even some series of definitives appeared in deliberately small printings. There were also miniature sheets printed, mainly to attract collectors. Offset, photogravure and recess printing of the stamps took place in Zagreb and Vienna. Co-operation with foreign artists resulted in varying styles of design. Portraits tended to predominate in the designs. From 1945 Yugoslav stamps came into use.

CZECHOSLOVAKIA (ČESKOSLOVENSKO)
Area 127,896 sq.km, **population** 15.42m (1983), **capital** Prague (Praha).

Socialist republic, federation of two national republics, the Czech Socialist Republic and the Slovak Socialist Republic. Developed economy with industry and agriculture. Member of the U.P.U. indirectly since 1 July 1875 as part of the Austro-Hungarian Empire and directly from 18 May 1920 as Czechoslovakia.

Czechoslovakia came into existence on 28 October 1918 after the disintegration of the Austro-Hungarian Empire. Slovakia became part of Czechoslovakia on 30 October 1918 under the Martin Declaration adopted at a session of the Slovak National Council, whose participants did not know that Czechoslovakia as such had been proclaimed in Prague on 28 October 1918. Trans-Carpathian Russia was added in 1919. According to the Treaty of Versailles, Hlučínsko became part of Czechoslovakia; and Vitoraz and the Valtice region under the Treaty of St Germain from 9 August 1920. The dispute with Poland over the Těšín region was to be solved by plebiscite (see *Eastern Silesia*), but in the end it was divided between the two countries by decision of the Council of Ambassadors on 28 July 1920. Poland also received part of the territory of Slovakia at Spiš and the River Orava, but in 1923 the Javorina region was added to the Czechoslovak Republic. In 1938 the Bohemian and Moravian borderland and a smaller area near Bratislava was ceded to Germany under the Munich Agreement (1–10 October and 24 November 1938), Poland occupied two-thirds of the Těšín region and part of the Čadca district (2–11 October), the Javorina region and part of Orava, Lysa and Majery on the River Dunajec and Lesnica in the Pieniny Hills, Medzibrodie in the Poprad River (1–30 November). Hungary occupied the borderland in southern Slovakia and part of Trans-Carpathian Russia (5–10 November); Slovakia and Trans-Carpathian Russia (i.e. Carpathian Ukraine) were given the promise of autonomy (6 October and 11 October 1938). After all these events the state formally became Czecho-Slovakia and was regarded legally as the Second Republic. The Slovak Assembly proclaimed the establishment of an independent Slovak state in Bratislava on 14 March 1939, whereby Czechoslovakia ceased to exist, but the situation was resolved the following day (15 March), when German units occupied Czech territory, from which the Protectorate of Bohemia and Moravia was formed on 16 March. Following Slovakia, the Carpathian Ukraine declared independence on 14 March 1939, but was immediately occupied by the Hungarian army, which took over the adjacent strip of the eastern Slovakian territory. The struggle of the Czechs and Slovaks for the re-establishment of the Czechoslovak state and its sovereignty reached its climax in 1944 in Slovakia, and in 1945 the Czech National Uprising took place, with the country gradually being liberated throughout 1944 and 1945 from the east by the Soviet, Czechoslovak, Rumanian and Polish armies, while the American army occupied Western Bohemia. Czechoslovakia was re-established within the original frontiers of 1938. In an agreement with the Soviet Union of 29 June 1945 the Trans-Carpathian Ukraine became part of the Soviet Union, to which a small part of the borderland of Eastern Slovakia was added. Under the Paris Peace Treaty of 1946 the Bratislava bridgehead (Rusovce and surroundings) was added to Czechoslovakia. Minor alterations of the original state frontier were carried out at an even later stage in agreement with Austria and Poland.

From 1918 definitive stamps were issued bearing the wording 'POŠTA ČESKO-SLOVEN-SKÁ', then 'POŠTA ČESKOSLOVENSKÁ' and, finally 'ČESKOSLOVENSKO'. In 1939 stamps once again bore the name as 'ČESKO-SLOVENSKO', expressing the dualism of the state of the time, when Slovakia was given autonomy. The stamps were printed by varying processes, mainly recess printing, which is typical of Czechoslovak production. Multi-colour rotary recess printing has been used effectively for some issues. From an artistic point of view peak achievements in the earlier productions were made by Mucha and Švabinský; more recently by artists like Svolinský, Liesler, Šváb, Strnad, Lukavský and others. Outstanding engravers are Švengsbír, Schmidt, Herčík, Housa, Jirka and others, some of whom also work on stamp designing. Annual production at the present time is about 60 different stamps. Apart from themes publicizing the country there are many issues covering different general subjects. Printings are usually in the millions, the higher values with limited issues being around 400,000. Purely 'philatelic' items are produced in much lower quantities. Typical of Czechoslovakia are coupons which began to appear in the 1930s. Curios include the special souvenir sheets of 15 of each value of the Czech National Anthem Centenary stamps of 1934. Each sheet of the 1Kr. and 2Kr. stamps was printed on thick carton paper (ungummed) measuring 17.5 × 28.5cm. Words and music of the anthem were printed above and below the stamps in the sheet.

Philatelic bureau Artia, Prague.

DANZIG (GDAŃSK)

Hanseatic town occupied by Prussia in 1792, separated from Germany under the Treaty of Versailles in 1919 and proclaimed, with the surrounding territory, a free city (Freie Stadt Danzig, 1,893 sq.km). Towards the end of 1924 the Free City of Danzig ceded to Poland a plot of land on which a Polish post office, Port Gdańsk, was established on 5 January 1925. On 1 September 1939 the entire territory was occupied by Germany and after the war it became part of Poland.

From 1920 German stamps with the overprint 'DANZIG' or 'Danzig'; later, definitives with the words 'FREIE STADT DANZIG' or 'Freie Stadt Danzig': a total of 308 + 98 stamps. Apart from numerous overprinted provisionals, definitive stamps with subjects publicizing the region, mostly made by M. Buchholz, with striking influences of German stamp production, especially when printing was transferred to Berlin. Danzig also reflected the German inflation in the year 1923 with face values up to 500 million Marks. After 1939 German stamps were used and from 1945, Polish ones. From 1925 the Polish post office in Gdańsk used Polish stamps with the overprint 'PORT GDAŃSK'. In 1938 a pictorial issue marked the tenth anniversary of Polish independence. A total of 37 stamps, mostly overprinted provisionals; the four-value commemorative issue of Polish origin shows Polish stamp characteristics. From 1934 the Gdańsk stamps were also valid in Poland. In September 1939 the Polish post office in Gdańsk was closed.

DEDEAGACH

Dedeagach, today Alexandroúpolis, seaport in Western Thrace (now Greece), until 1912 part of Turkey. In 1912–13 it was occupied by the Bulgarians and in 1913 by Greece for several months. In October 1913 it was ceded to Bulgaria, which ruled it until 1918, then it became once again part of Greece, though there was another Bulgarian occupation in the years 1941–5.

In 1874–1914 a French post office was in operation here and issued its own stamps from 1893 on, using ordinary French stamps and surcharged issues of French post offices in the Turkish Empire overprinted 'Dédéagh' (a total of 16 stamps). In 1913, during the Greek occupation, 22 primitive provisional stamps and overprints on Bulgarian stamps were issued in two and a half months. The inscriptions are in Greek script and include the name Dedeagatz. The true postal function of these overprints has never been fully clarified.

DENMARK

Area 43,080 sq.km, **population** 5.12m (1983), **capital** Copenhagen.

Developed economy with industry, agriculture and intensive livestock breeding. Constitutional monarchy with overseas territories, Greenland and the Faeroe Islands. Norway belonged to Denmark until 1813, as did Schleswig-Holstein until 1864. Iceland was Danish until 1918 when an independent kingdom with the Danish king as monarch was declared. Iceland became a republic in 1944. In 1920 the northern part of Schleswig was returned to Danish nationality. In 1917 Denmark sold its territory in the West Indies to the USA for $ 25,000,000. In the years 1940–5 the country was occupied by the German army. Direct UPU membership of Denmark, including Greenland, as of 1 July 1875.

Definitive issues from 1851, initially without the name of the country, but from 1870 onwards with the word 'DANMARK'. From its first issue of 1851 Denmark has maintained a very conservative stamp-issuing policy, stamps being sold primarily for postal use rather than to philatelists. A total of 588 + 124 stamps (in over 130 years!). The stamps are produced in Denmark and, since 1933, exclusively by recess printing. They are striking designs of national interest. Apart from numerals and portraits present-day production includes symbolic topics. A number of stamp designs are of a high artistic standard. Most of the commemorative issues are single stamps. Definitive issues are long-lived and added to as postage rates alter. The designs of these have been simple portraits of the monarch. The design of postage due stamps was unchanged from 1921 until their withdrawal in 1968. Outstanding among present-day designers are Nellemann, Stage, Schwalbe, S. and A. Havsteen-Middelsen. The chief engraver in recent years has been C. Slania of Sweden. The present-day production does not exceed 20–25 stamps annually. Greenland has had stamps of its own since 1938 and the Faeroe Islands since 1975. Greenland parcel stamps were used for parcels from Denmark to Greenland.

Philatelic bureau Postens Filateli, Copenhagen.

DURAZZO
Seaport in central Albania on the Adriatic coast. The Albanian territory was under the administration of the Ottoman Empire. From 1902 the Italians opened a post office in the port (see *Albania*), and from 1909 to 1916 Italian stamps were in use with the overprint 'DURAZZO' and a local currency surcharge. When the Italian post office was closed in 1916 a total of 9 stamps had been issued.

EASTERN KARELIA
Russian territory occupied in 1941–3 by the Finnish army which fought on the side of Germany against the USSR.

In 1941-3 Finnish stamps with the overprint 'ITÄ KARJALA' were issued for the occupied parts of Karelia: a total of 27 stamps, all in printings of many thousands. In 1943 a single charity stamp (3.50m + 1.50m) appeared additionally inscribed 'SUOMI-FINLAND'. (See also *Karelia*.)

EASTERN RUMELIA
Turkish territory in southern Bulgaria which, after the Russo-Turkish War, was to become part of Bulgaria under the peace negotiations of San Stefano (3 March 1878) but which, according to the resolutions of the Congress of Berlin that same year, became a semi-autonomous Turkish province (**area** 32,720 sq.km, **capital** Philippopolis, today Plovdiv). A rising in Plovdiv in September 1885 led to the occupation and annexing of the territory by Bulgaria on 14 July 1886.

When issues of the Ottoman Empire became invalid in the area they were given the overprint 'R.O.' (= ROUMELIE ORIENTALE) in 1880, then definitives were issued similar to contemporary Turkish stamps, inscribed 'Eastern Rumelia' in four languages, French, Turkish, Bulgarian and Greek. A total of 18 stamps appeared until 1885 when they were replaced by stamps of *Southern Bulgaria*.

EASTERN SAXONY
The eastern part of Saxony, one of the territories in the Soviet Occupation Zone in Germany established in 1945, (**area** 16,922 sq.km, **capital** Dresden).

First, in 1945, primitive designs with the word 'POST', followed in 1946 by one definitive issue of two stamps with the inscription 'BUNDESLAND SACHSEN' (together with 'DEUTSCHE POST') depicting buildings in Dresden and printed at the local newspaper office in Dresden.

EASTERN SILESIA
In 1919–20 territory consisting of part of Těšin (2,278 sq.km), part of Orava (1,206 sq.km) and Spiš (539 sq.km) where in 1920 a plebiscite was called to decide whether it should be incorporated into Poland or Czechoslovakia. The interim demarcation line was stipulated by the Inter-Allied Commission in 1919. Voting did not take place, however, and on 28 July 1920 the Conference of Ambassadors allotted 1,009 sq.km of Těšin, 358 sq.km of Orava and 217 sq.km of Spiš to Poland. The border with Těšin was moved a little to the east for Czechoslovakia as compared with the line of demarcation. In 1923 Javorina (92 sq.km) was returned to Czechoslovakia, and in 1924 Hladovka (18 sq.km) and Suchá Hora (22 sq.km) were incorporated into the Czechoslovak Republic in exchange for part of Dolná Lipnica, called Slovenská Lipnica (70 sq.km).

At the instigation of the Commission, with its seat in Těšín, from 2 February 1920, stamps were issued in Czechoslovakia (a total of 37 provisionals on Czechoslovak stamps) and in Poland (a total of 10 provisionals on Polish stamps) all overprinted 'S.O. 1920' (= Silésie Orientale). The Czechoslovak issue was valid in the Czech part of Těšín, in Orava and Spiš. The Polish issues were valid in the rest of the territory.

ESTONIA

Baltic country (**area** 47,549 sq.km, **capital** Tallinn, formerly Reval), originally part of Tsarist Russia, occupied by the Germans in 1918, and an independent republic from 1918 to 6 August 1940 when it became part of the USSR. In the Second World War, Estonia was once again occupied by the German army (1941–4) and incorporated into the region known as Ostland, but it reverted to being part of the USSR after the war.

Definitive stamps with the inscription 'EESTI POST' began to be issued in 1918, later as 'EESTI VABARIK', and then just 'EESTI'. A total of 164 stamps made locally, mostly in the state printing house in Tallinn. The designs were of local historical interest. A number of issues were in small printings, which is typical of stamps produced for the collectors' market. After the establishment of the Estonian Soviet Socialist Republic in 1940, 5 stamps appeared inscribed 'EESTI POST'. Estonian stamps were postally valid until 31 January 1941 and were then replaced by Soviet stamps. After the attack on the USSR by the German army in 1941, German stamps were valid throughout Estonia. In August 1941 stamps with the inscription 'ESTLAND-EESTI' were issued by the Germans. A total of 9 stamps appeared in the year 1941 in two issues, one symbolic (including the swastika) and the other pictorial in character. The second issue was in circulation until 30 April 1942. In the following stage of the German occupation, German stamps were valid in Estonian territory with the overprint 'OSTLAND' (see *Ostland*). In the autumn of 1944 Soviet stamps were given validity throughout Estonia.

EUPEN

Belgium acquired the small German territory of Eupen by plebiscite in 1920. In March 1920 16 + 5 Belgian stamps with the overprint 'EUPEN' were issued, and remained valid until 30 April 1931. These stamps could also be used in Malmédy (and vice versa). Belgian stamps were in use after 1925. In the years 1940–44 the territory was occupied by Germany.

EUPEN AND MALMÉDY

German territory (Prussian from 1815) which was ceded to Belgium in 1920 (**area** 1,056 sq.km) on the basis of a decision under the Treaty of Versailles of 1919 and a plebiscite. In the years 1940–44 it was again occupied by Germany.

From 1920 Belgian stamps with the overprint 'EUPEN & MALMÉDY'. A total of 7 stamps, all overprinted provisionals, which remained valid until 31 March 1920. They were followed by issues for Eupen and for Malmédy.

FAEROE ISLANDS

Area 1,399 sq.km, **population** 44,479 (1982), **capital** Thorshavn.

Autonomous region of Denmark with separatist tendencies. The islands were Norwegian from 1035 on, but were ceded to Denmark under the Calmar Union of 1397. During the First World War they remained Danish. During the Second World War the British occupied the Faeroe Islands, but Danish stamps (which were imported, with British permission, via neutral Portugal) continued to be valid. UPU membership through Denmark.

Separate definitive stamps, bearing the name 'FØROYAR' (in the Faeroese language) appeared in 1975, replacing Danish issues, which had been valid until that time. Present-day annual production is around 10 stamps, the designs depicting the life and history of the inhabitants and the nature of the Faeroe Islands.

Philatelic bureau Postverk Foroya, Faeroese Postal Service, Philatelic Office, Thorshavn.

FEDERAL REPUBLIC OF GERMANY
Area 248,690 sq.km, **population** 61.64 m (1982), **capital** Bonn.

Highly developed industrial country with advanced agriculture, in value of production fourth in the world. Direct UPU membership as Germany from 1 July 1875; as Federal Republic of Germany from 1955.

The Federal Republic of Germany issues stamps that, since 1950, have been inscribed 'DEUTSCHE BUNDESPOST'. Stamps are printed by various methods including line-engraving at the Bundesdruckerei in Berlin. Many designs are of specifically national interest although, more recently, general themes of international interest have increased, all being on a high artistic level, both naturalistic and stylised. Many issues are portraits of famous Germans and there is a tendency towards symbolic designs, all printed to a high standard. Leading designers include O. Blase, E. Ege, H. and H. Schillinger, H. Michel, G. Kieser, H. Kern and others. Printings of around 30 million ensure a wide distribution for both publicity purposes and postal use. Present annual output is about 40 stamps. Stamps of the Federal Republic are also valid for postage in West Berlin, where they are sold only at the philatelic counters.

Philatelic bureau Versandstelle für Sammlermarken, Frankfurt-am-Main.

FINLAND
Area 338,145 sq.km, **population** 4.84m (1982), **capital** Helsinki.

A republic with developed industry and agriculture. In 1809 Finland left Sweden and became an autonomous Grand Duchy in Russia; after December 1917, it became an independent country, and has had a republican constitution since 1919. In the years 1939–40 Finland fought the 'Winter War' with the Soviet Union, and was again in a state of war in the years 1941–4 when the Finns occupied *Eastern Karelia*. Indirect UPU membership since 1 July 1875 (through Russia), direct member from 12 February 1918.

Definitive issues from 1856, first only with arms and face value (in Latin and Cyrillic), but after 1875, with the words 'FINLAND/SUOMI'. From 1891 joint design with Russian stamps, the distinction being small circles added to the Russian designs. In 1901 stamps of Russian design appeared inscribed with Finnish currency, and then in 1917, when the republic was established, again with the words 'SUOMI/FINLAND'. Until independence the stamps were produced both in Finland and in Russia. After the Second World War, Finnish stamps were produced in the printing house of the Finnish Bank by recess printing. Current production is now almost exclusively lithographic, and most issues are confined to a single stamp. The designs are concerned with Finnish events and people, and are of a high artistic standard. The leading designers include T. Ekström, O. Vepsälainen, P. Huovinen and P. Rahikainen, who have been responsible for the majority of present-day Finnish stamp production. Engravers include R. Achrén, B. Ekholm and S. Rönberg. Issues usually have a printing of some two million. Where philatelic sales are intended rather than broad public sales, the print order is around 400,000. Typical of Finnish productions are parcel stamps for transportation in buses, military stamps (without indication of the nominal value) issued for soldiers on active service and, finally, a definitive issue which remained in use for over 50 years (with the motif of the lion of the country's coat-of-arms). The annual production at the present time is some 25 stamps. The first issues are valuable classic stamps. In the first period — until independence was recognized in 1917 — some Finnish issues were valid only in Finland or abroad with the exception of Russia; or, alternatively, only in Russia. From 1901 Russian stamps were on sale in Finland and were used for mail to Russia and abroad, and were also valid in Finland.

Philatelic bureau Philatelic Section, General Direction of Posts and Telecommunications, Helsinki.

FIUME (RIJEKA)
The town of Fiume (now Rijeka) belonged to Austria until 1867, as part of the Croatian-Slovenian kingdom, then to Hungary, and after the First World War was claimed by both Yugoslavia and Italy. In the period 20 October to 17 November 1918 it was part of Croatia,

but was then occupied by the Italian army, France, Great Britain and the USA, and on 18 November 1918 a National Council took over the administration of the town. After less than a year, on 12 September 1919, the Italian poet Gabriele d'Annunzio arrived with his Italian Free Corps, and in the following year (after declaring Fiume a free state) they occupied also the islands of *Arbe* and *Veglia* (Rab and Krk) in Kvarner Bay. In the Treaty of Rapallo of 12 November 1920 Fiume was proclaimed a free state, and on 6 January 1921 a provisional government was established. But on 12 January 1924, under the Treaty of Rome, Fiume was ceded to Italy, and Yugoslavia retained only the suburb of Sušak. In 1941 Sušak was occupied by Italian troops who remained there until September 1943. The occupied country was given the name Fiume-Kupa from the river Kupa. After the Second World War, Fiume, now called Rijeka, became part of Yugoslavia.

From 1918, overprint 'FIUME' on Hungarian stamps, later definitive stamps with the same name inscribed. A total of 195 + 30 stamps. Definitive issues, which are of local and Italian origin, had political and pictorial themes, the designs of the best being by G. Marussig or executed from sketches by d'Annunzio. Italian stamps superseded the Fiume issues in 1924. In 1941, when Italian troops occupied Yugoslav Sušak, a total of 21 overprinted provisionals were issued (on Yugoslav stamps) bearing the words 'ZONA OCCUPATA FIUMANO KUPA'. They were valid until 1942 when Italian stamps came into use. If we consider that the individual stamps of the first issue were limited to a printing of not more than 10,000, that the smallest issue amounted to a mere 60 stamps and that stamps without overprints were being used postally, these overprinted provisionals must be considered commodities for the collectors' market, since their real postal function is dubious.

In 1945, when the territory of Fiume was occupied by the Yugoslav army, an issue of Italian stamps (7 values) appeared with the overprint 'FIUME/RIJEKA'.

FRANCE
Area 547,026 sq.km, **population** 54.35m (1982), **capital** Paris.

Republic, with a highly developed economy, industry and agriculture. One of the Great Powers in Western Europe, and leading country in the French Community, which includes, apart from France, other member countries, overseas departments and territories, the remnants of the once extensive French colonial empire. In the years 1848–52 France was a republic (Second Republic), in 1860 Nice and part of Savoy were added; in 1852–70 came the Second Empire, followed by the Third Republic. In 1914–18 France was at war with the Central Powers, and from 1939 at war with Germany (1940 with Italy also). On 22 June 1940 the Pétain Government signed the capitulation, two-thirds of the country was occupied and the government, collaborating with the Germans, moved to Vichy. On 9 November 1942 the German and Italian armies occupied the rest of France until 1944. In 1940, General de Gaulle established the Free French movement, which administered certain French colonies from London, England. He then formed a provisional government in Algeria. In 1944 the Fourth Republic was established and in 1959 the Fifth Republic. UPU membership since 1 January 1876.

France was one of the first European countries to introduce stamps on 1 January 1849 (after Great Britain and the Swiss cantons). Definitive stamps from 1849 were inscribed 'REPUB FRANC'. Then, after changes in the system of government in 1853, 'EMPIRE FRANC' or 'EMPIRE FRANCAIS'. In 1870 came a return to the Republican wording once again with 'REPUB FRANC' which became the unabbreviated 'RÉPUBLIQUE FRANÇAISE' in 1876, on occasions abbreviation to 'RF'. Other inscriptions used were 'POSTES FRANCE', 'FRANCE', 'ÉTAT FRANÇAIS' (during the Pétain regime) and similar combinations, while after the Second World War the name was standardized to 'RÉPUBLIQUE FRANÇAISE', and then from 1975 just 'FRANCE'.

Most of the stamps were printed by the recess method, which is typical of French stamp production. From 1961 a new press was used which made multicoloured engraving possible. A large number of French engravers have contributed to French stamp production, many even designing stamps, which explains the trend towards a traditional 'look' for French stamps. The engravers concerned are Gandon, Piel, Durrens, Pheulpin, Combet, Cottet,

Decaris, Mazelin, Cami and others. Apart from commemorative portraits of famous French-men, landscapes are frequently the subjects of design but many other subjects also project the image of the country. Printings of many millions (4–30 million) emphasize this publicity value as well as the postal function of the stamps. The annual output is between 40 and 50 stamps. The first issue includes some highly coveted items such as the *tête-bêche* varieties. Some definitive stamps were in use over several decades (e.g. Roty's 'Sower' was first issued in 1903 and was re-introduced in 1960). Among other types France has pre-cancelled stamps (*affranchissements*) for official mail and bulk posting; also, military stamps (like Swe-den) for use by soldiers on compulsory military service who are exempt from postage for two letters monthly. A number of issues of Free France appeared in different places during the struggle for liberation in the Second World War. Their postal use was doubtful, some of the stamps probably being bogus issues. (For issues of the government of Free France in Algeria see also *French Colonies*.)

French stamps were also valid in the overseas departments of French Guiana, Guadelou-pe, Martinique and Réunion for the period 1946–9; and from 1976 onwards, also on the island of Mayotte and on St Pierre et Miquelon.

In 1919 Hungarian stamps with the overprint 'Occupation Française' were used in the region of Arad in former Hungary occupied by the French army 1919–20 and then ceded to Rumania. A total of 55 provisionals.

Philatelic bureau Service Philatélique des Postes et Télécommunications, Paris.

GENEVA
Swiss canton (282 sq.km) with capital of the same name, which had its own postal author-ities.

Geneva is the fourth oldest stamp-issuing territory in the world. From 1843 definitive stamps with the inscription 'Genève' or without name: a total of 5 stamps in a heraldic design, locally produced. The first issue in particular is a highly coveted classic stamp. From 1850 stamps of the Swiss Federal postal authorities were used; in 1849 they had taken over the postal services previously in the hands of the cantons.

GERMAN AUSTRIA
After the defeat and disintegration of the Austro-Hungarian Empire in 1918 the core of the former monarchy adopted the name German Austria (Deutsch-Österreich). Under the Peace Treaty of St Germain, on 10 September 1919, Austria had to relinquish the possibility of linking up with Germany, and the use of the name German Austria was prohibited.

In 1918 Austrian stamps were issued with the overprint 'Deutschösterreich', followed in 1919 by definitives with the same inscription. The designs, by F. J. Renner, were strongly influenced by Art Nouveau. A total of 113 + 30 stamps were issued.

GERMAN DEMOCRATIC REPUBLIC
Area 108,333 sq.km, **population** 16.74m (1981), **capital** Berlin.

Country with developed industry and agriculture. Democratic republic, created out of the former Soviet Occupation Zone of Germany on 7 October 1949. Direct UPU membership from 1 July 1875 as Germany, from 1955 as G.D.R.

The German Democratic Republic began issuing stamps in 1949 with the inscrip-tion 'DEUTSCHE POST'. In 1950 this became 'DEUTSCHE DEMOKRATISCHE RE-PUBLIK', sometimes abbreviated to 'DDR'. Most of the stamps are printed in Leipzig, usually in offset-lithography and/or photogravure. The earlier propaganda subjects of design have more recently been complemented by general themes. Designs by Gott-schall, Naumann, Detlefsen, Stauf, Riess, Bläser, Deutschendorf, Dorfstecher and others working with great graphic precision. Miniature sheets are issued for collectors (about 50) and some stamps have low printings. Annual output 80–100 stamps. A distinctive feature of the German Democratic Republic issues are official stamps of the Central Courier Service (1958–9).

Philatelic bureau Deutscher Buchexport und Import GmbH, Leipzig.

GERMAN MILITARY COMMAND AREAS

Postal area of the German occupation authorities during the First World War on the Eastern Front comprising by stages, after 1915, Latvia and southern Lithuania, and from 1918 also northern Lithuania and Estonia. The first stamps appeared in 1916: German issue with the overprint 'Postgebiet Ob. Ost.' (= Oberbefehlshaber Osten): a total of 12 overprinted provisionals. The German post offices in the Baltic republics were closed at the end of 1918. ('Deutsche Post Osten' is the wording on an overprinted set of 13 stamps, which were issued in 1939 for the territory of Poland occupied by the German Army; see *Poland: General Gouvernement*.)

GERMANY

When the German Confederation disintegrated in 1866, its place was taken by the North German Confederation, which signed treaties with Baden, Hessen, Bavaria and Württemberg in 1870 and became the German Empire. When France was defeated in the Franco-Prussian War, King Wilhelm I was proclaimed German Emperor at Versailles on 18 January 1871 and the treaties were ratified in Berlin on 29 January 1871. This brought into existence the German Empire, a federated state which from 1871 included Alsace-Lorraine. During the era of colonial expansion, Germany acquired territories in Africa — Togo, Cameroon, German East Africa, German South-West Africa (and gave Zanzibar to Great Britain in exchange for Heligoland); and in Oceania — German New Guinea with the Bismack Archipelago, the Marshall Islands, Mariana Islands, Caroline Islands and German Samoa. In Europe, Germany became the leading member of the Triple Alliance but was defeated in the First World War and lost not only her colonial empire but also certain territories in Europe — Posen, Western Prussia, Danzig, Klaipeda, part of Upper Silesia, Alsace-Lorraine, Eupen-Malmédy, northern Schleswig, Hlučín region and, for a time, also the Saar. In 1918 a republic was proclaimed which came to be called the Weimar Republic after the Constitution adopted in 1919 in that town. In 1923 French and Belgian troops occupied the Ruhr and Rhineland because reparations had not been fully made. In 1933 Hitler became Chancellor, established Nazism and led Germany into the Second World War. After the unconditional surrender on 8 May 1945 the four Great Powers took control of the country, and Four Occupation Zones were established — the Soviet, American, British and French. In 1946 the American and British Zones were linked into one, and in 1948 the French Zone was joined to this. On 21 September 1949 these three Zones became the *Federal Republic of Germany*. On 7 October 1949 the *German Democratic Republic* was established in the former Soviet Zone.

The stamps of the *North German Postal District* were replaced from 1872 by those of the German Reichspost bearing the wording 'DEUTSCHE REICHSPOST'. The stamps of the North German Postal District remained valid in Hamburg until 1874. Bavaria retained its own postal sovereignty until 1920 and Württemberg until 1902 (although in Württemberg separate official stamps continued until 1920 and municipal postage stamps until 1924). The first issues of the North German Postal District expressed the face value in two currencies. Stamps in groschen were valid in the northern district and stamps with kreuzer values in the southern district. In 1875 the whole of Germany adopted a new currency: 100 pfennige = 1 mark. Until the end of the Second World War the following inscriptions were used: 'REICHSPOST', 'DEUTSCHES REICH', 'GROSSDEUTSCHES REICH', 'DEUTSCHE FLUGPOST' (1919) and 'DEUTSCHE NATIONAL VERSAMMLUNG' (1919). A total of 910 + 195 stamps, of local origin, printed in Berlin and, from 1938 to 1945, in Vienna, using various techniques. Issues with symbols or numerals were followed by portrait and pictorial stamps. The stamps demonstrate runaway inflation from August to November 1923 when almost every week stamps with a new range of face values had to be issued, running as high as ten billion marks. During the First World War the German stamps were surcharged in centimes and francs for use in Belgium and Northern France, which were occupied by the German army.

In 1919 a total of 17 Belgian stamps appeared with the overprint 'ALLEMAGNE DUITSCHLAND' to be used by the Belgian army of occupation in the Rhineland. These remained valid for use until 30 April 1931.

After the Second World War, a wide range of issues were used in the territory of Germany for individual and merged Occupation Zones and for individual parts of these Zones: *Berlin-Brandenburg, Mecklenburg-Western Pomerania, Eastern Saxony, Western Saxony, Province of Saxony, Thuringia, Baden, Rhineland-Palatinate, Württemberg, French Occupation Zone of Germany, Soviet Occupation Zone of Germany*. The unifying element for most of the issues was the inscription 'DEUTSCHE POST', even though they appeared in different regions, Occupation Zones and territories. This is true of the issues for the American, British and Soviet Zones in 1946–8, while the French Zone and, later, its individual territories issued their own stamps. On the joint American-British Zone issues of 1948–9 and the Federal Republic of Germany issues in 1949 and onward from 1950, the inscription was changed to 'DEUTSCHE BUNDESPOST'. In the western sector of Berlin the same inscriptions were used until 1952, when 'BERLIN' was added to 'DEUTSCHE POST'. This was changed to 'DEUTSCHE BUNDESPOST BERLIN' (see *West Berlin*) in 1955. Finally, there are the issues of the Soviet Occupation Zone: in 1945–6 in the territory of Western Saxony, and from 1948 and 1949 in the general Soviet Occupation Zone, which in 1949 became the *German Democratic Republic*. Initially, the inscription 'DEUTSCHE POST' was used, to be replaced in 1950 by 'DEUTSCHE DEMOKRATISCHE REPUBLIK'. In the territory of *Eastern Saxony* stamps simply inscribed 'POST' were used in 1945. In 1945–6 stamps were issued for the Anglo-American Zone with the inscription 'AM POST DEUTSCHLAND'. Symbolic in design, these were first printed in Washington, later in London and, finally, in Brunswick, Germany. A total of 366 stamps, of local origin (with a few exceptions).

GERMANY, FRENCH OCCUPATION ZONE
After the capitulation of Germany on 8 May 1945 sovereignty over the territory then occupied by the French army fell to the Government of France. The French Occupation Zone included the Rhineland-Palatinate, southern Baden, southern Württemberg and the Saar region (**area** approx. 60,000 sq.km, **capital** Mainz).

From 1945 definitive stamps bearing the words 'ZONE FRANÇAISE', a total of 13 stamps, printed in Baden, the designs being influenced by French production (symbols and portraits). After 1947 stamps appeared for individual *Länder* of the French Occupation Zone (Rhineland-Palatinate, Baden, Württemberg). The stamps of the French Occupation Zone were valid in the years 1945 to 1947 also in the *Saar*.

GERMANY, SOVIET OCCUPATION ZONE
After the capitulation of Germany on 8 May 1945, sovereign power in the territory occupied by the Soviet army passed to the government of the USSR. After moving the demarcation line to the west on 30 June 1945, the Soviet Occupation Zone covered an area of 102,298 sq.km and Berlin became the capital. Administratively it was divided into Berlin-Brandenburg, Mecklenburg-Vorpommern, Thuringia, Province of Saxony and Eastern Saxony, Western Saxony, which mostly issued their own stamps under their own names until 1946, when stamps for three Occupation Zones (American, British and Soviet) were issued jointly with the inscription 'DEUTSCHE POST.'

In 1948, after a currency reform in the Western Zones on 21 June, various overprints were issued in the Soviet Occupation Zone on local postage stamps distinguishing the town of origin and, by surcharge, amending the face values as required. Non-overprinted stamps could then be used only at one tenth of the original face value. From 3 July the valid stamps were then given the overprint 'Sowjetische Besatzungszone'. A total of 32 different overprinted provisionals were issued.

These were followed again by an issue with the inscription 'DEUTSCHE POST' and when, on 7 October 1949, the *German Democratic Republic* was established, stamps appeared from 1950 with the text 'DEUTSCHE DEMOKRATISCHE REPUBLIK'.

GIBRALTAR
Area 5.5 sq.km, **population** 31,183 (1982).

Strategically important base with a military and a commercial port, British since 1704;

colony 1713, status of Crown Colony from 1830, Gibraltar acquired extended internal autonomy under the 1969 Constitution. Indirect UPU membership from 1 January 1876 (through
Great Britain).

From 1886 Bermuda stamps with the overprint 'GIBRALTAR', then definitives with
the same word. Royal portrait stamps to 1931, then pictorials with subjects relating to the
territory and its British associations. Production largely British, some issues by Enschedé
of Holland. At the present time, the principal designer is A. Ryman, and printing is offset
and photogravure. Gibraltar normally takes part in any British Commonwealth 'omnibus'
issues, and maintains a modest output of different stamps each year, normally about
5 issues. From 1857 to 1885 stamps of Great Britain were used at British post offices
in Morocco. From 1886 to 1898 Gibraltar stamps were used there without any distinguishing
overprint. However, from 1898 to 1907 stamps of Gibraltar with the overprint 'Morocco Agencies' were in use.

Philatelic bureau c/o Gibraltar Post Office, Gibraltar. **Trade sales** Crown Agents' Stamp
Bureau; Inter-Governmental Philatelic Corporation.

GREAT BRITAIN AND NORTHERN IRELAND
Area 244,103 sq.km, **population** 56.34m (1982), **capital** London.

Economically highly developed commercial and industrial country. Constitutional monarchy. In the 19th and early 20th centuries Great Britain was the greatest colonial power in the
world, and is today the leading country in the British Commonwealth of Nations. The larger
part of Ireland became an independent republic in 1937. The present composition of the
British Commonwealth is:
1. The United Kingdom of Great Britain and Northern Ireland (including the dependencies of Guernsey, Jersey and the Isle of Man). 2. **Dominions and monarchies:** Canada,
Australia, New Zealand, Malaysia, Jamaica, Mauritius, Barbados, Lesotho, Swaziland,
Western Samoa, Tonga, Fiji, Grenada, Bahamas, Papua-New Guinea, Solomon Islands,
Tuvalu, St Lucia, St Vincent, Grenadines, Brunei, St. Kitts-Nevis, Antigua, Belize. 3. **Republics:** India, Ghana, Cyprus, Tanzania, Nigeria, Uganda, Kenya, Zambia, Botswana, Sin-
gapore, Malawi, Guyana, Nauru, The Gambia, Sierra Leone, Sri Lanka, Bangladesh, Malta,
Trinidad and Tobago, Seychelles, Dominica, Kiribati, Zimbabwe. 4. **Dependent territories
and protectorates:** Gibraltar, Hong Kong, British Indian Ocean Territories, St Helena (with
dependencies Ascension Island and Tristan da Cunha), Bermuda, British Virgin Islands,
Montserrat, Cayman Islands, Turks and Caicos Islands, Anguilla, Falkland Islands (with
South Georgia), Pitcairn Islands, British Antarctic Territory.

Of the former territories of the British Empire the following are no longer members of the
Commonwealth: Burma (1947), Ireland (1949), Sudan (1956), South African Republic
(1961), South Cameroon (1961), Kuwait (1961), Maldives (1963), Democratic Yemen
(1967), Oman (1970), Bahrain (1971), Qatar (1971), United Arab Emirates (1971), Pakistan
(1972).

Direct UPU membership since 1 July 1875.

Great Britain was the first country in the world to issue an adhesive postage stamp, in the
year 1840. It has been rather conservative in its stamp issues, although wider production
has taken place in recent years. Stamps are of local production from high-quality printers
(Perkins Bacon, De la Rue, Harrison, etc.), and different techniques are used, including
die-stamping. Priority is given to postal function and publicity of the country (large editions,
in many millions). Stamps are predominantly portraits, and even the present-day issues,
often of pictorial or general topics, always include a portrait of the monarch (the only exception is postage-due stamps). This portrait is used instead of the country of issue, as Great
Britain is the only country in the world which does not have to include this on its stamps. The
franking devices (meter marks), however, bear the mark of Great Britain since there is no
portrait.

In 1964 a change in stamp production took place in response to marketing and philatelic
trends, and annual production rose to 15 (now 20–30) stamps, with an emphasis on high
artistic level (designers include David Gentleman, Marjorie Saynor, Andrew Restall, etc.).

Regional stamps, issued for individual territories (without name), are generally sold only in the given territory, but are valid for the whole of Great Britain, differing only in their symbols: Scotland, Northern Ireland, Wales, Jersey and Guernsey and the Isle of Man. The last three have now become independent stamp-issuing countries: Jersey and Guernsey since 1969 and the Isle of Man since 1973.

During the last century British stamps were used in a very wide network of British post offices abroad.

Philatelic bureau The British Post Office Philatelic Bureau, Edinburgh.

GREECE

Area 131,990 sq.km, **population** 9.7m (1981), **capital** Athens.

Republic on the south of the Balkan peninsula, economically a not very highly developed agricultural country where tourism plays an important role. Modern Greece proclaimed its independence from Turkey in 1822, but Turkey did not acknowledge this until after the Russo-Turkish War in 1829. In 1830 Greece became a kingdom (its area measured 48,976 sq.km at that time). By 1832 it had acquired the Northern Sporades and the Cyclades; in 1864 the Ionian islands; in 1881, Thessalonica and part of Epirus; and in 1908, Crete. After the Balkan Wars in 1913, Southern Macedonia, Southern Epirus, part of Western Thrace and the Aegean Islands were added to the kingdom. In 1919 the whole of Thrace (Bulgarian and Turkish), Gallipoli, the European coast of the Dardanelles and the surroundings of Smyrna were incorporated, but after the defeat in the war with Turkey in 1923 Greece lost most of these territories. For a time it also held Southern Albania (Northern Epirus, 1919–23). During the Second World War, after the Italian invasion from Albania in 1940, Greece for a short time occupied Southern Albania, but was then itself occupied by Italian and German army units and temporarily lost Macedonia, Western Thrace and the Ionian Islands, but gained the Italian Aegean Islands (Dodecanese) after the war. It was a republic from 1924 to 1935 and again after 1973. Direct UPU membership from 1 July 1875.

Definitive stamps from 1861, which at first bore the abbreviation 'ELL' in Greek script, later 'ELLAS', and from 1966 onwards 'HELLAS' is shown in Latin script. In 1912 an overprint reading 'Greek Administration' in Greek script was used on Greek stamps issued in acquired territory. The design of the first Greek stamps, produced in Paris, was based on contemporary French stamps, the head of Mercury replacing the goddess Ceres. Subsequent designs, of varying quality, were influenced also by other foreign printing houses. Various printing techniques were used, including line-engraving, but at present offset-lithography of local origin (Aspiotis) is normally used. The revival of the Olympic Games served as the occasion for the issue of pictorial stamps in 1896, these being among the earliest of true pictorial stamps. Greek stamp designs include many themes of publicity and a large share of themes taken from Greek mythology apart from more general subjects designed to appeal to collectors. An exceptionally low printing occurred with the Greek Youth Organisation issue of 1940 with only 8,570 and 9,435 of the top values of the two sets which prompted speculation. Present-day production is much higher. A typical feature is charity tax stamps, of which 91 have appeared since 1914. Present annual output is 30–50 stamps.

Greece ran a number of post offices abroad. In 1881 the Greek post office in the Ottoman Empire was closed and a Turkish-Greek postal war broke out when other countries had to take over the delivery of mail between the two countries.

Philatelic bureau Hellenic Post Office (ELTA), Philatelic Service, Athens.

GUERNSEY

Area 65 sq.km, **population** 53,268 (1981), **principal town** St Peter Port.

The most westerly of the Channel Islands off the French coast, including the islands of Herm, Jethou, Sark and Alderney. Occupied by the German army 1940–5.

British stamps continued to be used even after the German occupation in 1940. In 1941 local stamps with the inscription 'GUERNSEY' were issued (a total of 5 stamps produced locally). After liberation in 1945 there were again British stamps, with the existing local issue remaining valid until 1946.

The postal authorities of Guernsey became independent of the British post office on 1 October 1969, when a definitive issue with the words 'GUERNSEY BAILIWICK' appeared (bailiwick being the name of the administrative unit), now as 'BAILIWICK OF GUERNSEY'. Mainly pictorial stamps for collectors, printed in Switzerland and Great Britain; the pictorial stamps always bear a small silhouette portrait of the monarch. Annual output of new stamps around 10–20.

Prior to 1969 the British postal authorities issued regional stamps (1958 to 1969) with the normal royal portrait and a symbol of the island of Guernsey (a lily) but without the name of the island. They were valid in the entire territory of Great Britain, even though they were on sale only on the island. Apart from this, a number of local private issues appeared. Of these, the issues for Herm were authorized for conveying mail to Guernsey, and *Alderney* began to issue its own stamps in 1983 under Guernsey's control. Other issues for Jethou and Sark (except for the Commodore Shipping Line parcel stamps) were of dubious validity.

Philatelic bureau States Philatelic Bureau, Head Post Office, St Peter Port, Guernsey.
Trade sales Crown Agents' Stamp Bureau; Inter-Governmental Philatelic Corporation.

HAMBURG
Free Hanseatic town (410 sq.km), the biggest port in Germany. Member of the German and North German Confederation and then in 1871 of the German Empire. In 1867 the territory of Hamburg was enlarged by the purchase of Bergedorf.

From 1857 definitive stamps with the word 'HAMBURG'. A total of 22 stamps of local origin, all with bold numerals of value as the basic design. They are popular classic stamps among collectors, having primarily served a postal function. Validity ended on 31 December 1867; from 1868 they were followed by stamps of the *North German Confederation*. The unsold remainders of the unused Hamburg stamps were sold to one merchant in 1868 but do not have the brown gum of the issued stamps. There were also a number of foreign post offices in Hamburg, which used their own stamps: Schleswig-Holstein, Hanover, Prussia, the Thurn and Taxis post offices, Denmark, Mecklenburg-Schwerin. The post offices of Sweden and Norway in Hamburg did not use their own stamps but purchased Hamburg stamps for use on outgoing mail. Hamburg stamps could be used in Bergedorf, Hanover and on Heligoland until 1867 when the British-issued stamps for *Heligoland* appeared.

HANOVER (HANNOVER)
Kingdom (**area** 38,500 sq.km, **capital** Hanover) from 1815, but supported Austria in the Austro-Prussian War, was annexed by the Prussians in 1866 and proclaimed a province of Prussia.

Definitive stamps from 1850 to 1866 bearing the inscription 'HANNOVER'. A total of 25 stamps of local origin, mostly with numerals or symbols. Popular classic stamps. They fulfilled a postal function and remained valid until 31 October 1866, even though, from 1 October 1866, Prussian stamps were issued when Hanover became a Prussian province. Hanover stamps were also in use in Hamburg and Bremen.

HELIGOLAND
Island in the North Sea (0.9 sq.km), originally part of Danish Schleswig. After 1807 it was British, but in 1890 was ceded to Germany in exchange for concessions about Zanzibar. After the Second World War the island was used for bombing practice by the RAF, but from 1952 it was again settled by civilians.

Before 1867, postal services were provided by a branch post office of Hamburg, using its own stamps. From 1867, definitives with the name 'HELIGOLAND' and, until 1876, Queen Victoria's head in embossed relief. A total of 20 stamps including portraits and symbols. Some give dual currency, German and British. All the stamps of Heligoland were produced in Berlin. Stamps were issued until 1890, although the postal use of the last issue has never ben fully established. After Germany re-possessed Heligoland in 1890, the printing plates for the stamps passed into commercial hands and many worthless reprints of the stamps flooded the philatelic market.

HOLSTEIN

Former German duchy, linked with Schleswig under the Danish crown in 1386 and remaining with it in a political union until 1486. In 1815 it became a member of the German Confederation, in 1864 it became a Condominium under the administration of Prussia and Austria; from 1865 it was ceded to Austria under the Treaty of Gastein (without the southern duchy of Lauenburg, which was ceded to Prussia). During the Austro-Prussian War Holstein was occupied by Prussia (1866) and, with Prussia, became a member of the North German Confederation in 1867.

From 1850 local stamps were issued in conjunction with neighbouring Schleswig. In 1853–1864 Danish stamps were in use. In 1864, during the Prussian-Austrian occupation, stamps were again issued without the name of the country, but with the identifying inscription 'HRZGL POST FRM'. Later, there were issues for Schleswig-Holstein, which remained valid until 31 October 1865.

In the period 1 November 1865 to the year 1866, under the Austrian occupation, 7 stamps appeared with the name 'HERZOGHT. (or 'HERZOGTHUM') HOLSTEIN'. They were produced locally at Altona, the designs being numerals of value. After the invasion by Prussia, from 29 December 1866, there were again stamps for Schleswig-Holstein, which were replaced in 1868 by the stamps of the *North German Postal District*.

HUNGARY

Area 93,036 sq.km, **population** 10.7m (1983), **capital** Budapest.

Industrial and agricultural country, socialist republic. In 1526 Hungary became part of the Hapsburg monarchy, from 1804 the Austrian Empire, which in 1867 became a dualist state, within which Hungary enjoyed a measure of autonomy. After the disintegration of the Austro-Hungarian Empire, Hungary was proclaimed a republic (16 November 1918). From March to August 1919 power was in the hands of the Hungarian Republic of Soviets, the monarchy was re-established in 1920, headed by a regent, Admiral Nicholas Horthy. Under the Peace Treaty of Trianon the frontiers between Hungary, Czechoslovakia, Rumania, Yugoslavia and Austria were laid down on 4 June 1920. After 1938 Hungary occupied part of the territories of the neighbouring countries: in 1938 southern Slovakia, 1939 the Carpathian Ukraine and eastern Slovakia, 1940 part of Transylvania, 1941 part of Slovenia, Croatia and Serbia (Vojvodina). After the war, on 1 February 1946, Hungary was proclaimed a republic and in 1949 a people's republic. Under the Paris Treaty of 1947 its frontiers of 1 January 1939 were re-established, with minor corrections in favour of Czechoslovakia (Rusovce). Direct UPU membership from 1 July 1875.

Until 1867 Austrian stamps were in use. With the settlement of 1867 the Hungarian postal authorities became independent of Austria. The stamps of Austria were in use in Hungary until distinctive separate issues first appeared in 1871, the first issue still without a country name, until 1880 when stamps inscribed 'MAGYAR KIR POSTA' were usual. After the proclamation of the republic in 1918 the stamps then in use were overprinted 'KÖZTÁRSASÁG', and the inscription on the definitives became 'MAGYAR POSTA'. Under the Hungarian Republic of Soviets (1919) the name 'MAGYAR TANÁCSKÖZTÁR-SASÁG' was used, both as overprint and on definitive stamps. With the proclamation of the republic in 1946 the stamps were again inscribed 'MAGYAR POSTA', which is mainly used to this day. (Occasionally 'MAGYARORSZÁG' is to be found both in the inter-war and post-war periods.) Exceptions were 'MAGYAR NÉPKÖZTÁRSÁG' on two issues of 1949 and the Latin inscription only, 'RESPUBLICA HUNGARICA', on an issue commemorating the proclamation of the republic in 1946. With its total production of 4,000 stamps and an annual output of 80–100 stamps Hungary is one of the world's major stamp producers.

Nearly all are printed in Budapest, and designs are by Légrád, Vertel, Bokros, Zombory, Kékesi, Gál and Cziglényi. Overprinted provisionals, with symbolic and numerical treatment, are typical of the period up to the Second World War. At the present time a broad range of designs publicizing the country are used. Pictorial stamps are issued for stamp collectors with and without perforation (the latter with low printings), as well as numerous miniature sheets (with and without perforation). Interesting stamps are those printed on aluminium foil, representing the Hungarian aluminium industry. The exceptionally high rate of inflation after 1945 produced stamps with a denominational value that is a world record. The face value rose to 500,000 billion pengös, and shortly after to a currency denomination adópengő (= a tax pengo), amounting to 2000 trillion pengős, and reached 5 million adópengős. At the beginning of the period of inflation overprinted issues came into use, to indicate the stamp had been paid for in cash to meet a specific postal rate (e.g. 'Helyi levél' indicated a local charge for a letter; 'ájánlás' the charge for a registered letter, and so on). The currency was stabilized on 1 August 1946 in filler and forint.

Philatelic bureau Philatelia Hungarica, Budapest.

ICARIA
One of the islands in the Aegean Sea (261 sq.km), Turkish until the Balkan War. In July 1912 it was proclaimed a republic, but at the end of that year was occupied by the Greek army and has been Greek since 1913.

In October 1912, Provisional Government definitives (8 values) depicting Hermes' head appeared. There followed provisionals consisting of Greek definitives overprinted 'GREEK ADMINISTRATION' in Greek characters.

ICELAND
Area 103,000 sq.km, **population** 235,453 (1982), **capital** Reykjavik.

Economically underdeveloped country but with an important fishing industry. From 1380 Iceland was under Danish domination, becoming autonomous from 1874, and formally independent from 1918, though linked to Denmark in a political union for twenty-six years. In 1940 and 1941 British and then American soldiers landed on the island. The Icelandic Parliament adopted a republican constitution in 1941 and severed all links with Denmark. This was confirmed by a referendum held in 1944, and on 17 June 1944 Iceland was proclaimed a republic. UPU membership (indirect) from 1 July 1875 (Denmark), direct from 15 November 1919 as independent Iceland.

From 1873, definitives (in Danish definitive design) with the word 'ISLAND' (prior to this Danish stamps were valid), later written 'ÍSLAND'. In over a hundred years only some 500 different stamps were issued, which is a very small number. The overall production is very mixed, with strong Danish influences until 1925, and later, influences from other regions. Most of the post-1925 stamps were printed by recess in Great Britain, Austria and Switzerland. Typical designs relate to Icelandic history or current life and, nowadays, are mainly pictorial stamps printed by photogravure. Printings are sufficient for normal public and philatelic demand. The current annual output is about 10 stamps a year.

Philatelic bureau Frimerkjasalan, Reykjavik.

IONIAN ISLANDS
Islands off the west coast of Greece — Corfu, Paxos, Levkas, Ithaca, Cephalonia, Zante, and Cerigo lying to the south. From 1815 to 1864 a British protectorate, ceded to Greece on 2 June 1864. In 1923 Italy for a short time occupied Corfu; in April 1941 the islands were occupied by Italy and in 1943 Germany occupied Zante.

In 1859, 3 definitive stamps in differing colours but without figures of value were issued with the wording 'IONIKON KRATOS' in Greek script, meaning 'Ionian Government'. The stamps issued under the British protectorate were printed in London and have a portrait of Queen Victoria. They remained valid until 1864 when Greek stamps replaced them.

In 1941, during the Italian occupation, 9 + 4 Italian stamps were issued with the overprint 'ISOLE JONIE'. The stamps were put into circulation on the islands of Corfu and Paxos on 16 August, and on Ithaca, Cephalonia, Levkas and Zante on 1 September 1941. On the island of Cerigo Greek stamps remained valid even during the Italian occupation in the years

1941–3. Some catalogues give a large number of local overprinted provisionals. e.g. for Cephalonia and Ithaca, Cerigo, Santa Maura, Paxos etc., but their postal use has not been proved. They are more likely to be regarded as commercially inspired philatelic labels.

When the German army occupied the islands in October 1943, Greek stamps were re-introduced, but the overprinted provisionals for the island of Zante consisted of the Italian occupation issues further overprinted 'GREECE' in Greek characters) and the date '2.X.43'.

On the island of Corfu, the Serbian government in exile established itself in 1916 (see also *Serbia*).

IRAKLION (CANDIA).

British administrative territory (formerly called Candia) in central Crete after the island was occupied by the Great Powers in the years 1898–1909 (see *Crete*).

From 1898 to 1899, 5 primitive handstamped and lithographed stamps appeared on which the name 'IRAKLION' is included in Greek script. The British post office existed from 25 November 1898 to the end of the year 1899. Other stamps were issued by the Austrian and French post offices in Candia.

IRELAND (EIRE)

Area 70, 283 sq.km, **population** 3.44m (1981), **capital** Dublin.

Agricultural country with predominant livestock breeding. Independent state since 1921 (previously part of Great Britain) with the exception of six counties in Northern Ireland (Ulster), which remain British. In 1937 a republican constitution was proclaimed within the British Commonwealth of Nations but in 1949 the independent republic left the Commonwealth. UPU membership (indirect) from 1 July 1875 (Great Britain), direct from 6 September 1923 (Irish Free State, renamed Eire on 29 December 1937).

In 1922 overprints on British stamps indicating the provisional Irish government; from 1923, definitives with the name 'EIRE'. Most of the stamp output is commemorative in purpose with portraits predominating, these and pictorial motifs being well designed in a simplistic style, typical of most issues. The definitive issues have been long-lived, the 1923 definitive designs serving until 1968. The subsequent L.s.d. and decimal definitives were unchanged from 1968 to 1968. Overall production is very conservative, the annual output at present being some 15 stamps. In the past, stamps were not even issued every year, a rare occurrence in world stamp production. All stamps are printed in large quantities to encourage full public use and publicity for the events commemorated.

Philatelic bureau The Controller, Philatelic Section, General Post Office, Dublin.

ISLE OF MAN

Area 588 sq.km, **population** 64,679 (1981), **capital** Douglas.

British Crown dependency under a Lieutenant-Governor. UPU membership through Great Britain.

Like the Channel Islands of Jersey and Guernsey, the Isle of Man has postal autonomy within the British post office. From 1958 some stamps based on British definitives carried the Legs of Man symbol. On 5 July 1973, the first definitives inscribed 'ISLE OF MAN' appeared. The stamps depict scenes from the life of the island and reflect its long history. All stamps bear the portrait of the British monarch, who rules the Isle of Man. Most of the pictorial designs are based on photographs. The chief designers are local artists, John Nicholson and Victor Kneale. Printing is mainly in Britain, sometimes in Switzerland. Annual production is about 20 stamps. The name 'ELLAN VANNIN' appeared on a series of 1975 side by side with the English 'ISLE OF MAN'. The former is in the local Celtic Manx, which virtually became extinct in the middle of the 20th century. It used to be the official language before English was introduced.

Philatelic bureau Isle of Man Post Office Authority, Douglas, I.O.M., Great Britain. **Trade sales** Crown Agents'Stamp Bureau; Inter-Governmental Philatelic Corporation.

ISTRIA AND THE SLOVENE COAST

Territory occupied by the Yugoslav army after the Second World War (1945–7).

From 1945, overprints on Italian stamps with the word 'ISTRA', then definitives with the bilingual 'ISTRA, SLOVENSKO PRIMORJE/ISTRIA, LITTORALE SLOVENO' on pictorial stamps of Yugoslav origin. A total of 48 + 24 stamps (a large number of postage due stamps, made by the overprint 'PORTO' on postage stamps), mostly of little postal necessity. Influences of the collectors' market are seen in printings of 300,000 down to 1,200. Postage dues included those of Yugoslavia with the overprint 'Vojna Uprava Jugoslavenske Armije'. Apart from forgeries there are bogus issues that could not have had any postal use.

ITALY
Area 301,278 sq.km, **population** 56.74m (1982), **capital** Rome.

Industrial and agricultural country with republican government. Tourism plays an important role in the national economy.

In the middle of the 19th century Italy was split up into a number of independent monarchies, Lombardy and Venice belonging to Austria from 1815. The process of unification was begun by the Kingdom of Piedmont, which acquired Lombardy in 1859 but ceded to France, in return, Nice and Savoy in 1860, and annexed Parma, Modena, Tuscany, Romagna, the northern part of the Papal States, Naples and Sicily in the same year. The Italian Kingdom was proclaimed on 17 March 1861 and Victor Emmanuel II, the central figure in the unification movement, became the first king of united Italy. Turin was then the capital city, but later Florence acquired that status. After the Austro-Prussian War, in which Italy was on the side of Prussia, the Venice region was added, and during the Franco-Prussian War (1870) the rest of the Papal States was occupied, with Rome (which had been under French protection), and that city became the capital. This completed the creation of the Italian state.

From the end of the 19th century, Italian colonial expansion intensified and Italy seized Eritrea (1882), Somaliland (1889–1905), Libya (1912) and the Aegean Islands (1912). Though originally a member of the Triple Alliance, Italy entered the First World War in 1915 on the side of the Allies and acquired the Tridente region in the south of the Tyrol in 1919, Istria with Trieste in 1920, Zadar, certain islands in the Adriatic Sea and Castelrosso. In 1935–6, Italy conquered Ethiopia and in 1936 concluded a Treaty of Co-operation with Germany (the Berlin-Rome Axis). In 1939 Italy occupied Albania, and until 1943 fought in the Second World War as an ally of Germany, occupying a considerable part of the Yugoslav coast. After the Italian capitulation in 1943 the northern and central parts of the country were occupied by the German army, and Mussolini proclaimed the Fascist Italian Socialist Republic (September 1943 to April 1945), while the unoccupied part of Italy declared war on Germany. The monarchy was abolished in 1946, and a republic was established. In 1947 Italy signed the peace treaty, ceding Istria, Zadar, the Pelagos Islands, Sazan, the Aegean Islands including Castelrosso and smaller areas near Nice and in Savoy. It also lost its colonies, Somaliland alone remaining under the Italian Protectorate Administration from 1950 to 1960. Trieste was proclaimed a free zone and was returned to Italy in 1954 after an agreement with Yugoslavia, but without any hinterland. UPU membership from 1 July 1875 (direct).

From 1862 definitive issues, the first being identical to the last Sardinian stamps except that the issues for Italy were perforated and the original stamps were imperforate. These issues have no country name. In 1863 came issues inscribed, 'FRANCO-BOLLO POSTALE ITALIANO' or more usually, 'POSTE ITALIANE'. From 1969, the name has been sometimes given as 'ITALIA'. During 1943, the Italian Socialist Republic used the name 'REPUBBLICA SOCIALE ITALIANA' as an overprint and on definitive stamps. After the period of the regular definitives from 1862 to 1912 with restrained designs of royal portraits, numerals, and coats-of-arms, pictorials more original in conception began to appear in the 1920s.

Typical of Italian production is the use of letterpress printing, photogravure and, less often, recess-printing. From 1945 all issues have been printed in the State Printing House in Rome, and highly artistic stamps have been designed by Mancini, Franzoni, Mezzana and others. Issues directed to the philatelic market between the two world wars include the issue for the Italian Philatelic Congress at Trieste in 1922 with a limited printing of 15,000 stamps, and that issued on the occasion of the fleet sailing to South America with a printing of 25,000. Modern curios include the triptych stamps of 1933 in honour of Balbo's mass flight from Rome to Chicago and return flight from New York to Rome. Exceptional to the Italian post office are the small two-part parcel post stamps which have appeared in identical form since 1914. Otherwise, Italian stamps include a noticeable predominance of propaganda themes giving publicity to the country's many historical and cultural associations. The present annual output is around 40 stamps.

In 1943, after the Anglo-American landing in Sicily, 9 stamps of American origin were issued for the civilian population with the inscription 'ALLIED MILITARY POSTAGE — ITALY'.

Philatelic bureau Direzione Generale Poste e Telecommunicazioni, Vendita Francobolli per Collezioni, I-00 100 Rome.

YANINNA (IOANNINA)
A town in Greek Northern Epirus, belonging to Turkey from 1431 to 1913, and then occupied by Greece. The Italian post office was working here during the Greek occupation in 1913. (See also *Levant*).

In 1909–10 a total of 8 Italian stamps were issued bearing the overprint 'Janina' or 'JANI-NA'. Prior to that, Italian stamps were used with overprints in Turkish currency.

JERSEY
Area 116 sq.km, **population** 76,050 (1980), **principal town** St Helier.

The largest of the Channel Islands, occupied by Germany during the Second World War. UPU membership through Great Britain, where Jersey is specifically named.

British stamps continued to be used on the Channel Islands after German occupation in 1940. From 1941 to 1943, 8 locally produced stamps with the name 'JERSEY' were issued. The British postal authorities granted the Jersey post office independence on 1 October 1969, and a definitive issue with the name 'JERSEY' appeared. They are pictorial stamps designed by the designers of British postage stamps, and most of them were printed in Switzerland. Stamp production is aimed strongly at the philatelic market. The subjects of the issues are Jersey life and history, except for the joint issues for the British sphere (e.g. Royal Wedding). Every stamp bears the portrait of the monarch. Most issues appear in series of 4 stamps with an average annual output of 16.

Regional stamps were previously issued by the British post office with the symbol of the island of Jersey but without the name. They were valid throughout Great Britain and are, therefore, British stamps. Apart from that, a number of private local issues exist on the philatelic market both for Jersey and the rest of the Channel Islands (as in *Guernsey*).

Philatelic bureau Jersey Philatelic Bureau, P.O. Box 304, Postal Headquarters, St Helier.
Trade sales Crown Agents' Stamp Bureau; Inter-Governmental Philatelic Corporation.

KARELIA (CARELIA)
Territory east of the Finnish border (capital city Petrozavodsk), which declared independence in 1921 but was incorporated into the USSR in the spring of 1922. It became an autonomous republic of the USSR on 25 July 1923, and from 31 March 1940 to 16 July 1956 was called the Karelo-Finnish Soviet Socialist Republic. Part of Karelia was occupied by Finland in 1941–3 (see *Eastern Karelia*).

In 1922 one definitive issue of 15 stamps bearing the name 'KARJALA', of Finnish origin in a symbolic design, was issued in a printing of 15,000 (low values) to 2,000 (high values) stamps. Valid only at Uchta from 31 January to 18 February 1922.

KINGDOM OF THE SERBS, CROATS AND SLOVENES
After the disintegration of the Austro-Hungarian Empire an independent state of Serbs, Croats and Slovenes was proclaimed on 29 October 1918. It comprised the territory of Bosnia-Herzegovina, Croatia, Slovenia, Dalmatia, Carniola and southern Styria and Carinthia. On 1 December 1918 this state united with the Serbian Kingdom and Montenegro to

form the Kingdom of Serbs, Croats and Slovenes. In 1929 the name was changed to Yugoslavia.

From 1918, the individual territories of Bosnia, Herzegovina and Croatia produced their own issues, using overprints on stamps of Bosnia and Hungary with the wording 'DRŽAVA SHS' (or only 'SHS'), and 'KRALJEVSTVO Srba, Hrvata i Slovenaca'. Croatia issued definitive designs in 1919. Slovenia produced definitive designs ('Chainbreakers') with the full name. After 1921 came a single series for the entire territory with the words 'KRALJEVSTVO (or KRALJEVINA) SRBA, HRVATA I SLOVENACA' in both Latin and Cyrillic script. A total of 192 + 53 stamps, largely overprinted provisionals. The second printing of the definitive Slovenian 'Chainbreaker' issues were printed cheaply by letterpress in Vienna. The 'Kingdom' issues of 1921 to 1925 were finely executed in line-engraving, first in the USA, later in London, the designs being mainly portraits of King Peter I and King Alexander.

KORYTZA (KORYTZAN REPUBLIC)
In the unsettled conditions in the territory of Albania the Greek army had to withdraw from Northern Epirus in the autumn of 1916. The French army from Thessalonica occupied the eastern part and established the Korytzan Republic in early 1917; the occupation ended in 1920.

In 1917–18 a total of 17 stamps was issued, either primitive definitives or variously inscribed overprints as: 'KORÇË', 'SHQIPERE VETQEVEITABE' (KORYTZA INDEPENDENT ALBANIA), 'KORÇË REPUBLIKA SHQIPETARE' (KORYTZA ALBANIAN REPUBLIC) and 'QARKU POSTES KORÇES' (LOCAL POSTS OF KORYTZA).

KOTOR
After the occupation of Yugoslavia in 1941, Kotor (Cattaro, 547 sq.km), Split (Spalato, 976 sq. km) and Italian Zadar (Zara, 3,719 sq.km) became the territory of Italian Dalmatia until the capitulation of Italy in 1943. Then it was occupied by the German army.

In 1944 Italian stamps were overprinted with the text 'Deutsche Militärverwaltung Kotor', in October of that year the former Yugoslav stamps were overprinted 'Boka Kotorska'. A total of 10 stamps with the insignificant printing of 5,000 of each points to an issue intended for collectors rather than for public use.

KVARNER
Kvarner Bay in the Adriatic Sea near Rijeka (formerly Fiume) and the Yugoslav islands of Rab (Arbe) and Krk (Veglia), were occupied by d'Annunzio's Italian volunteers from 13 November 1920 to 5 January 1921 (see also *Arbe, Fiume, Veglia*), but the islands remained Yugoslavian.

In 1920 Fiume stamps were issued with the overprint 'Reggenza Italiana Del Carnaro'. A total of 20 overprinted provisionals.

LA CANEA (CANIA, CHANIA)
Territory in western Crete administered by Italy after the occupation of the island of Crete by the Great Powers in 1898–1909.

From 1900 Italian stamps with the overprint 'LA CANEA', a total of 20 overprinted provisionals. The Italian post office ceased operations in 1914.

LATVIA
Baltic country (**area** 65,791 sq.km, **capital** Riga), formerly part of Tsarist Russia, occupied by the Germans in the First World War, independent republic after 1918. After 5 August 1940, one of the republics of the USSR. In the Second World War Latvia was occupied by the German army (1941–5) and incorporated into Ostland. Since 1944-5 it has been part of the USSR.

After 1918 definitive issues with the name 'LATVIJA'. The first Latvian stamps (5 kop.) were printed on the backs of military maps (left by the German army) because of a paper shortage. Production was large for its time — a total of 304 stamps, which points to the influence of collector demand. Designs, aimed at publicizing of the country, were modelled on Russian pictorial issues, and most of the stamps were produced in the State Printing House in Riga. Some of the stamps were printed in very small quantities (a number or airmail stamps ran to no more than 7,000). During the First World War *Ostland* issues were in use, these being German stamps overprinted 'Postgebiet Ob. Ost' in Gothic characters. After the proclamation of the Latvian Soviet Socialist Republic in 1940 an issue of 13 definitives, printed in Riga, with the name 'LATVIJAS PSR' appeared. After the occupation by the German army in 1941, Soviet stamps were overprinted 'LATVIJA 1941.1.VII' (six overprinted provisionals). In that same year German stamps overprinted 'OSTLAND' were in use until, in 1944, Russian stamps were issued for public use.

LEMNOS
One of the Italian Aegean Islands (475 sq.km) under Turkey until the Balkan Wars, in 1912–1913 under Greek military government, then part of Greece.

In 1912–13 first Turkish stamps with Greek overprint meaning 'Lemnos', then Greek stamps with the same overprint. A total of 37 stamps, all overprinted provisionals.

LERO (LEROS)
One of the Italian Aegean Islands (**area** 55 sq.km, **capital** Portolago), Italian 1912–47.

From 1912 to 1932, overprints on Italian stamps 'Leros' or 'LERO'. A total of 26 stamps, all overprinted provisionals. Issues probably designed for the collector's market (printings 10,000 to 12,000), and of dubious postal status. (See also *Rhodes and the Dodecanese Islands*.)

LIECHTENSTEIN
Area 160 sq.km, **population** 26,380 (1982), **capital** Vaduz.

Duchy in the Alps, its present frontiers dating back to 1434. From the early 18th century the property of the Liechtensteins, becoming an imperial duchy in 1719. Independent since 1719 but in economic union with Austro-Hungary 1876-1918. After 1923, customs union with Switzerland, which represents the principality abroad. Indirect UPU membership from 1 July 1875 (Austria), indirect after 1 February 1921 (Switzerland), direct from 13 April 1962 (Liechtenstein).

Until 1921 Austrian stamps were valid in Liechtenstein even though Liechtenstein had its own stamps from 1912 onwards. The first definitives after 1912 bore the inscription 'K.K. ÖSTERR. POST IM FÜRSTENTUM LIECHTENSTEIN'. Later issues were inscribed only 'FÜRSTENTUM' (or FUERSTENTUM) LIECHTENSTEIN'. The first stamps were printed in Austria and were influenced by the Austrian stamp design of the time. Later came Swiss printing (photogravure by Courvoisier and recess in Bern), also a series of line engraved stamps by the Austrian State Printing House. The influence of Swiss and Austrian production can be seen in the high-quality printing and design as well as the direct participation of Austrian or Swiss designers. At the present time, Liechtenstein stamps are influenced by the striking work of G. Malin and L. Jäger of Vaduz. Subjects are mainly tourist publicity for the country as well as a smaller number of general topics. There are numbers of pictorial and portrait stamps while other designs tend towards modern symbolism. Annual output roughly 20 stamps. The regard for the collector market has no negative effect because the production is at a high level of general appeal. In the inter-war period there were low printings (roughly 30,000 stamps or only 7,788 of miniature sheets) but at the present time production rarely falls below 100,000 of each stamp. More often the print is 200,000 to 300,000 stamps.

Philatelic bureau Official Philatelic Service, Vaduz.

LIPSO (LISSO)
One of the Italian Aegean Islands (**area** 17 sq.km, **capital** P. Socoro), Italian 1912–47.

In the years 1912 to 1932 overprints on Italian stamps 'Lipso' or 'LISSO'. A total of 26 stamps, all overprinted provisionals probably designed for the collector market (printings of

10,000 to 12,000), of dubious postal use. (See also *Rhodes and the Dodecanese Islands*.)

LITHUANIA

Baltic state (**area** 52,882 sq.km, **capital** Kaunas, later Vilnius), formerly part of Tsarist Russia. During the First World War occupied by German troops and from 1918 an independent republic, including Klaipéda (Memel) in the years 1923–39. In October 1939 Lithuania included the region of Vilnius (see *Central Lithuania*) and on 5 August 1940 became a republic of the USSR. During the Second World War the country was occupied by the German army and incorporated into Ostland. Since 1945 it has again been part of the USSR.

In the years 1916–18 Ostland stamps were in use and after 1918 came first primitive locals, then definitives with the inscription 'LIETUVOS PAŠTAS', later 'LIETUVA'. Numerous overprinted provisionals and definitives with themes of state propaganda. The influence of the collector's market can be seen in the relatively large number of airmail stamps (almost 100). There were a total of 456 stamps, printed by various methods in local and foreign printing houses, whose influence merges with elements of Polish stamp design. In 1940, after incorporation in the USSR, Lithuanian stamps were given the overprint 'LTSR' (Lithuanian Soviet Socialist Republic). In 1941, after the occupation by German troops, Soviet stamps were overprinted 'LIETUVA' (see *Vilnius*). In 1923 Polish rebels occupied the village of Warwiszki in the neutral zone, where they issued 3 Polish stamps with the overprint 'SAMOSAD WARWISZKI', an insignificant printing of 200 stamps, which underlines doubts as to their postal necessity.

LJUBLJANA

After the defeat of Yugoslavia in 1941 Slovenia was divided among Germany, Hungary and Italy, which acquired the south-western part of the country, the Ljubljana Basin, and this was given the status of an Italian province (**area** 4,585 sq.km, **capital** Ljubljana). After the capitulation of Italy this region was occupied by the German army in 1944 and a Slovenian provincial administration was established.

In 1941 Yugoslav stamps were overprinted 'Territori Sloveni Occupati LUBIANA'; prior to this, Yugoslav stamps had been used with the overprint 'Co.Ci.' (for 'Commissario Civile'). A total of 49 stamps with small printings of 5,000 down to 700 sets, most of which appeared after the Italian stamps were introduced in Slovenia by a decree of 3 May 1941. This suggests that the provisional issues were mainly for sale to collectors.

After the occupation by the German army in 1944 the Italian stamps were overprinted 'PROVINZ LAIBACH/LJUBLJANSKA POKRAJINA'. One definitive issue of pictorials appeared with the same text. A total of 69 stamps, many in printings of less than 15,000 stamps.

LORRAINE

Lorraine became part of France in 1735. In the Franco-Prussian War in 1870 it was occupied and in 1871 incorporated into the German Empire. In 1919 under the Treaty of Versailles Lorraine became once again part of France. During the Second World War, in 1940, the country was again occupied by the German army but since 1945 it has been part of France (**area** 5,598 sq.km, **capital** Metz).

During the first occupation in 1870–71 the German postal authorities issued stamps (with numerals of value but without the name of the country) which were valid in Alsace and Lorraine and in the occupied part of France. During the second German occupation in 1940 German stamps appeared with the overprint 'Lothringen' in Gothic characters; a total of 16 stamps, which remained in use until 1941, and were then replaced by German stamps until the end of the war. (See also *Alsace*.)

LÜBECK

Free Hanseatic city (**area** with 10 other enclaves 298 sq.km), member of the German and North German Confederations; after 1871, the German Empire.

From 1859 definitive issues inscribed 'LÜBECK' or 'LUEBECK': a total of 14 stamps, all heraldic in character, were in use. On 1 January 1868 Lübeck joined the *North German Confederation,* and from that date the stamps of the Confederation were used.

LUXEMBOURG
Area 2,586 sq.km, **population** 365,500 (1982), **capital** Luxembourg.

Developed industrial country, once the estate of the Luxembourg dynasty; after 1815 independent as a grand duchy in direct union with the Netherlands until 1890. In the First and Second World Wars the country was occupied by the German army. Since 1948 a member of the Benelux customs union (until 1919 with Germany, after 1920 with Belgium). UPU direct membership from 1 July 1875.

Definitive stamps from 1852, the first issue without name, subsequent issues inscribed with 'G.D. DE LUXEMBOURG', 'GRAND DUCHÉ DE LUXEMBOURG', later just 'LUXEMBOURG'. Printed mostly in the Netherlands, in recent years in France and Switzerland by various techniques. Strikingly influenced by Netherlands, French and Belgian designs, especially where foreign designers participated. Most subjects deal with publicity for the country, either in the form of portraits or pictures, but symbolic heraldry is also to be found. Collectors' interests are reflected in the relatively small printings (as low as 30,000 stamps in some cases); at the present time printings are far larger. Exceptionally, Luxembourg has issued almost 200 'official' stamps. Present annual output is roughly 15–20 stamps. In 1923 Luxembourg was the first country in the world to issue a miniature sheet.

During the German occupation in the Second World War German stamps with the overprint 'Luxemburg' were introduced, and existing Luxembourg stamps were surcharged with values in German currency, to a total of 41 overprinted provisionals. German stamps were used after 1 January 1942, Luxembourg stamps again from 6 November 1944.

Philatelic bureau Direction des Postes et Télécommunications, Office des Timbres, Luxembourg.

MACEDONIA
After the defeat of Yugoslavia in 1941, Macedonia became part of Bulgaria, which was an ally of Germany. But, with the advance of the Soviet army, a democratic government was established in Bulgaria, which declared war on Germany, and then German troops occupied Macedonia and a puppet government was set up, which proclaimed the country's independence (8 September 1944). The existence of independent Macedonia (**area** 25,990 sq.km, **capital** Skopje) came to an end with the withdrawal of the German army on 13 November 1944. Macedonia was again incorporated into Yugoslavia.

In 1944 eight Bulgarian stamps with the overprint 'Makedonija' in Cyrillic were issued in a small printing of 24,000 sets.

MALMÉDY
A small territory which in 1815 belonged to Prussia, and by plebiscite in 1920 became Belgian (see also *Eupen*).

After issues for *Eupen and Malmédy* Belgian stamps with the overprint 'Malmédy' appeared in 1920. They remained valid until 1931. A total of 15 + 5 overprinted provisionals, which could also be used in Eupen, appeared. After 1925 Belgian stamps were used. German stamps were used in Malmédy from 1940 to 1944.

MALTA
Area 316 sq.km, **population** 326,178 (1982), **capital** Valletta.

Island in the Mediterranean Sea, with an important port. In 1530 the island became the property of the Order of St John, which adopted the name of the Order of the Knights of Malta. From 1800 (legally, 1813) the island was British, but in 1964 it gained independence and became a dominion within the British Commonwealth of Nations. First internal autonomy granted in 1921; full autonomy in 1946. Since 13 December 1974 Malta has been a republic in the Commonwealth. Indirect UPU membership from 1 July 1875 (Great Britain), direct from 21 May 1965.

Before Malta's own stamps were issued, British stamps were valid from 1857 until the first definitives appeared in 1860 bearing the name 'MALTA' (although until membership — through Britain — in the UPU in 1875 only British stamps were valid for overseas mail). After the declaration of independence English texts continued on the stamps, to be replaced by Maltese and, on a few occasions, Italian and Maltese texts, as in 1974: 'Twelid ta Malta/ Repubblica Malta'. The normal royal portraits and pictorial issues of a distinctive nature were common to the period of British colonial rule. In 1958 Chevalier E. Cremona became the chief designer of Maltese stamps, giving them a highly artistic and unified style. Maltese stamps were printed in London until 1965. The annual output is about 20 stamps.

Philatelic bureau The Philatelic Bureau, General Post Office, Valletta.

MARIENWERDER

East Prussian territory including Marienwerder, Stuhm, Rosenburg and Marienburg (2,494 sq.km), occupied by an Allied Commission after the Treaty of Versailles. A plebiscite held 11 July 1920 decided that the territory should be part of Germany.

In 1920 definitives, printed in Milan, were issued with the inscription 'COMMISSION INTERALLIÉE MARIENWERDER', then German stamps with an overprint of the same wording; finally there were again definitives printed for the Allied Commission in Milan, this time with German and Polish wording 'MARIENWERDER/KWIDZYN'. A total of 43 stamps, both overprinted provisionals and definitives. Following the plebiscite, German stamps came into use on 16 August 1920.

MECKLENBURG-SCHWERIN

Grand duchy (**area** 13,304 sq.km, **capital** Schwerin), member of the German and North German Confederation, after 1871 the German Empire.

After 1856 definitive issues inscribed 'MECKLENB. SCHWERIN'. A total of 8 stamps, heraldic in character. The first issue was 1 × 1 cm in size, making these stamps (printed in blocks of four for convenience) some of the smallest in the world ever issued for public use. On 1 January 1868 stamps of the *North German Postal District* came into use.

MECKLENBURG-STRELITZ

Grand duchy (**area** 2,930 sq.km, **capital** Neustrelitz), member of the German and North German Confederation; after 1871, the German Empire.

After 1864 definitive stamps with the inscription 'MECKLENB. STRELITZ'. A total of 6 stamps in an heraldic design. All were freely used for postage. They remained valid until 1867 and in 1868 stamps of the *North German Postal District* replaced them.

MECKLENBURG-WESTERN POMERANIA

Part of the Soviet Occupation Zone of Germany (**area** 22,938 sq.km, **capital** Schwerin) formed after 1945.

From 1945 to 31 October 1946 a total of 32 stamps were issued, mostly primitive designs locally printed, some without a name, others with 'MECKLENBURG-VORPOMMERN'.

MEMEL (KLAIPÉDA)

Seaport and district on the Baltic (**area** 2,829 sq.km), until the end of the First World War part of Germany. Ceded by Germany under the Treaty of Versailles and from February 1920 under Allied control administered by France. Became part of Lithuania 16 February 1923, as Klaipéda, an autonomous region. Germany occupied the region 22 March 1939; since 25 January 1945 part of the Soviet Union.

During the French administration (1920–23) German stamps were issued with the over-print 'Memelgebiet' (in Gothic characters) and French stamps with the overprint 'MEMEL'. A total of 120 overprinted and/or surcharged provisionals until the end of the French occupation.

After 1923 Lithuanian stamps with the overprint 'KLAIPÉDA (MEMEL)', and a German currency surcharge; then definitives with the words 'Klaipéda (Memel)' and on them provisional surcharges: a total of 114 stamps, mostly overprinted provisionals and definitives of Lithuanian origin, all issued in one year, 1923. In 1924 Lithuanian stamps came into use. Because of inflation (and collector demand) there were frequent printings, only a small portion of which were used for postal purposes. After the annexation by Germany in 1939, there were local issues of doubtful status.

MODENA

Italian duchy (**area** 2,590 sq.km, **capital** Modena) from 1452 and again after 1815 under the rule of the house of Austria-Este. The last ruler, Francis IV, was exiled in 1859, and from 1860 Modena became incorporated into the Kingdom of Sardinia (and after 1861 into the Kingdom of Italy).

After 1852 definitive stamps of local origin, symbolic in character, without the name of the duchy at first, but bearing the name of the ducal rulers, 'POSTE ESTENSI', later with 'PROVINCIE MODENESI'. A total of 15 stamps, which fulfilled the classical postal purpose in the first place and are in great demand among philatelists. In 1860 they were replaced by stamps of *Sardinia*.

MOLDAVIA and WALACHIA

Princedom within the territory of present-day Rumania (**area** 37,716 sq.km, **capital** Jassy). Under Turkish rule from the 16th century, autonomous from 1829 when, under the Treaty of Drinopol, the Russian Protectorate was confirmed. During the Crimean War Moldavia was occupied by the Austrian army (1854–7), in 1859 it was united with Walachia, and in 1861 the Rumanian princedom was proclaimed within the Ottoman Empire.

In 1858 primitive stamps without the name of the country were handprinted locally : a total of 7 stamps, popularly called 'Moldavian Bulls' from the bull's head depicted on each stamp. They are among the valuable classic stamps of Europe. The inscription 'PORTO SCRISORI' means 'letter stamp' and 'PORTO GAZETTI', 'newspaper stamp'. These stamps with the emblem of Moldavia were valid only in Moldavian territory. Issuing continued until Moldavia united with Walachia to form Moldo-Walachia (territorially identical to the later Romania). Even though the unification took place in 1859, the stamps of Moldavia continued to be issued until 1862. They bear an eagle and bull's head with a posthorn below, but have no name of the state, although in the meantime the name *Rumania* came into use, but did not appear on stamps until 1865.

MONACO

Area 1.8 sq.km, **population** 27,063 (1982), **capital** Monaco.

Constitutional princedom under French protection. A large part of the national income derives from tourism and the casino. In 1793 Monaco was joined to France; in 1815 it became a protectorate of Sardinia; in 1861 it came under French protection as a semi-sovereign princedom ceding the towns of Menton and Roquebrune. A customs union with France has operated since 1912. UPU membership, indirect through France, from 1 April 1879, direct from 12 October 1955.

Before the introduction of Monaco stamps those of Sardinia were in use until 1860, and then French stamps until 1885. After 1885 definitives were issued inscribed 'PRINCIPAUTÉ DE MONACO', and from 1938 only 'MONACO'. Typical French designs, printed in France but with certain local features until 1948. Later issues incorporate a wider range of subjects in a variety of stamp shapes and a large number of airmail stamps and other features that reflect the strong appeal to the collector market. Apart from portraits, designs are largely pictorials (landscapes and other subjects). Printings mostly around 250,000, occasionally fewer (50,000). Present annual output about 50 stamps.

Philatelic bureau Office des Emissions de Timbres-postes, Monte Carlo, Monaco.

MONTENEGRO

From 1852 an absolute princedom, whose independence was officially acknowledged by Turkey in 1878. Proclaimed a kingdom in 1910 (**area** 14,000 sq.km, **capital** Cetinje).

After the Balkan War of 1912–13 it was joined to the Novibazar sanjak and in 1915–16 was occupied by Austro-Hungarian troops. The government went into exile in Bordeaux in France. In 1918 Montenegro became part of the *Kingdom of the Serbs, Croats and Slovenes*. After the defeat of Yugoslavia during the Second World War the Italian army occupied Montenegro on 12 June 1941 and turned it into a monarchy under an Italian regent. After the capitulation of Italy the German army occupied the country in September 1943 and established a military régime. On 10 November 1943 a civil administration was formed under a National Committee. After the retreat of the German army in November 1944 the territory of Montenegro was once again incorporated into Yugoslavia and, in 1945, became a people's republic. Since 1963, it has been a socialist republic in Federated Yugoslavia.

Definitive stamps since 1874 with Cyrillic script indicating 'Montenegrin Post' and 'Montenegro'. A total of 98 + 26 stamps, mainly portraits, but also symbolic. Landscape sets have been issued since 1896, a very early date. The stamps were printed by letterpress and recess printing in Vienna, those produced after 1910 to designs by Kolo Moser were very finely engraved by Schirnböck, who also designed the famous landscape stamps of Bosnia and Herzegovina. Those stamps, which show a strong Austrian influence, were issued until 1913. In 1917 two stamps of the Austro-Hungarian field post were issued in Montenegro territory bearing the overprint 'K.U.K. MILIT. VERWALTUNG MONTENEGRO'.

During the Second World War, after the entry of the Italian army in 1941, there appeared first a 'MONTENEGRO' overprint on Italian and Yugoslav stamps, and later a definitive issue simply with the name Montenegro in Cyrillic script. A total of 74 + 10 stamps, both overprinted provisionals and pictorial designs. The overprinted sets are strongly angled towards the collector's market, as shown by the small issues, at times no more than 1,000, 500 and sometimes as few as 100 stamps! When in 1943 the German administration replaced the Italian, the former Yugoslav and Montenegrin stamps were issued with an overprint, where the word 'MONTENEGRO' is to be found. A total of 35 stamps, all overprinted provisionals. In November 1944, after the retreat of the German army, the territory became once again part of *Yugoslavia,* and Yugoslav stamps came into use.

MYTILENE

Capital of Lesbos in the Aegean Sea which, until the Balkan Wars, was Turkish; occupied by Greece in 1912 and has been Greek since 1913. (See also *Levant.*)

Russia also operated a postal agency which, in 1910, issued overprinted provisionals on Russian stamps with 'Mételin' in Latin script: a total of 9 stamps. In 1912 a total of 18 Turkish stamps were overprinted with a Greek text meaning 'Greek Occupation of Mytilene'. Their real postal purpose has not been fully clarified.

NAPLES

Kingdom (**area** 119,000 sq.km, **capital** Naples) linked politically with the Kingdom of Sicily to form the Kingdom of the Two Sicilies in the middle of the 19th century under the rule of the Bourbon dynasty, which was driven out by Garibaldi in 1860. After a popular plebiscite Naples was joined to the Kingdom of Sardinia in 1860 and has been part of Italy since 1861.

In 1858 definitive issues inscribed 'POSTA NAPOLETANA'. A total of 17 stamps by 1861, the last issue of the Neapolitan Provinces of the Kingdom of Italy being without the name of the country. The stamps of Naples are heraldic. The Neapolitan Provinces issues have portraits of King Victor Emmanuel II. All are coveted classical stamps.

NETHERLANDS

Area 41,160 sq.km, **population** 14.34m (1983), **commercial capital** Amsterdam, **political capital** The Hague.

Developed country with industry and agriculture. Constitutional monarchy and a former colonial power. The last dependent territory — the Netherlands Antilles — has been declared a member of the Netherlands Union. At the Congress of Vienna in 1815 the United Provinces and the Austrian Netherlands were unified under Wilhelm I, Belgium later separated although its independence was not acknowledged until 1839 and Luxembourg, linked by the common monarchy, broke away in 1890. In 1948 the BENELUX customs union was formed of Belgium, the Netherlands and Luxembourg. UPU membership from 1 July 1875.

Definitive stamps from 1852, first without the name of the country ('postzegel' = 'postage stamp'); from 1867 with the inscription 'NEDERLAND'. Printing was by the Mint, Utrecht and J. Enschedé in Haarlem. Stamp designs concentrate on national events and anniversaries. Issues include the earliest charity stamps in Europe (1906). There are a number of common designs for all Netherlands stamp-issuing territories. The entire production is based on exacting artistic treatment (numerals, artistic use of photographs, stylized symbols, etc.) represented in the work of experienced designers, e.g. Krimpen, Hertz, Chr. de Moor, Treumann, Vossen and others. Exceptional features include telegraph stamps in the shape of a hexagon and the 1921 marine insurance stamps paying for mail carried in unsinkable safes that would survive a shipwreck on the way to the Netherlands Indies. A common design is used for a set of Netherlands postage-due stamps valid also in the colonies, the different colour of each set being the distinguishing feature: Netherlands, blue; Netherlands Indies, red; Curaçao, green; Surinam, violet. Annual output is about 35 stamps. Special official stamps are issued for the International Court of Justice. The Netherlands are often incorrectly referred to as 'Holland', which is one of the historical provinces of the Netherlands.

Philatelic bureau Filatelische Dienst, 9700 RN-Groningen.

NISIRO (NISIROS)
One of the Italian Aegean Islands (**area** 48 sq.km, **capital** Nisiro), Italian from 1912 to 1947.

In 1912–32 overprints on Italian stamps with the name 'NISIROS' or 'NISIRO', a total of 26 overprinted provisionals. The issues were speculative in character with small printings ranging from 10,000 to 12,000 stamps. Their postal function remains doubtful. (See also *Rhodes and the Dodecanese Islands*.)

NORTHERN EPIRUS
After the proclamation of the independence of Albania in 1912 and the accession of Prince Wilhelm of Wied it was necessary to fix the frontier between Greece and Albania. Some areas of Northern Epirus (1,024 sq.km) inhabited by Greeks, and liberated by the Greek army from the Turks, were to become part of Albania. The Greeks left under protest but set up a provisional revolutionary government under the chairmanship of the one-time Greek minister Zorographos, who was born in Epirus. They had their own units which occupied the territory and proclaimed the independent republic of Epirus at Chimara and Argyrocasta in February 1914. When the Greek army occupied this territory at the beginning of the First World War it was given the name of Northern Epirus, but in the autumn of 1916 the Greeks had to withdraw because the French army entered its eastern parts from Thessalonica and established the *Korytzan Republic*, while the western part was occupied from Valona by the Italians, and the Albanian Republic under Italian protection was proclaimed at Gjirokastro. The Greeks were forced to withdraw to the frontier originally stipulated. They tried again to gain Epirus in 1920 but were not successful. At the beginning of the Second World War, when the Italians attacked Greece from Albania, the Greeks occupied the territory of Epirus once again for a short time (in 1940).

In 1914 there were stamps of primitive design (incorporating a skull and crossbones) followed by overprinted provisionals on stamps of Turkey and, finally, definitives of Greek origin (Corfu) inscribed 'IPEIROS' in Greek script. In December 1914 overprints on Greek stamps reading 'V. IPEIROS' (= Northern Epirus) in Greek script were issued: a total of 63 stamps, most of them overprinted provisionals. Albanian stamps were brought into use after 1919.

In 1914, also, local issues for Himara with the words 'Greek Chimara' in Greek script, as overprints on Greek stamps, and portrait definitives of Greek origin (Aspiotis, Corfu): a total of 17 stamps. Also two local stamps for Koritza as overprints, on Epirus stamps, with the word 'KORITZA' in Greek script.

In 1940–41 Greek stamps were valid with a Greek overprint, reading 'Greek Administration.'

NORTH GERMAN POSTAL DISTRICT

After the defeat of Austria in the Austro-Prussian War of 1866 and the disintegration of the first German Confederation, Prussia (following its occupation of Holstein, Hanover, Hessen, Nassau and Frankfurt) negotiated the North German Confederation with the northern states of Germany in 1867, assumed the leading role in it (capital, Berlin) and agreed on a customs union with the states of southern Germany. The postal territory of the North German Confederation was called 'Norddeutscher Postbezirk' (= 'North German Postal Union') from 1 January 1868 and was divided into two regions according to the currency used: Groschen and Kreuzer.

The Groschen region: Bremen, Brunswick, Hamburg, Lübeck, Mecklenburg-Schwerin, Mecklenburg-Strelitz, Oldenburg, Prussia (including Bergedorf, Hanover, Schleswig-Holstein, and the northern parts of the Thurn and Taxis postal territory (i.e. Hessen-Kassel, Saxony-Weimar-Eisenach, Gotha, Schwarzburg-Sondershausen, Reuss-Gera, Reuss-Greiz, Lippe-Detmold, Lippe-Schaumburg and Camburg) and Saxony.

The Kreuzer region: the southern part of the Thurn and Taxis postal territory (Hessen-Darmstadt, Hessen-Homburg, Nassau, Frankfurt-am-Main, Saxony-Meiningen, Coburg, Schwarzburg-Rudolstadt and Hohenzollern).

From 1868 definitive stamps were issued with the wording 'NORDDEUTSCHER POSTBEZIRK'. In the Groschen region values were given in Groschen, in the southern region in Kreuzer, and for the city mail in Hamburg without indication of currency: a total of 35 stamps in numeral designs and of local origin. They were valid until the end of 1871. On 1 January 1872 they were replaced by the stamps of *Germany*.

NORTH INGERMANLAND

Russian territory between Lake Ladoga and Narva which in 1920 (with the support of Finland) demanded to be incorporated into Finland under the name of Pohjois (= Northern) Inkeri. In 1920, under the peace treaty of Dorpat (Tartu), it became part of the Russian S.F.S.R.

In 1920 definitive stamps with the name 'POHJOIS INKERI', a total of 14 stamps with heraldic devices and pictorial designs. Only one post office functioned, at Kirjasalo. The first issue was used for the post to Finland and of the first four values only 200,000 were printed. Of the highest value (10 markka) only 1,000 were printed.

NORWAY

Area 323,895 sq.km, **population** 4.12m (1983), **capital** Oslo.

Country with developed industry and agriculture and an important timber industry. Constitutional monarchy. After declaring its independence from Denmark, a hereditary part of which it had formed from 1508 to 1814, Norway became a joint kingdom with Sweden from 1815 to 1905, being ruled by the same monarch. It remained neutral in the First World War, and at its conclusion acquired Spitzbergen and Jan Mayen Island. In 1930 Norway laid claims to the Peter I Island in the Antarctic and to the Bouvet Islands, and in 1939 to the Bouvet Sector of the Antarctic. During the Second World War the country was occupied by the German army (1940-5) and a government-in-exile was set up in London. The country was liberated by the British and the Soviet armies (north). UPU membership — direct — from 1 July 1875.

Definitives since 1855, first without the name of the country ('Frimaerke' = postage stamp). After 1856, the inscription was 'NORGE' or 'NOREG'. The stamps are usually produced in Oslo. The Norwegian government-in-exile in London issued stamps in 1943 (with printings up to 22 million) which from 1945 were valid in the liberated territory of Norway. The majority of designs are tourist-orientated but include some with symbolic and numerical treatment. Artistically, production is rather uneven, the definitives being basically numerals. The numeral and posthorn design of the 1872 definitives remained in use for almost a hundred years (last re-issue in 1978) which is a world record. Typical of Norway is restrained issuing of stamps, mainly to fulfil the postal function and provide postal propaganda for the country. At the present time the annual new issue output is some 20 stamps.

Philatelic bureau Postens Filatelitjeneste, Oslo.

OLDENBURG

Former grand duchy with two enclaves (**area** 6,414 sq.km, **capital** Oldenburg), a member of the German and North German Confederation; since 1871 member-country of the German Empire.

From 1852 definitives with the name 'OLDENBURG': a total of 19 stamps in heraldic designs, mostly of local origin (the last issue was printed in Berlin), which fulfilled the classic postal function. Prussian stamps were used in the Birkenfeld enclave. After 1 January 1868 the stamps of the *North German Postal District* came into use.

OSTLAND

During the Second World War, in 1941, the German occupation authorities introduced over-prints on German stamps with the word 'OSTLAND'. These were valid in the territory of the Reichskomissariat Ost, i.e. Estonia, Latvia, Lithuania, and parts of White Russia until 1944. A total of 20 overprinted provisionals.

PAPAL STATES

Came into existence in central Italy in 755 as the domain of the Pope, and its stature was renewed by the Congress of Vienna after the Napoleonic Wars (after temporary French annexation) in 1815 (then 41,152 sq.km in area). In 1860 the Kingdom of Sardinia annexed its northern parts — Romagna, the Marches and Umbria and the enclaves of Pontecorvo and Benevento, so that only the province of Lazio (Latium) remained (11,770 sq.km) under the protection of the French. It was conquered together with the city of Rome by the Italian army on 29 September 1870, and thus the Papal States ceased to exist. The Pope, residing only in the Vatican, became a voluntary 'Vatican Prisoner'. Politically, the Papal States were re-established in 1929 in the form of the Vatican City.

From 1852 onwards stamps of symbolic character without the name of the state (the Italian text alone indicates that they are postage stamps), with the insignia of the crossed keys of St Peter surmounted by the papal crown. There were a total of 25 classic stamps, much sought after by collectors. From 1870 these were replaced by Italian stamps.

PARMA

Former duchy in Italy known as the United Duchy of Parma-Piacenza (**area** 3,206 sq.km, **capital** Parma). In 1859 a provisional government came to power which proclaimed union with the Kingdom of Sardinia, which was established in 1860, and in 1861 the territory was absorbed in the new Italian kingdom.

From 1852 definitive stamps with the text 'STATI PARM', 'STATI PARMENSI', 'DUC. DI PARMA PIAC. ECC': a total of 18 stamps in heraldic designs and of local origin. All these stamps are regarded as valuable classic issues.

PATMO (PATMOS)

One of the Italian Aegean Islands (**area** 57 sq.km, **capital** Patmos), Italian 1912–47.

In 1912–32 Italian stamps overprinted 'PATMO' or 'PATMOS': a total of 26 overprinted provisionals. These issues are considered speculative in view of limited printings of 10,000 and 12,000, and their postal function is doubtful. (See also *Rhodes and the Dodecanese Islands*.)

PISCOPI (TILOS)

One of the Italian Aegean Islands (**area** 64 sq.km, **capital** Pigadia), Italian 1912–47.

In the years 1912–32 overprints on Italian stamps were inscribed 'PISCOPI': a total of 26 overprinted provisionals. These issues are considered to be speculative in view of the limited printings of 10,000 and 12,000, and their postal function is doubtful. (See also *Rhodes and the Dodecanese Islands*.)

POLAND

Area 312,683 sq.km, **population** 36.57m (1983), **capital** Warsaw.

Socialist republic, industrial and agricultural country with an important coal-mining industry. Historical Poland came into existence in 1795, and this was confirmed by the Congress of Vienna in 1815; an autonomous Congress Kingdom was established at that time with Warsaw as capital, linked in political union with Russia. After the defeat of the Polish January Rising (1863) the autonomy was abolished, and in 1864 a Russian province was set up — the Warsaw General Gubernia. During the First World War, after a temporary occupation by Russia, this was taken over by the German and Austro-Hungarian armies. Berlin and Vienna formally acknowledged the revival of Poland on 5 November 1916 and set up a regency in Warsaw. The Alliance proclaimed Poland a member on 3 June 1918. The Polish state was renewed as a republic in 1918 within new frontiers. These were fixed in relation to Germany by the Treaty of Versailles in 1919, by plebiscite in Upper Silesia in 1921, with Czechoslovakia by the Conference of Ambassadors in 1920, and in relation to the USSR by the Riga Peace Treaty of 1921, so that the area of Poland then measured 388,634 sq.km. In the years 1939–44 part of the Polish territory came under the General Gouvernement and the other parts, occupied by the German and the Soviet armies, were incorporated into those countries. Some parts of Spiš and Orava came under Slovakia. Poland was re-established with new frontiers in 1944.

Indirect UPU membership from 1 July 1875 (Germany, Austria and Russia); direct from 1 May 1919.

The first definitive Polish stamps (a single 10 kopecks) was issued in 1860 as an expression of the political autonomy of the Polish Kingdom. It does not bear the name of the country, and was based on the design of contemporary Russian stamps, from which it differed only in colour and in the bilingual inscriptions in Russian and Polish: the inscription 'ZA LOT KOP 10' marks the charge of 10 kopecks for a letter weighing 1 lot. Russian stamps were introduced in 1865 and remained in use until 1915. In 1915–16 German stamps appeared overprinted 'Russisch Polen' and 'Gen. Gouv. Warschau' in Gothic characters. (See *Russian Poland* and *Poland: General Gouvernement Warschau*.) From 1918 Polish stamps appeared both in northern Poland (the former Russian Poland), the General Gouvernement area, and in southern Poland (the former General Gouvernement, Lublin, Galicia and Austrian Silesia, the region that had formerly belonged to Austria). The first to appear were overprinted provisionals with the name 'Poczta Polska'. In the area of northern Poland these overprints were on unissued stamps of the Warsaw Citizens' Post and overprinted provisionals of Russian Poland. In the other regions of Poland there were overprints on Austrian stamps and then definitives produced in Cracow. The definitive issues of Poland in the years 1919–20 expressed the face value in two currencies — in pfennige and marks for the region of northern Poland and in halerzy and korona for the rest of the country. From 1 February 1920 the German currency stamps were valid for use in the whole of Poland. Zloty-based currency was introduced in 1924 to replace the currency debased by inflation, which reached its climax in 1924, when the high value overprinted provisionals reached a denomination of 2,000,000 marks (and of 3,000,000 marks for the postage due issue).

In the years 1918–39 a total of 359 + 119 different stamps were printed in Warsaw, mainly by letterpress, although occasionally stamps were produced by line-engraving. Most of the designs relate to Polish history and Polish personalities of national importance. Some issues depicted Polish landscapes, and these show a striking artistic level. The Polish stamps of 1922–3 with values in German currency, were intended for the region of Upper Silesia, which was added to Poland and where the German mark was in circulation.

On new issues which appeared after 1944, the inscription 'POCZTA POLSKA' was shortened to 'POLSKA'. Present-day annual output amounts to 40–60 stamps. These post-war issues tend to cover wider themes in addition to national propaganda, the majority of designs being pictorial. Regard for the philatelic market is shown by the large and less common formats, as well as curious materials such as artificial silk and other constituents of paper manufacture. The most striking designers include Kaczmarczyk, Malecki, Desselsberger, Heidrich and others. Most of the stamps are printed in Warsaw, occasionally by recess printing. In 1950 there appeared a large number of overprinted provisionals.

In the years 1915–19 and 1941–5 there existed a large number of local post offices responsible for various issues (government-in-exile, Polish army at Monte Cassino, etc.), where the postal need was usually lacking and the stamps' status remains dubious.

Philatelic bureau Ars Polona, Warsaw.

POLAND: GENERAL GOUVERNEMENT

After the occupation of part of Poland in 1939 most of the country was incorporated directly into Germany. The rest was proclaimed a 'General Government' on 12 October 1939 and everything Polish was eradicated, even the geographical term Poland was abolished. The area encompassed 93,871 sq.km, and from 1 July 1941, when eastern Galicia was added, this increased to 144,968 sq.km (capital Cracow). In 1944 this occupation status came to an end.

From 1939 German stamps with the overprint 'Deutsche Post OSTEN' were valid; from 1940 Polish stamps with the overprint 'General-Gouvernement'. Definitive stamps appeared in 1941 with the overprint 'DEUTSCHES REICH'; from 1943 'GROSSDEUTSCHES REICH'. A total of 112 + 40 stamps were produced in Vienna; designs, German in style, covered propaganda subjects, portraits, symbols and landscapes.

POLAND: GENERAL GOUVERNEMENT WARSCHAU

The region of *Russian Poland* (the gubernias of Warsaw, Plock, Lomža, Kalisz and part of Piotrkow) was occupied by the German army during the First World War. In the years 1916–17 overprinted provisionals appeared on German stamps with the wording (in Gothic characters), 'Gen.-Gouv. Warschau' (a total of 11 stamps).

PORT LAGOS

Town on the coast of the Aegean Sea in Western Thrace, until 1912 Turkish, today on Greek territory.

The French post office here used French stamps in the years 1874–93; in 1893 six French stamps of Peace and Commerce design were issued with the overprint 'Port-Lagos'. The French post office was closed in 1898. (See also *Levant.*)

PORTUGAL

Area 92,072 sq.km (including Madeira and the Azores), **population** 9.93m (1983), **capital** Lisbon.

Republic (kingdom until 1910), the economy is largely agricultural, with mining of mineral ores. In the past, Portugal possessed a vast colonial empire, of which only Macao in Asia remains. Direct UPU membership from 1 July 1875 (including Madeira and the Azores).

Definitive issues from 1853, but the word 'PORTUGAL' appeared only from 1866 on, being changed to 'REPUBLICA PORTUGUESA' after the proclamation of the republic and, later, again followed by 'PORTUGAL', which is used at the present time. Most of the stamp printing is of local origin in Lisbon but, at present, some printing is in Switzerland, at Courvoisier. Design stress is on publicity for the country based on a striking graphic presentation. One of the main designers is C. C. Pinto, who has greatly influenced Portuguese stamp design. The early definitives were noted for long sets of up to 30 values. At the present time the annual output is about 40 new stamps.

When in 1980 the Azores and Madeira renewed their own stamp issuing, their stamps were also valid in continental Portugal and vice-versa.

Philatelic bureau Servicos de Filatelia, Lisbon.

PRUSSIA

The largest and economically most developed part of Germany, a kingdom from 1701, and after 1772 its name was adopted for all territories ruled by the Brandenburg Hohenzollerns. Member country of the German Confederation, and after the victory in the Austro-Prussian War (1866) occupied Holstein (Schleswig was already occupied from 1864), the regions of Hanover, Hessen-Nassau and Frankfurt-am-Main and formed the North German Confederation (1867). After the victory over France, the King of Prussia was proclaimed German Emperor at Versailles on 18 January 1871, and Prussia (**area** 347,509 sq.km, **capital** Berlin) became the leading country of the German Empire.

Definitive issues from 1850, at first merely inscribed 'FREIMARKE', but later with the name 'PREUSSEN': a total of 26 stamps (printed in Berlin), heraldic, royal portraits and numeral designs. They are regarded as classic stamps by collectors. With Prussia's entry into the North German Confederation the Prussian stamps lost validity at the end of 1867 and were replaced by those of the *North German Postal District* in 1868.

Prussian stamps were also used in Anhalt, Waldeck, the Oldenburg part of Birkenfeld and the Weimar enclaves of Allstedt, Schwarzburg-Rudolstadt and Schwarzburg-Sonderhausen; after 1866-7 likewise in Lauenburg, Schleswig-Holstein and Bergedorf.

PSKOV (PLESKAU)

Town and district at the southern end of Lake Pskov in the Russian Soviet Federal Socialist Republic, south-west of Leningrad, occupied by the German army 1941-4. The German name is Pleskau.

From 1941 overprints on German and Soviet stamps 'PLESKAU', then definitive stamps: a total of 18 stamps, all in small printings of only a few thousand, so that their postal function is doubtful. Some authorities claim that these are bogus stamps without any official backing.

RETHYMNON

Part of Crete in the Russian sphere of administration after the occupation of the island in 1898-1909 by England, France, Russia and Italy (see *Crete*).

A total of 10 stamps were issued for the Russian post office on the territory administered by Russia from 13 May to 29 July 1899. The first stamps were hand-struck locally, while further issues were printed in Athens. Most of them have Russian inscriptions, a few bear the name 'RETYMNO' in Latin script. Printings did not exceed 10,000 and in some cases only 1,200 or even 960 stamps are thought to have been issued. Forgeries of the rarer stamps are known to exist.

RHINELAND-PALATINATE

Part of the French Occupation Zone of Germany (in 1945: **area** 19,828 sq.km, **capital** Mainz); formally established on 30 August 1946; today part of the Federal Republic of Germany.

After a general issue for the entire French Occupation Zone ('ZONE FRANÇAISE') in Germany, separate definitive stamps were issued from 1947 inscribed 'RHEINLAND-PFALZ': a total of 52 stamps (printed in photogravure by F. Burda in Offenburg, Baden) influenced by the then current French and German stamp designers. After the establishment of the Federal Republic of Germany in 1949 with its own stamps, issues of the Rhineland-Palatinate remained valid for the entire territory of the Federal Republic until 31 March 1950. (See also *Germany, French Occupation Zone*.)

RHODES AND THE DODECANESE ISLANDS

The group of islands (**total area** 2,682 sq.km, **capital** Rhodes) in the south-eastern part of the Aegean Sea were all originally under Turkish domination. They include Rhodes, the islands of the Dodecanese (*Calino, Carchi, Caso, Cos, Lero, Lipso, Nisiro, Patmo, Piscopi, Scarpanto, Simi, Stampalia*) and *Castellrosso*. They proclaimed independence in 1912, but were shortly afterwards occupied by Italy in the war against Turkey and Tripolitania. In 1913 the islands were promised to Greece, but were not ceded, and in 1923, under the Treaty of Lausanne, they became Italian (together with Castelrosso). In 1943–5 they were under German occupation, then temporarily occupied by British troops, and in 1947 were finally ceded by Italy to Greece.

Italian stamps were valid in the islands from 1912 bearing first the overprint 'EGEO' and then with an overprint for each of the islands. Next came an issue with 'ISOLE ITALIANE DELL EGEO' as an overprint. From 1929 all the Italian Aegean Islands used the Rhodes issue for regular postal use, while other issues were printed mainly for collectors: a total of 113 stamps, mostly overprinted provisionals. The definitives are of Italian origin.Most of the sets were issued simply for sale to collectors, as shown by the very low printings of around 10,000. Of the high values of the 1933 issue for the twentieth anniversary of the Italian occupation only 2,900 were printed, suggesting that there was no attempt to provide stamps for public use. Apart from issues for the Italian Aegean Islands, stamps appeared for each of the twelve islands separately.

In 1945–7, during the British occupation, British stamps were in use with the overprint 'MEF' (Middle East Forces). In 1947 these were replaced by Greek stamps with an overprint meaning 'Greek Administration'. The use of normal Greek stamps followed soon after.

The grand total for all the stamps issued for individual Italian Aegean Islands during Italian occupation is over 500, strongly suggesting that the philatelic demand, rather than public requirements, prompted the issue of many of the stamps.

ROMAGNA

A province of the Papal States (**area** 11,375 sq.km, **capital** Ravenna), actually from the 8th century, but officially only from 1500. In 1859–60 independent, and from 1860 part of the Kingdom of Sardinia (from 1861, Italy).

When in 1859 Romagna separated from the Papal States in preparation for joining Sardinia, the stamps of the Papal States were still valid. One issue of 9 stamps appeared in September 1859 bearing the name 'ROMAGNE'. They are considered to be classic stamps of simple design (numerals and text). In February 1860 these stamps were superseded by Sardinian stamps (see also *Sardinia*).

RUMANIA (ROMANIA)

Area 237,500 sq.km, **population** 22.6m (1984), **capital** Bucharest.

Agricultural and industrial country with resources of oil. Romania came into existence in 1859 by the unification of the principalities of Moldavia and Walachia. The resulting Romanian principality (within the framework of the Ottoman Empire) was proclaimed in 1861 and the name Romania was introduced in 1862. In 1878 it became independent from Turkey and in 1881 was declared a kingdom. During the First World War, the country stood on the side of the Entente until 1916, and in 1917 it was almost entirely occupied by the Austrian, Hungarian, German, and Bulgarian armies with the exception of the eastern parts of Moldavia. After the war, Romania incorporated Transylvania, Bucovina, Bessarabia, and eastern Banat. In 1940 Bessarabia and northern Bucovina were ceded to the USSR, part of Transylvania to Hungary and southern Dobruja to Bulgaria. In 1941–4 Romania temporarily regained Bessarabia and northern Bucovina and administered the Soviet territory between the Dnieper and the Bug (called Transnistria). Transylvania was regained in 1944 during the Second World War while Romania was on the side of Germany. Late in 1944, Romania fought against Germany. In 1947 a People's Republic was proclaimed and from 1965 Romania has been a socialist country. Direct UPU membership from 1 July 1875.

After issues for Moldo-Walachia, which did not bear the name of the territory, definitive issues appeared in 1865 with the wording 'POSTA ROMÂNĂ', later 'ROMÂNIA'; from 1948, 'REPUBLICA POPULARĂ ROMÂNĂ'; then, 'ROMINA', and, at the present time, again 'POSTA ROMANA'. With its total output of nearly 4,000 stamps, Romania is one of the major stamp-issuing countries. The present annual output amounts to about 70 stamps. The printing, all in Romania, includes offset, letterpress and photogravure. Stamp designs favouring propaganda for the country have now been replaced by general topics, with a view to encouraging collectors' interest, which is also evident in the large number of miniature sheets. Most of the stamps are pictorials with some portraits of prominent national figures.

At first Romanian stamps were valid only locally, foreign mail services of the Romanian post office did not begin until 1869. Foreign mail was handled on Romanian territory by post offices of Austria-Hungary, France, Greece and the Ottoman Empire.

During the First World War, when German, Austro-Hungarian and Bulgarian troops occupied the larger part of Romania, these administrations used their own stamps: German stamps with the overprint 'M.V.I.R.' or only 'RUMÄNIEN' (12 stamps, whose postal function has not been reliably proved); Bulgarian stamps with an overprint in Cyrillic script meaning 'Post Office in Romania' (4 stamps). The Austro-Hungarian issue Military Post (Feldpost) issued special stamps with face value overprinted in Romanian currency.

After the occupation of the newly acquired Romanian territories of Transylvania and adjacent regions (which until 1918 belonged to Hungary) Hungarian stamps were overprinted 'REGATUL ROMANIEI' (Kingdom of Romania) and surcharged in Romanian currency: a total of 81 overprinted provisionals issued in 1919. In 1919–20 Hungarian stamps with the overprint 'ZONA DE OCUPATIE ROMÂNĂ' for the region of Debrecen, occupied by Romanian soldiers: a total of 123 overprinted provisionals.

On the occasion of the inauguration of the joint Romanian-Yugoslav Iron Gate Dam on the Danube in 1965, stamps with the names of the two countries were issued giving face value in both currencies; these stamps were valid both in Romania and in Yugoslavia.

Philatelic bureau Illexim, Bucharest.

RUSSIA
The Russian state formed around Muscovite Russia and was ruled by a tsar from 1547. From the beginning it was multi-national and covered an enormous area in Europe and Asia. The tsarist absolutism and social injustice brought forth a number of revolutionary movements, and the monarchy was overthrown during the First World War after the February Revolution in 1917, and a Provisional Government was set up. The October Revolution of that same year established a government of Soviets, and on 7 November 1917 the Russian Soviet Federated Socialist Republic came into existence (called the Russian Republic until 1918) as well as other Soviet Republics. On 30 December 1922 the Union of Soviet Socialist Republics (see *Soviet Union*) was formed by the merger of the Russian Soviet Federated Socialist Republic with the Ukrainian Soviet Socialist Republic, the Byelorussian S.S.R. and the Transcaucasian S.F.S.R.

From 1857 definitive stamps, for a number of years, had only the name of the post office or the words 'Postal stamp' in Cyrillic script. The word 'ROSSIJA' or 'RSFSR' in Cyrillic script appeared only on isolated stamps after 1917: a total of 266 stamps, at first symbolic in character, later with portraits and socialist symbols, apart from the overprinted provisionals. They were generally of local origin (most of them printed in St Petersburg), using various printing techniques of varying quality (hand-struck primitive lithographic prints and fine line-engraving in 1921). A great variety of artistic conception is present, from simple line drawing to involved design. Between 1 January 1919 and 15 August 1921 inland letters were mailed free of charge and no stamps were issued. In 1922 inflation raised the face value of some stamps to as much as 100,000 roubles.

In 1918–20 Russian stamps continued to be used on the territory where the fighting against the Red Army took place. Additionally, many special issues without regional names appeared, and these are dealt with as separate stamp-issuing territories. These issues were mostly provisionals surcharged in different currencies, or are poorly printed definitives, most of them without the name of the area in which they circulated. Occasionally an inscription in Cyrillic script read 'Post Office of the Red Army' or simply 'Russia', 'Russian Post' and so on. The postal validity of many of these issues has never been reliably confirmed.

RUSSIAN POLAND

After the defeat of the Polish January Rising in 1863 Polish autonomy was abolished, and in 1864 the Warsaw General Gubernia was set up, which was a Russian province. In the First World War the Russian army was driven out and the territory of the Gubernia was occupied by German and Austro-Hungarian soldiers.

In 1915 five German stamps were given (in Gothic characters) the provisional overprint 'Russisch-Polen' to be used in this territory. They were followed in 1916 by an issue of the General Gouvernement Warsaw (see *Poland: General Gouvernement Warsaw*). The services of the German post office were limited to the regional towns of Warsaw, Sosnoviec, Zawiercie, Częstochowa and Lodz. Delivery in smaller places followed special regulations and involved extra charge.

SAAR

As an administrative unit, the Saar was established in 1920 from territory that had belonged to Prussia and Bavaria (Palatinate) with the capital Saarbrücken, and was administered for fifteen years by the League of Nations. A plebiscite was held on 13 February 1935 whereby the territory was returned to Germany. In 1945 it became part of the French Zone of Occupation of Germany, achieved autonomy in 1947 and, economically, became part of France. After a plebiscite in 1955 Saarland became politically a member of the Federal Republic of Germany (1 January 1957). Its area changed several times in 1946–9. Today its area is 2,567 sq.km.

Until 31 March 1920, German and Bavarian stamps were in use. From January 1920, German and Bavarian stamps used the overprint 'Sarre' and then German stamps only the overprint 'SAARGEBIET'. Some of these overprinted provisionals are considered speculative, as when an issue had only 16 complete sets and the stamps were allocated only to certain persons at the post office in Saarbrücken and St Ingert. Those were followed by definitives of French origin influenced by French stamp designing, with subjects publicizing the territory in pictorial form. The small printings (mostly 20,000–40,000) indicate some exploitation of the speculator's market. German stamps again became valid in 1935. A total of 205 + 32 stamps.

After the Second World War, issues of the French Occupation Zone in Germany (see *Germany: French Occupation Zone*) were valid in the Saar territory, and they were followed in 1947 by definitive issues with the name 'SAAR'. Until 1956 these stamps were of local and French origin, often influenced by French stamp design; at other times of conservative character, all mainly pictorial and designed as publicity for the territory. When the Saar returned to German control in 1957, German stamps took over with values given in French currency and the words 'DEUTSCHE BUNDES-POST SAARLAND' in the design. Several single stamps were issued in designs used for the equivalent issues in Germany. After 1959 stamps of the Federal Republic of Germany became valid. A total of 242 + 12 stamps. While all the stamps were postally valid, there was a deliberate endeavour (through low printings of 100,000–300,000) to encourage collector interest. In the case of the miniature sheet on the occasion of the 1947–8 floods, only 38,000 were printed. Special Saar issues under the German postal authorities had printings which ran into millions, fulfilling both publicity purposes and their postal functions. In 1959 Germany took complete control of the postal service, German stamps only being used.

SALONICA

Greek port, Turkish until 1912, then Greek, occupied by the British army 1916–18. Foreign post offices were in operation here.

In 1909–11 Italian stamps with the overprint 'SALONICCO' and surcharge in Turkish currency: a total of 8 overprinted provisionals. In 1909–10 Russian stamps were issued with the overprint 'Salonique' and a surcharge in Turkish currency to a total of 9 values. During the British occupation of 1916–18, British stamps overprinted 'Levant' were in use. These are rare and numerous forgeries are known. (See also *Levant*).

SAMOS

One of the islands in the Aegean Sea (**area** 472 sq.km, **capital** Vathy), Turkish until the Balkan Wars (princedom dependent on the Ottoman Empire), Greek occupation in 1912 with a local provisional government (until 1915).

The postal authorities of the princedom provided mail sevices only on the island with its forty villages; foreign mail services were set up only by the provisional government in 1912. Until that time such mail was handled by the Ottoman Empire, Austria and France (post offices at Vathy). Primitive issues from 1878, a definitive issue with the Greek name of the island 'SAMOS' (in Greek) after 1912. Samos issued its own stamps until 1913 and they were then replaced by overprinted provisionals from Greece. A number of these were dubious issues with a total of 20 stamps, some in very small printings for which detailed postal justification is lacking. (See also *Vathy*).

SAN MARINO

Area 61 sq.km, **population** 21,240 (1982), **capital** San Marino.

Republic on the eastern slopes of the Italian Appenines around Mount Titano. Tourism is the chief source of income. Customs and currency union with Italy, which represents San Marino in its international relations. This tiny republic is a remnant of the medieval feudal division of Italy. Indirect UPU membership from 1 July 1875 (Italy); direct since 1 July 1915.

Sardinian stamps (1862) and Italian stamps (until 1877) were used before San Marino issued its own. Definitive stamps from 1877 bearing the name 'REPUBBLICA DI SAN MARINO', or various abbreviations of this; at the present time, just 'SAN MARINO'. Annual output of about 25 stamps.

Stamps exhibit the characteristic influence of Italian designers and printers, in some cases even to the extent of using Italian stamp designs. The line-engraved issues of 1927 onwards (printed in London) show the influence of stamp production in Britain and America. Pictorial stamps were issued even as early as 1892 and they prevail in San Marino today. The mainly national publicity designs have now given way to general topics and participation in omnibus issues. The influence of the collector's market is shown by the stress on attractive pictorial stamps with sometimes small printings (often less than 10,000 sets), long sets (mostly 10 or more values), and a large number of airmail stamps (over 100). Typical of San Marino are parcel stamps of small size based on similar Italian issues.

Philatelic bureau Ufficio Filatelico di Stato, San Marino.

SARDINIA

The Duke of Savoy and Piedmont exchanged Sicily for Sardinia in 1720, and in this manner the Kingdom of Sardinia (**area** 64,094 sq.km, **capital** Turin) came into existence, ruled by the Savoy dynasty. Under Victor Emmanuel II this kingdom began the process that led to the unification of Italy. In 1859 it acquired Austrian Lombardy while ceding Nice and Savoy to France, annexing Parma, Modena, Tuscany, Romagna and the north of the Papal State, Naples and Sicily in 1860. In 1861 the entire territory was proclaimed the Kingdom of Italy (see *Italy*) and Victor Emmanuel II was proclaimed king.

From 1851 a total of 17 definitive stamps appeared, without the name of the issuing country, in portrait and numeral designs. They are highly coveted stamps among the top collectors. Produced in Turin, partly by embossing of the portraits. From 1862 Sardinian stamps were replaced by Italian issues.

Sardinia also had post offices abroad in Tunis, Monaco, Alexandria and Constantinople (during the Crimean War). Sardinian stamps were valid in Savoy and Nice until 1860, and they were used from 1859 to 1862 in all the countries that gradually became linked to Sardinia, and also in San Marino.

SASENO (SAZAN)

Albanian island in the Strait of Otranto guarding the entrance to the port of Valona, occupied by Italy in 1914–47 and turned into a naval base.

In 1923 provisional Italian stamps with the overprint 'Saseno' were issued.

SAXONY

From 1806 a kingdom (**area** 14,993 sq.km, **capital** Dresden). Saxony was an ally of Austria but also a member of the German and the North German Confederation and, from 1871, part of the German Empire.

Stamps were issued from 1850 inscribed 'SACHSEN', which makes Saxony one of the oldest stamp-issuing countries in the world: a total of 19 stamps with numerals and portraits (printed in Leipzig by letterpress and in Dresden by line engraving) all of which are regarded as classic stamps. Stamps of the first issue in particular — the famous Saxon 3 pf. in various shades of red — are nearly all regarded as valuable collectors' items. Saxony's stamps were also valid in Saxony-Altenburg. They were replaced by stamps of the *North German Postal District* in 1868.

SAXONY, PROVINCE OF

One of the parts of the Soviet Occupation Zone in Germany created in 1945 (**area** 24,669 sq.km, **capital** Halle).

A total of 26 stamps were issued in the years 1945–6; most of them were printed in Leipzig and bore the inscription 'PROVINZ SACHSEN'.

SCARPANTO (KARPATHOS)

One of the Italian Aegean Islands (**area** 304 sq.km, **capital** Pigadia), Italian 1912–47.

In 1912–32 Italian stamps overprinted with the word 'Scarpanto': a total of 26 overprinted provisionals. The issues were speculative in character with small printings ranging from 10,000 to 12,000. Their postal function remains dubious. (See also *Rhodes and the Dodecanese Islands*.)

SCHLESWIG

Duchy, Danish territory from 1035; from 1386 linked with Holstein, and from 1848 a member of the German Confederation. After the Danish war against Prussia and Austria it became a Prussian-Austrian condominium in 1864, and in 1865 was incorporated into Prussia under the Convention of Gastein, becoming a member of the North German Postal District in 1867. After the First World War, on the basis of the Versailles Peace Conference, a plebiscite was held in northern Schleswig in 1920; the territory was divided into two zones. Voting, which took place in the first zone on 10 February 1920, decided on joining Denmark (which occupied it on 19 May). The second zone decided (on 14 March) to remain part of Germany.

The first stamps began to appear during the Prussian-Austrian occupation in 1864. There were two definitive stamps with the inscription 'HERZOGTH.SCHLESWIG' and numerals of value (in Danish currency), which remained valid until 1865 when similar stamps also inscribed 'HERZOGTH.SCHLESWIG' were issued by the Prussian administration (with values in German currency) and remained valid until 1867. During the involved political conditions, stamps of *Schleswig-Holstein* were valid in the interim period. From 1868 stamps of the *North German Postal District* were used.

In 1920 German-currency definitives inscribed 'SLESVIG' and 'PLEBISCIT' appeared. These were of Danish origin. These stamps were overprinted 'C.I.S' for official use by the Commission Interalliée Slesvig seated in Flensburg, from 26 January to 16 June 1920. Printings were limited to only a few thousand (all that were required since only a hundred or so of each value were actually used). The definitive issue newly inscribed in Danish currency was given the overprint '1. ZONE'. A total of 42 stamps were issued between January and May 1920. After the plebiscite, Danish stamps were introduced in the first zone, and German stamps in the second zone.

SCHLESWIG-HOLSTEIN

United duchies (**area** 19,018 sq.km, **capital** Schleswig), divided by the river Eider, associated with Denmark from 1386 and integrated from 1468. In 1815 Holstein became a member of the German Confederation, followed by Schleswig in 1848. Disputes over this territory led to a war with Prussia and Austria allied against Denmark in 1848–50 and again in 1863–4, when Denmark had to renounce the territory. Schleswig-Holstein and the Duchy of Lauenburg came under the joint administration of Prussia and Austria. In 1865 under the Treaty of Gastein, Schleswig and Lauenburg were incorporated into Prussia, and Austria was given Holstein. During the Austro-Prussian War in 1866, Prussia occupied Holstein and the two duchies became members of the North German Postal District.

In 1850 two definitive stamps were introduced for the duchies, without names but inscribed 'S' and 'H'. These were valid until 1851 when they were replaced by Danish stamps until 1864. After issues for Schleswig and for Holstein in 1865 (5 numeral designs), stamps appeared with the wording 'SCHLESWIG-HOLSTEIN. That same year separate issues appeared for Schleswig and for Holstein. From 1866, after Prussia occupied Holstein, joint issues were again introduced which remained valid until the end of 1867. From 1868 stamps of the *North German Postal District* went into circulation. (See also *Holstein* and *Schleswig*.)

Schleswig-Holstein also operated a post office in *Bergedorf* and in *Hamburg*.

SCUTARI (SKADAR, SHKODËR)
Town in northern Albania on the shores of Lake Skadar.

From 1902 the Italian post office in Albania used Italian stamps overprinted 'ALBANIA' and surcharged in Turkish currency. From 1909 these were replaced by stamps for the individual post offices in the territory of Albania. Thus, 10 Italian stamps were given the overprint 'SCUTARI DI ALBANIA' (some in capital letters, others mixed capital and small letters). The last issue appeared in 1916 when Scutari was occupied by the Austro-Hungarian army, and the Italian post office was closed.

In 1914 and 1915 Albanian stamps were overprinted 'SHKODRE', but remained valid only for three days, when the post office was closed. It was opened again in January 1919 when one Albanian stamp came out with the overprint 'SHKODËR': a total of 7 + 3 stamps.

After the proclamation of the truce at the end of the First World War, foreign troops were in the country; Italian until August 1920; French until June 1920; Yugoslav until December 1921. The Allied Council was stationed in Scutari. In 1919 and 1920 overprinted provisionals appeared on Austrian fiscal issues bearing the words 'POSTA E Shkodres SHQYPNIS', 'SHKODRA' and 'SHKODËR', a total of 58 stamps.

SERBIA
Autonomous princedom under Turkish domination from 1817, independent from 1878, proclaimed a kingdom in 1882. In 1914 it was attacked by Austria-Hungary and the Serbian government took refuge on the island of Corfu, where in 1917 it issued a declaration on the establishment of the Kingdom of Serbs, Croats and Slovenes with Serbia as the dominant country. In 1929 the name of Yugoslavia was adopted. After occupation by the German army in the Second World War, a Serbian State (**area** 51,000 sq.km, **capital** Belgrade) was set up under German military government which treated the Serbs as defeated enemies. In 1945 Serbia became once again part of Yugoslavia.

From 1866 definitive stamps with wording in Cyrillic script, first bearing only the abbreviation, 'K. S. POŠTA', then 'K. SRBSKA POŠTA'; after spelling changes in the last century the inscription became 'SRPSKA POŠTA' or most often 'SRBIJA'. A total of 144 + 15 stamps, both of local and French origin, mainly portraits. When the Serbian government went into exile on the island of Corfu, it issued, at first, French stamps with the overprint 'POSTES SERBES' (1916), then definitives with wording in Cyrillic script reading 'KRAJEVINA SRBIJA' (at first printed in Paris, and after the war in Belgrade), which were then valid on the territory of Serbia where they were used until 1920. In 1921 they were replaced by the stamps of the *Kingdom of the Serbs, Croats and Slovenes*.

During the First World War a large part of Serbia was occupied by the Austro-Hungarian army. At that time stamps of Bosnia and Herzegovina with the overprint 'SERBIEN' were in use. In the period 1914–16 a total of 42 overprinted provisionals were isssued. From 1941, during the German occupation, Yugoslav stamps appeared with the overprint 'SERBIEN' (in Latin script), the definitive issue then had a bilingual text; later only 'SRBIJA' in Cyrillic script:

155

a total of 107 + 22 stamps. Apart from the overprinted provisionals, the definitives were of local origin, the designs being aimed at publicity for the country. The speculative nature of some issues is apparent from the low printing figures (these are as low as 20,000 for some stamps).

SICILY

Kingdom (25,426 sq.km) which merged with the Kingdom of Naples in the middle of the 19th century to form the Kingdom of the Two Sicilies, under the rule of the Bourbon dynasty. This, after numerous uprisings, was overthrown by Garibaldi in 1860. The country was then linked to the Kingdom of Sardinia and, from 1861, became part of Italy.

In 1859, 7 definitive portrait stamps (of King Francis II) were issued with the inscription 'BOLLO DELLA POSTA DI SICILIA'. All are coveted classic stamps. A strange cancellation consisting of a stamp-size rectangular ornament frame permitted postmarking the stamp without defacing the portrait of the monarch, who earned the nickname 'King Bomba'. These stamps were withdrawn in 1860 and replaced by those of Sardinia.

SIMI

One of the Italian Aegean Islands (**area** 58 sq.km,**capital** Simi), Italian 1912–47.

In 1912 to 1932 overprints appeared on Italian stamps with the name 'SIMI'; a total of 26 overprinted provisionals, generally considered speculative in view of the very small printings of 10,000 to 12,000. Their postal function was dubious. (See also *Rhodes and the Dodecanese Islands*).

SLOVAKIA

Slovakia lost its border areas in 1938 when they were occupied by the Polish and the Hungarian armies. On 14 March 1939 it proclaimed itself a separate country, and a republic on 21 July 1939. This put an end to the second Czechoslovak republic, which was Czecho-Slovakia at the time. Hungary occupied the Carpathian Ukraine on 15–18 March 1939, and in April of that year took over a further part of eastern Slovakia, while after the defeat of Poland in 1939 Slovakia gained part of the Spiš, Javorina and Orava regions. At that time its total area measured 37,620 sq.km, and Bratislava was the capital. The Slovak state ceased to exist in 1945 and Slovakia became once again part of Czechoslovakia.

By 21 March 1939 Czechoslovak stamps were given the overprint 'SLOVENSKÝ ŠTÁT', and unissued Czecho-Slovak stamps were given the same overprint and bore a portrait of A. Hlinka, the definitives then being inscribed 'SLOVENSKÁ POŠTA' and, finally, 'SLOVEN-SKO': a total of 161 stamps + 38. Most of the designs are nationalistic graphically or in portrait form, providing basic propaganda. In 1945 the issue of Czechoslovak stamps was resumed, even though their validity differed from that in the Czech *Länder*. Some Czechoslovak stamps were issued in Slovakia in 1945 and their validity was then extended to the other territories of Czechoslovakia while certain issues put out in the Czech *Länder* were not valid in Slovakia. Czechoslovak official stamps, valid until 1948, were issued in Slovakia only for Slovak authorities.

SLOVENIA

Part of Yugoslavia (**area** 20,251 sq.km, **capital** Ljubljana) and from 1918 a member country of the Kingdom of Serbs, Croats and Slovenes. After the occupation of Yugoslavia in 1941 the territory was divided between Germany, Italy and Hungary. The Italians established the province of Ljubljana, which was then occupied by the German army. Ljubljana issued its own stamps. From 1945 Slovenia again became part of Yugoslavia.

In 1945 stamps of Ljubljana province and further stamps of Germany were overprinted 'SLOVENIJA JUGOSLAVIJA': a total of 46 overprinted provisionals. The low printings of 7,600 for some values and 1,500 for others, permitting only 1,500 sets, suggests that speculation in these stamps was anticipated.

SOUTH BULGARIA

Formerly Eastern Rumelia, a Turkish province in southern Bulgaria (**area** 32,720 sq.km, **capital** Philippopolis, now Plovdiv), which was occupied and annexed by Bulgaria (14 July 1886) after the Bulgarian uprising in Plovdiv.

The stamps of *Eastern Rumelia* were replaced in 1885 by an issue for South Bulgaria. At first Eastern Rumelian stamps were overprinted with the Bulgarian crowned lion emblem, then with a Bulgarian inscription in Cyrillic characters meaning Bulgaria: a total of 16 stamps, all overprinted provisionals. In 1886 normal Bulgarian stamps were introduced.

SOVIET UNION

Area 22,402,200 sq.km, **population** 272.5m (1983), **capital** Moscow.

The most highly developed industrial and agricultural country in the socialist world, and now a federated republic. The USSR was established on 30 December 1922 by a union of the Russian S.F.S.R., the Ukrainian S.S.R., the Byelorussian S.S.R.and the Transcaucasian S.F.S.R. Its first constitution was passed in 1924. The number of republics gradually increased and has now reached 15. Direct UPU membership from 1 July 1875 as Russia and from 24 June 1924 as the USSR.

From 1923 the inscription 'POCHTA S.S.S.R.' appeared in Cyrillic script and then became generally used. The USSR holds the world record for the total number of different stamps issued, which amounts to over 5,000. Production rose rapidly after the Second World War, since when the annual output has been more than 100, sometimes as many as 150 stamps. The stamps are all of local origin printed by various processes but only occasionally in line-engraving. Most of the designs are based on Soviet propaganda themes, including home and foreign anniversaries and events, international co-operation, the development of the country, five-year plans, space research, and so on. There is a large group of designers, each with his own characteristic style but with an overall approach which is clearly national: for example, Kalashnikov, Levinovski, Martynov, Aniskin, Pimenov, Strelnikov, Axamit, Sokolov, Shevcov, Tifonov, the Lesegri group and others. The philatelic market is catered for by commemorative miniature sheets, *se-tenant* printings (joined pairs of stamps of differing value or design) and small sheets of definitives.

Philatelic bureau Mezhdunarodnaya Kniga, Moscow.

SPAIN

Area 504,782 sq.km, **population** 38.22m (1980), **capital** Madrid.

A monarchy with industry and agriculture. Divided into 50 provinces, among which the Canary Islands and North African settlements belong, geographically, to Africa. Nothing remains today of the once extensive colonial empire. When the first stamps were issued in 1850 Spain was a kingdom. In 1868 Queen Isabella II was overthrown which caused an uprising by of the supporters of Don Carlos in the northern and eastern provinces. The first Spanish Republic was established in 1873–4, but the Bourbon dynasty returned to the throne in December 1874. In the Spanish-American War of 1898 Spain lost Cuba, Puerto Rico, the Philippines, and Guam and in 1899 it sold the Caroline and Marianas Islands to Germany. In the years 1931 to 1939 a second republic existed, but in 1936 a military *putsch* was carried out by General Franco who, with the aid of Germany, Italy and Portugal took over power in the whole of Spain by 1939. The first province to succumb (in 1937) was Asturias. After a formal plebiscite in 1947 the monarchy was re-established in the country but did not assume power until after the death of Franco and the accession of King Juan Carlos to the throne in 1975. Direct UPU membership from 1 July 1875.

From 1850 definitive stamps. At that time Spain was a country with frequent issues of stamps, at first without the name of the country; then from 1862 with 'ESPAÑA', except for some issues on which the country's name was still missing. In 1931–8 the words used were mainly 'REPUBLICA ESPAÑOLA', while from 1936 the territory under the nationalist government issued stamps with 'ESPAÑA', which is used to this day. Stamp production is of highly varying standard, with printing by local and foreign firms using various printing methods. In present-day production photogravure predominates, but the State Printing House in Madrid also uses the recess-printing process. Designs tend to favour state propaganda and general subjects. The appeal to the collector's market is evident in attractive pictorial stamps, while in the past numerous miniature sheets were issued; there are unusual shapes with small issues of 1,100 to 2,660 stamps. Present printings run into several million and the annual output is 60-90 stamps.

Unique in world stamp issuing policy are the annual changes and issues of new sets, which began with the Spanish classic issue of 1850. This was intended to limit the possibility of forgeries being produced and used postally at the expense of the post office. Characteristic of older issues are continuous control numbers at the back of the stamps. A number of the older issues were greatly influenced by the designs of British and French stamps and those of Brunswick and other countries.

At the time of the Carlist post office, in the years 1873–6, the stamps were valid in Spanish territory, where there were also issues for Catalonia and Valencia, and in 1929 supplementary compulsory stamps of Barcelona were issued to pay the cost of holding the World Exhibition in Barcelona. In 1963–4 there was a special issue for Valencia, supplementary stamps for Asturias in 1937, and numerous local issues during the Civil War. The postal functions of some of these remain open to doubt.

Philatelic bureau Dirección General de Correos y Telecomunicaciones, Madrid.

STAMPALIA (ASTIPALAIA)
One of the Italian Aegean Islands (**area** 99 sq.km, **capital** Stampalia), Italian 1912–47.

In the years 1912–32 Italian stamps were overprinted with the word 'STAMPALIA': a total of 26 overprinted provisionals. The issues were speculative in character with small printings of 10,000 to 12,000 stamps. Their postal function remains dubious. (See also *Rhodes and the Dodecanese Islands*.)

SWEDEN
Area 449,964 sq.km, **population** 8.33m (1982), **capital** Stockholm.

Constitutional monarchy. Economically developed industrialized country with important ore mining. In 1815–1905 Norway was linked to Sweden, sharing the same monarch. Direct UPU membership from 1 July 1875.

From 1855 definitive stamps inscribed 'SVERIGE'. Swedish stamp production has many characteristic features. It has used stamps for publicizing the country, the printings running into the millions and thus readily available for postal purposes. The graphic designs of Hjortzberg were of a high standard and influenced Swedish stamp production mainly in the period between the two wars. Predominant features are a striking terseness and stylization, although more recently a number of normal pictorial stamps have appeared. Sweden is one of a few countries which continue the tradition of recess-printing by local printing firms or the Post Office itself. Since stamps are largely sold in rolls or booklets, a considerable part of the production is perforated only along two or three sides. An unusual feature is the military stamps without nominal value. The first issue of 1855 is a highly coveted one among collectors. Annual output about 40 stamps. Present production frequently uses photographic bases for the engraving by engravers Slania, Wallhorn, Franzen and Jakus.

Philatelic bureau PFA, The Swedish Post Office, Stamps and Philatelic Service, Stockholm.

SWITZERLAND
Area 41,288 sq.km, **population** 6.43m (1981), **capital** Bern.

Industrialized country with important livestock breeding and a large share of the tourist industry. This is the oldest republic in the world (since 1291), today comprising 26 cantons. Swiss history, in the later centuries, was dominated by the religious reform movement and religious wars. After the French Revolution, the Helvetian Republic came into existence in 1798. This historical tradition is the reason why the stamps bear the name of the country in Latin ('HELVETIA'), a convenient compromise in view of the fact that the country has four official languages: German, French, Italian and Romansch. UPU membership from 1 July 1875.

On the territory of the Swiss Confederation, stamp issuing was first in the hands of individual cantons: *Zurich, Geneva, Basle*. The Swiss postal authorities were established on 1 January 1849, but the definitives (1850) did not bear the name of the country. From 1862 the name was expressed as 'HELVETIA' and this is still the practice. In some Pro Patria issues the words 'CONFOEDERATIO HELVETICA' are used.

Swiss stamps are strongly nationalistic in design but are very popular with collectors because of their excellent graphic qualities and very high printing standards. Apart from heraldic and portrait stamps the majority are pictorials. There is an individualistic stylization of landscape motifs on many stamps and a striking simplicity on other issues, both types demonstrating a high standard of graphic design. All printing is either by the Swiss firm of Courvoisier (in photogravure) or by the recess-printing works of the Swiss post office in Bern. Design innovation allied to precision printing ensures a ready market for all new issues of Swiss stamps. A considerable number of miniature sheets of modest face value are popular, as are annual issues such as Pro Patria and Pro Juventute and the occasional issues for special air flights with short-term validity. Issues run into large quantities: in the case of miniature sheets from 200,000 to 400,000 each, otherwise mostly ranging from one to 30 million, so that they fulfil the dual purpose of postal requirements and state publicity. Most of the texts are in Latin (e.g. Pro Patria, Pro Aero, Pro Juventute) to avoid having to repeat them in several languages. Annual output about 30 stamps.

Switzerland is the seat of many international institutions which issue their own stamps.

Philatelic bureau Swiss PTT, Postage Stamp Division, Philatelic Office, Bern.

THURINGIA

One of the *Länder* in the Soviet Occupation Zone of Germany (**area** 15,598 sq.km, **capital** Erfurt) established in 1945.

Between 1945 and 31 October 1946 a total of 24 definitive stamps were issued bearing the name 'THÜRINGEN', among them 4 miniature sheets of 4 stamps each limited to printings of about 30,000 designed for the philatelic market rather than public use. The stamp designs publicized the country in the typical German manner.

TRANS-CARPATHIAN UKRAINE

The most easterly part of Czechoslovakia (see *Carpathian Ukraine*), where after liberation at the end of the Second World War in October 1944 a Czechoslovak Government delegation arrived at the basis of an agreement with the USSR on 8 July 1944 and took up its seat at Khust. But at the Conference of National Committees at Mukachevo on 26 November 1944 a manifesto was adopted proposing the unification of Trans-Carpathian Ukraine with the Ukraine, and on 29 June 1945 an agreement was signed in Moscow under which this territory (**area** 12,617 sq.km, **capital** Uzhgorod) became part of the USSR. In 1946 the Trans-Carpathian Region was established within the framework of the Ukrainian S.S.R.

In 1944 overprints appeared on Hungarian stamps, which bear the wording, 'Zakarpatskaya Ukraina' and 'Pochta Zakarpatskaya Ukraina' in Cyrillic script. Then definitives appeared with the same wording; first, primitive prints of local origin, showing symbols of liberation. A total of 101 stamps, whose true postal function is not fully confirmed in all cases. Issues ceased in 1945 when Soviet stamps were introduced (see also *Soviet Union*).

TRENTINO

Territory of southern Tyrol, lying to the south of the Brenner Pass. (**Area** 8,961 sq.km, **capital** Trento.) In 1918 the territory was occupied by the Italian army and Italy acquired it from Austria under the Treaty of St Germain in 1919. The territory was subsequently called Trentino-Alto Adige.

In 1918 Austrian stamps were issued with the overprint 'Regno d'Italia Trentino': a total of 19 stamps. In 1918–19 a total of 12 Italian stamps with the overprint 'Venezia Tridentina' were issued.

TRIESTE

After the occupation by the Yugoslav and the Anglo-American armies in May 1945, Trieste became a Free Territory under international supervision in the years 1947–54 (**area** 738 sq.km, **capital** Trieste). A Zone A was established (town and port, 223 sq.km), which was occupied by the British and American forces and was handed over to Italy on 5 October 1954; and Zone B (515 sq.km), occupied by the Yugoslav army. This and a narrow strip of Zone A became part of Yugoslavia (largest town, Koper-Capodistria).

Zone A used Italian stamps with the overprint 'AMG VG' (Allied Military Government Venezia Giulia) from 1945 to 1947 (see *Venezia Giulia.*) From 1947 to 1954 Italian stamps with the overprint 'AMG FTT' (Allied Military Government Free Territory Trieste) were in use: a total of 240 + 59 stamps, all overprinted provisionals. Printings averaged 200,000 for the lower values and fewer for higher denominations. Since 1954 normal Italian stamps have been in use.

Zone B used stamps of Istria and Slovene Coast from 1945 to 1947. A Trieste issue of Italian stamps with the overprint 'TRIESTE/TRST' dates from 1945. From 1948 Zone B issued its own definitives. The first issue was in three languages (each of the three stamps had one text). In Slovenian the text read 'VOJNA UPRAVA J. A. SVOBODNO TRZASKO OZEMIJE'; in Italian, 'AMMINISTRAZIONE MILITARE A. J. TERRITORIO LIBERO DI TRIESTE'; in Croat, 'VOJNA UPRAVA J. A. SLOBODNI TERITORIJ TRSTA', frequently abbreviated to 'STT VUJA' or, from 1952, to 'STT VUJNA' (Slobodni Teritorij Trsta Vojna Uprava /Narodne/ Jugoslavenske Armije). Definitive and commemorative issues were numerous; 139 + 28 stamps of Yugoslav origin. Some of the first issues are artistically interesting, from 1952 almost exclusively overprints on Yugoslav stamps. Most of them appeared in low printings of 15,000 to 30,000, suggesting speculation in the collector's market. All Trieste Zone B issues were replaced by Yugoslav stamps from 1954.

TUSCANY

Italian coastal duchy on the Ligurian Sea and the Tyrrhenian Sea with the island of Elba and other smaller islands (**area** 24,104 sq.km, **capital** Florence), incorporated into the Kingdom of Sardinia in 1860 and became part of Italy in 1861.

From 1851 definitive stamps with the wording 'FRANCOBOLLO POSTALE TOSCANA': a total of 23 stamps of local origin in heraldic designs, which collectors regard as valuable classic stamps. In 1860 they were replaced by stamps of *Sardinia.*

UKRAINE

After the October Revolution the Ukraine was declared a Soviet Republic (on 25 December 1917), but the Central National Council in Kiev proclaimed it independent as the Ukraine People's Republic. In 1918, the country was occupied by German and Austrian soldiers, in 1919 it was partly liberated by the Red Army which was fighting the Denikin, Polish and Wrangel Armies (1919–20). On 30 December 1922, the Soviet Ukraine joined the USSR. In the Second World War (1941–4), the country was occupied by the Germans, who set up a Reichskommissariat Ukraine (which did not include Transnistria, which was under Rumanian administration).

From 1918 first came Russian stamps with the local overprint of a trident which varied in size and style for each main town. Later in the same year, definitives with a Ukrainian text reading 'Ukrainian People's Republic' were issued. Since in 1919 the larger part of the country was liberated by the Red Army further definitive stamps were prepared in Vienna but were never issued for postal use and were sold to stamp dealers. After these complicated military and postal conditions settled down, definitive issues appeared in 1923 inscribed 'USSR Post' (in Cyrillic script) and in 1924 Russian stamps with the overprint 'USSR' (in Cyrillic script). They were replaced by Soviet stamps from 1924.

During the Second World War, at the time of the German occupation from 1941 to 1943, a total of 20 German stamps were issued with the overprint 'UKRAINE'.

UPPER SILESIA

Coal-mining region (10,949 sq.km) with the towns of Opole, Bytom, Gliwice, Katowice. In 1919–21 this was a plebiscite territory between Germany and Poland. The plebiscite (21 March 1921) was favourable to the Germans, which led to unrest in the Polish-dominated areas. This forced the Conference of Ambassadors to the decision that the south-eastern part of the territory (3,146 sq.km) should belong to Poland, and the rest to Germany.

From 1920 definitive stamps printed in Paris with wording in three languages, 'COMMISSION DE GOUVERNEMENT HAUTE SILÉSIE/GÓRNY ŚLASK/OBER SCHLESIEN'. German stamps with the overprint 'CIHS' or 'CGHS' were also issued for official use on Inter-Allied Commission correspondence: a total of 63 stamps, mostly overprinted provisionals, definitives being either numerals or pictorials (of Silesian coalmines) produced in Paris. After the departure (23 June 1922) of the International Commission which was responsible for holding the plebiscite, German stamps came into use in the territory that was attached to Germany. In the south-eastern parts Polish stamps were introduced, with the face value expressed in Deutsche marks, which were in circulation there. Their validity ended on 30 April 1923 and they were followed by the normal Polish stamps (see *Poland*).

VALONA

Albanian port on the Strait of Otranto, Turkish until 1912.

During the Turkish rule, an Italian post office was set up which used its own stamps from 1902, first with the overprint for the whole of Albania; after 1909, for the individual post offices in individual towns.

In 1909–16 'VALONA' or 'Valona' was overprinted on 10 Italian stamps which were also surcharged in Turkish currency. (See also *Albania, Koritza, Northern Epirus.*)

VATHY

Capital of the island of Samos in the Aegean Sea, which was Turkish until 1912, and which from that time has belonged to Greece.

For the use of the French post office, French stamps with the overprint 'Vathy' were introduced in 1893: a total of 9 overprinted provisionals, which were valid until 1900. From 1901 they were replaced by French stamps until 1914 when the post office was discontinued. (See also *Levant.*)

VATICAN CITY

Area 0.44 sq.km, **population** approx. 1,000.

Modern ecclesiastical state in Rome, set up on the basis of the Lateran Agreement between the Holy See and Italy in 1929 and called the Vatican. Indirect UPU membership from 1 July 1875 (Italy); direct from 1 June 1929.

From 1929 all stamps have been inscribed in Italian, 'POSTE VATICANE'. Stamp designing and printing reflects its Italian origin, both for recess printing and other methods in the Italian State Printing House. Recently, some Vatican stamps have also been printed in the Austrian State Printing House. Frequent designers include Grassellini and Dabrowska. Themes relate mainly to the Vatican, with numerous portraits of the Pope and of saints. Annual output is at present about 30 stamps, which are in popular demand among collectors, especially in Catholic countries. Current printing orders for each issue are 300,000 to 500,000 stamps.

Philatelic bureau Ufficio Filatelico del Governatorato, Stato della Citta del Vaticano.

VEGLIA (KRK)

Yugoslav island (Veglia is the Italian name) in Kvarner Bay, which was temporarily occupied by Italian d'Annunzio volunteers (13 November 1920 to 5 January 1921). The island remained Yugoslav (see also *Arbe, Fiume, Kvarner*).

In 1920 on Fiume issues overprints reading 'VEGLIA'. A total of 8 overprinted provisionals.

VENEZIA GIULIA
Territory of Istria and Trieste and the coastal regions of Slovenia (**area** 9,312 sq.km, **capital** city Trieste). Trieste was occupied by Italy in 1918 and annexed under the Treaty of Rapallo in 1920 after being part of the Austro-Hungarian monarchy. In 1945 this territory was occupied by the Allied armies, and Trieste by the Yugoslav army. From 1947 to 1954 Trieste and surroundings constituted a Free Territory.

In 1918 Austrian stamps with the overprint 'Regno d'Italia Venezia Giulia' and the date '3.xi.18', were followed by Italian stamps with the overprint 'Venezia Giulia': a total of 39 stamps, all overprinted provisionals, which were valid until 1919.

After the Second World War, in the years 1945–7, Italian stamps with the overprint 'AMG V G' (Allied Military Government Venezia Giulia). A total of 31 stamps, all overprinted provisionals. Replaced by *Trieste* stamps in 1947.

VILNIUS (VILNA)
Capital of Lithuania, for whose southern territories stamps were issued during the German occupation in the Second World War (see also *Lithuania*).

In 1941 Soviet stamps were given the overprint 'VILNIUS' in Latin script: a total of 9 overprinted provisionals. Later in 1941 they were replaced by *Ostland* issues.

WEST BERLIN
Area 480 sq.km, **population** 1.88m (1982).

Territory of the three western sectors (American, British and French), which separated from the Soviet sector (which covered 54 per cent of the area of Greater Berlin) in 1948. Although the area has a special status since, formally, the occupation administration of Berlin by the Four Powers continues, the Federal Republic of Germany in 1951 proclaimed West Berlin one of the *Länder* of its federation, even if of special standing.

Stamp issues of the territory of West Berlin began on 1 September 1948, when the existing German stamps, which had been in common use by the American, British and Soviet zones, were given the overprint 'BERLIN'. (Note: Forgeries of these overprints exist.) Then followed a definitive issue without that name, only 'Deutsche Post', and from 1952 it became 'DEUTSCHE POST BERLIN', and from 1955 'DEUTSCHE BUNDESPOST BERLIN'.

Since 1950 West Berlin stamps have been valid in the territory of the Federal Republic, but are sold only at the philatelic counter in Frankfurt. The stamps are issued by the West Berlin Senate, not the postal authorities of the Federal Republic of Germany. Most of the stamp designs are based on that of the German stamps of the preceding period. Apart from the special designs approved by the West Berlin Senate since 1959, the designs are close to the artistic conception of the Federal Republic, and there are even common designs to which the word 'BERLIN' has been added. The stamps are printed in the State Printing House in West Berlin, where the stamps and bank notes of the German Federal Republic are also printed. In some cases recess-printing is used. When the designs differ from those of the G.F.R. they depict all aspects of local life in West Berlin. Printings are increasing in numbers adequately fulfilling the purposes of publicity and postal use. The first issues in 1949 had limited printings (less than one million in some cases). In a few cases there were only 150,000 while the present-day printings amount to 7–10 million stamps. Annual output 15–20 stamps.

Philatelic bureau Versandstelle für Sammlermarken, Berlin 12.

WESTERN HUNGARY
According to the Trianon Agreement a plebiscite in 1921 was to decide on the adherence of Western Hungary (Burgenland) to Hungary or Austria. Hungarian rebels prevented the holding of the plebiscite and occupied the whole territory. In the end, Sopron and its environs remained in Hungary.

In 1921 Hungarian stamps with various overprints such as 'NYUGAT-MAGYARORSZÁG', 'LAJTABÁNSÁG', 'WESTUNGARN ORGLAND', appeared followed by definitive issues:

a total of 85 stamps. Equally doubtful is a 1956 issue when, during the events in Hungary in October, Hungarian stamps were given the overprint 'SOPRON'. The authority for issuing the stamps is unclear and their postal validity has not been proved.

WESTERN THRACE

Greek territory on the Turkish border (**area** 8,343 sq.km, **capital** Gümülsina, or Komotiné). As Turkish territory it was occupied by Bulgarian troops on 20 August 1913 after the Peace of Bucharest. The local Muslim population, however, expelled the invaders and proclaimed independence on 10 October 1913. At the end of that month, the Bulgarians occupied the territory anew and annexed it. After the defeat of Bulgaria in September 1918, Western Thrace was occupied by French and British-Indian units. Under the Peace of Neuilly in 1919 the territory of Gümülsina and Xanthé was ceded to Greece, whose army occupied the area in 1920.

In 1913, stamps of the Ottoman Empire, and then Bulgarian and Greek stamps, were overprinted in Arabic script. In 1919–20 Bulgarian stamps appeared with the overprint 'THRACE INTERALLIÉE' or 'THRACE OCCIDENTALE' and, finally, in the period of Greek occupation Greek stamps were issued with overprints in Greek script meaning 'Administration of Western Thrace'. A total of 115 + 7 stamps were issued. On 10 August 1920, Greek stamps became valid when the Treaty of Sèvres incorporated Western Thrace into Greece.

WESTERN UKRAINE

After the disintegration of the Austro-Hungarian Empire a Western Ukrainian People's Republic was established on 19 October 1918, and its administration was taken over by the Ukrainian National Council on 1 November 1918, with Lvov as capital. The Republic covered the eastern and central parts of former Galicia as far as the San, Dukla and Bucovina. However, by the end of November, Rumania had occupied the whole of Bucovina so that the Western Ukraine was limited to the Galician territory. On 22 June 1919 the Western Ukraine merged with the Ukraine, but in July 1919 it was occupied by Poland. The Conference of Paris in 1921 added Eastern Galicia to this with right of control for 15 years.

In 1919 Austrian stamps appeared with an abbreviated overprint in Cyrillic script meaning Western Ukrainian People's Republic. Most issues had virtually no postal use and were largely sold to collectors. Very small printings, in some values a mere 60 to 100 stamps and in one case an alleged printing of 2 stamps. It is, therefore, difficult to regard the 70 different stamps as being authorized even though they are listed in most general catalogues. In the part occupied by Romania, in Bucovina, Austrian stamps were given the overprint 'CMT' (= Comandamentul Militar Teritorial): a total of 38 overprinted provisionals, whose postal function is as doubtful as the preceding issue.

WÜRTTEMBERG

Kingdom from 1806 (**area** 19,507 sq.km, **capital** Stuttgart); from 1815 member of the German Confederation and from 1871 the German Empire. Status of a republic from 1919. After the Second World War, Württemberg was divided into Württemberg-Baden (American Occupation Zone) and Württemberg-Hohenzollern (French Zone). In 1952 these two parts formed Baden-Württemberg as one of the *Länder* of the Federal Republic of Germany.

From 1851 definitive issues with the name, 'WÜRTTEMBERG' or 'K. WURTT. POST'. Most issues have numeral designs, a total of 62 + 181 stamps. In 1902 Württemberg ceased to issue its own postage stamps and used German stamps, but the official stamps continued to be issued and used by Württemberg, which explains the abnormally large output of these issues.

After issues for the French Occupation Zone of Germany definitive stamps appeared in 1947 inscribed, 'WÜRTTEMBERG': until 1949 a total of 52 stamps of local origin but influenced by French stamp designs. German stamps took their place in 1949. (See *Germany* and *Germany, French Occupation Zone.*)

YUGOSLAVIA

Area 255,804 sq.km, **population** 22.85m (1983), **capital** Belgrade.

Industrial and agricultural country, developed tourist trade, socialist federal republic.

Yugoslavia came into existence after the collapse of the Austro-Hungarian Empire in 1918, and was formed by the union of Bosnia-Herzegovina with Croatia, Slovenia, Dalmatia, Vojvodina and Slavonia. After the unification with the Kingdom of Serbia and Montenegro, a Kingdom of the Serbs, Croats and Slovenes was formed, and formally proclaimed in December 1918. From 1929 this was known as the Kingdom of Yugoslavia. In 1941 the country was attacked by the Germans and Italians and split up into Serbia, Croatia and Montenegro, while the rest of the country was annexed by Italy, Germany, Hungary, Albania and Bulgaria. In 1944–5 the whole country was liberated, and on 29 November 1945 the monarchy was abolished and a federal people's republic proclaimed (from 7 April 1963, federal socialist republic). Indirect UPU membership from 1 July 1875 (Montenegro and Serbia); direct from 24 December 1921 (Kingdom of the Serbs, Croats and Slovenes; name changed to Yugoslavia in 1929).

The former *Kingdom of the Serbs, Croats and Slovenes* was officially re-named the Kingdom of Yugoslavia on 6 January 1929, and the first stamps appeared with the new name in 1931. They were definitives with the inscription 'KRALJEVINA JUGOSLAVIJA', given in Latin and Cyrillic script; later only 'JUGOSLAVIJA'. After the Second World War 'DEMOKRATSKA FEDERATIVNA JUGOSLAVIJA' was given in Latin and Cyrillic script, with the postal abbreviation PTT JUGOSLAVIJA. Production is of varying quality, caused by poorly used printing methods. Themes on state policy have, in present-day production, been replaced by general subjects with a wide collector appeal. Printings are rather limited, some of the higher values in sets being 60,000. Apart from conventional designs, present production includes exacting graphic art (stylized landscapes and symbols), the work of Kršic, Gorbunov, Jakač and others. Every year Yugoslavia issues stamps with a charity premium above the postal value of the stamps. The annual output at present is around 40–50 stamps. The joint Yugoslav-Rumanian issue of 1965 in celebration of the technical engineering feat of the Iron Gate on the Danube (Djerdap Hydro-Electric Project) had face values in Yugoslav and Rumanian currency and was valid in both countries.

Philatelic bureau Bureau for Postage Stamps, Belgrade.

ZARA

Italian territory on the Dalmatian coast of Yugoslavia (**area** 3,719 sq.km, **capital** Zara), ceded to Italy after the disintegration of the Austro-Hungarian Empire in 1920 as a free city under its sovereignty (Treaty of Rapallo). After the capitulation of Italy in 1943 the German army occupied the territory until 1945. In 1947 it was ceded to Yugoslavia by treaty.

During the German occupation in 1943, Italian stamps were given the overprint 'Deutsche Besetzung Zara': a total of 49 overprinted provisionals, whose true postal function has not been clarified. Several appeared in very small printings, allowing for only 47 complete sets to the top values. This suggests speculation in the collector's market.

ZÜRICH

Swiss canton (1,729 sq.km) with capital of the same name, which issued its own stamps because, until 1 January 1849, the postal arrangements in Switzerland were in the hands of the cantons. After Great Britain, the second oldest stamp-issuing territory.

In 1843 definitive stamps with the wording 'ZÜRICH': a total of 2 stamps with bold numeral designs, locally produced, which remained valid until 30 September 1854, although by 1850 stamps of the Swiss federal postal authorities came into use. The Zürich stamps are among the valuable classic issues.

ASIA

ABU DHABI

The largest of the countries of the former Trucial States in the south-eastern part of the Arabian peninsula (73,450 sq.km). Oil drilling. Since 1971 part of the United Arab Emirates.

Stamp issuing under the name of 'ABU DHABI' by the postal authorities of Great Britain began in 1964. When the treaty with Great Britain expired on 31 December 1966 the sheikhdom of Abu Dhabi took over the postal service and with it stamp issuing. This situation remained until the establishment of the *United Arab Emirates* in 1972. A total of 95 stamps appeared, mostly pictorials. Abu Dhabi was the only one of the sheikhdoms of the peninsula which kept its stamp issuing on a restrained level and devoted it mainly to national propaganda subjects, often depicting the ruler and emphasizing the economic importance of oil.

ADEN

British territory in the south of the Arabian peninsula, from 1839 part of British India, from 1937 Crown Colony (**area** 207 sq.km, **capital** Aden). In 1963 it became part of the South Arabian Federation. It is now in the Yemen People's Democratic Republic. Not to be confused with the Aden Protectorate (South Arabian Protectorate) with Kathiri and Qu'aiti State in Hadramaut, Mahra and Upper Yaf'á.

Before the country issued its own stamps, Indian stamps were in use. From 1937 definitive issues with the name ADEN. Until 1964, 85 stamps of British origin, mostly normal definitive postage stamps in pictorial designs relating to the country of issue and in a style common to the British stamp-issuing regions. Stamps did not appear every year. Issuing ceased in 1964 although politically Aden joined the *South Arabian Federation* in 1963, and its stamps were valid here.

AFGHANISTAN

Area 652,225 sq. km, **population**, 16.35m (1982), **capital** Kabul.

Agricultural country with important sheep-rearing, especially the karakul breed. It became a unified country in 1747, and fully independent in 1919 (Kingdom of Afghanistan). UPU membership from 1 April 1928.

Although stamp issuing began in 1871, Afghanistan joined the UPU only in 1928, the previous stamps being only valid as locals to be used inside the country. Mail going abroad needed Indian stamps until 1928. Since these early issues were only of local validity, they had no Latin text until 1927 when 'AFGHAN POSTAGE' appeared for the first time, followed by 'POSTES AFGHANES' and, for a time 'AFGHANISTAN'. After the proclamation of the Republic in 1973 and the Afghan Democratic Republic in 1978 most of the stamps bore the French 'POSTES AFGHANES' in Latin script; some had the English 'AFGHANI POST'.

Afghani stamp designs first had variations of letters (in Arabic script) and symbols; pictorial stamps began to appear in the 1930s. Restrained issuing, 1–2 issues a year, which in the 1960s changed to up to 140 stamps a year produced basically for the collector's market (perforated and imperforate stamps and miniature sheets in very small quantities, some only 2,000 to 3,000). The stamp designs were mainly conventional, and indifferently printed, often being just photographic reproductions. This was largely due to several agencies which, in the years 1961–4, issued up to 500 different stamps which most world stamp catalogues did not even list in detail, and whose postal validity is highly dubious. When the agency contracts expired the Afghani postal authorities resumed a restrained issuing policy, and stamps were again sold at all post offices. Mainly propaganda themes, some of which repeat year by year, as the Anniversary of Independence in 1928, Pakhtunistan Day 1951. Current annual output ranges from 5 to 20 stamps.

Philatelic bureau Ministry of Communications, Postal Department, Philatelic Section, Kabul.

AJMAN

The smallest of the countries of the former Trucial States in the south-eastern part of the

Arabian peninsula (250 sq.km) with two dependencies, of which *Manama* has its own stamps. Since 1971 part of the United Arab Emirates.

Very lively issuing of definitive stamps with the name AJMAN began in 1964, and continued until 1972, when the country ceased its own stamp-issuing activity after the establishment of the *United Arab Emirates*. Insofar as it was possible to keep an accurate record, it appears that over 1,150 Ajman stamps appeared, more than half of them air stamps. The stamps were typical commodities for the collector's market, usually without any postal function. In 1971 alone, 448 stamps were issued, something which no other postal authority anywhere in the world has achieved. At one stage these issues were distributed by two competing agencies at the same time, one using the name of 'Ajman' on its stamps and the other 'AJMAN/AND ITS DEPENDENCIES'.

ALAOUITES

French territory on the coast of Syria (**area** 5,905 sq.km, **capital** Latakia) originally Turkish, part of the French Mandate of Syria from 1920. Became a republic independent of Syria in 1922 and an autonomous part of Syria again in 1926, and was fully incorporated in 1942. Renamed *Latakia* in 1930.

In 1925 French stamps with the overprint 'ALAOUITES' in Arabic and Latin script, then stamps of Syria overprinted similarly. A total of 63 + 10 stamps, all overprinted provisionals, appeared until 1930, when stamps of Latakia succeeded the Alaouites issues.

ALEXANDRETTA

Part of the French Mandate of Syria (**area** 260 sq.km, **capital** Alexandretta), originally a Turkish sanjak, a semi-autonomous part of Syria from 1920, with Turkish as the official language, with a greater degree of autonomy from 1925. In 1938 it was proclaimed as the Republic of Hatay, which was incorporated into Turkey as Hatay Province, with French agreement, on 30 June 1939, when France gained certain concessions.

From 1919 to 1938 Syrian stamps were valid here; from 1938 Syrian stamps with the overprint 'SANDJAK D'ALEXANDRETTE' were in use: a total of 25 + 6 stamps, all overprinted provisionals. The Turkish Administration, from 1939, used the name *Hatay* for the territory and used Turkish stamps suitably overprinted.

ALWAR

Feudatory state (**area** 8,143 sq.km, **capital** Alwar) in north-western India, under British influence since 1803.

From 1877 to 1901 a total of 4 definitive stamps of local origin. These were followed by stamps of India from 1902.

AMUR PROVINCE

The territory was a gubernia from 1882 (**area** 449,500 sq.km, **capital** Blagovestchensk) and part of the Far Eastern Republic from 1920. During a temporary shortage of stamps in 1921 it used 5 definitives of local origin bearing the words 'AMURSKAYA OBLASTNAYA PO-SHTOVAYA MARKA', in Cyrillic script, meaning 'Amur Province Postage Stamps'. They remained in use until new supplies of the stamps of the *Far Eastern Republic* were sent from Chita.

ANNAM AND TONKIN

The French protectorate of Annam (147,600 sq.km) and the colony of Tonkin (115,700 sq.km) were occupied in the years 1882–4, and were incorporated into the neighbouring regions of French Indochina.

In 1888 the general French colonial stamps were issued with the overprint 'A & T' (Annam & Tonkin), a total of 6 overprinted provisionals. The stamps of *French Indochina* were used from 1892.

ARMENIA

After the secession of the Caucasian territory from Russia an Armenian Republic came into being with Yerevan as capital. It was occupied first by Turkish, and then British, troops. After a new Turkish invasion in August 1920 the Red Army set up a Soviet Republic on 29 November 1920 in the eastern part of the country, while the western part remained Turkish and the south-east came under the control of Iran. In 1922, Armenia joined Azerbaijan and Georgia to form the Transcaucasian Soviet Socialist Republic.

From 1919 Russian stamps with overprints and surcharges were in use, then from 1922 definitive stamps of the Soviet Republic of Armenia, with the name only in Armenian script; a total of 193 stamps, mostly overprinted provisionals. The definitives were crudely printed, the pictorial designs and symbolic treatment relating to the country. In the case of the definitives the true postal status has not been clarified. Issuing continued until 1923, when the stamps of Transcaucasia were introduced, followed, from 1924, by stamps of the Soviet Union.

AZERBAIJAN

After the secession of the Caucasian countries from Russia on 27 May 1918, the Azerbaijan Republic was established, which was then occupied by Turkish, and later British, troops. After a people's rising, the country was proclaimed a Soviet Socialist Republic in 1920 (**area** originally 141,000 sq.km, **capital** Baku). In 1922 Azerbaijan joined Georgia and Armenia to form the Transcaucasian Soviet Socialist Republic, and with them became part of the Soviet Union that year. It has been a separate republic within the Soviet Union since 1936.

In 1919 definitive republic issues appeared with the inscription 'RÉPUBLIQUE D'AZERBAIDJAN'. Subsequent issues of the Soviet Republic have the text in Cyrillic and Arabic script instead of Latin, as the former two were used by the Azerbaijan population at the time. A total of 59 stamps appeared. The definitive issues have pictures and symbols of life in the country. The rapid inflation of 1922–3 brought about the many surcharged provisionals. From 1923, stamps of the *Transcaucasian Federation* became valid and then were replaced from 1924 by stamps of the Soviet Union.

BAGHDAD

Iraqi province with the capital city of the same name, part of the Ottoman Empire until 1917, and then occupied by British and Indian troops from Basra (1917–20). In 1921 the town became the capital of the British Mandate of Iraq.

In 1917 a total of 25 Turkish stamps appeared with the overprint 'BAGHDAD IN BRITISH OCCUPATION'. •

BAHAWALPUR

Feudatory state in India (**area** 45,480 sq.km, **capital** Bahawalpur) in south-western Punjab (now in Pakistan), under British influence from 1838.

In 1947 Indian stamps appeared with a star and crescent overprint for use within Bahawalpur only. The state ceded to Pakistan on 3 October 1947. In 1948 definitive issues with 'BAHAWALPUR': a total of 46 + 28 stamps. All the definitives were printed by the exacting line-engraving process in London, England. Since 1949 only the stamps of Pakistan have been in use.

BAHRAIN

Area 661 sq.km, **population** 350,798 (1981), **capital** Manama.

Arabian island sheikhdom in the Persian Gulf, a British protectorate from 1861, now with an important international airport and oil industry. An independent emirate since 14 August 1971. Indirect UPU membership from 1884 (British India); indirect from 1 April 1948 (through British post office); indirect from 1 January 1966 (autonomous postal authorities represented by Great Britain); direct from 21 December 1973.

Before the country issued its own stamps Indian stamps were in use. From 1933 Indian stamps with the overprint 'BAHRAIN'; from 1948 stamps of Great Britain with the same overprint; from 1960 definitives of its own, with the same inscription, produced in Great Britain. An issue of definitive stamps with the portrait of the ruler of Bahrain were issued from

167

1953 to 1966 for internal use only. The British post office was closed down in 1965. From then on the Bahrain postal authorities took over stamp issuing, and maintained a restrained programme. In recent years 1 to 4 issues have appeared each year, mainly with national subjects or general international themes.

Philatelic bureau The Philatelic Bureau, Director of Posts, Manama.

BAKU

Capital of *Azerbaijan* where, in 1922, 10 overprinted provisionals appeared on Azerbaijan stamps with the inscription (in Cyrillic), 'BAKINSKOY OK', 'BAKINSKAGO GPTO' or BAKU.

BAMRA

Feudatory state (**area** 5,149 sq.km, **capital** Bamra) in eastern India.
Primitive stamps were issued in 1888 and 1889 typographed from hand-drawn text: a total of 13 stamps bearing the inscription 'BAMRA'. In 1894 stamp issuing ceased and the post office was taken over by India in 1895.

BANGKOK

Capital of Siam (today Thailand), called Krung Thep in the Thai language.
In 1882 stamps of the Straits Settlements with the overprint 'B' (Bangkok) for use at the British post office in Siam. From 1882–5 22 overprinted provisionals were issued for use abroad. From July 1885 Siamese stamps came into use on closure of the British post office.

BANGLADESH

Area 143,998 sq.km, **population** 92.62 m (1982), **capital** Dhaka.
Largely an agricultural country. Republic, since 1972 member of the Commonwealth. Until 26 March 1971 part of Pakistan (Eastern Pakistan). Indirect UPU membership from 1 July 1876 (British India); indirect from 10 November 1947 (Pakistan); direct from 7 February 1973.
Before liberation, during 1971, stamps with the inscription 'BANGLA DESH' were issued by a London agency, but in view of the real situation these must have been of political and propaganda character rather than for postal use. After the civil war and the proclamation of independence several values of this issue were overprinted 'BANGLADESH LIBERATED' and were officially issued for public use. Stamp issuing is limited, usually to 3 short sets per annum. The stamp designs have themes mainly of national interest with, in addition, participation in some of the omnibus issues of international interest.

Philatelic bureau General Post Office, Dhaka.

BARWANI

Feudatory native state (**area** 3,080 sq.km, **capital** Barwani) in south-western India.
Stamp issuing began in 1921, the stamps bearing the portrait of the ruler, and continued with definitive portrait issues and the name 'BARWANI STATE' until 1938: a total of 29 stamps. They were replaced by Indian stamps in 1948.

BATUM

Adzhar town and port, Russian from 1878. In December 1918 it was occupied by British troops, who withdrew in July 1920.
Stamp issuing began in 1919 with stamps bearing the words 'Batumi Post' in Cyrillic script. These were either definitives or bore the overprint 'BATUM. OB.' or 'BATUM OBL.' on Russian stamps in Cyrillic script and with a Latin text, referring to the British occupation. A total of 53 stamps, most of them overprinted provisionals.

BEIRUT

Town in present-day Lebanon, Turkish until the First World War. A number of foreign post offices operated here, each using its own stamps.
In 1909–19 the Russian post office issued Russian stamps with the overprint 'Beyrouth': a total of 9 overprinted provisionals. The French post office issued 1 overprinted set in 1905.

They were French stamps with the overprint 'Beyrouth'. Both post offices were closed in 1914.

BHOPAL

Feudatory state (**area** 17,814 sq.km, **capital** Bhopal) in the south of Central India, under British influence from 1817.

From 1876 primitive definitive stamps made by the litho process with the name of the ruler forming the frame: 'H. H. NAWAB SHAH JAHAN BEGAM' (including some errors reading 'BEGAN'). From 1908, when Indian stamps began to be used, even for internal mail in Bhopal, official stamps were introduced inscribed, 'BHOPAL STATE' and over-printed, 'SERVICE'. Later issues omitted the name of the state but incorporated the word 'Service' in the design. From 1950 Indian official stamps came into validity. A total of 29 + 49 stamps.

BHOR

Feudatory state (**area** 2,357 sq.km, **capital** Bhor) in the Bombay Presidency in western India.

Between 1879 and 1901, 2 stamps of primitive handstruck production were issued, and 1 portrait stamp of the ruler, inscribed in English 'BHOR STATE POSTAGE'. Genuinely used examples of all three stamps are rare, especially on the original envelope.

BHUTAN

Area 46,620 sq.km, **population** 1.25 m (1983), **capital** Thimbu.

Independent kingdom in the Himalayas. It was formally independent until 1971, but in fact under Indian protection on the basis of a treaty of 1949, which renewed the British-Bhutan Treaty of 1910. Direct UPU membership from 7 March 1969.

A definitive issue (originally intended for fiscal use) with the name 'BHUTAN' appeared in 1955, symbolic in character, and authorized for use on internal mails. From 1962 there was a rapid increase in stamp production with an eye to the collector's market (pictorial stamps, general international subjects, general topics). The stamps were produced by a number of different foreign printing houses which employed artists of varying style and ability. Present-day annual production amounts to some 100 stamps, largely issued for purchase by collectors. Some catalogues do not even include data on overprinted stamps, which is a further indication that the postal function of Bhutan issues is open to dispute, if it exists at all. Well-known curiosities of Bhutan are 'three-dimensional stamps' with space exploration and other themes. The stamps were printed on curious thick materials and, being without adhesive backs, cannot normally be used for mail purposes. If regarded as valid postage stamps, the output to date is over 700 stamps and 70 miniature sheets.

Philatelic bureau Philatelic Bureau, c/o P. O. Punakha. **Trade sales** Inter-Governmental Philatelic Corporation.

BIJAWAR

Feudatory state (**area** 2,520 sq.km, **capital** Bijawar) in Central India.

From 1935 to 1937 a total of 10 stamps appeared with the portrait of the Maharaja and the name 'BIJAWAR STATE'. The postal validity of these stamps has not been clarified, and there are few letters with such stamps. In 1939 Indian stamps began to be used, and in 1941 all stamps of Bijawar were finally withdrawn.

BRITISH NORTH BORNEO

Territory which, from 1877, was administered by the British North Borneo Company and in the years 1886–92 had the official name of British North Borneo.

After issues for North Borneo in 1886 came definitive stamps inscribed 'BRITISH NORTH BORNEO': a total of 35 stamps. The first definitives, of British origin, adopted the stamp designs of the preceding stamps of *North Borneo*, followed by surcharged provisionals giving new values. From 1894 again stamps of North Borneo.

BRUNEI
Area 5,765 sq.km, **population** 191,770 (1981), **capital** Bandar Seri Begawan.

Sultanate under British protection (from 1888) on the island of Borneo; in 1941–5 under Japanese occupation. Brunei did not join the Malaysian Federation in 1963 because of disputes over the question of sharing profits from oil drilling. It was an independent state from 1984. Indirect UPU membership from 1 January 1916.

From 1906 Labuan stamps with the overprint 'BRUNEI'; later definitives with the same name; now 'BRUNEI DARUSSALAM'. Typical stamps of British origin, except that the portrait of the British monarch is replaced by a portrait of the local ruler. Apart from individual pictorial issues there has been participation in British Commonwealth and world-wide omnibus issues. During the Japanese occupation (1942–5) Brunei stamps were valid with Japanese occupation overprints, and Japanese stamps proper were also in circulation. The Japanese-overprinted provisionals on Brunei stamps were valid also in Sarawak and North Borneo. From September 1944 stamps of *North Borneo* with Japanese overprints were valid in Brunei. In 1945–7, stamps of North Borneo and Sarawak with overprints of the British Occupation Authorities. From 1947 again stamps with the name Brunei. A policy of limited issues, usually not more than 3 per annum.

Philatelic bureau Postmaster General, Philatelic Service, Brunei. **Trade sales** Crown Agents' Stamp Bureau.

BUKHARA
Territory occupied by Russia in 1866–8, then a protectorate under the tsar. Proclaimed Bukhara People's Soviet Republic on 2 September 1920 (capital, Bukhara) and concluded a treaty with the Russian Soviet Federated Socialist Republic in March 1921, to become a socialist republic on 19 September 1924, entering the Soviet Union the following day. Today, the territory is divided among the Union Republics of Uzbekistān and Tadzhikhistān.

At the end of 1923, 3 stamps were issued with a Turkish text.

BUNDI
Feudatory state (**area** 5,698 sq.km, **capital** Bundi) in north-western India, under British influence since 1818; from 1947 part of the state of Rajasthan.

From 1894 primitive stamps in native text, later portraits, which used the name of 'BUNDI' in Latin script (as overprint on official service stamps) only after 1918. Later definitives (1947) were inscribed 'BUNDI STATE': a total of 47 + 37 stamps, with text, symbols and portraits. Issuing continued until 1947 with breaks in the years 1902–5 and 1920–40, when Indian stamps were valid, and in 1948 stamps of Rajasthan came into use. In most cases, postal use is not clearly proved.

BURMA
Area 678,031 sq.km, **population** 35.31m (1983), **capital** Rangoon.

Agricultural country with large-scale rice production. In 1811–86 it was gradually occupied by the British, and in 1886 became a province of the Indian Empire. In 1937 Burma separated from India and came under direct British administration. After the Japanese occupation (1942–5), when a puppet government proclaimed independence, Burma came under British military rule in 1945 and civil administration in 1946. In 1947 an interim government was formed, and on 4 January 1948 the country gained full independence as the Union of Burma. On 4 January 1974 the name was changed to the Socialist Republic of the Union of Burma. Indirect UPU membership from 1 July 1876 (British India); indirect from 1 April 1937 (British territory); direct from 4 October 1949.

Before the country issued its own stamps, Indian stamps were in use from 1854. From 1937 Indian stamps with the overprint BURMA, followed by definitives with the same name. Later, after independence, the inscription 'UNION OF BURMA' was used and, from 1974, 'SOCIALIST REPUBLIC OF THE UNION OF BURMA'. Stamp-issuing policy is restrained, with an output of not more than 3 issues per annum, essentially for public use but, through the designs, having a propaganda purpose. British influence was seen in the first pictorial issue (1938), but subsequent issues are more typically Burmese, printing being carried out by various techniques at different foreign printing houses. During the period of the Japanese occupation (1942–5) numerous provisionals with a peacock overprint were issued by the pro-Japanese Burmese army in the delta of the Irrawaddy, and other issues by the Japanese occupation authorities. The latter even released a crudely printed definitive. In all cases the name Burma remained, whether in Latin, Burmese or Japanese script. From the period of Japanese occupation, see also *Shan State*.

Philatelic Bureau Mei Philatelic Section, Export Division, Rangoon.

BUSHIRE

Important seaport in Persia (now Iran), occupied by British troops from 8 August to 16 October 1915. Captured Persian stamps were given the overprint 'BUSHIRE Under British Occupation': a total of 29 stamps, all overprinted provisionals. The use of Persian stamps was resumed on 16 October 1916.

BUSSAHIR

Feudatory state (**area** 8,599 sq.km, **capital** Bussahir) in north-western India, eastern Punjab.

From 1895 definitive stamps in symbolic designs with the English inscription 'BUSSAHIR STATE': a total of 18 stamps. Followed from 1901 by Indian stamps.

CAMBODIA see KAMPUCHEA.

CANTON)

Town in southern China with a French post office. In the years 1901–11 *French Indo-China* stamps with the overprint 'CANTON' were used by the Indo-Chinese postal authorities in the Chinese town: a total of 83 overprinted provisionals. The post office was closed in 1922.

CENTRAL CHINA

The provinces of Anhwei, Chekiang, Hunan, Hupeh and Kiangsu with the capital Nanking, subordinate to the puppet government in Nanking, which was set up under Japanese aegis in 1940.

Even during the Japanese occupation, Chinese stamps remained valid until 1941. From that time Chinese stamps with surcharges of new values; then further surcharged provisionals on various occasions (e.g. the return of the Shanghai concession to China in 1943). In 1944, a definitive issue. A total of 107 + 4 stamps, mostly surcharged provisionals. All names and surcharges in Chinese.

From 1948 the territory of Central China produced overprinted provisionals in the provinces of Hupeh, Hunan and Kiangsu, followed by definitives with the portrait of Mao Tse-tung and other propaganda subjects. A total of 159 stamps appeared until 1950, mostly surcharged provisionals, all inscriptions and surcharges being in Chinese script.

CEYLON

From 1862 a British Crown Colony off the southern coast of India (**area** 40,750 sq.km, **capital** Colombo). Independence with the status of dominion came in 1948. In 1972 the name was changed to *Sri Lanka* and the country became a republic within the Commonwealth.

From 1857 definitive stamps with the name 'CEYLON': a total of 444 + 17 stamps, based on the pattern of the British colonial stamp designs up to 1947, all printed in Great Britain. From independence in 1949, designs showed local influence, and printing was by various methods and by different printers in Great Britain, Switzerland, Austria and elsewhere. Limited issuing, often a single commemorative stamp; national propaganda subjects and certain common international themes. The first Ceylonese stamps are coveted among collectors.

CHAMBA

Indian convention state (**area** 8,099 sq.km, **capital** Chamba) in north-eastern Punjab, under British influence from 1846.

From 1886 Indian stamps with the overprint 'CHAMBA STATE', which were issued until 1948. From 1950 Indian stamps were used: a total of 108 + 72 stamps.

CHARKHARI
Feudatory state (**area** 2,279 sq.km, **capital** Charkhari) in the north-east of Central India.

From 1894 primitively produced stamps with 'CHARKHARI STATE' inscription and symbolic in character; later pictorials with the same name: a total of 40 stamps, with limited postal validity. Since 1950 stamps of India alone have been usable.

CHE-NAN (HONAN)
Chinese province (**area** 167,000 sq.km, **capital** Chengchow or Kaifeng) in Northern China, occupied by the Japanese 1938–45.

In 1941 Chinese stamps appeared with the Chinese overprint 'For Honan': a total of 53 stamps until 1942, all overprinted provisionals.

CHINA (CHINESE PEOPLE'S REPUBLIC)
Area 9,596,961 sq.km, **population** 1,008m (1982), **capital** Peking (Beijing).

Agricultural and industrial country with rapidly developing industry. Until 1911 the country was ruled by an Emperor of the Manchu dynasty of Ch'ing. On 29 December 1911 a Republic was proclaimed and Sun Yat-sen became the first president. China participated in the First World War on the side of the Allies. After the war there were three civil wars (1924–7, 1929–36, 1946–9). In 1931 Japan attacked, leading to the 1937 war against the whole of China. In 1937 the Japanese established an interim government and in 1940 a 'national' pro-Japanese puppet government in Nanking led by Wang T'ing-wei. This brought about the war of national liberation (1937–45) in which China won back its occupied territories: Manchuria (lost in 1932), Taiwan (1894), and leased territory. In 1949 the Chinese People's Republic was proclaimed and the Nationalist Army of Chiang Kai-shek withdrew to Taiwan. Direct UPU membership from 1 March 1914.

China's relatively late membership of the UPU (in 1914) indicates that postal conditions were highly complicated up to that date. There were foreign post offices on the territory of China, particularly in the most important trade centres, and they used the stamps of their own country, stamps with the overprint of Chinese towns or stamps with the name China in various languages. For example, the French post office, from 1894 until its closure in 1922, used French stamps with the overprint 'CHINE' : a total of 48 + 29 stamps, mostly overprinted provisionals or designs common to the French colonial issues. From 1899 to 1920 the Russian post office used Russian stamps with the overprint 'KITAY' in Cyrillic script. The Russian post office closed down in 1920 on the basis of a mutual agreement. A total of 34 overprinted or surcharged provisionals. The Japanese post office issued a total of 49 overprinted provisionals from 1900 to its closure in 1922, using Japanese stamps. The overprints mean 'China' in Japanese, and some printings were as low as 5,000 stamps. French Indo-China, in 1902–5, used stamps of French Indo-China with the overprint 'CHINE': a total of 28 overprinted provisionals. From 1917 to 1930, when the last British post office was closed down, the British postal authorities used Hong Kong stamps with the overprint 'CHINA': a total of 27 overprinted provisionals. German stamps with 'China' were issued for the German post office in 1898 to 1917, when the post office was closed down by China after the declaration of war: a total of 47 stamps, all overprinted provisionals.

Even though issues with the name 'CHINA' appeared as early as 1878, being issues of the marine customs authorities, the first issues of the Chinese Imperial Post appeared as late as 1897, first as overprinted and surcharged provisionals, then as definitives with the name, in Chinese and English, 'IMPERIAL CHINESE POST', or 'CHINESE IMPERIAL POST'. From 1912 the name 'REPUBLIC OF CHINA' began to be used. It is paradoxical that after joining the UPU (whose regulations prescribe that stamps must bear the name of the issuing country in Latin script), Latin disappeared from many of the Chinese stamps. A number of issues have the characteristic stylized symbol of the sun. Up to 1949 a total of 1,378 stamps appeared. At first, stamp issuing was not on a large scale. Up to 1938 fewer than

300 stamps were issued, mostly normal postage stamps in symbolic or portrait designs, but also a number of overprinted provisionals. In the 1940s new issues grew considerably in numbers due to currency devaluation, issues for individual territories, issues for occupied territories, then inflation in 1948 and involved internal political conditions. There can be no simple survey of issuing policy and postal use of issued stamps, with certain issues being valid under various political and postal authorities at the same time. The territory occupied by the Japanese formally belonged to the puppet Chinese government in Nanking. Here current Chinese stamps were used until 1941, then the Japanese began to issue occupation stamps, for *North China*, *Central China* and *South China*. Meng-tien had its own issue by its autonomous government, even though it came nominally under the Nanking government.

From 1949 on, stamps of the Chinese People's Republic appeared, numbered in the lower margin. The first number is the set, then the total number of stamps in the set, then the number of the stamp in the set, and on the right the total number of stamps issued up to this point. They bear only a Chinese text. The stamps were printed by various techniques in Chinese printing houses, up to 1957 mostly by recess printing. Striking designs are based on subjects of national and political interest and propaganda in a broad sense (e.g. gymnastics on 30 stamps with pictures of exercises). New issues now appear frequently: up to 100 stamps per year, most of them attractive pictorials without political overtones.

For modern stamps with the inscription 'REPUBLIC OF CHINA' see *Taiwan*. For stamps bearing the name of 'FORMOSA/CHINA' see *Formosa*.

Philatelic bureau China National Stamp Corporation, Peking (Beijing).

CHRISTMAS ISLAND
Area 135 sq.km, **population** 3,214 (1983), **capital** Flying Fish Cove.

Since 1958, an overseas territory of Australia in the Indian Ocean. The island was annexed by Great Britain in 1888 and became part of the Straits Settlements in 1889. Between 1946 and 1948 it was under Military Administration, and from 1948 to 1958 came under the control of the Crown Colony of Singapore. UPU membership as Australian territory.

From 1958 Australian stamps with the overprint 'CHRISTMAS ISLAND', then definitives of Australian origin and production. In 1968 the inscription became 'CHRISTMAS ISLAND/ INDIAN OCEAN' to avoid confusion with the Christmas Island in the Pacific Ocean, formerly administered by the Gilbert and Ellice Islands. The stamps that were issued there were of an entirely private character, thus not qualifying as an official issue. Limited production of 1–2 issues per year, one always at Christmas, the designs varying each year but with a Christmas theme for each issue. The other issues relate to island life and history.

Philatelic bureau Christmas Island Post Office, Indian Ocean. **Trade sales** Crown Agents' Stamp Bureau.

CILICIA
Turkish territory on the Iskenderun Straits of the Mediterranean (**area** 16,161 sq.km, **towns** Mersin and Adana), occupied in 1918–21 by the French and in September to October 1919 by Anglo-Egyptian troops. In 1920 became a mandate as part of Syria. The return of Cilicia to Turkey in December 1921 was confirmed in 1923 under the Treaty of Lausanne.

Turkish stamps with the overprint 'CILICIE' in 1919: a total of 68 overprinted provisionals, which were valid until 23 May 1919. After the temporary Anglo-Egyptian occupation overprinted provisionals again appeared from 1920 on Turkish and French stamps, bearing the wording 'OCCUPATION MILITAIRE Française CILICIE' or the abbreviation 'OMF Cilicie': a total of 114 stamps, all overprinted provisionals. From 1922 they were followed by Turkish stamps.

COCHIN
Feudatory Indian state (**area** 3,853 sq.km, **capital** Ernakulam) in the south of India, British from 1814, joined to Travancore in 1949.

From 1892 definitive issues with the inscription 'COCHIN': a total of 110 + 102 stamps, a large number of officials. Numerous overprinted provisionals and definitive issues in symbolic and portrait designs. After 1949 see *Travancore-Cochin*.

COCHIN CHINA

Territory occupied by the French in 1859–67 (**area** 67,622 sq.km, **capital** Saigon) and in 1887 incorporated into French Indo-China, later part of Vietnam.

In 1886 stamps of the French colonies ('commerce' type) with a currency surcharge and the letters 'C. CH.': a total of 5 overprinted provisionals. From 1892 the stamps of *French Indo-China* came into use.

COCOS (KEELING) ISLANDS

Area 14 sq.km, **population** 579 (1983), **capital** Home Island.

An island group of 27 atolls in the Indian Ocean, from 1955 under Australian administration. Earlier administrations were: from 1857, British; from 1878, Ceylonese; from 1886, Straits Settlements; from 1903, Singapore; in 1942–6, Ceylonese again; from 1946, the Governor of Singapore. UPU membership through Australia.

In 1963 pictorial definitive stamps with 'COCOS (KEELING) ISLANDS' printed in Australia. Very limited issues, with a moderate programme of commemorative stamps. The stamps with the old £. s. d. currency ceased validity on 15 February 1966, and until new ones were issued in decimal currency on 8 July 1969 stamps of *Australia* were in use. The stamps of the Cocos Islands are also valid up to 1979 in the territory of Australia.

Philatelic bureau Cocos (Keeling) Islands.

CYPRUS

Area 9,251 sq.km, **population** 645,000 (1982), **capital** Nicosia.

Republic in the Commonwealth from 1960. The strategic location of the island has caused frequent changes in rulers. In 1571 the Turks took it from the Venetians, and during their rule a Turkish minority grew up. After the Russo-Turkish war, at the Congress of Berlin in 1878, the administration was taken over by Great Britain who annexed it in 1914 since Turkey was on the side of the Central Powers. Great Britain was allotted the island under the Treaty of Lausanne in 1924, and Cyprus was proclaimed a Crown Colony in 1925. After the establishment of an independent republic in 1960, armed clashes began in 1963 and 1964 between the Turkish and the Greek inhabitants, and UN Peace-Keeping Forces were stationed on the island. The dispute came to a head on 15 July 1974 with a coup inspired by the junta in Athens. The Turkish army occupied the northeastern part of the island and on 13 February 1975 a Turkish-Cypriot Federal State was unilaterally proclaimed (Northern Cyprus). Indirect UPU membership from 1 July 1875 (Turkey); indirect from 1 July 1878 (Great Britain); direct from 23 November 1961.

From 1880 British stamps with the overprint 'CYPRUS', definitives with the same name. From independence the name was given in three languages – Greek, Turkish and English ('KYPROS', 'KIBRIS' and 'CYPRUS'); from 1966 in the changed order – 'KYPROS', 'CYPRUS', 'KIBRIS'. Since 1980 the name of the country has again been given on the stamps in Greek, Turkish and English. First stamps and all issues to 1960 were printed in Great Britain: pictorials, general Commonwealth issues, no local interest commemoratives. Since independence printing has been done in Greece in offset lithography by Aspiotis-Elka of Athens. Mainly subjects of national interest, but also participation in international omnibus issues (with designs in common), which makes overall production rather uneven. Present-day output amounts to 10 to 20 stamps per year. (See also *Cyprus-Turkish Administration*.)

Although geographically Cyprus belongs to Asia, it became the 19th member of the Council of Europe, contributed to the annual EUROPA issues and is included under Europe in all stamp catalogues.

Philatelic bureau Philatelic Branch, General Post Office, Nicosia. **Trade sales** Inter-Governmental Philatelic Corporation.

CYPRUS (Turkish Administration)

The north-eastern part of Cyprus was occupied by the Turkish army in July 1974, when an attempted coup d'état was staged on the island. The Turkish government concentrated virtually the entire Turkish population in the northern part of the island, along with about 35,000 refugees from the mainland and on 13 December 1975, under the aegis of the occupation forces, the Turkish Federated State of Cyprus (**area** 3,200 sq.km) was formed. The UN, however, does not recognize its existence.

From 1975 definitives have appeared with the inscription 'KIBRIS TÜRK FEDERE DEVLETI POSTALARI' (Post Office of the Turkish-Cypriot Federated State). Stamp production is of Turkish origin, the designs stressing political publicity. Annual output, 10 to 15 stamps.

Philatelic bureau The Directorate of the Postal Dept., Turkish Federated State of Kibris, Levkosia (Nicosia), Northern Cyprus.

DARDANELLES

The area of the Dardanelles Strait with post office at Canakkale on the Asian coast of Turkey.

A Russian post office was in operation here from 1910 using Russian stamps with the overprint 'Dardanelles': a total of 9 overprinted provisionals. The post office was closed down in 1914.

DHAR

Feudatory state (**area** 4,610 sq.km, **capital** Dhar) in north-western India, under British influence from 1819.

In 1897 primitive stamps with entirely native text. The second definitive issue bore the name 'DHAR STATE' in Latin script: a total of 8 stamps. Since 1901 Indian stamps have been in use.

DUBAI

One of the countries of the former Trucial States on the coast of the Persian Gulf (**area** 3,900 sq.km, **capital** Dubai), the only one that had a post office before 1963 (Indian from 1909, British from 1948). UPU membership is given as indirect in 1969, under Great Britain. From 1971 Dubai has been part of the United Arab Emirates.

British stamps were used (*Muscat and Oman*) before Dubai started issuing stamps. From 1963 to 1972 over 400 definitive stamps and commemoratives with 'DUBAI'. Many issues, although valid for postage, were designed for the collector's market and include numerous miniature sheets, large formats, and limited printings (a few restricted to 500 stamps), perforate and imperforate issues, etc. The pictorial stamps depict numerous international themes and general topics largely alien to Dubai. Printing is by photogravure and offset techniques by a wide range of printers. The postal use of many issues was minimal. In 1972 stamps of the *United Arab Emirates* were introduced.

DUTTIA

Feudatory state (**area** 2,391 sq.km, **capital** Duttia) in the north of Central India, under British administration from 1802.

From 1893 primitive stamps with the name 'DUTTIA STATE' and also 'DATIA STATE'. The first issue is possibly the rarest of all Indian states issues. A total of 29 stamps until 1920. From 1921 only Indian stamps were valid.

EAST INDIA

Issues with 'EAST INDIA' from 1855 to 1882: a total of 22 + 15 stamps, both definitives of British origin and overprinted provisionals. These succeeded the issues of the East India Company (with the name 'India') and preceded stamps of the Indian Empire which, from 1882, again used the name 'India'.

EASTERN CHINA

The territory of Anhwei, Kiangsu, Chekiang and Fukien (**area** 503,000 sq.km, **capital** Shanghai), occupied by the Japanese from 1938 to 1945; from 1949 a region of the Chinese People's Republic.

In 1949–50 a total of 91 + 14 stamps, both definitives and overprinted provisionals, none of which carried any inscription in Latin script. The design subjects were mainly propaganda and portraits of Mao Tse-tung.

FAR EASTERN REPUBLIC

Temporary state in eastern Siberia and in the Far East (1920–2), established as a buffer state to prevent direct contact between the Russian Soviet Federated Socialist Republic and Japan. It was about 1.5m sq.km in area. The first capital was Verkhnyeudinsk and then, from October 1920, Chita. In the spring of 1921 part of the republic was occupied by the army of the White General Diterichs and incorporated in Priamur District, but in November 1922 the republic was re-established. Soon after (on 15 November), it was joined to the Russian Soviet Federated Socialist Republic.

A total of 36 stamps were issued (Russian with the overprint 'DVR' = Dalnye-Vostochnaya Respublika, in Cyrillic script and definitives without the name of the territory) in the years 1920–2 and 18 stamps of the Soviet Far Eastern Republic in 1923 (Russian with the overprint 'D V').

FARIDKOT

Indian feudatory state in eastern Punjab; convention state from 1886 (**area** 1,585 sq.km, **capital** Faridkot), under British influence from 1809.

Primitive definitive stamps of local origin, text completely native (the name not in Latin script) from 1878. From 1887, when Faridkot became a convention state, Indian stamps with the overprint 'FARIDKOT STATE': a total of 14 + 9 stamps. In 1901 Indian stamps went into circulation.

FEDERATED MALAY STATES

During its first penetration of the Malayan Peninsula, Great Britain established the following protectorates: Perak (1873), Selangor(1874), Negri Sembilan (1876), Pahang (1888) and Sungei Ujong (1889 – merged with Negri Sembilan 1895). These were merged in 1896 to form the Federated Malay States (**area** 71,608 sq.km, **capital** Kuala Lumpur). They became part of British Malaya and today belong to *Malaysia.*

After the formation of the Federated Malay States the stamps of the individual states remained valid until 1899. In 1900 the stamps of Negri Sembilan and Perak were given the overprint 'FEDERATED MALAY STATES' (this was also used in Kedah, Kelantan and Perlis during 1909–1911), followed by definitives with the same name: a total of 79 + 27 stamps of British origin, typical of the Malayan region. While definitives continued to be issued until 1934, followed by stamps of the individual states in 1935, common postage-due stamps appeared under the name of the *Malayan Postal Union,* and were valid over a wider area (including Singapore) than the territory of the Federated Malay States.

FORMOSA (TAIWAN)

Island off the coast of China (**area** 35,970 sq.km, **capital** Taipei). Chinese until 1895 when it was taken over by Japan after the Sino-Japanese war of 1895. In 1945, after the Second World War, it was again Chinese, and since 1949 has been the seat of the government of National China under the late General Chiang Kai-shek and then his son. The Chinese name of the island is Taiwan.

Local issue in 1888, for use in north of Taiwan only, inscribed 'FORMOSA/CHINA'; then, in 1895, 7 values issued by the Black Flag Republic resistance group. From 1895 to 1945 Japanese stamps were in use. From 1945 see *Taiwan.*

FRENCH INDIA

Former French colonies on the coast of India (513 sq.km) occupied in the 17th and 18th centuries, ruled by the governor in Pondichéry. From 1947 they held the status of five free towns of French India: Pondichéry (291 sq.km); Karikał (135 sq.km); Yanaon (18 sq.km); Chandernagor (10 sq.km) and Mahé (59 sq.km). In 1950 Chandernagor became part of India, followed by the other four territories in 1954.

Indian stamps were in use before the colonies' own stamps appeared. From 1892 French colonial stamps of key-and-duty type with 'ETABLISSEMENTS DE L'INDE'; later, 'ETA-BLISSEMENTS FRANÇAIS DANS L'INDE': a total of 309 + 28 stamps of French origin with numerous overprinted provisionals and designs common to French colonial issues. During the Second World War there were Pétain issues released in Vichy (which had no validity in French India) and issues of Free France. An issue showing local subjects appeared in 1948, and was designed and printed in France. Stamp issuing ceased on the transfer of the French Indian Settlements to India in 1954, and Indian stamps were introduced.

FRENCH INDOCHINA
French territories of Tonkin, Annam, Cochin China and Cambodia linked into one administrative unit in 1887. To this was added Laos in 1893 and the port of Kouang-Tchéou-Wan in south China in 1898. French Indochina covered an area of 740,000 sq.km with Hanoi as capital. After the Second World War, French Indochina split up into the separate countries of *Vietnam, Cambodia* and *Laos*.

From 1889 French colonial stamps (General Issue) with the overprint 'INDO-CHINE', followed by key-and-duty types inscribed 'INDO-CHINE'. A total of 360 + 120 stamps until 1951, of French origin, a number of designs common to the majority of the French colonial issues, but also issues individual to Indochina, with numerous portrait stamps and some pictorials, the subjects being on historic themes and life in Indochina.

FUJEIRA
One of the countries of the former Trucial States on the coast of the Gulf of Oman (**area** 1,175 sq.km, **capital** Fujeira). From 1971 Fujeira has been part of the United Arab Emirates.

The state began to issue its own stamps in 1964, when definitives with the name 'FUJEI-RA' appeared: a total of 784 + 18 stamps, a very large number for the relatively short period and few inhabitants. Fujeira is one of the states which exploited the philatelic market with unnecessary thematic issues, frequently produced perforated and imperforate and with miniature sheets. The pre-Olympic set had 31 values, several Napoleonic issues 20 stamps each, and there were a number of printings on gold and silver foil. Although some have been cancelled-to-order postmarked, few of the stamps performed any postal function. Since 1972 stamps of the *United Arab Emirates* have been used.

GEORGIA
After the secession of the Caucasian territory from Russia a Georgian Republic was established on 26 May 1918 (area then 86,458 sq.km), which concluded a treaty with Turkey and was occupied by Turkish and, later, British troops. After the whole country had been liberated by the Red Army a Soviet republic was formed in 1921, which merged with Armenia and Azerbaijan to form the Transcaucasian Soviet Federated Socialist Republic and became part of the Soviet Union that year. It has been a Soviet republic since 1936.

In 1919 definitive stamps with the French text 'LA GEORGIE' or 'RÉPUBLIQUE GEORGIENNE'. The 1922 Soviet republic issue does not give the name in Latin script. A total of 62 stamps, with a number of overprinted provisionals apart from definitive issues of local origin. From 1923 see *Transcaucasian Federation;* from 1924, see *Soviet Union.*

GWALIOR
Convention state (**area** 68,291 sq.km, **capital** Gwalior) in the north of Central India, one of the five leading states of India.

Indian stamps with the overprint 'GWALIOR' appeared in 1885. A total of 121 + 62 stamps, all overprinted on Indian issues until 1949; replaced by Indian stamps in 1950, even though the Gwalior stamps remained valid until 1 January 1951.

HATAY

Former sanjak of Alexandretta (**area** 260 sq.km, **capital** Iskenderun – the Turkish name for Alexandretta). From 1920 to 1938, part of French Syria; in 1938, Republic of Hatay, which was incorporated into Turkey as a province on 30 June 1939.

The stamps of *Syria* were valid in this territory from 1919 to 1938; and, in 1938, those of *Alexandretta*. Separate stamp-issuing dates from 1939, when first Turkish stamps appeared with the overprint 'HATAY DEVLETI' ('State of Hatay'), then definitives with the same inscription. The first issue was not acknowledged by the French Commission in Beirut, so that mail to Great Lebanon and Syria was surcharged. A total of 39 + 13 stamps of Turkish origin. In 1939 Turkish stamps were introduced.

HEILUNGKIANG AND KIRIN

The Chinese province Heilungkiang and Kirin in northern Manchuria (552,525 sq.km) issued Chinese stamps from 1927 with a Chinese overprint meaning 'Only for the Province of Heilungkiang and Kirin'. Currency in the province was valued at about 30 % of the national currency and the overprint was to prevent transfer of stamps from the province. A total of 32 of these overprinted provisionals appeared until 1931.

HEJAZ

Kingdom on the Arabian Peninsula (**area** 472,000 sq.km, **capital** Mecca), whose independence was proclaimed on 30 May 1916 after a rising against the Turks. In 1925 it was occupied by Ibn Saud, the ruler of Nejd, and merged with it in 1932 to form *Saudi Arabia*.

From 1916 definitive stamps of ornamental oriental design. Until 1925 a total of 111 + 34 stamps, definitives as above and overprinted provisionals. From 1926 see *Hejaz and Nejd*.

HEJAZ AND NEJD

In 1926 definitive stamps of oriental design which only later (1928) had the name of the country, 'HEJAZ NEJD' or 'HEDJAZ NEDJDE' in Latin script: a total of 57 stamps, definitives and overprinted provisionals. Stamp issuing continued until 29 September 1932, when Nejd and Hejaz and dependent territories were renamed *Saudi Arabia,* with which name stamps began to be issued in 1934.

HOIHAO

Town on the northern coast of the Chinese island of Hainan with a French post office.

From 1901 stamps of French Indochina with the overprint 'HOI-HAO': a total of 82 provisionals. Stamp issuing ceased in 1919, and the post office was closed in 1922.

HOLKAR

Feudatory state in Central India, also called Indore (**area** 25,728 sq.km, **capital** Indore), under British influence from 1818.

In 1886 a portrait issue with the name 'HOLKAR STATE': a total of 7 stamps issued. From 1904 see *Indore,* with which name further stamps were issued.

HONAN see CHE-NAN

HONG KONG

Area 1,065 sq.km, **population** 5.31m (1983), **capital** Victoria.

Important port for transit trade to the Chinese People's Republic and for the re-export of goods. British from 1842 (the island) and 1860 (peninsula), while the New Territories were leased by China to Great Britain in 1898 for a period of 99 years. In 1941–5 occupied by the Japanese, then the status of British Crown Colony was renewed. Indirect UPU membership from 1 April 1877.

From 1862 definitive issues with the name 'HONGKONG', followed by a certain number of surcharged provisionals, all of British origin. Mainly royal portrait issues, and a few pictorials. When Hong Kong has joined in Commonwealth omnibus issues, the Hong Kong stamps have varied from the normal, and the inscriptions have been in English and Chinese. Very limited new issue programme, which at present amounts to 3–4 issues a year, often with only 2 stamps to a set.

Hong Kong stamps (at first without the overprint 'CHINA') were used in British post offices in China. During the Japanese occupation of 1942–5 three special stamps were issued and Japanese stamps were also valid in Hong Kong.

Philatelic bureau General Post Office, Hong Kong. **Trade sales** Crown Agents' Stamp Bureau.

HOPEI (HOPEH)

Chinese province (**area** 202,700 sq.km, **capital** Tientsin) in Northern China, occupied by the Japanese 1938–45.

In 1941 Chinese stamps were issued with the Chinese overprint 'For Hopei': a total of 55 stamps, all overprinted provisionals.

HYDERABAD

Feudatory state (**area** 213,191 sq.km, **capital** Hyderabad) in Deccan in Central India, under British influence from 1800. In 1947 its government refused to join the Indian Union but was forced by military pressure to do so in 1948.

From 1869 definitive stamps, which bore the name of Hyderabad in local characters only. Other stamps from 1947 have the inscription 'H.E.H. THE NIZAM'S GOVT. POSTAGE' but the name of the country does not appear in English. A total of 49 + 46 stamps of symbolic and pictorial character. In 1950 Indian stamps were introduced.

IDAR

Feudatory state (**area** 4,320 sq.km, **capital** Himmatnagar) in western India, part of Rajasthan since 1947.

Stamps were issued from 1939 to 1944, a total of 6 definitives with the portrait of the Maharaja and the inscription 'IDAR STATE POSTAGE'.

INDIA

Area 3,280,483 sq.km, **population** 684m (1981), **capital** New Delhi.

Developing agricultural country with some industry. In 1947 declared a dominion in the British Commonwealth; proclaimed a republic on 26 January 1950.

In 1600 The East India Company was established to develop Indian trade with Britain. Territorial expansion began in 1757, and by the 19th century almost the whole of India was under British control. In 1858 the Company was abolished and India became a Crown Colony with a Viceroy. In 1877 the British monarch began to use the title of Emperor of India. Until 1947 the Empire of India was divided into British India (2,241,605 sq.km), i.e. the territory occupied by the East India Company until 1858; and the Indian States (1,854,247 sq.km) i.e. the territory of about 600 states which recognized British sovereignty from 1858 on. In 1929 there were 562 such states, in 1948, 584. Until 1937, Burma and Aden came under Indian administration. In 1947 two countries came into existence, India and Pakistan. In 1950–54 France handed over to Indian sovereignty five small territories of French India; in 1961 Indian troops occupied three territories of Portuguese India; in 1975 Sikkim was proclaimed an Indian state. Direct UPU membership from 1 July 1876.

Some of the Indian states issued their own stamps. These are divided into:

1. **Convention states:** Chamba, Faridkot, Gwalior, Jind, Patiala, Nabha. These states had an agreement with India and a postal convention whereby from 1864 to 1886 they joined the Indian postal system and used Indian stamps with the overprint of their own name. Until 1950 these stamps were valid in the entire Indian territory.

2. **Native (feudatory) states:** (27). Most of these produced definitive issues that were valid only within the borders of the issuing state.

3. **Modern (feudatory) states:** (9).

From 1854 definitive stamps with the portrait of Queen Victoria and the name 'INDIA' as issues of the East India Company. In 1855–82 they were replaced by crown issues (*East India*), followed by issues of the Indian Empire again with the name 'INDIA'. Long-term definitive stamps with numerous official stamps. Until 1946 very small number of stamps, only 182 in all, mostly portraits. From the 1930s pictorial stamps and portraits. Production intensified from 1947 on, growing in quantity with pictorial subjects of Indian interest and numerous portraits. First the stamps were of British origin and under the influence of the British stamp designers, and from the middle 1920s most of them were printed in India. Since independence, an Indian conception has been worked out, for which photographic adaptations have been widely used. Annual production is about 20–40 stamps (often a single stamp issued on its own) which are issued in printings of about two million.

Indian stamps were also used in a number of other countries where Indian post offices existed, and in British territory under Indian administration: until 1867 in the Straits Settlements, until 1896 in Zanzibar, until 1903 in British Somaliland, until 1923 in Kuwait, until 1933 in the Bahrain Islands, until 1937 in Aden and the Aden Protectorate, likewise in Burma, until 1947 in Pakistan, Muscat and Oman, and until 1954 in Bhutan.

Philatelic bureau Presidency Postmaster, Philatelic Bureau, Bombay.

INDONESIA
Area 1,904,569 sq.km, **population** 154m (1981), **capital** Jakarta.

Developing agricultural country. Originally Netherlands Indies, occupied by the Japanese 1942–45; after the war (on 17 August 1945) the national liberation movement proclaimed Indonesia an independent republic, but the Netherlands did not acknowledge this and fought against it. In 1948 the Netherlands Indies were renamed Indonesia, but the colonial status continued until 27 December 1949, when it was agreed to form the United States of Indonesia in union with the Netherlands. It was an association of sixteen states, the largest of which was the Indonesian Republic comprising Java, Madura and the larger part of Sumatra, but excluding Western Irian. The United States of Indonesia were changed into a unified Indonesian Republic on 17 August 1950, and in 1960 seceded from the union with the Netherlands. In 1963 Indonesia acquired Western Irian, and in 1975 it occupied the territory of Portuguese Timor. Indirect UPU membership from 1 May 1877 (Dutch colony), direct from 1 January 1922 (Netherlands Indies) and as a sovereign country from 27 December 1949.

Official issues since 1948, when the stamps of the Netherlands Indies were first given the overprint 'INDONESIA', and then definitives with the same name; from 1950 the name expressed as 'REPUBLIK INDONESIA'. Various unofficial issues were already dated. In 1945, both overprinted provisionals and definitive stamps with the words 'REPOEBLIK INDONESIA' appeared in Java. There were also unofficial local overprints which had no postal validity. Similarly, official and local overprints appeared in Sumatra in 1946 together with definitives inscribed 'N.R. INDONESIA'. From 1949 pictorials of the United States of Indonesia were issued at frequent intervals and in large quantities, the themes being mainly national. Present annual production about 30 stamps.

Philatelic bureau Philatelic Section, Postal Service, Bandung. **Trade sales** International Philatelic Agencies, Netherlands.

INDORE
Also known as *Holkar,* feudatory state (**area** 25,729 sq.km, **capital** Indore) in central India, under British influence since 1818.

Stamp issuing of the state of Indore continued in 1904 with stamps bearing the new name of 'INDORE STATE' (in place of 'HOLKAR'): a total of 33 + 6 stamps. The Indian postal authorities took over mail services in Indore State in 1908, but after that time official stamps (with a 'SERVICE' overprint) continued to be issued in Indore. Since 1950 only stamps of India have been valid.

INNER MONGOLIA see MENG-CHIANG

NORTH-WESTERN CHINA
The territory of Sinkiang, 'Chinghai, Kansu, Shensi provinces and Inner Mongolia's Ningsia (**area** 3,205,000 sq.km, **capital** Urumchi).

Stamps were issued in the years 1946–9, when 84 stamps appeared, all without Latin script. They were overprinted provisionals and definitive issues with, in 1949, the portrait of Mao Tse-tung and the Great Wall of China.

NORTHERN CHINA
A territory covering five provinces: Honan, Hopeh, Shantung, Shansi and Supeh. **Total area** about 680,000 sq.km, **capital** Peking (Beijing). Occupied by Japan 1938–45, when it existed as an autonomous region of Nanking China. From 1949 a region in the Chinese People's Republic.

From 1941 Chinese stamps with overprints, then definitives, with no Latin script: a total of 112 stamps up to 1945, mostly overprinted provisionals. The definitives have propaganda subjects (e.g. the anniversary of an independent post office; the declaration of war on the Nanking Government by the Allies, etc.). The issues either adopted the Chinese-style stamp designs or were influenced by Japanese stamps. In 1949–50 overprinted provisionals and definitive stamps (e.g. with the portrait of Mao Tse-tung), again without Latin script: a total of 76 + 25 stamps.

OMAN
Area 271,950 sq.km, **population** 1.5m (1982), **capital** Muscat.

Independent sultanate on the Arabian peninsula with developing oil industry, formerly known as *Muscat and Oman*. That name was abolished after a palace coup on 23 July 1970 when a new sultan took power and introduced the name of Sultanate of Oman. Indirect UPU membership from 1 July 1876 (British India); indirect from 1 April 1948 (British Post Office); indirect from 30 April 1966 as autonomous postal services; direct as of 17 August 1971.

Definitive stamps and overprinted provisionals with 'SULTANATE OF OMAN' and the same name in Arabic script appeared in 1971. Limited issuing with subjects of national propaganda, mostly on pictorials, dominated by the portrait of the ruler or the emblem of the country. Annually, normal maximum of 3 issues.

Philatelic bureau Directorate of Posts, Telegraphs and Telephones, Muscat. **Trade sales** Crown Agents' Stamp Bureau.

ORCHHA
Feudatory state (**area** 5,177 sq.km, **capital** Tikamgarh) in central India.

From 1913 definitive issues of symbolic character in primitive print with the name 'OR-CHA'; later, stamps with the portrait of the ruler and 'ORCHHA STATE': a total of 43 stamps. Since 1950 only Indian stamps have been in use. (**Note:** An earlier issue was prepared in 1897 but was not issued for postal use.)

OTTOMAN EMPIRE (TURKEY)
Vast and powerful state founded in the late 13th century by the Ottoman Turks. It ruled extensive territories in south-eastern Europe, the Near East and North Africa. Gradually losing its dominant position from the 19th century on, it had to abandon nearly all its European holdings after the Balkan Wars (1912-13), at the same time losing its influence in Africa, so that its territory became limited basically only to the Asian continent. In the First World War the Ottoman Empire stood on the side of the Central Powers, and it capitulated in 1918, bringing the Empire virtually to an end. The countries of the Allies took over the Arab territories and began military occupation. In June 1920 the Greek army, supported by Great Britain, began its attack towards the core of the Ottoman Empire from Izmir, which the Greeks had occupied in May 1919. On 10 August 1920, the Treaty of Sèvres confirmed the dissolution of the Ottoman Empire, which then gave up three-quarters of its territory inhabited mainly by Arabs, keeping only about 500,000 sq.km. That same year Mustafa Kemal (Ataturk)

formed a new Turkish government with its seat in Ankara and began to fight against the Allies as well as against the old government of the Ottoman Empire at Constantinople. Of the abandoned territories he conquered western Armenia in 1920, gained Cilicia from the French in 1921, beat back the Greek attack, and in 1922 occupied Smyrna and Constantinople. In the same year the sultanate was officially abolished, and the Turkish Republic came into being with Mustafa Kemal at its head.

From 1863 definitive issues, mostly in Arabic scripts, but at times with text in Latin script reading, 'EMP. OTTOMAN', or 'POSTES OTTOMANNES': a total of 689 + 46 stamps. Ornamental and symbolic designs of local origin with a great many overprinted provisionals, which in the period around the First World War were issued alternately with pictorial stamps. Although printed in Great Britain or Austria, these showed strong local influences in the designs. In 1911, stamps with the overprints 'MONASTIR', 'PRISTINA', 'SALONIQUE' and 'USKUB' were issued when the Sultan visited these areas — these are commemorative stamps only, and do not represent separate stamp territories. In 1917, stocks of Turkish stamps from 1865 to 1905 were revalidated by an overprint reading (in Arabic) '1333' (= AD 1917) and 'PTT' (= Postes, Télégraphes et Téléphones). In some cases only 1,100 stamps were involved, of which 388 went to Berne to the UPU. Many foreign post offices operated in the territories of the Ottoman Empire up to the First World War, and they used the stamps of their own countries as well as those of the *Levant*. From 1922 stamps of Turkey came into use, and for that reason many stamp catalogues give the issues of the Ottoman Empire under Turkey.

PACKHOI
Chinese Peihei; southern Chinese town with a French post office.

From 1903 stamps of French Indo-China with the overprint 'PACKHOI', 'PAK'HOI' or 'PA-KHOI': a total of 67 overprinted provisionals until 1919. The post office was closed down in 1922.

PAHANG
Area 35,931 sq.km, **capital** Kuantan. Member state of the Malaysian Federation since 1963.

British protectorate from 1888, from 1895 one of the Federated Malay States. In 1941–5 occupied by Japan, and in 1945 by the British army. From 1948 part of the Malayan Union, in 1957–63 a member of the independent Malayan Federation. Indirect UPU membership of Negri Sembilan, Pahang, Perak and Selangor from 1 April 1915 as Federated Malay States (British colony); direct from 17 January 1958 (Malayan Federation); direct from 16 September 1963 (Malaysia).

From 1890 stamps of the Straits Settlements, later also stamps of Perak with the overprint 'PAHANG'. The name appeared alone on definitive issues in 1891–5, and in 1935 onward as part of 'MALAYA' or 'MALAYSIA' which were also named. Some stamps of 1950 have the name of Pahang in Arabic script only but also with 'MALAYA'. Production of British origin. Apart from overprinted provisionals, all issues are in designs common to the other states in Malaya, mostly portraits of local ruler or pictorials of Malayan scenes. Stamps are not issued every year. From 1900 to 1935 the stamps of the Federated Malay States were valid in this territory. Then the country's own stamps were issued until the Japanese occupation, when a total of 25 stamps of Pahang appeared with overprints of the Japanese postal authorities, and Japanese stamps themselves were valid. Separate stamp-issuing resumed after the British occupation (see *Malaya*) from 1948 on. Stamps of the Malaysian, formerly Malayan, Federation are also in circulation in the territory of Pahang, and the stamps of all the states of *Malaysia* are likewise valid. Similarly, the stamps of Pahang are valid in the entire territory of the Federation.

PAKISTAN
Area 803,942 sq.km, **population** 88m (1983), **capital** Islamabad.

' Independent republic; underdeveloped agricultural country. Pakistan came into existence on 15 August 1947 when the former British Indian Empire split up into two independent countries, India and Pakistan, which became separate dominions. In 1956 the country was proclaimed a republic, the Islamic Republic of Pakistan. Until 1971 the country was divided into two large provinces, separated by more than 1,600 km of India. East Pakistan became independent of West Pakistan (with Indian assistance) on 26 March 1971, and became the independent Republic of Bangladesh. In 1972 Pakistan left the Commonwealth. The former Indian stamp-issuing states of Las Bela, Scinde and Bahawalpur are incorporated into the territory of present-day Pakistan. Indirect UPU membership from 1 July 1876 (British India); direct from 10 November 1947.

From 1947 Indian stamps with the overprint 'PAKISTAN', and in 1948 definitives inscribed 'PAKISTAN'. Occasionally since 1956 stamps have been issued inscribed 'ISLAMIC REPUBLIC OF PAKISTAN'. The name of the country is given in Arabic, English and formerly also Urdu. The first pictorials were recess-printed in Great Britain. Subsequently, other printers and other techniques were employed. The designs are strongly Muslim (art, history and religion), but in recent years there has been participation in international issues. Artistically, some issues are outstanding, particularly stamps designed by Rashid ud Din, while others are merely reproductions of photographic concepts. Annual output at the present time ranges from 10 to 40 stamps.

Philatelic bureau The Manager, Philatelic Bureau, GPO, Karachi.

PALESTINE
Turkish territory until 1918, then occupied by the British and Egyptian armies and entrusted to Great Britain as a mandate in 1920. This continued until 1948 (**area** 27,100 sq.km, **capital** Jerusalem). At that time, the Jewish state of Israel was formed on Palestinian territory, and at the same time the first Arab-Jewish war (1948–9) broke out. Israel added further occupied territories to its own territory, as did Transjordan (renamed Jordan in 1950) and Egypt, which occupied Gaza and proclaimed it a territory of a future Arab Palestine.

Until Turkey entered the First World War, the stamps of the individual post offices of the Levant were valid in Palestinian territory, otherwise Turkish stamps until 1918. Next came stamps of the occupying British army (Egyptian Expeditionary Force) which are inscribed 'E.E.F.' but do not bear the name of the territory. When the British Mandate came into existence in 1920 these stamps were given the overprint 'PALESTINE' (in English and Arabic), and this was, in fact, the beginning of the country's own stamp issuing. A total of 73 + 20 stamps, mostly overprinted provisionals, and only 2 definitive issues. The 1927 set remained in circulation for 21 years. The name of the territory is tri-lingual, in English, Hebrew and Arabic. In 1948 Israeli stamps went into circulation on part of the Palestine territory. From 1948 to 1950 the overprint of 'PALESTINE' (in English and Arabic) appeared on Jordanian stamps: a total of 33 overprinted provisionals. From 1948 the overprint of 'PALESTINE' (in English and Arabic) appeared on Egyptian stamps, issued for the Gaza strip: a total of 93 + 7 stamps until 1958, including airmail sets, all overprinted provisionals. Such issues continued after 1958 on stamps of the United Arab Republic – Egypt (part of a short-lived UAR which included Syria), again with the overprint 'PALESTINE', followed by definitive and commemorative stamps as issued in Egypt but in changed colours and additionally inscribed 'PALESTINE': a total of 79 + 7 stamps running into printings of 250,000. The issue of these special stamps continued until 1967, when the Gaza strip was occupied by Israeli forces.

PATIALA
Indian Convention state (**area** 15,393 sq.km, **capital** Patiala) in the Punjab, under British influence from 1809.

From 1884 Indian stamps with the overprint 'PUTTIALLA STATE', later 'PATIALA STATE': a total of 109 + 76 stamps, all overprinted provisionals. Their validity ended on 1 January 1951, Indian stamps having been introduced on 1 April 1950.

PEKING
In the years 1917–19 the Italian post office in Chinese territory used Italian stamps with the

overprint 'PECHINO' or 'Pechino': a total of 31 + 12 stamps, which were said to be for the Italian soldiers in Russian captivity to facilitate postal links with their homeland. These overprints, however, include postage-due and express stamps, some of which were sold only at philatelic counters in Rome, so that they could not serve a postal function. The demand of the collector's market clearly played a major role here.

PENANG
Area 1,036 sq.km, **capital** Penang. Member state of the Malaysian Federation since 1963, comprising the island of Penang in the Straits of Malacca (285 sq.km) and the territory of Wellesley on the Malayan peninsula (745 sq.km).

The British settled on the island in 1786, and on the mainland in 1800. In 1826 Penang came under the administration of the British East India Company and became part of the Straits Settlements colony — a Crown colony after 1867. In 1941–5 it was occupied by the Japanese, and in 1945 by the British army. Colonial status was terminated in 1946, and from 1948 Penang became part of the Malayan Union, and in 1957–63 a member of the Independent Malayan Federation. In 1965 the Malay name 'PULAU PINANG' was introduced. UPU membership (indirect as Malacca and Penang) from 1 April 1877 (Straits Settlements — British colony); direct as Malayan Federation from 17 January 1958; direct as Malaysia from 16 September 1963.

From 1948 definitive issues with 'PENANG' and 'MALAYA'; from 1965 the Malay name 'PULAU PINANG' was used with the addition of 'MALAYSIA'. Most of the designs are common to the British and Malayan issues for the region. Stamps are not issued every year, and only in limited quantities. In the territory of Penang there are also stamps of the Malaysian (formerly Malayan) Federation, and all the stamps of the member states of the Federation are valid. Likewise, Penang stamps can be used in the whole territory of the Federation.

In 1942, during the Japanese occupation. Straits Settlements stamps appeared with the overprint 'DAI NIPPON PENANG', to be used in Penang and Province Wellesley: a total of 13 stamps of doubtful postal usage.

PERAK
Area 20,668 sq.km **capital** Ipoh. Member state of the Malaysian Federation since 1963.

From 1873 a British protectorate; from 1895 one of the Federated Malay States. In 1941–5 occupied by the Japanese, and in 1945 by the British army. In 1948 part of Malayan Union; in 1957–63 in the Independent Malayan Federation, then Malaysia. Indirect UPU membership (Negri Sembilan, Penang, Perak and Selangor) from 1 April 1915 (Federated Malay States, British colony); direct from 17 January 1958 (Malayan Federation); direct from 16 September 1963 (Malaysia).

From 1878 stamps of the Straits Settlements with the overprint of a star and half-moon and the letter 'P'; later, the overprint 'PERAK'. This name then appeared on the definitive issues from 1891. From 1900 to 1935 stamps of the Federated Malay States were in use. From 1935 issuing was renewed with 'PERAK' and 'MALAYA', later changed to 'MALAYSIA'. All the stamps were of British origin, and there were numerous overprinted provisionals. Designs were those common to the British or Malayan issue of the region. In 1942–5 Perak stamps appeared with overprints of the occupying Japanese postal authorities: a total of 45 stamps, all overprinted provisionals, some limited in number to 47 complete sets, which encouraged speculation. From 1945 issues of the British Military Administration in *Malaya*; from 1948 renewed individual issues. Malaysian (formerly Malayan) stamps are in circulation on the territory of Perak, and all the stamps of the other member states of the Federation are valid here and vice versa.

PERLIS
Area 803 sq.km, **capital** Kangar. Member state of the Malaysian Federation since 1963.

Until 1909 under Siamese domination, then British protectorate as an Unfederated Malay State until the 1941 occupation by Japan. In 1943 ceded to Thailand by Japan and in 1945 occupied by the British army. From 1948 part of the Malayan Union; in

1957–63 in the independent Malayan Federation. UPU membership: indirect (Kedah, Kelantan, and Perlis) from 1 January 1916 (Unfederated Malay States, British colony); direct from 17 January 1958 (Malayan Federation); direct from 16 September 1963 (Malaysia).

In view of its small area and limited number of inhabitants Perlis, unlike the other Malayan states, originally did not issue its own stamps, using those of the neighbouring state of Kedah. Independent stamp issuing began in 1948, and in 1951 definitive stamps with the name 'PERLIS' and, in addition, 'MALAYA', later 'MALAYSIA'. Infrequent new issues. Production is British, mostly in designs common to the British and Malayan issues of the region. The stamps of Malaysia are in circulation in Perlis, including those of all the member states of the Federation, and vice versa.

PERSIA

The modern Persian empire arose at the turn of the 16th to 17th century, and during the 19th and the 20th centuries the country was gradually divided into spheres of British and Russian influence. In 1905 a constitutional state came into existence. The old name of Persia was replaced by the new name of Iran on 22 March 1935.

From 1870 definitive stamps in symbolic designs or with portraits of the monarch, first without the name in Latin script, later with 'POSTE PERSANE', 'POSTES PERSANES': a total of 648 + 98 stamps issued until 1935. Until the end of the last century most stamps were designed and produced in foreign printing houses. This was followed by a period of overprinted provisionals, among them occasional pictorial stamps and further portrait issues, most of which kept to the classic conception of Persian stamps. Some of the provisionals were in very limited printings, e.g. in 1909 a provisional issue of only 500 stamps, and in 1927 provisional airmail stamps, some values being restricted to only 600. After 1935 see *Iran*.

In 1867–1923 the Indian post offices in Persia used Indian stamps.

PHILIPPINES

Area 300,000 sq.km, **population** 51.95m (1983), **capital** Manila.

Developing agricultural country, independent since 4 July 1946. In 1571–1898 under Spanish domination; then there was an uprising, followed from 1899 by American domination, and in 1941–4 Japanese occupation, during which a puppet government was set up in the Philippines in 1943. Indirect UPU membership from 1 June 1877 (Spanish colony); indirect from 11 April 1899 (USA); direct as from 1 January 1922.

The first stamps with the name 'FILIPINAS' appeared in 1872. Before this, from 1854, stamps of Spanish origin had existed, but without the name of the country. In 1898–9 definitive stamps of the revolutionary government with the same name. After American occupation in 1899 American stamps with the overprint 'PHILIPPINES'; later definitives inscribed 'PHILIPPINE ISLANDS' and the additional 'UNITED STATES OF AMERICA'. From 1935 when the Philippines were granted greater autonomy, the name on the stamps was changed to 'COMMONWEALTH OF THE PHILIPPINES'. In 1942–4, during the Japanese occupation, there were stamps with a Japanese text, then with the name as 'PILIPINAS' or 'REPUBLIKA NG PILIPINAS'. After the gaining of independence in 1946 again 'PHILIPPINES', 'REPUBLIC OF THE PHILIPPINES'; from 1962 again 'PILIPINAS', occasionally also 'FILIPINAS'.

In the first period, Philippine stamps were printed in Spain (and the designs conformed with contemporary Spanish colonial issues: portraits and symbolic designs). Under American influence the islands finally found their own original form of expression. Printing is now done by various world stamp printers. The designs are largely based on national propaganda and appear in issues of many millions, an exception being a 1926 set of airmail stamps of which only 500 were produced. Present production 20–30 stamps annually, most of them pictorials.

Philatelic bureau Postal Fiscal Service Chief, Stamp and Philatelic Section, Bureau of Posts, Manila.

POONCH
Feudatory state (**area** 4,214 sq.km, **capital** Poonch) in India; vassal state of Kashmir.

In 1876 primitive definitive issues appeared without any Latin script: a total of 12 + 5 stamps of symbolic design until 1894, when India took over the postal services.

PORT ARTHUR AND DAIREN (KWANTUNG)
Territory in the south-western Liaodong peninsula in north-eastern China (**area** 3,463 sq.km, **capital** Lüda): once called Port-Arthur and Dairen. In 1898–1905 leased to Russia, then to Japan until 1945. In 1945–52 under the joint administration of the USSR and China, since then part of the Chinese province of Liao-ning.

From 1946 overprints on Japanese and Manchurian stamps, then definitives with a Chinese text: a total of 83 stamps until 1950.

PORTUGUESE INDIA
Three small territories on the coast of India, occupied by the Portuguese from the 16th century. (1) Diu Island and the mainland territory of Gogola and Simlor (38 sq.km). (2) Damao (Daman) with the territory of Dadra and Naga-Aveli (545 sq.km). (3) Gôa with the islands of Angedova, Sao Jorge and Morceges (3,370 sq.km). **Total area** 3,953 sq.km **capital** Vila Nova da Gôa. On 18–19 December 1961 Indian troops occupied this area and incorporated it into India.

In 1871 definitive stamps with 'INDIA PORT.' (or 'PORTUGUEZA'); from 1946 also 'ESTADO DA INDIA': a total of 590 + 83 stamps of Portuguese origin with a number of designs common to the Portuguese stamp issue region, overprinted provisionals mainly at the time when the Portuguese Republic came into being. After the Second World War there was a trend towards pictorial stamps, largely concerned with local social and religious history. The influence of the speculator's market is reflected in low issues, particularly in the early period. Recently, printings of 150,000–200,000 are normal. In 1962 Portugal had prepared an issue for release (in common with other Portuguese territories), but these were not issued in Portuguese India. Stamps of Portuguese India were taken off sale on 28 December 1961, but remained valid for use until 7 January 1962.

PRIAMUR DISTRICT
When the Red Army took Nikolayevsk during the Russian Civil War the Priamur territory was occupied by the Japanese in 1921. In May they set up a White Russian government which, towards the end of the year, under General Diterichs, began operations against the Far Eastern Republic. It occupied a large part of the territory but with the withdrawal of the Japanese army the whole region was taken over by the Red Army and a Far Eastern Republic was established once again.

In April 1921 a set of 24 Russian stamps was issued with the Cyrillic overprint 'N na A/PVP' ('Nikolayevsk na Amure / Priamurskoye Vremennoye Pravityelstvo'), and the following year seized stamps of the *Far Eastern Republic* with the overprints 'V P P' ('Vremennoye Priamurskoye Pravityelstvo') and 'PRIAM.ZEMSKIJ KRAJ'. The same overprint occurred later on Russian stamps and those of the Central Siberian Kolchak Army, always in Cyrillic script (a total of 31 values). The postal use of these stamps has not been fully clarified.

QATAR
Area 11,437 sq.km, **population** over 260,000 (1982), **capital** Doha.

Sheikhdom under British protection from 1916, independent since 1971. Major oil producing country, insignificant agriculture; UPU membership (indirect) from 11 May 1950 (British post office); direct from 31 January 1969.

Before special Qatar stamps were introduced, British stamps, were used with currency overprints (see *Muscat and Oman*). From 1957 British stamps with the overprint 'QATAR', later definitives with the same name. From 1971 'STATE OF QATAR'. Annual output amounts to about 50 different stamps, issued in relatively small numbers but mainly for the collector's market (16,000 sets). The subjects include common international issues and general subjects on pictorial stamps. Postal use is limited.

Philatelic bureau The Director, Philatelic Bureau, Department of Posts, Doha. **Trade sales** Inter-Governmental Philatelic Corporation.

QU'AITI

One of the Aden states, from 1965 South Arabian Protectorate; capital, Mukalla. From 1967 part of the South Yemen People's Republic.

From 1942 definitive stamps with 'QU'AITI STATE OF SHIHR AND MUKALLA' and the heading 'ADEN'. Until 1952 a total of 28 stamps of British origin, characteristic pictorial issues engraved and printed in Great Britain. From 1955 the name changed to 'QU'AITI STATE IN HADRAMAUT' and the heading 'SOUTH ARABIA' instead of 'ADEN': a total of 59 stamps including commemorative issues released at infrequent intervals. After 1967 see *South Yemen*.

RAJASTHAN

Union of 14 feudatory Indian states (**area** 337,236 sq.km, **capital** Jaipur) set up in June 1947 in north-western India to ensure the better administration and maintenance of the monarchic form of government. Three state members, Bundi, Jaipur and Kishangarh, continued to issue their own stamps, although co-operating in postal matters. In 1950 Rajasthan became a state in the Indian Union.

In 1949 the existing stamps of the states of Bundi, Jaipur and Kishangarh were given overprints validating them for use in Rajasthan, but only one issue (Jaipur) bears the name of Rajasthan overprinted in Latin script. The postal use of these issues was very limited, some stamps not being listed in the standard catalogues.

RAJPIPLA

Feudatory state (**area** 3,933 sq.km, **capital** Nandad) in western India. In 1880, 3 definitive stamps of symbolic character and without any identifying features in Latin script were issued. Replaced by Indian stamps in 1886.

RAS AL-KHAIMA

One of the former Trucial States on the coast of the Persian Gulf (**area** 1,625 sq.km, **capital** Ras al-Khaima), with territory stretching far inland and divided into two parts by the narrow promontory of Fujeira. Since 14 February 1972 part of the United Arab Emirates.

From 1964 definitive stamps with 'RAS AL KHAIMA': a total of 617 + 6 stamps of British origin. The first issue adopted a design of the seven palms from the stamps of the British-controlled Trucial States. Very frequent issues with little postal demand but more than adequate stocks for the collector's market. From 1967 to 1972, the constant flow of thematic sets and miniature sheets and frequent high value airmail stamps for which there was no commercial demand has resulted in these issues not being fully catalogued, as their postal use was virtually nil. Stamp issuing ceased when Ras al-Khaima became part of the United Arab Emirates, which set up their own postal authorities in 1972.

RIAU-LINGGA ARCHIPELAGO

Indonesian islands of Riau and Lingga off the eastern coast of Sumatra, south of Singapore (**area** 8,100 sq.km, **capital** Tangjungpinang on the island of Bintan).

Between 1954 and 1960 a total of 40 Indonesian stamps with the overprint 'RIAU', all overprinted provisionals. The stamps were valid on the islands of Riau and Lingga and were sold for Singapore currency. The stamps were withdrawn in 1965 following the revaluation of the Indonesian rupiah.

RIZEH (RIZE)

Town in northern Turkey on the shores of the Black Sea. Nine Russian stamps with the overprint 'Rizeh' were issued for the Russian post office, which closed down in 1914.

ROUAD ISLAND

Small island on the coast of Syria to the south of the town of Tartus. In the First World War this was the first place on the Syrian coast to be occupied by the French (1915) In 1916 they opened a post office which issued a total of 16 stamps of the French Levant with the overprint 'ILE ROUAD'. In 1920 the island became part of the French Mandate of Alaouites and later Syria, the stamps of which came into use in 1923.

RYUKYU ISLANDS (OKINAWA)

A group of islands of strategic importance (**area** 2,196 sq.km, **capital** Naha), particularly in the case of Okinawa; Japanese territory under US administration from 1945 until 1952, when part autonomy was granted. In 1972 the islands were given back to Japan.

From 1948 own issues; prior to that date Japanese stamps and various provisionals. Later the stamps bore the name 'RYUKYUS' in Latin script: a total of 249 stamps of Japanese origin but differing in appearance from Japanese stamps in that the graphic work is of a more exacting standard. Mainly nationalistic designs but also general themes. At first printings were limited to approximately 200,000, but later printings were up to 1,000,000. From 1972 Japanese stamps have been in use.

SABAH

Area 76,115 sq.km, **capital** Kota Kinabula. Member state of the Malaysian Federation since 1963.

Before this, until 31 August 1963, the area was the autonomous British colony of Sabah, previously known as *North Borneo*. Indirect UPU membership (North Borneo – Sabah) from 1 February 1891 as British colony; direct as of 16 September 1963 (Federation of Malaysia).

In 1964 North Borneo stamps with the overprint 'SABAH'. The following definitive issues bore the same inscription with the addition of 'MALAYSIA'. New issues are infrequent. Malaysian stamps are valid in the territory of Sabah and those of all the individual states of the Federation, and **vice versa.**

SARAWAK

Area 124,967 sq.km, **capital** Kuching. Member state of the Malaysian Federation since 1963.

Until 1840 part of the sultanate of Brunei. In 1841 the English officer James Brooke acquired the north of the country (originally some 19,000 sq.km) and set up the independent state of Sarawak with himself as rajah. Further territory was added in 1861, 1882 and 1884. In 1888 Brooke accepted the status of a British Protectorate. In 1941–5 Sarawak was occupied by the Japanese, in 1945 by the British army, and in 1946 it became a British Crown Colony (until 1963). Indirect UPU membership from 1 July 1897 (British colony); direct as of 16 September 1963 (Federation of Malaysia).

In 1869 definitive issues with the name 'SARAWAK', Indian stamps having been in use previously. Until UPU membership was granted, all foreign mail bore stamps of the Straits Settlements. The stamps were of British origin, although they were not at first printed by firms specializing in stamp printing. As a result the conception differed from normal British colonial issues. A number of pictorial stamps and designs common to the British Empire characterize the subsequent period from 1946. Japan occupied Sarawak in 1941, and Sarawak stamps were valid until the end of 1942, although in the course of that year, the stamps bore a Japanese overprint reading (in translation) 'Imperial Japanese Government'. The issues of the subsequent British military administration (1945–6) were the pre-war issues overprinted 'B.M.A.'. At the present, Sarawak does not issue stamps every year. Since 1965 Sarawak stamps have borne the name 'MALAYSIA' as well as Sarawak. Malaysian stamps are valid in Sarawak territory, and so are the stamps of the other member states of the Federation, and vice versa.

SAUDI ARABIA
Area 2,400,900 sq.km, **population** 9.68m (1982), **capital** Riyadh.

Undeveloped agricultural and pastoral country with extremely important oil drilling. Came into existence on 29 September 1932 when Nejd and Hejaz and dependent territories were renamed the Kingdom of Saudi Arabia. In 1964 part of the neutral territory of Wafra was added. Indirect UPU membership as Hejaz from 1 July 1875 (Turkey); direct from 1 January 1927 as Kingdom of Hejaz and Nejd and dependencies; transferred to Saudi Arabia on 1 June 1934.

In 1934 definitive stamps with the French inscription 'ROYAUME DE L'ARABIE SOU-DITE', then '. . . SAOUDITE'. Later the English version 'KINGDOM OF SAUDI ARABIA', appeared and, finally, only 'SAUDI ARABIA' or 'ARABIE SOUDITE' in addition to the Arabic text. From 1975 the abbreviation 'K.S.A' has been used in conjunction with Arabic texts. Stamps are of local and Egyptian origin, the influence of the latter being evident in the designs of pictorial issues. Propaganda permeates many designs, though in symbolic rather than pictorial form. At the present time 10–30 stamps appear each year.

Philatelic bureau Philatelic Service, General Post Office, Riyadh.

SAURASHTRA
The United State of Saurashtra was formed from 31 Indian states and 191 smaller estates in 1948 on the Kathiawar peninsula in western India (**area** 54,760 sq.km, **capital** Rajkot). Former stamp-issuing states were Saurashtra (Soruth), Jasdan and Morwi, Nawanagar and Wadhwan. The United State of Saurashtra existed until 1956. It is not to be confused with Saurashtra-Surat to the south of the Kathiawar peninsula, which is only part of this larger state. In 1949, the 1929 Saurashtra pictorials and court fee stamps of Bhavnagar were overprinted and surcharged for use in Junagarh when that state joined the Union: a total of 11 overprinted provisionals. Indian stamps went into use in 1950.

SCINDE
Province in north-western British India, from 1947 part of the territory of Pakistan (**area** 125,150 sq.km, **capital** Karachi). British from 1850. Sir Bartle Frere, who became the first ruler of Scinde, developed the local 'dawk' (postal system) in which runners were used to transport the mail, and introduced the first postage stamps on Indian territory in 1852.

In 1852 a definitive issue of 3 stamps made by embossing, circular in shape with the text 'SCINDE DISTRICT DAWK'. They are considered a rare classical issue. They were in use until 30 September 1854. As from 1 October of that year the first general issue of Indian stamps came into existence, issued by the East India Company.

SELANGOR
Area 8,203 sq.km, **capital** Shah Alam. Member state of the Malaysian Federation since 1963.

British Protectorate from 1874 and, from 1895, one of the Federated Malay States. In 1941–5 occupied by Japan; in 1945 by the British army. From 1948 part of the Malayan Union, in 1957–63 in the independent Malayan Federation. Indirect UPU membership from 1 April 1915 (Negri Sembilan, Pahang, Perak and Selangor as Federated Malay States, British colony); direct from 17 January 1958 (Malayan Federation); direct as of 16 September 1963 (Malaysia).

In 1878 a 2c. brown stamp of the Straits Settlements with the overprint of a star and crescent and the letter 'S'. This is thought to be Selangor's first stamp. In 1881 stamps of the Straits Settlements appeared with the overprint 'SELANGOR', followed in the same year by definitive issues which, from 1935, had in addition 'MALAYA'; later, 'PERSEKUTUAN TANAH MELAYU' and, lastly, 'MALAYSIA'. All issues of British origin (apart from the overprinted provisionals), in designs common to others of Malaya. Separate issues for Selangor were interrupted in the years 1900–35 when the stamps of the Federated Malay States were valid in the territory, and again during the Japanese occupation when issues of the Japanese authorities were in circulation (from 1942–5) with a number of overprinted provisionals, until the British occupation. The stamps of Selangor began to be issued again only in 1948. The stamps of *Malaysia* (*Malaya*) are now in circulation in Selangor, and those of the other states of the Federation are equally valid there, and vice versa.

SHAN STATE
At the time of the Japanese occupation, the semi-autonomous puppet Shan State was formed in 1943 in the territory of Burma under Japanese administration (**area** 149,744 sq.km, **capital** Taund'i), but on 24 december 1943 it was incorporated into the newly-formed Burmese puppet state under Japanese aegis.

In 1943-7 stamps appeared with a Japanese text including the name of 'SHAN' which, however, was not given in Latin script. The stamps were based on Japanese stamp designs and were printed in the Netherlands East Indies, then occupied by the Japanese. After the establishment of the all-Burma puppet government these stamps were given the overprint 'BURMA STATE' (in Burmese) and were valid in the entire territory of Burma.

SHANGHAI
Foreign traders in Shanghai urged the Municipal Council to set up an official local post in place of the very expensive private Min Chu services. In 1864 the Council set up a local post office to which participants paid an annual subscription, but the public were able to buy stamps for their own use when posting letters. Agencies of the Shanghai Local Post Office eventually opened in sixteen Chinese cities before the service was, in 1898, taken over by the Imperial Chinese postal authorities.

From 1865 definitive issues with 'SHANGHAI' and at times, additionally, 'L.P.O.' (meaning local post office): a total of 113 + 18 stamps, mostly of British origin and printed by Nissen and Parker of London, who were not specialist stamp printers. The main design feature throughout is a Chinese dragon. There are numerous overprinted and surcharged provisionals. In 1897 Chinese stamps were introduced.

Seven foreign post offices were in operation in Shanghai, some until the end of 1922: Great Britain, France, Germany, Italy, Russia, Japan and the USA. All used the stamps of their respective countries. The American post office used American stamps with the overprint 'SHANGHAI CHINA' from 1919 to 22: a total of 18 overprinted provisionals.

SHANSI
Chinese province (**area** 157,100 sq.km, **capital** Yangku) in Northern China, once the 'model province'. In 1937–45 occupied by the Japanese, but the scene of guerilla warfare. Units of Red China occupied it in 1948–9.

In 1941 Chinese stamps with the Chinese overprint, 'For Shansi', and no Latin script at all: a total of 55 stamps, all overprinted provisionals, were issued until 1942.

SHANTUNG
Chinese province (**area** 153,300 sq.km, **capital** Tsi-nan) in Northern China, occupied by Japan 1937–45 and by units of Red China in 1948.

In 1941–2 a total of 55 overprinted provisionals on Chinese stamps with the Chinese text 'Shantung', and no Latin script at all.

SHARJAH
Since 1971 part of the United Arab Emirates (**area** 2,600 sq.km, **capital** Sharjah). The more important of the countries of the former Trucial States on the coast of the Persian Gulf with three dependencies on the Oman coast: Dibba, Khor Fakkan and Kalba.

Stamp issuing from 1963 to 1972; definitive issues with 'SHARJAH' to which sometimes '& DEPENDENCIES' was added. A rough total of 1,000 stamps, a third of these airmails. There are no reliable data on exact production, a fact that characterizes the issuing policy of the sheikhdoms carried out through an agency. This large output of stamps could not be justified by postal demand, and was a blatant attempt to supply the collector's market. Perforated and imperforate issues, low printings (at times no more than 5,000 of a stamp), printing on gold foil and other 'gimmicky' issues. The pictorial issues were colourful and attractive to the young collector. In 1973 stamps of the United Arab Emirates were introduced.

SIAM

Kingdom from the 1880s (**area** 514,521 sq.km, **capital** Bangkok), a buffer state between the colonial empires of Great Britain and France, whereby it managed to keep its independence even though the two Great Powers took away many of its provinces. In 1939 the name was officially changed to Thailand; in 1946 the name of Siam was re-introduced, but since 1949 it has again become *Thailand*. During the Second World War an ally of the Japanese, who ceded to it part of occupied Malaya, Laos and Cambodia, which Siam had lost in the years 1902–9.

From 1883 definitive royal portrait stamps which originally did not bear the name of the country in Latin script; only after joining the UPU in 1885 did the name 'SIAM' appear on the stamps, and remained until 1939 when 'Thailand' came into use until 1946. In 1947 Siam appeared once again, with official reversion in 1949 to Thailand. A total of 273 stamps produced by British, German and other printers in designs of local origin and character. Apart from a considerable number of overprinted provisionals there then appeared definitive stamps, mainly illustrating national religious and political monuments and scenes. Many of the early overprinted provisionals were issued in very limited printings of 500, especially in the years 1918–20. From 1949 see *Thailand*.

SINGAPORE

Area 618 sq.km, **population** 2.5m (1983), **capital** Singapore.

Since 9 August 1965 an internally self-governing state; a republic within the British Commonwealth from 28 December 1965. Important trading port with the largest rubber exchange in the world, and the biggest tin smelting plant. The English settled here in 1819, and in 1826 Singapore became one of the Straits Settlements administered by the East India Company. From 1836 it was the administrative centre. In 1907–12 the island of Labuan belonged to Singapore. After the Japanese occupation of 1942–5 (when it was called Shonan), it was separate from British Malaya in 1946 and constituted as a separated Crown Colony with its dependencies of Christmas Island (until 1958) and the Cocos (Keeling) Islands (until 1955). In 1959 it was given internal autonomy and regarded as a state, proclaiming its independence on 31 August 1963. As a state it entered the Malaysian Federation on 16 September 1963, but left it in 1965. Indirect UPU membership from 1 January 1877 (Straits Settlements, British colony); indirect from 16 September 1963 (Malaysia); direct from 8 January 1966.

From 1948 definitive issues with 'SINGAPORE' and 'MALAYA' followed by just 'SINGAPORE' or 'STATE OF SINGAPORE'. The stamps, commemorating the first anniversary (1966) of the republic, bear the inscription 'REPUBLIC OF SINGAPORE'. All inscriptions are in English. Most stamps are of British design and origin although recent issues have employed local designers, and printing has been done in Japan and Austria as well as in Britain and Singapore itself. Many designs are based on national propaganda (e.g. since 1960 stamps are issued annually for National Day). The present production amounts to 15–20 stamps annually and demonstrates efforts towards progressive artistic treatment.

While Singapore was a member of the Malaysian Federation the stamps of Malaysia and Malaya and those of all the member states of the Federation were valid in the territory of Singapore, and Singapore stamps were valid throughout the Federation. Postage-due stamps of the Malayan Postal Union were valid in Singapore until 31 January 1968, that is, longer than in Malaysia itself.

Philatelic bureau Postal Services Dept., Singapore. **Trade sales** Crown Agents' Stamp Bureau; Inter-Governmental Philatelic Corporation.

SINKIANG

Province in North-Western China (**area** 1,646,800 sq.km, **capital** Urumchi). Until about 1911 the province had only official courier routes, for example to Kulji, where, on the basis of a Russian-Chinese treaty, a postal exchange station existed as early as 1851. In 1911 the Imperial Chinese Post Offices were introduced in this territory.

From 1915 Chinese stamps with a Chinese overprint of the name of the province. These were necessary because of heavy currency devaluation in the province, stamps with the overprint only being valid in Sinkiang. Issuing continued until 1945, all overprinted provisionals (a total of 199 stamps) followed by stamps of *North-Western China*.

SIRMOOR

Feudatory state (**area** 2,826 sq.km, **capital** Nahan) in the Punjab in north-western India.

From 1879 definitive stamps with 'SIRMOOR STATE': a total of 19 + 16 stamps, both of primitive native designs and with good portrait printing. On one of the issues an elephant is depicted. The stamps of India were introduced in 1902.

SMYRNA

Town and port on the Turkish coast of the Aegean Sea. Until 1914 foreign post offices were in operation here. In 1919 Smyrna was occupied by the Greek army and from there, in 1920, it opened its attack on inland Turkey. The terms of the peace treaty of Sèvres, in 1920, allocated Smyrna to Greece for five years, but the Turks occupied it in 1922.

From 1909 until 1914 the Russian post office used Russian stamps with the overprint 'Smyrne': a total of 9 overprinted provisionals. The Italian post office issued a total of 8 Italian stamps with the overprint 'Smirne' or 'SMIRNE' and surcharged in Turkish currency in 1909. In 1922 the Italian post office issued a further 5 overprinted and surcharged provisionals for the intended re-opening of its post office in Smyrna, but in view of the occupation of the town by the Turks these stamps were sold only at philatelic counters in Turin. They could not fulfil any postal function and cannot, therefore, be regarded as true postage stamps.

SORUTH (SAURASHTRA)

Feudatory state (**area** 8,643 sq.km, **capital** Junagadh) on the Kathiawar peninsula in western India. The name of Junagadh would be more correct for the entire state.

Own stamps from 1864, first with the inscription in Devanagari; from 1877 in Latin script reading 'SORUTH'; from 1923 'SOURASHTRA' and from 1929 'SAURASHTRA'. Stamp issuing continued until 1949 when the stamps of the United State of Saurashtra (see *Saurashtra*) took over. A total of 45 stamps.

SOUTH ARABIAN FEDERATION

Territory of 17 small South Arabian countries in the Protectorate of Aden including Aden (**area** 61,894 sq.km, **capital** Ittihad), which in 1963 adopted this name. From 1959 it had been known, on a smaller scale, as the Federation of South Arabian Emirates. The Federation broke up on 30 November 1967 when the South Yemen People's Republic was formed from it and from the South Arabian Protectorate.

In 1963, 2 Red Cross centenary stamps were issued, followed in 1965 by definitive stamps with the name 'FEDERATION OF SOUTH ARABIA' and further commemoratives until 1966: a total of 29 stamps of British origin. From 1968 see *South Yemen*.

SOUTH CHINA

Territory of the provinces of Kwangtung and Kwangsi (**area** 451,800 sq.km, **capital** Canton), from 1950 part of the Chinese People's Republic.

In the years 1949–50 a total of 23 stamps, most of them overprinted provisionals, but also definitives issued for South China, which did not bear the name in Latin script. In 1938–45 during the Japanese occupation see *Kwangtung*.

SOUTH KOREA see KOREAN REPUBLIC

SOUTH VIETNAM (REPUBLIC OF VIETNAM)

From 26 October 1955 to 20 April 1975 republic with the official name of the Republic of Vietnam (**area** 170,806 sq.km, **capital** Saigon).

Agricultural country, south of the 17th parallel. In 1960 the National Liberation Front was set up here which took over the whole of South Vietnam in 1975 (South Vietnamese Republic). The union of North and South Vietnam into the *Vietnamese Socialist Republic* took place in 1976.

After issues for the *Vietnamese Democratic Republic,* when the government withdrew to the northern regions of Vietnam, the stamps of French Indochina were valid in the territory controlled by the French army. From 1951 definitive issues with the text 'VIET-NAM BUU-CHINH' (Vietnamese Post), printed mostly in France and Great Britain. These stamps were until 1954 valid also in the northern parts of Vietnam controlled by the French (e.g. Hanoi): a total of 37 stamps with propaganda subjects in pictorial, portrait and symbolic designs. After the establishment of the republic, issuing continued under the same name, but from 1956 the stamps were given a new text 'VIET-NAM CONG-HOA BUU-CHINH' (Cong-hoa = republic; Buu-chinh = post): a total of 492 + 24 stamps. Printed in various techniques in different foreign printing houses (often France), but they were mostly designed by local artists and reflected national characteristics. The subjects are largely propaganda for the country, often expressed in symbolic form. Printings range around 1 million of each stamp. With the military defeat of 1975 the existence of the country as a stamp-issuing territory came to an end.

SOUTH VIETNAM – N.L.F. ISSUES

From 1960 the National Liberation Front of South Vietnam was active in the territory of the Vietnamese Republic, known also as South Vietnam, and from 1961 it had a regular army at its disposal. In 1966 it controlled four-fifths of the total territory, and in 1969 established a provisional government of the South Vietnamese Republic, taking over the whole of South Vietnam on 30 April 1975. From 2 July 1976 part of the *Vietnamese Socialist Republic.*

From 1963 definitive issues with the wording 'MAT-TRAN DAN-TOC GIAIPHONG MIEN-NAM VIET-NAM' (National Liberation Front of South Vietnam), printed in the Vietnamese Democratic Republic and using its currency. In 1970 the inscription became 'CONG HOA MIEN NAM VIET NAM (Republic of South Vietnam).

SOUTH-WEST CHINA

The territory of the provinces of Szechwan, Sikang, Yunnan and Kweichow (**area** 1,209,200 sq.km, **capital** Chungking); from 1949, part of the Chinese People's Republic.

In 1949–50 a total of 61 + 3 stamps, most of them overprinted provisionals, issued for South-West China. None of the stamps had any Latin script in the designs.

SOUTH YEMEN

Area 287,683 sq.km, **population** 2.09m (1982), **capital** Aden.

Under-developed pastoral and agricultural country. Came into existence on 30 November 1967 after the withdrawal of the British from the South Arabian Federation and the South Arabian Protectorate, which comprised the stamp-issuing territories of Qu'aiti, Kathiri, Mahra and Upper Yafa. After the proclamation of a new constitution in October 1970 the country was re-named Yemen People's Democratic Republic (not to be confused with the Yemen Arab Republic – see *Yemen*). Indirect UPU membership from 1 July 1876 (British India); indirect from 1 April 1937 (British colony); direct from 28 June 1968.

In 1967 overprinted provisionals on stamps of the South Arabian Federation, with wording in Arabic and Latin script, 'PEOPLE'S DEMOCRATIC REPUBLIC OF SOUTHERN YE-MEN'; from 1971, 'PEOPLE'S DEMOCRATIC REPUBLIC OF YEMEN'. Designs mainly concerned with national interests. Annual output about 10 stamps.

Philatelic bureau GPO, Aden. **Trade supplies** Crown Agents' Stamp Bureau.

SRI LANKA
Area 65,610 sq.km, **population** 15.19m (1982), **capital** Colombo.

Republic since 1972, when the name of *Ceylon* was replaced by that of Sri Lanka. Member of the Commonwealth. Indirect UPU membership from 1 April 1877 until 1948 (British colony); direct from 13 July 1949.

The first stamps with the name Sri Lanka appeared in 1972. The stamp design followed up the previous Ceylonese production. Stamp issuing is limited to about 10 stamps a year, with a stress on national events and postal anniversaries.

Philatelic bureau The Director, Philatelic Bureau, P T Department, Colombo. **Trade sales** Crown Agents' Stamp Bureau; Inter-Governmental Philatelic Corporation.

STRAITS SETTLEMENTS
British colony on the Malayan peninsula on the Strait of Malacca (**area** 3,716 sq.km, **capital** Singapore). Established in 1826 out of the scattered British enclaves under the administration of the East India Company: Penang, Wellesley, Dindings, Malacca and Singapore, with the dependencies of the Cocos Islands until 1955, Christmas Island until 1958 and Labuan, separate after 1907. In 1867 the Straits Settlements were accorded the status of Crown Colony, which continued until 1946.

Before separate issues appeared, Indian stamps were in use; from 1867 Indian stamps with currency surcharges in cents; in 1868 a definitive issue inscribed 'STRAITS SETTLEMENTS': a total of 227 + 6 stamps until 1941, when the Japanese occupation began. Stamps of British origin, with numerous portrait designs similar to other British Commonwealth issues, and a large number of overprinted provisionals. Stamps of high face values of 25 to 500 dollars were intended for fiscal purposes, but being inscribed 'POSTAGE AND REVENUE', were valid for postal purposes and are catalogued as postage stamps. The postage-due stamps of the *Malayan Postal Union* replaced those of the Straits Settlements in 1936.

SUMATRA
During the Japanese occupation of the Netherlands East Indies in 1943–4, 1 pictorial issue of 12 stamps appeared for Sumatra. The designs were similar to contemporary Japanese stamps and there was no Latin inscription other than the face value being expressed in Dutch 'cents'.

SUNGEI UJONG
Former Malayan sultanate (capital Seremban), a British protectorate from 1889. In 1895 it merged with the sultanate of Negri Sembilan and then became one of the Federated Malay States.

In 1878 stamps of the Straits Settlements with the overprint 'SU' and the star and crescent; in the following years with the overprint 'SUNGEI UJONG' and then, on definitive stamps only, 'S.UJONG': a total of 19 stamps of British origin, mostly overprinted provisionals. Stamps continued to be issued until 1895, when the stamps of *Negri Sembilan* came into use.

SUPEH
Chinese territory in Northern China with Hsinheilien as capital, the northern part of the province of Kiangsu, occupied by the Japanese from 1938 to 1945.

From 1941 to 1942 overprinted provisionals on Chinese stamps with the inscription 'For the Territory of Supeh', in Chinese: no Latin script.

SYRIA – GREATER LEBANON
In 1922 a Syrian Union was set up composed of five smaller states, one of which was the autonomous Greater Lebanon, which left the Union in 1926.

The first issue after the establishment in 1923 of the French mandate over the Syrian region including Lebanon (**area** about 194,500 sq.km, **capital** Damascus) was made up of provisionals, being French stamps with the overprint 'SYRIE-GRAND LIBAN' (a total of 24 stamps). Then Great Lebanon became an independent stamp-issuing state and from 1924 issues appeared for *Syria* and for *Lebanon.*

SYRIA (SYRIAN ARAB REPUBLIC)
Area 185,180 sq.km, **population** 9.84m (1982), **capital** Damascus.

Agricultural country on the eastern shores of the Mediterranean Sea. Indirect UPU membership from 1 July 1875 (Turkey); indirect from 30 October 1923 (French colony); indirect from 12 May 1931 (Levant); direct from 15 May 1946.

During the First World War, Turkish troops were expelled from Syria, and in 1918 Arab and French soldiers occupied the country. On 8 March 1920 the Arab Kingdom of Greater Syria was established under King Faisal, but the French army then occupied the country again, Faisal had to leave Syria and France took over the mandate. In 1922 a Syrian Union was established made up of the states of Damascus and Aleppo, the autonomous regions of Alaouites (Latakia) and Hauran and Greater Lebanon (until 1926). A republican constitution was introduced in 1930. After the capitulation of France in the Second World War, Syria was administered by a German-Italian control commission. In 1941 it was occupied by the forces of the Free French and the British army and declared an independent republic on 16 September 1941. The Allied military garrison, however, did not leave until 1946. In 1958–61 the country became a province of the *United Arab Republic* and after leaving this union (25 September 1961), it adopted the name, 'Syrian Arab Republic'.

After stamps of the Ottoman Empire there appeared various overprinted provisionals, either of the occupation forces in Syria or issues of the Arab Kingdom of Greater Syria. Until 1920 French stamps overprinted 'SYRIE' and in addition 'OMF' (Occupation Militaire Française); from 1933 with 'RÉPUBLIQUE SYRIENNE' and then 'SYRIE', for a time replaced by the name of the republic. Up to 1958 there was a total of 769 stamps with a large number of overprinted and surcharged provisionals. The definitive issues are of varying origins according to the political spheres of influence. The long French influence was replaced by Egyptian influence on the stamp designs even though the stamps were printed in Syria. Various pictorial issues, many scenic subjects, but others stressing national propaganda. A characteristic feature is the many airmail stamps which, in certain periods, exceeded other types of stamps. In the years 1947–57 133 airmail stamps were issued, and only 93 other issues. The clear influence of philatelic speculation can be seen in the large numbers of miniature sheets (47) and low printings (often 1,500 although some are as low as 200). From 1958 to 1961 stamps were issued under the name of *United Arab Republic–Syria.*

In 1961 definitive stamps with 'SYRIAN ARAB REPUBLIC' in Latin and Arabic script. Most of these stamps are of local origin, mostly portraits, symbolic designs and propaganda issues: also participation in several international omnibus issues. Even though some issues do not have large editions (the lowest being around 50,000) they are designed to meet postal rather than philatelic demand as in the preceding period up to 1957. At the present time issuing is restrained and does not take place every year.

Philatelic bureau General Post Establishment, Directorate of Postal Services, Philatelic Office, Damascus.

SZECHWAN
Chinese province (**area** 569,000 sq.km, **capital** Cheng-tu).

In 1933–4 Chinese stamps with the overprint of the name of the province in Chinese. This was because of the devaluation of the local currency, and prevented stamps being bought cheaply in Szechwan and used in provinces where devaluation had not occurred: a total of 23 overprinted provisionals. In 1950 overprints of East and West Szechwan appeared on stamps of *South-West China.*

TAIWAN
Area 36,000 sq.km, **population** 18.64m (1983), **capital** Taipei.

Chinese island, also known as Formosa, since 1949 the seat of the Nationalist Chinese

Republican government which had been established under the leadership of the late Chiang Kai-shek.

Previous issues *Formosa*. From 1895 to 1945 Japanese stamps were in use. In 1945 stamps of the Japanese occupation of Taiwan with the name of the Japanese postal authorities (with large Arabic numeral and stylized chrysanthemum) were printed and sold only in Taiwan (although without its name) and issued on 21 October. Taiwan was formally returned to China on 25 October 1945. On 4 November Chinese issues followed, the Chinese overprint reading, 'Taiwan Province, Chinese Republic'. Overprints on previous Japanese issues, then on Chinese stamps with the name 'Taiwan', in a Chinese script. The name 'REPUBLIC OF CHINA' in English followed later. Definitive stamps, mostly of Japanese or local origin, though other printing houses were also used. Mostly propaganda subjects, some especially notable both artistically and symbolically; though photographic reproductions are also used, which shows the influence of Japanese stamp design. Annual production at present about 50 stamps.

Philatelic bureau Philatelic Dept., Directorate General of Posts, Taipei, Taiwan.

TANNU-TUVA

Small country to the south of Siberia between the USSR and Mongolia (**area** 170,500 sq.km, **capital** Kyzyl). From 1914 a Russian protectorate; in 1921–44 an independent people's republic; since 1944 part of the USSR. Today, Tuva ASSR.

In 1926 a definitive issue (in 'wheel of destiny' symbolic design) with the text in Mongolian script; then a further one with 'TOUVA' in Latin script. Stamps were issued up to 1943 after which stamps of the USSR were used: a total of 103 stamps, printed in Moscow in designs showing the influence of Soviet stamp production. Pictorial stamps of various shape, obviously aimed at the junior stamp market; the postal function of some issues has not been fully established.

CHUNG-KING

The largest town in the Chinese province of Szechwan, where a French post office was in operation. The Indochinese postal authorities in China used the stamps of French Indochina in the years 1903–22 with the overprint 'TSCHONGKING' or 'TCH'ONG K'ING': a total of 67 overprinted provisionals.

THAILAND

Area 514,121 sq.km, **population** 49.59m (1983), **capital** Bangkok.

Under-developed agricultural country with mineral mining. Constitutional monarchy since 1932. Formerly known as Siam (until 1939 and again in 1946–9). During the Second World War Thailand was an ally of the Japanese who ceded to it parts of Laos, Cambodia and Malaya, which had been taken away from Siam in 1902–9. Direct UPU membership from 1 July 1885.

Following issues inscribed 'Siam', the official change of name in 1939 resulted in definitive issues in 1940 with the name 'THAILAND' and, during the Second World War, also 'THAI'. In 1947 these were replaced by stamps with the old name of Siam, but from 1950 the name THAILAND was restored. Most of the stamps since 1964 are of Japanese origin and are influenced by Japanese stamp design. National life and propaganda, together with international omnibus issues, are normally treated in pictorial form, sometimes involving symbolism. A blend of traditional and modern art combine to achieve a striking and above-average graphic treatment. Present-day annual production is between 30 and 50 stamps in large printings, running into millions.

Thailand issues of the year 1943, with currency expressed in cents, were valid in all the occupied Malayan states of Kedah, Kelantan, Perlis and Trengganu.

Philatelic bureau Chief of Philatelic Section, Philatelic Division, Communications Authority, Bangkok.

TIBET

Territory in the south-western part of China (**area** 1.22 million sq.km, **capital** Lhasa) dependent on China since 1751.

In 1903 the British came to Tibet, and in 1912 the country was granted autonomy. In 1950 China began to occupy the country, which led to the 'Treaty on the Peaceful Liberation' (1951) and the incorporation of Tibet into the Chinese People's Republic as an autonomous region (1965).

Between 1911 and 1956 a total of 23 + 11 definitive stamps of symbolic design and primitive production which, in some cases, bear the name of 'TIBET' in Latin script.

Foreign post offices were in operation in the territory of Tibet, and a Chinese post office in the years 1910–11 used Chinese stamps with a surcharge and overprint (11 values). The office was reopened in 1950. An Indian post office became a postal agency in 1904 in charge of foreign mail to and from Tibet, and it operated until 1955, when it closed down.

TIENTSIN

The Italian post office in Chinese Tientsin used Italian stamps with the overprint 'TIENTSIN' in the years 1917–19: a total of 25 + 12 stamps, all overprinted provisionals. These were claimed to be for the Italian soldiers in Russian captivity, to facilitate postal links with their own country. However, some of the stamps were sold only at philatelic counters in Rome, which, together with certain other features which have not been properly explained, throws doubt on the postal function of this issue. The Italian post office, which used Italian stamps surcharged in Chinese currency, was closed down in 1922.

TIMOR

One-time overseas territory of Portugal (**area** 14,925 sq.km, **capital** Dili) on the eastern part of the island of Timor in the Lesser Sunda Islands (Eastern Timor) and on its northern shore (the Ocussi Ambeno enclave). It belonged to the Portuguese from 1586 to 1975. On 28 November 1975 an East Timor People's Democratic Republic was proclaimed, but the Indonesian army immediately occupied the whole territory. First the Ocussi Ambeno enclave was annexed, and on 26 June 1976 East Timor became an Indonesian province.

In 1885 (the first issue) Macao stamps with the overprint 'TIMOR'; from 1948 also 'TIMOR PORTUGUÊS'; later, again 'TIMOR' and 'REPÚBLICA PORTUGUESA': a total of 353 + 52 stamps of Portuguese origin, a number of designs common to the Portuguese colonial issues and numerous overprinted provisionals, mainly with the 'REPUBLICA' overprint. From 1948 pictorial stamps with local history as the main topic.

TRANSCAUCASIAN FEDERATION

Transcaucasus split off from Russia and proclaimed itself as a republic in April 1918; but in May 1918 it split up into three republics – Armenia, Azerbaijan and Georgia – which were then occupied by German, Turkish and British army units. After their liberation by the Red Army, they were merged in 1922 to form the Transcaucasian Soviet Federated Socialist Republic, which joined the Soviet Union at the end of that year. Transcaucasia came to an end as a unified territory in 1935 when all three of its member states were proclaimed individual Soviet Union Republics.

In 1923 overprints on Russian stamps, then definitives with the letters 'ZSFSR' in Cyrillic script within a five-pointed star: a total of 33 stamps. The face values indicate the rapidly advancing inflation with stamps of 700,000 roubles before a new currency was expressed in gold kopeks. Until 1 October 1923 stamps for the individual countries of Transcaucasia were issued; from October to December of that year only Transcaucasian stamps were valid, issued from April 1923. After 1924 only stamps of the Soviet Union were valid.

TRANSJORDAN

Until 1918 part of the Ottoman Empire, then liberated by Arab units fighting on the side of the Allies and proclaimed a mandate of Great Britain in 1920, linked with Palestine. In 1921 an emirate of Transjordan was established, covering the territory east of the River Jordan (**area** 89,975 sq.km, **capital** Amman). In 1923 it was partitioned off from Palestine and in 1946, on the withdrawal of the British mandate, it became an independent kingdom. After the proclamation of the merger of Palestinian territory on the Western Bank of the Jordan in 1948 the country began to be known as Jordan.

In 1920 overprints for Palestine in Arabic meaning 'East of Jordan'; later 'Arab Government of the East', then definitive stamps in 1927 with the name 'TRANSJORDAN' in English: a total of 294 stamps, mostly overprinted provisionals. The definitives are of British origin, but retained the original style of stamps of this part of the Arab world. After 1949 see *Jordan.*

TRAVANCORE
Feudatory state (**area** 19,844 sq.km, **capital** Trivandrum), in the south of India, under British influence from 1795; linked with Cochin in 1949.

From 1888 definitive stamps of heraldic characters with 'TRAVANCORE', later pictorial stamps with the same name: a total of 50 + 48 stamps, both definitives and overprinted and surcharged provisionals. In 1949 they were replaced by stamps of *Travancore-Cochin.*

TRAVANCORE-COCHIN
Southern Indian feudatory state since 1949 (**area** 23,697 sq.km, **capital** Trivandrum).

In 1949 overprinted provisionals which bore the letters 'U.S.T.C.' (United State of Travancore - Cochin) on Cochin stamps; in 1950 definitives with 'STATE OF TRAVANCORE-COCHIN'. A total of 13 + 13 stamps were issued. From 1951 they were replaced by the stamps of India.

TREBIZONDE (TRABZON)
Turkish town on the coast of the Black Sea where the Russian post office used its own stamps from 1909 with the overprint 'Trebizonde' or 'Trebisonde': a total of 9 overprinted provisionals. The post office closed in 1914.

TRENGGANU
Area 13,080 sq.km, **capital** Kuala Trengganu. Member state of the Malaysian Federation since 1963.

Until 1909 dominated by Siam, then a British protectorate as one of the Unfederated Malay States. Occupied by Japan in 1941, which ceded it to Thailand in 1943. In 1945 occupied by the British army. From 1948 part of the Malayan Federation; in 1957–63 in the independent Malayan Federation. Indirect UPU mermbership (Johore and Trengganu) from 1 July 1928 (British colony); direct from 17 January 1958 (Malayan Federation); direct from 16 September 1963 (Malaysia).

In 1910 definitive issues with 'TRENGGANU', later with the addition of 'MALAYA', then 'MALAYSIA'. Stamps of British origin in the style of other stamps for the Malayan region and also overprinted provisionals. During the Japanese occupation from 1942 numerous Japanese overprints validating the stamps for use in Trengganu, then Thai stamps; from 1945 British occupation, with own stamp issuing renewed in 1948. At present, stamps are not issued every year. The stamps of high nominal face value (up to $100) issued in 1921 were intended for fiscal purposes. The stamps of Malaysia (formerly Malaya) are in circulation in the territory of Trengganu and those of the other member states are valid there, and vice versa.

TRUCIAL STATES
Region on the coast of the Arabian peninsula (83,600 sq.km), composed of seven sheikdoms and their dependencies: Abu Dhabi, Ajman, Dubai, Fujeira, Ras Al-Khaima, Sharjah and Umm al-Qiwain. It was not a unified state but a group of countries along the former Pirates' Coast, which, in 1892, concluded an agreement on protection with Great Britain and

abandoned piracy. Since 1971–2 the countries have been called United Arab Emirates.

From 1909 Indian stamps came into use; from 1948 British stamps with a surcharge in the currency of the countries on the Persian Gulf (see *Muscat and Oman*). In 1961 the only stamps with 'TRUCIAL STATES' appeared. Their validity ended in 1963 when the British post office in Dubai, the only one in the whole region, was closed down, and postal services were provided by the post office of Dubai and the other countries, which gradually opened their own post offices. One definitive issue appeared with 11 stamps of British origin. The design with seven palm trees symbolized the seven princedoms of the group. After 1963 issues of the individual princedoms; from 1972 see *United Arab Emirates*.

TURKEY

Area 779,452 sq.km, **population** 47m (1983), **capital** Ankara.

Republic in Asia Minor and south-eastern Europe with rather under-developed agriculture. Successor to the Ottoman Empire which ended in 1922. Two years earlier, Mustafa Kemal (Ataturk) had already formed a new Turkish government with its seat in Ankara and begun the fight against both the Allies and the old government in Constantinople. He conquered Western Armenia in 1920, gained Cilicia from the French, beat back the Greek attack (begun in 1920) and in 1922 occupied Smyrna and Constantinople. The Ottoman sultanate was abolished, and in 1923 the Allies abandoned their plan for the division of Turkey, set out in the Treaty of Sèvres, and at the Conference of Lausanne they recognized the country's independence and revised the Treaty of Sèvres. Turkey retained Eastern Thrace in Europe. On 20 October 1923 it became a republic. Direct UPU membership from 1 July 1875.

In 1922 the inscription 'Turkish Post' appeared (in Arabic script) for the first time on stamps of the nationalist government of Mustafa Kemal. After the proclamation of the republic, from 1926 on, the name began to appear in Latin script 'TURK POSTALARI', 'TÜRKIYE POSTALARI' (= Turkish post), 'TÜRKIYE CUMHURIYETI' (= Turkish republic), or just 'TÜR-KIYE'. Stamps mostly of local origin, at first occasionally British, but after the Second World War usually printed by other foreign printing houses, particularly those in Switzerland and Austria. Overall design conception rather uneven, with numerous pictorial stamps, often based on photographic reproductions. A good many stamps are symbolic in character, and some are interesting artistically. Numerous issues for tourist propaganda purposes resulting in an increased collector demand. Annual output is between 30 and 50 stamps, with numerous postage-due and charity stamps (250). In 1958 to 1960 stamps began to be issued with pictures of all the Turkish district towns, the full set amounting to 134 stamps.

Philatelic bureau PTT General Murudlugu, Post Dairesi, Ankara.

TURKISH CYPRIOT POSTS see CYPRUS (Turkish Administration)

UMM AL-QIWAIN

One of the countries of the former Trucial States on the coast of the Persian Gulf (**area** 700 sq.km, **capital** Umm al-Qiwain). Since 1971 part of the United Arab Emirates.

In 1964 a definitive issue with 'UMM AL QIWAIN'. Soon the number of issues grew greatly. The agency advising the government issued numerous stamps with designs not associated with the state and few of these were available or necessary for public use. Before the *United Arab Emirates* took over in 1972 some 600 different stamps had been issued, imperforate stamps, printings on gold foil and many miniature sheets, some printings being as low as 4,000.

UNITED ARAB EMIRATES

Area 83,600 sq.km, **population** 1.18m (1982), **capital** Abu Dhabi.

Federation of seven emirates in the eastern part of the Arabian peninsula, established on 2 December 1971 – Abu Dhabi, Ajman (with Manama), Dubai, Fujeira, Sharjah (with Khor Fakkan), Umm al-Qiwain and Ras al-Khaima, which joined on 14 February 1972. This is the territory of the former Trucial States. Direct UPU membership as of 30 March 1973.

The postal union of the Emirates put an end to the notorious issuing policies of the individual sheikhdoms, since their stamps ceased to be valid and were replaced by the stamps of the United Arab Emirates. In 1972 the Abu Dhabi stamp with the overprint 'UAE' and limited validity appeared. The first issue of definitive stamps dates from 1973 and bears the inscription 'UNITED ARAB EMIRATES'. There are about 5 issues per year, which fully satisfies postal needs and the collector's market. The stamps have almost exclusively national and propaganda subjects.

Philatelic bureau General Post Office, Dubai. **Trade sales** Crown Agents' Stamp Bureau.

UNITED ARAB REPUBLIC – SYRIA

Agricultural region on the eastern shores of the Mediterranean Sea (**area** 185,180 sq.km, **capital** Damascus). With the establishment on 1 February 1958 of the UAR, linking Egypt and Syria, given the status of the Syrian province. After the collapse of the UAR on 25 September 1961 again *Syria (Syrian Arab Republic)*.

In 1958 definitive issues with 'THE UNITED ARAB REPUBLIC SYRIA' also the French text 'RÉPUBLIQUE ARABE UNIE'; most often the English abbreviation 'UAR'. Issuing was merged so that some stamps have designs identical to those in the Egyptian province (*United Arab Republik – Egypt*). Some designs were identical but were printed by a Syrian printing house, and displayed small differences from the stamps printed in Egypt. Some texts differ: apart from 'UAR', the stamps have the name of Syria while the Egyptian issues bear the word 'Egypt'. They also differ in currency, which was not identical in Syria and Egypt. In a number of cases Syria went its own way and issued different stamps to those of the Egyptian province. A total of 90 stamps, mainly with propaganda designs.

UPPER YAF'A

One of the states of Aden, from 1965 South Arabian Protectorate (**area** 1,550 sq.km, **capital** Hilyan). Since 1967 part of South Yemen.

Issuing of stamps began on 30 September 1967 with 10 definitives. From April 1968 stamps of South Yemen were valid here. A total of 93 stamps were issued, but other than the definitives, doubt exists as to whether these issues were put to commercial use. All issues were with the inscription 'STATE OF UPPER YAF'A'. The South Yemen ministry of posts proclaimed illegal all issues after the administration of Upper Yaf'a was taken over by the Front of National Liberation on 13 September 1967. At the time when stamps were issued there was not a single post office in Upper Yaf'a but commercial mail franked with Upper Yaf'a stamps may have been accepted by a friendly neighbouring state with UPU membership and passed into the international system.

VIETNAMESE DEMOCRATIC REPUBLIC

Former state of south-east Asia (**area** 164,103 sq.km, **capital** Hanoi), since 1976 part of the unified country of Vietnam. Originally the country was conquered by the French, divided into three areas, Tonkin, Annam and Cochin-china, and in 1887 incorporated into French Indo-china. Occupied by Japan from 1940 to 1945. A nationwide rising took place in August 1945, and on 2 September 1945 the Democratic Republic of Vietnam was proclaimed. The French government recognized this in 1946 as a free state within the French sphere of influence, but soon fighting broke out and the government was forced to retreat to the mountains in the north of the country. In 1949 the French set up a government of the former Emperor of Annam Bao Dai in Saigon. The war came to an end with the Geneva Conference in 1954 and the country was divided into two parts: the forces of the Democratic Republic withdrew to the north with the support of the socialist countries, and in the south the Republic of Vietnam (see *South Vietnam*) was formed on 26 October 1955 with the support of the USA.

In 1945 former Indo-China stamps overprinted 'VIET-NAM DAN-CHU CONG-HOA' (Democratic Republic of Vietnam) were issued for the entire territory of Vietnam: a total of 60 stamps until 1946, mostly overprinted provisionals of local origin. When, after the split with France, the government withdrew into the mountains, the existing stamps were used while in stock. The rest of Vietnam used first the stamps of French Indo-China; from 1951 South

Vietnamese issues inscribed 'BUU-CHINH' ('Postal Service') which, officially, were valid throughout the entire territory of Vietnam but, in practice, only in the territory controlled by the French. From 1946 definitive stamps, of local manufacture, with 'VIET-NAM BUU-DIEN' (= 'Official Post') and, later, 'VIET-NAM DAN-CHU CONG-HOA' ('Democratic Republic of Vietnam'): a total of 854 + 36 stamps, mostly of local origin but with some printed in Prague. The originally exclusive propaganda subjects were, in the 1960s, replaced increasingly by general themes designed to attract collectors, with limited printings of 15,000 sets, perforated and imperforate stamps, etc. On 2 July 1976 the Democratic Republic of Vietnam merged with the Republic of South Vietnam to become one state, which is called the *Vietnamese Socialist Republic*.

In the 1950s, a time of shortages, the face values of stamps were expressed in terms of weights of rice; e.g. official stamps of 1953 – 0.6 kg, 1 kg, 2 kg, 5 kg rice. During the war rice, as the main source of food, formed the basis of the state budget, and all public expenditure was calculated in relation to it.

Apart from recognized issues, certain other locally produced issues are sometimes mentioned: e.g. for Nga-khe, the 4th and 5th interzone (Lien-khu 4 and 5), but the postal status of such stamps has not been established.

VIETNAMESE SOCIALIST REPUBLIC
Area 329,556 sq.km, **population** 57.02m (1983), **capital** Hanoi.

Since 2 July 1976 a socialist republic formed by the merging of the South Vietnamese Democratic Republic and the Republic of Vietnam. Agricultural country where industry is being introduced. Indirect UPU membership from 1 July 1876 (French colony); indirect from 1 January 1899 as Indo-China; direct from 20 October 1951 (Republic of Vietnam known as South Vietnam); direct from 23 August 1976 as Vietnamese Socialist Republic.

After the unification of the two countries the first stamps bore the inscription 'BUU CHINH VIET NAM' ('Vietnamese post').

Philatelic bureau Xunhasaba, Hanoi.

WADHWAN
Feudatory state (**area** 6.4 sq.km, **capital** Wadhwan) on the Kathiawar peninsula in western India.

Two definitive stamps, produced by primitive lithography, were issued between 1888 and 1892 bearing the name 'WADHWAN STATE'. The stamps became invalid for postage on 1 January 1895.

YEMEN
Area 195,000 sq.km, **population** 7.16m (1981), **capital** San'a.

Undeveloped agricultural and pastoral country. After major risings against the Turkish Rule, Yemen achieved autonomy in 1911, and on 1 December 1918 was proclaimed an independent kingdom under the rule of an Imam. After his overthrow a republic was proclaimed on 27 September 1962 with the support of the United Arab Republic, but the Imam's supporters, who held sway with the aid of Saudi Arabia in the northern, eastern and western parts of the country, continued to acknowledge the monarchy. But in 1970 Saudi Arabia officially acknowledged the Yemen Arab Republic and ceased all support for the Yemeni royalists, some of whom were even then given high positions in state institutions of the Republic. Indirect UPU membership from 1 July 1875 (Turkey); direct from 1 January 1930.

In 1926, before entry into the UPU, primitive stamps with entirely local inscriptions; from 1930 with 'YEMEN'; later with 'ROYAUME DE YEMEN', 'THE MOUTAWAKILITE KINGDOM OF YEMEN', 'YEMEN ARAB REPUBLIC', 'Y.A.R.'. Very varied quality of production. In 1948 unissued stamps looted from official stores reached the philatelic market. Printings in some cases of the issued stamps were very limited. Before 1947 designs were basically oriental patterns, but later issues were pictorial, and from 1952 the more frequent issues were made specifically for the collector's market. Some small printings were of only a few hundred stamps, perforated and imperforate. A large number of miniature sheets, overprints in different colours, were not placed on public sale but sold to collectors. The design subjects varied and the stamps were printed in a number of foreign printing houses. A total of 158 stamps until 1962. From that year there was a rapid increase to about 1,000 stamps, all those produced unofficially being included. Annual output varies from 50 to 100, of which over one half are airmail stamps. The postal necessity for all those stamps must be doubted and the assumption be that they are largely produced for the philatelic market.

From November 1962 when civil war was taking place there appeared issues of the iman (royalist) government for use in royalist-held territory. Overprinted provisionals, later definitive stamps with the name 'MUTAWAKELITE KINGDOM OF YEMEN': a total of 781 stamps with numerous miniature sheets, different coloured overprints, the latter in very small printings of only 44 in some cases. Most of these were produced by agents more concerned to provide items for the collector's market, particularly as there was very little postal demand or use for royalist issues. When the new Yemeni government was recognized by Saudi Arabia on 22 July 1970 the royalist issues lost their basis, even formally. After 1972 issuing slowed down, and Yemen now issues about 5 stamps per year in adequate quantities to achieve the propaganda purpose behind most of the designs.

Philatelic bureau Philatelic Section, General Dept. of Posts, Ministry of Communications, Sana'a.

YUNNAN
South Chinese province (**area** 436,000 sq.km, **capital** Kunming) which issued stamps from 1926 to 1933, a total of 60 overprinted provisionals. They are Chinese stamps with a Chinese overprint for this province, required because the local currency was devalued in relation to other provinces.

YUNNAN-FU (KUNMING)
Town in the South Chinese province of Yunnan with a French Indochinese post office, which in 1903–19 issued Indo-Chinese stamps with the overprints 'YUNNANSEN', 'Yunnan-Fou' and 'YUNNANFOU': a total of 66 overprinted provisionals. The post office was closed in 1922.

AFRICA

ALEXANDRIA

A French post office was opened in Alexandria (today in the Arab Republic of Egypt) in 1830. Before Alexandria issued its own stamps, French stamps were in use. From 1899 French stamps overprinted 'ALEXANDRIE', then definitives of French key-and-duty types with the same name. A total of 80 + 17 stamps. From 1922 Alexandria had its own postage-due stamps (French postage-due stamps had been used previously). The French post office in Alexandria was closed on 31 March 1931. Some stamps of the first issue with the Alexandria overprint were also valid in Port Said and vice versa.

As well as the French post office, there were also at various times British, Austrian, Greek, Italian and Russian post offices in Alexandria, but they used different stamps from those described above.

ALGERIA

Area 2,381,740 sq.km, **population** 21m (1982), **capital** Algiers (Al-jezair).

An agricultural country, considerably more advanced than most African countries, with important oil and mineral production and expanding industry. The country was occupied by the French from 1830, but it was never a French colony, being always regarded as an overseas department of France. The country became independent, under the name of Democratic People's Republic of Algeria, in 1962. UPU membership from 1 January 1876 (France); direct from 1 October 1907; and from 28 May 1964 as a sovereign state.

French stamps were used until Algeria's own issues appeared. Stamp-issuing began in 1924 with French stamps overprinted 'ALGÉRIE'; definitives with the same name came later. In 1958 stamps inscribed 'RÉPUBLIQUE FRANÇAISE' in addition to the name 'ALGÉRIE', also began to appear. From 22 July 1958, Algerian stamps were no longer used (they were valid until 31 August 1958) having been supplanted by French stamps.

On 3 July 1962, the country's independence was proclaimed, and this was first reflected in the overprint 'EA' ('État Algérien') on French stamps . Later, definitives appeared reading 'RÉPUBLIQUE ALGÉRIENNE' or 'ALGÉRIE' and with the name in Arabic. The early stamps were mostly pictorials of French origin, typical of French colonial issues, but the later issues showed a more distinctly Arab influence. When the country gained its independence, Algerian graphic designs also became independent, and national customs and history provided themes for designs. Current annual production is 20 to 30 stamps.

Algerian stamps with the overprint 'E F M' (Expeditionary Force Messages) were used by the Anglo-American military forces in 1943-4; they were sold at post offices in Algiers.

Philatelic bureau Agence Comptable des Timbres-Poste, Alger. **Trade sales** Agence des Timbres-Poste d'Outre-Mer.

ANGOLA

Area 1,246,700 sq.km, **population** 8.3m (1983), **capital** Luanda.

A developing agricultural country with mineral mining. Portuguese from the 15th century, officially a colony from 1885; from 1951 an overseas province of Portugal. Angola was declared an independent people's republic on 11 November 1975 in Luanda. Indirect UPU membership from 1 July 1877 (Portuguese possessions); direct from 3 March 1977.

Definitives in 1870 with the name 'ANGOLA'; later also 'PROVINCIA DE ANGOLA', and from 1954 bearing the text REPUBLICA PORTUGUESA. The stamps are of Portuguese manufacture, and in the initial period were in the Portuguese colonial key-plate design. After 1911 a large number of overprinted provisionals appeared with the word 'Republica' (after the Republic of Portugal was proclaimed). In 1939 there was an issue limited to 2,000 sets for the New York World's Fair and sold only in New York. This was the same issue as for other overseas Portuguese territories, by a decree of 15 August 1939. Pictorial stamps appeared from 1938. A characteristic feature is long sets (about 20 values). Restrained production in other ways with a maximum of 4 issues annually. Since independence most stamps have borne the name 'REPUBLICA POPULAR DE ANGOLA', but some only 'ANGOLA', the designs promoting the national interest politically and historically.

Philatelic bureau Philatelic Service, PTT, Luanda.

ANGRA

An administrative district of the Azores consisting of Terceira, São Jorge and Graciosa islands (**area** 704 sq.km, **capital** Angra do Heroísmo).

Portuguese stamps until 1868, followed by issues for the Azores. Later, in 1892–1905, the district's own issues (although the contemporary Azores commemoratives and postage-due stamps were valid in the district). Definitives with the name ANGRA: a total of 34 stamps of Portuguese origin (in the colonial key-types). From 1905 stamp-issuing was halted, and from 1906 issues with the name Azores were used again (these were valid for Angra territory, Horta and Ponta Delgada). From 1932 they were replaced by Portuguese stamps.

ANJOUAN

Between 1886 and 1908 an island sultanate and French protectorate in the Comoros (**area** 359 sq.km, **capital** Mutsamudu). In 1908, Anjouan, together with the islands of Mayotte, Grande Comore and Mohéli, was joined to Madagascar as the Province of Mayotte et dépendances, and was declared a colony in 1912. Today it is part of the Comoro Islands.

From 1892 French issues of the key-and-duty types with the name 'SULTANAT D'ANJOUAN'. Until 1908, 2 issues with a total of 19 stamps.

ASCENSION

Area 88 sq.km, **population** 1,372 (1983), **main settlement** Georgetown.

A volcanic island in the Atlantic Ocean, British since 1815, a dependency of St Helena since 1922. Indirect UPU membership since 1 October 1879.

In 1922 stamps of St Helena with the overprint 'ASCENSION', then definitives with the same name. At present, the name 'ASCENSION ISLAND' also appears. Characteristic pictorial stamps of British origin including regular participation in British Commonwealth omnibus issues. Following very moderate stamp-issuing activity, when stamps did not appear every year, there are now 2 to 4 issues annually.

Philatelic bureau Postmaster, Philatelic Services, Ascension. **Trade sales** Crown Agents' Stamp Bureau.

AZORES

Area 2,335 sq.km, **population** 251,352, **capital** Ponta Delgada.

An island group in the Atlantic Ocean, divided into three districts. These are: Angra (the islands of Graciosa, São Jorge, Terceira); Horta (Corvo, Faial, Flores, Pico); and Ponta Delgada (Santa Maria, São Miguel). From 1892 to 1905 they issued their own stamps. Today the Azores are considered an integral part of Portugal (not an overseas province) with Portuguese currency. Membership in the UPU is specifically as a part of Portugal.

Until 1868 the Azores used the stamps of Portugal, and from 1868, Portuguese stamps with the overprint 'AÇORES'. From 1892 to 1905 stamps were also issued separately for each district (Angra, Horta and Ponta Delgada) and issues were simultaneously produced for the whole Azore group. A sizeable total of 403 stamps issued until 1930. Issues of Portuguese origin in standard Portuguese colonial designs, with many overprinted provisionals. From 1931 the stamps of Portugal were used, the rest were used up in the Azores and in Portugal (obligatory postage-due stamps issued in 1925 could be used as postage stamps from 1935 to 1945). In 1980 stamp issuing was revived in the Azores, with these stamps valid also in the territory of continental Portugal.

Philatelic bureau Servicos de Filatelia, Estaçao de Correio de Ponta Delgada, Azores.

BASUTOLAND

A British protectorate in southern Africa from 1868 (from 1871 to 1884 it was joined temporarily to Cape Province); a British colony from 1884. In 1965 it became autonomous, on 4 October 1966, it proclaimed its independence as the Kingdom of Lesotho (**area** 30,344 sq.km, **capital** Maseru).

Until 1933 Cape of Good Hope and South African stamps were used, but from 1933 Basutoland had its own issues, definitives bearing the name 'BASUTOLAND'. The South African Victory stamps of 1945 were overprinted 'Basutoland' for use in the territory: a total of 86 + 12 stamps. Typical pictorial stamps of British origin with some issues common to the British Commonwealth. From 1966 see *Lesotho*.

BECHUANALAND

The northern part of Bechuanaland, in Southern Africa, was a British protectorate from 1885 to 1966. (Not to be confused with *British Bechuanaland*, the southern part.) From 1965 self-governing; on 30 September 1966, declared the independent Republic of Botswana (**area** 600,372 sq.km, **capital** Mafeking in British Bechuanaland from 1965, Gaborones, now Gaborone).

From 1888 overprinted provisionals of British Bechuanaland with the additional overprint 'Protectorate'; also stamps of Cape of Good Hope with the overprint 'BECHUANALAND PROTECTORATE'. From 1890 to 1895 the protectorate was united with the colony British Bechuanaland. This was reflected by the issue of overprinted provisionals on stamps of Cape of Good Hope with the text 'BRITISH BECHUANALAND' and the stamps of Great Britain overprinted 'BECHUANALAND PROTECTORATE'. Definitives issued with the latter inscription starting in 1932. A total of 128 + 12 stamps of British origin, many pictorial issues and also joint issues characteristic of the British Commonwealth, as well as a great many overprinted provisionals. Limited printing quantities. From 1966 see *Botswana*.

BELGIAN CONGO

The explorations of David Livingstone and H. M. Stanley during the 19th century revealed the economic potential of the Congo, and King Leopold II of Belgium became interested in its acquisition and development. In 1878 he commissioned Stanley to make treaties with the rulers, and in 1885 he organized the Congo Free State, with himself as monarch. It became a Belgian colony in 1908, and an independent country (Congo) on 30 June 1960 (**area** 2,345,409 sq.km, **capital** Léopoldville).

From 1909, Belgian colonial issues; Congo stamps with the overprint 'CONGO BELGE'. Definitives, often with a bilingual text, in French and Flemish, 'CONGO BELGE – BELGISCHE CONGO'. Up to 1960 a total of 383 stamps, some with designs by Belgian artists – later, especially, by van Noten – printed in various countries. Most stamps are typical pictorials usually in the style of Belgian stamp designing. Many issues exist in small printings of up to 10,000. From 1960 see *Congo (Kinshasa)* and from 1971 see *Zaire*.

BENADIR

Italian territory on the coast of Somalia (capital Mogadishu). The Italians began to settle here from 1889, when they acquired Obbia, and in 1892–3 most of the settlements of Benadir were leased to Italy by the sultan of Zanzibar, who in 1905 gave them this territory as compensation. In 1908 Italy combined all its territories in this area into the colony of Italian Somaliland.

From 1903 definitive pictorial stamps of Italian origin with the name 'BENADIR', issued by the Benadir Company. In later years (up to 1924) these stamps had currency surcharges, while issues were printed with the name 'Somalia Italiana' (Italian Somaliland) from 1907. A total of 33 stamps, predominantly overprinted and/or surcharged provisionals. The Company's offices were opened in 1903; the post office in 1905.

BENGASI

A city of Cyrenaica (today's Libya), Turkish until 1912. During Turkish rule there was an Italian post office, which in 1901 and in 1911 issued 2 Italian stamps with the overprint 'BENGASI' and surcharged in Turkish currency.

BENIN

Area 112,622 sq.km, **population** 3.91m (1983), **capital** Porto Novo.

A developing country with underdeveloped agriculture. From 1889 to 1899 there was a small French colony at the Gulf of Benin, whose capital was Assini, but in 1899 it became a part of *Dahomey*. The name Benin was revived on 30 November 1975, when Dahomey was proclaimed the People's Republic of Benin. Indirect UPU membership from 1 July 1876 (as a French colony); direct as from 27 April 1961 (Dahomey).

Before Benin issued its own stamps, French stamps were used, followed by the key-plate issues of the French colonies with the overprint 'BÉNIN'. These were replaced in 1893 by French colonial key-plate stamps with the inscription 'GOLFE DE BÉNIN', or just 'BÉNIN': 46 stamps. From 1899 to 1976 the stamps of Dahomey were used. The first issue with the name 'RÉPUBLIQUE POPULAIRE DU BÉNIN' appeared in 1976. Lively stamp-issuing activity, which now results in about 40 stamps per annum, mostly large pictorials whose subjects focus on propaganda themes and also cater to the collector's market. An unusually large number of airmail stamps, representing roughly half of entire production — once again endeavouring to influence the collector's market.

Philatelic bureau Office des PTT, Section Philatélique, Cotonou, Benin. **Trade sales** Agence des Timbres-Poste d'Outre-Mer.

BIAFRA

An agricultural region with oil production, formerly the Eastern Region of Nigeria which, on 30 May 1967, proclaimed its independence as the Republic of Biafra (**area** 76,364 sq.km, **capital** Enugu). Biafran territory grew smaller with the passing of time, and in 1970, Nigerian troops occupied the remaining strip of Biafra and it ceased to exist as an independent territory.

The first stamps appeared as overprinted provisionals on Nigerian stamps; definitives in 1968 with the inscription 'REPUBLIC OF BIAFRA'. Later a number of overprints reading 'SOVEREIGN BIAFRA' or, only, 'BIAFRA'. These were produced in Lisbon, Portugal. Biafra's stamp-issuing activities were fairly large for a small and short-lived area, particularly considering postal conditions and the country's problems: a total of 42 recognized postage stamps and a further 12 of doubtful postal status. More than half are overprinted provisionals and most of them went through European agencies directly into philatelic hands rather than to the Biafran public.

BOPHUTHATSWANA

Area 44,000 sq.km, **population** 2.6m (1980), **capital** Mmabatho.

The second South African bantustan, set up in 1961 for the Tswana (Bechuana) people. It consists of seven separate parts and was given autonomy in 1972, and independence under the name Republic of Bophuthatswana (not recognized by any other country except the Republic of South Africa) on 6 December 1977. It is a poor agricultural region, many of whose inhabitants work in South African mines.

The first — and a definitive — issue appeared in 1977 bearing the name 'BOPHUTHAT-SWANA'. The stamps depict propaganda and general subjects and are of South African design and production. The annual output is 3 to 4 short issues.

Philatelic bureau Philatelic Services and Intersapa, GPO, Pretoria, South Africa.

BOTSWANA

Area 582,000 sq.km, **population** 941,027 (1981), **capital** Gaborone.

A backward country (formerly called Bechuanaland); its main economic source is livestock farming. An independent republic from 30 September 1966. Indirect UPU membership from 1 March 1901 (Bechuanaland); direct from 12 January 1968.

The first stamps appeared in 1966 as overprinted provisionals with the text 'REPUBLIC OF BOTSWANA' on Bechuanaland stamps previously valid (see *Bechuanaland*). Definitives from 1967 carry only the name 'BOTSWANA'. Relatively small production, of British origin.

Primarily pictorial stamps printed by the photogravure or offset-litho process. Annual new issues about 15 to 30 stamps.

Philatelic bureau Dept. of Posts and Telecommunications, Gaborone. **Trade sales** Crown Agents' Stamp Bureau.

BRITISH BECHUANALAND

The southern part of Bechuanaland between the Rivers Molopo and Oranje; proclaimed a British Crown Colony in 1885 (while the northern part became a British protectorate – see *Bechuanaland*); in 1895 joined to Cape Province (Cape of Good Hope) and together with it incorporated into the Union of South Africa in 1910 (**area** 133,960 sq.km, **capital** Mafeking).

In 1886 stamps of *Cape of Good Hope* with the overprint 'British Bechuanaland' or 'BRITISH BECHUANALAND': 28 stamps were issued up to 1889 (overprinted provisionals). From 1891 joint issue for colony and protectorate — 7 provisionals with the overprint 'BRITISH BECHUANALAND' on Cape of Good Hope stamps and 'BECHUANALAND PROTECTORATE' on British stamps. After the colony was merged with Cape Province, Cape of Good Hope stamps became valid.

During the Boer War (1899–1902) there were also British emergency issues, and in 1900 there was an issue for Mafeking, the town captured by the British in 1900 after being briefly occupied by the Boers. These included Cape of Good Hope or Bechuanaland stamps with the overprint 'MAFEKING BESIEGED' (in varying quantities for different values, but only 840 of some so that only 840 complete sets ever existed). There were also 2 definitives produced locally. Military authorities in Vryburg (a town in British Bechuanaland, which, after being temporarily occupied by the Boer troops of the South African Republic in 1899, was recaptured by the British in 1900) issued 4 Transvaal stamps with the overprint 'V. R. SPECIAL POST'.

BRITISH CAMEROONS

A British trusteeship territory, though administered as part of Nigeria from 1922 to 1961. As part of the German colony of Kamerun, the territory was occupied by British troops in 1915–16 (**area** 89,270 sq.km, **capital** Bouea). In 1961 the larger part of British Cameroons was joined to Nigeria, while the southern part, together with the Republic of Cameroun (formerly French Cameroun), formed a federation.

In 1915 German stamps of Kamerun (seized on a captured German steamship) with the overprint 'C.E.F.' (Cameroons Expeditionary Force) until the stamps of Nigeria were used. From 1 October 1960 to 19 September 1961, Nigerian stamps were issued with the overprint 'CAMEROONS U.K.T.T.' (United Kingdom Trusteeship Territory — 12 values) for use in both Southern and Northern Cameroons. A total of 25 overprinted provisionals appeared altogether in both periods.

BRITISH CENTRAL AFRICA

A British protectorate on the western shore of Lake Nyasa from 1891; known by this name between 1893 and 1907 (**area** 120,400 sq.km, **capital** Blantyre). From 1907 called Nyasaland.

From 1891 stamps of the British South Africa Company (Rhodesia) with the overprint 'B.C.A' (British Central Africa), and from 1895 definitives with the name 'BRITISH CENTRAL AFRICA' and 'BRITISH CENTRAL AFRICA PROTECTORATE'. Issues until 1907: a total of 70 stamps in heraldic and portrait designs, of British origin. Particularly high-face-value stamps (£10 and £25) were intended for fiscal purposes. They are among the most valuable philatelic rarities. From 1907 see *Nyasaland*.

BRITISH EAST AFRICA

The territory of British East Africa (**area** about 500,000 sq.km, **capital** Mombasa), which is today Kenya and Uganda, was ruled from 1885 to 1895 by the British through the British East Africa Company (they acquired the German protectorate of Swahililand or Witu in 1890). It then came under British government as the British East Africa Protectorate, and the coastline was given the name Protectorate of Kenya. The British East Africa Company issued stamps from 1890 to 1894. These were 3 stamps of Great Britain with the overprint 'BRITISH EAST AFRICA COMPANY', and 13 definitives inscribed 'IMPERIAL BRITISH EAST AFRICA COMPANY'. These stamps came out in small printings (the most frequently used value in a printing of 144,000, the least frequently used in only a few hundred). From 1895 to 1903 British colonial administration issues were in use and consisted of Company issues with the overprint 'British East Africa' followed by stamps of India or Zanzibar with the same overprint. Finally, definitives with the inscription 'BRITISH EAST AFRICA PRO-TECTORATE', produced in Britain by the line-engraving process, some in small printings. A total of 85 stamps appeared, chiefly overprinted provisionals. From 1903 see *British East Africa and Uganda*, whose stamps were valid here.

BRITISH EAST AFRICA AND UGANDA

In 1903 the British East Africa Protectorate was divided administratively into British East Africa (today Kenya) and Uganda. Stamps appeared for both territories with the name 'EAST AFRICA AND UGANDA PROTECTORATES' from 1903 until 1922: a total of 70 stamps, typical of British Commonwealth portrait issues. High face values of up to 500 rupees (for fiscal purposes) are among the acknowledged philatelic rarities. From 1922 see *Kenya and Uganda*.

BRITISH INDIAN OCEAN TERRITORY

A British Crown Colony (210 sq.km), established in 1967 from the Mauritian dependency of Chagos Islands and from the Seychelles Islands dependencies Aldabra, Farquhar and Des-roches. The last three dependencies were returned to the Seychelles in 1976, so that the territory was restricted to the uninhabited Chagos Islands, and thereby ceased to be a stamp-issuing territory.

The first stamps were issued in 1968 as overprinted provisionals on Seychelles stamps (15 values) with the overprint 'B.I.O.T.'. Definitives bear the name 'BRITISH INDIAN OCEAN TERRITORY'. A total of 89 stamps. Typical British Commonwealth pictorial issues, all print-ed in Great Britain by lithography.

BRITISH SOMALILAND

A British protectorate in East Africa from 1884, at first administered from Aden as an Indian dependency (**area** 176,113 sq.km, **capital** Hargeisa, formerly Berbera). In 1940–1 the territory was occupied by Italy. On 26 June 1960, it gained its independence and merged with the former Italian Somaliland on 1 July 1960, to form the Republic of Somalia.

In 1903 stamps of British India with the overprint 'BRITISH SOMALILAND'; later, definiti-ves with the inscription 'SOMALILAND PROTECTORATE'. By 1960 a total of 136 + 16 stamps issued. Very moderate stamp-issuing policy, almost all of British origin in typical portrait and pictorial designs of the British Commonwealth.

BRITISH SOUTH AFRICA COMPANY

Territory (now Zimbabwe) colonized by Sir Cecil Rhodes and united under the administration of the British South Africa Company in 1889–1923. Through the agreement of 27 September 1923, the British government acquired, by purchase, the territory of the British South Africa Company when the validity of its charter expired. From that time Northern and Southern Rhodesia were separate administrations.

In 1890 definitives were issued inscribed 'BRITISH SOUTH AFRICA COMPANY'; from 1909, overprinted 'RHODESIA'; from 1910 both these names on each definitive issue. Up to 1923 a total of 138 stamps was issued, characteristic of British design and printing and including heraldic and portrait issues, as well as many overprinted provisionals. See also *Rhodesia*.

BURKINA FASO see UPPER VOLTA

BURUNDI
Area 27,834 sq.km, **population** 4.92m (1983), **capital** Bujumbura.

A developing agricultural country created from part of the Belgian trusteeship territory of Ruanda-Urundi in 1962. An independent kingdom from 1 July 1962; declared a republic on 28 November 1966 after the king was overthrown. Indirect UPU membership from 1 April 1891 (German protectorate); indirect from 31 August 1923 (Belgian possession); direct from 6 April 1963.

In 1962 Ruanda-Urundi stamps with the overprint 'Royaume du Burundi'; then definitives with the same name. From 1967 stamps were inscribed 'RÉPUBLIQUE DU BURUNDI'. Until 1965 as many as 200 stamps were issued, mostly printed in photogravure by the Israeli State Printing House, Hakirya. Typical collector's market exploitation with some issues deliberately kept to small printings; many miniature sheets, perforated and imperforate stamps (in printings of only 2,500 to 5,000) in unorthodox shapes (some circular). Pictorial stamps with general subjects and joint issues, directed especially to stamp export business. Annual output 80–150 stamps, chiefly airmail, sometimes also in long sets (up to 24 values).

Philatelic bureau Agence Philatélique, Bujumbura.

CAMEROON (CAMEROUN)
Area 475,442 sq.km, **population** 9.06m (1983), **capital** Yaoundé.

An agricultural country with developed bauxite metallurgy. An independent republic from 1 January 1960 (until then it was a trusteeship territory of *French Cameroun;* autonomous from 1959). Following a plebiscite in British Cameroons, the latter's southern part joined the Republic of Cameroon to form a federation on 1 October 1961. On 20 May 1972, the federal system was abolished, and the country adopted the name United Republic of Cameroon. Indirect UPU membership from 1 June 1887 (as a German protectorate); from 1919 (French Cameroun); direct from 26 July 1960.

From 1960 stamps with the name 'ÉTAT DU CAMEROUN' and 'RÉPUBLIQUE DU CAMEROUN'; from 1961, overprints 'RÉPUBLIQUE FÉDÉRALE', definitives with the inscription 'HÉPUBLIQUE FÉDÉRALE DU CAMEROUN'. Later stamps used a dual-language text — in French, 'RÉPUBLIQUE FÉDÉRALE DU CAMEROUN', and English, 'FEDERAL REPUBLIC OF CAMEROON'. From 1972, in conformity with the new constitution, the French text has read, 'RÉPUBLIQUE UNIE DU CAMEROUN', and the English, 'UNITED REPUBLIC OF CAMEROON'. Stamp production first characteristically French, using line-engraving technique; then frequent changes in design and printed by photogravure. Outstanding graphic stamp work with expensive printing. Apart from strongly propagandist themes, predominantly pictorial stamps and participation in omnibus issues, with some issues specifically for collectors. Annual output 25 to 40 stamps. See also *Kamerun.*

Philatelic bureau Bureau Philatélique, Direction des Postes, Yaoundé. **Trade sales** Inter-Governmental Philatelic Corporation.

CAMEROONS see **BRITISH CAMEROONS; FRENCH CAMEROUN;**
             KAMERUN (German)

CAMEROUN, FRENCH see **FRENCH CAMEROUN**

CANARY ISLANDS
An island group off the north-western coast of Africa, regarded, administratively, as the Spanish province of Las Palmas and Santa Cruz (**area** 7,273 sq.km, **capital** Las Palmas). Independent postal territory only during the Spanish Civil War (1936–8), when airmail stamps were intended for German Lufthansa flights along the route Canary Islands – Lisbon – Spain.

From 1936 Spanish stamps with the overprint 'CANARIAS': a total of 101 stamps issued (some appeared in very small printings of 1,350, 1,700 or 3,000) but it is doubtful if all of them did postal service. After 1938, Spanish stamps once again.

CAPE JUBY

A Spanish possession, acquired when Morocco was partitioned in 1912 (**area** 26,000 sq.km, **capital** Villa Bens-Cabo Yubi); joined to Spanish Western Sahara in 1924. In 1958 it was returned to Morocco as Southern Morocco.

In 1916, Rio de Oro stamps with the overprint 'CABO JUBI'; then Spanish stamps and, later, stamps of Spanish Morocco with the overprint 'CABO JUBY'. By 1948 a total of 168 stamps, some in small printings of 1,000 to 5,000; otherwise, tens of thousands. Virtually all overprinted provisionals. In 1917–19 the stamps of Rio de Oro or Spanish Morocco were used. The territory of Cape Juby was incorporated into Morocco in 1958, and Moroccan stamps are now used there.

CAPE OF GOOD HOPE (CAPE PROVINCE)

Cape Province, in southern Africa, was originally Boer territory, but after being occupied by the British in 1806–14 it became a British colony. It gradually expanded by adding more territory (Kaffaria and up to Orange in the north, Tembuland, Pondoland, Transkei, Griqualand East, between 1871 and 1884 Basutoland, the Bay of Whales (Walvis Bay) in South-West Africa in 1878, Stellaland in 1884, and British Bechuanaland in 1895). In 1910 it became a province of the Union of South Africa (**area** 717,395 sq.km, **capital** Cape Town).

The first stamps (definitives) with the text 'CAPE OF GOOD HOPE' appeared in 1853. These are the first triangular stamps in the world, and are among the great rarities — especially the so-called 'Woodblock' issues printed locally during a temporary shortage of London-printed supplies. Actually, these were printed from engraved plates, but the coarse engraving gave the finished stamps the appearance of rough woodcuts. From 1910 the country was a province of the Union of *South Africa*, but the stamps of Cape of Good Hope were valid until 31 December 1937. A total of 61 + 5 stamps of British origin.

CAPE VERDE ISLANDS

Area 4,033 sq.km, **population** 296,093 (1980), **capital** Praia.

An island group in the Atlantic, west of Cape Verde. A poor agricultural region. From 1951 the islands were regarded as an overseas province of Portugal, to which they had belonged since 1495. They became an independent republic by proclamation on 5 July 1975. Indirect UPU membership from 1 July 1877 (Portuguese colony); direct from 30 September 1976.

Definitives from 1877 with the name 'CABO VERDE'. Later occasionally with the inscription 'PROVINCIA DE CABO VERDE'. The designs were largely Portuguese colonial key-types, and provisionals (overprinted 'REPUBLICA' in 1911–25) until 1938. From the 1950s typical printing by offset-lithography with many general themes. After the declaration of independence in 1976, stamps were inscribed 'REPÚBLICA DE CABO VERDE'; more recently only the name 'CABO VERDE'. Current output is about 10 stamps a year, with national propaganda themes dominating.

Philatelic bureau Service Philatélique, Services des PRR, Praia.

CENTRAL AFRICAN REPUBLIC

Area 622,984 sq.km, **population** 2.52m (1983), **capital** Bangui.

Underdeveloped agricultural country whose independence was proclaimed on 13 August 1960, after two years as an autonomous republic. The country was earlier known as Oubangi-Shari, and according to the new Constitution the name was changed on 4 December 1976 to Central African Empire. However, on 21 September 1979, a republic was re-established and the present name revived. Indirect UPU membership from 1 June 1876 (French colony); direct from 28 June 1961.

In 1959 definitives with the text 'RÉPUBLIQUE CENTRAFRICAINE'. After the establishment of the empire, 'EMPIRE CENTRAFRICAIN'; after its fall, once again 'RÉPUBLIQUE CENTRAFRICAINE', all stamps of French origin. Besides propaganda subjects, a far greater number of pictorial stamps intended especially for foreign customers. In 1977 a large number of overprinted provisionals (63 different stamps), when existing stamps were overprinted at the time the empire was established. An attempt to interest collectors is demonstrated by the production of large stamps on gold foil, a big quantity of airmail stamps and miniature sheets, pictorial postage-due stamps, etc. Current annual output about 70 stamps.

Philatelic bureau Office des PTT, Service Philatélique, Bangui. **Trade sales** Agence des Timbres-Poste d'Outre-Mer.

CHAD

Area 1,284,000 sq.km, **population** 4.97m (1983), **capital** N'djamena.

A developing country with underdeveloped agriculture. Originally part of the French Congo, occupied in 1897–1903, then from 1904 a dependency, and from 1914 a territory of the colony of Ubangi-Shari-Chad (from 1910 in the framework of French Equatorial Africa). The northern part of the territory was joined to it in 1913–14. On 17 March 1920, Chad set up as an independent colony. It became an autonomous republic on 28 November 1958 and its independence was proclaimed on 11 August 1960. Indirect UPU membership from 1 July 1876 (as a French colony); direct from 23 June 1961.

Stamp-issuing as a French colony from 1922; stamps of the Middle Congo (used there previously) with the overprint 'TCHAD', then additionally 'AFRIQUE ÉQUATORIALE FRANÇAISE'. Until 1931 quite restrained stamp-issuing activities: 61 stamps, overprinted provisionals and pictorial stamps in designs common to French production. From 1936 to 1969 Chad used the stamps of *French Equatorial Africa*.

Republican issues appeared only in 1959, on the first anniversary of the proclamation of the autonomous republic. These were definitives with the name 'RÉPUBLIQUE DU TCHAD', pictorial stamps of French origin and designed to promote the area. At present, interest in the collector's market has become more prominent (choice of subjects, issues on gold foil, a large number of airmail stamps — more than 200 — long sets devoted to winners of the Olympic Games in Mexico consisting of 30 values, and pictorial triangular postage-due stamps. The annual output is irregular, but up to 40 stamps.

Philatelic bureau Philatelic Service, PTT, N'djamena. **Trade sales** Agence des Timbres-Poste d'Outre-Mer.

CISKEI

Area 8,500 sq.km, **population** 2.1m (1981), **capital** Bisho.

The fourth South African bantustan, declared an 'independent' republic for the Xhosa people on 4 December 1981. The bantustan, set up on 24 March 1961, originally consisted of 14 scattered territories in Cape Province.

Stamps of South African origin first issued in 1981 with the inscription 'CISKEI'. Designs promote the country and also cover general subjects.

Philatelic bureau Philatelic Services and Intersapa, GPO, Pretoria, South Africa.

COMORO (COMOROS)

Area 2,236 sq.km, **population** 408,000 (1980), **capital** Moroni.

An island republic in the Mozambique Channel. The islands were French from 1841; from 1908 to 1950 they were a colony, from 1914 as a province of Madagascar under the name Province de Mayotte et dépendances (the islands of Mayotte, Anjouan, Great Comoro and Mohéli, which until 1908 had their own stamps), and the stamps of *Madagascar* were valid until 1950. In 1946 the Comoros obtained autonomy, and from 1950 they separated from Madagascar. In 1958 they became an overseas territory of France, from 1961 with special autonomy before proclaiming an independent republic on 6 September 1975. Today, the official name is Republic of the Comoros. However, France declared the island Mayotte a French overseas department. Indirect UPU membership from 17 July 1876 (as part of the French colonies); direct from 29 July 1976.

Definitives from 1950 with the name 'ARCHIPEL DES COMORES'. After winning independence the name was changed to 'ÉTAT COMORIEN'; then 'RÉPUBLIQUE DES COMORES' and, finally, 'RÉPUBLIQUE FÉDÉRALE ISLAMIQUE DES COMORES'. Standard stamps of French origin, as other colonial issues of France. After winning independence, stamp-issuing rose sharply to an annual output of 50 to 70 stamps. The issues catered for collectors with large stamps of pleasing pictorial themes, especially attractive to foreign customers, and also a large quantity of airmail stamps and miniature sheets.

Philatelic bureau Direction des PTT, Section Philatélique, Dzaoudzi, Mayotte. **Trade sales** Agence des Timbres-Poste d'Outre-Mer.

CONGO (Brazzaville)

Area 342,000 sq.km, **population** 1.66m (1983), **capital** Brazzaville.

A developing agricultural country. A republic since 15 August 1960 (an autonomous republic from 1958, a part of French Equatorial Africa from 1910 under the name Middle Congo). Since 31 December 1969, it has used the name People's Republic of the Congo. Indirect UPU membership from 1 July 1876 (French colony); direct from 5 July 1961.

Definitives issued in 1959 with the name 'RÉPUBLIQUE DU CONGO'; from 1970, 'RÉPUBLIQUE POPULAIRE DU CONGO'. Stamp production is characteristically French, using, predominantly, the line-engraving process based on interesting graphic work, usually by French designers. Mostly general subjects and joint issues common to the French-controlled areas, apart from several stamps with propaganda themes. Current production 50 to 70 stamps annually. Large percentage of airmail stamps (almost half of present output), reflecting keen interest in the collector's market.

Philatelic bureau Centre Philatélique de l'Office Nationale des Postes et Télécommunications, Brazzaville. **Trade sales** Agence des Timbres-Poste d'Outre-Mer.

CONGO (Kinshasa)

Now Zaire, a developing agricultural country with enormous mineral wealth (**area** 2,345,409 sq.km, **capital** Kinshasa). The country was owned by the Belgian King Leopold II from 1885, and in 1908 became a Belgian colony with the name Belgian Congo. It gained independence on 30 June 1960 and from 1964 was called Democratic Republic of the Congo. The name Zaire was introduced on 27 September 1971.

In 1886 a definitive issue (portrait of King Leopold II) of the independent country of the Congo with the inscription: 'ÉTAT INDÉPENDANT DU CONGO' (in an issue of only 6,000 complete sets). By 1900, 34 stamps had been issued (usually the work of Belgian artists), printed in Belgium and in Great Britain. Portrait issues were followed, from 1894, by pictorial stamps (representing the early period of pictorial issues). From 1909 see *Belgian Congo*.

In 1960 stamps of the Belgian Congo with the overprint 'CONGO' and definitives with the same inscription; later, 'RÉPUBLIQUE DU CONGO' and, finally, 'RÉPUBLIQUE DÉMOCRATIQUE DU CONGO'. A total of 446 stamps of Belgian origin, chiefly the designs of J. van Noten, produced in several European printing houses. General subjects, small printings (some of 25,000) and production of miniature sheets suggest that sales to the collector's market prevail over postal use. The designs include many popular pictorial themes with a limited number of propaganda designs. From 1971 see *Zaire*.

CYRENAICA

Until 1912 a part of a Turkish vilayet. After the Italian-Turkish war Cyrenaica formed the eastern part of the Italian colony of Libya. From 1942/3 to 1951 it was occupied by the British, then became a province of the Independent Kingdom of Libya (**area** 855,400 sq.km, **capital** Bengasi).

Preceded by stamps of the Italian post office in Bengasi, from 1911 Libyan stamps (valid together with those of Cyrenaica until 1935). The first stamps specifically for Cyrenaica were Italian stamps of 1923 with the overprint 'CIRENAICA'. Altogether, there was a total of 136 + 7 stamps characteristic of Italian design and printing. Printings tended to be limited — less than 1,000 sometimes — to tempt buying by collectors. Chiefly overprinted provisionals; later pictorial stamps also. Stamp issuing continued until 1934, when Libyan stamps became valid in the territory.

British stamps with the overprint 'M.E.F.' (Middle East Forces) were introduced during the Second World War and were valid until 1949 in Cyrenaica (also in the Mediterranean area).

Efforts to achieve political independence were reflected in 1950 by 2 issues, of British origin, with the inscription 'CYRENAICA'. A total of 13 + 7 definitives. See also *Libya*.

DAHOMEY

The one-time African Kingdom of Dahomey (**area** 112,622 sq.km, **capital** Porto Novo) was annexed by France in 1894, and in 1899 it was joined to coastal Benin and given the name of Dahomey. From 1895 a part of French West Africa; declared an autonomous republic on 4 December 1958. Dahomey obtained full independence on 1 August 1960, and on 30 November 1975 was renamed the People's Republic of Benin.

Stamp-issuing as a French colony from 1899, when stamps in designs common to the French colonial issues of the time appeared with the name 'DAHOMEY ET DÉPENDAN-CES'. Later issues were inscribed 'DAHOMEY' and 'AFRIQUE OCCIDENTALE FRANÇAISE'. Subsequently, 'DAHOMEY' alone was used. A total of 170 + 31 stamps issued, of French origin (produced by the line-engraving process). From 1941–60 stamps of French West Africa were issued. The first issues of the independent country date from 1960 with 'RÉPUBLIQUE DU DAHOMEY'. A total 259 + 27 stamps issued with a change in graphic concept and a switch to photogravure. Besides themes covering national activities, there have been a number of issues on joint subjects. Production geared to the demand of the collector's market; this includes a large number of airmail stamps (more than half), pictorial postage-due stamps and a general selection of attractive subjects. From 1975 see *Benin*.

DIÉGO SUAREZ

From 1885 to 1893 a French colonial territory on the northern shore of Madagascar, consisting of territory around the town of Diégo Suarez and the island dependencies of Sainte Marie de Madagascar and Nossi-Bé (the capital of Diégo Suarez). In 1893 the colony was divided into three independent units which in 1906 were joined to Madagascar.

In 1890, the standard French colonial key-type with the inscription (later the overprint) 'DIÉGO SUAREZ (ET DÉPENDANCES)'. Stamps of French origin, mostly of the colonial designs, but also primitives locally printed. A total of 50 + 13 stamps, of which several were also valid on Nossi-Bé and Sainte Marie de Madagascar. From mid-1898 the small postal territory of Diégo Suarez, Nossi-Bé and Sainte Marie de Madagascar was united with the main island, *Madagascar,* whose stamps were then used there.

DJIBOUTI

Area 23,000 sq.km, **population** 330,000 (1983), **capital** Djibouti.

A backward territory on the Red Sea coast. The French began to occupy it in 1869, and after building up the port of Djibouti in 1888, declared the town and its environs a protectorate. In 1894 the post office from *Obock* was transferred here, and after the colony of *French Somaliland* was established, Djibouti and Obock became a part of it, the former becoming the capital. In 1967 it was given the name, *French Territory of Afars and Issas.* On 27 June 1977, it obtained independence under the name Republic of Djibouti. Indirect UPU membership from 1 July 1876 as French Somaliland (French colonies); direct from 6 June 1978.

From 1894 the word 'DJIBOUTI' or only 'DJ' was overprinted on Obock stamps used here from 1892 to 1894, when definitives appeared inscribed, 'PROTECTORAT DE LA CÔTE DES SOMALIS DJIBOUTI', in French, Somali and Amharic: a total of 36 stamps, chiefly overprinted provisionals. The definitives were triangular and diamond-shaped. From 1902 stamps of *French Somaliland.* The name DJIBOUTI appeared once again, later, on some isolated stamps of French Somaliland (especially issues of Free France, issued in London during the Second World War). Stamps of French Territory of the Afars and Issas had overprinted on them in 1977, 'RÉPUBLIQUE DE DJIBOUTI' (following independence) and similarly inscribed definitives followed soon after. A predominance of pictorial thematic designs appealing to the collector's market. Annual output about 25 stamps, of which half are airmail.

Philatelic bureau Office des PTT, Service Philatélique, Djibouti. **Trade sales** Agence des Timbres-Poste d'Outre-Mer.

EGYPT
Area 1,002,000 sq.km, **population** 46m (1984), **capital** Cairo.

An agricultural country with developing industry. Until 1914 the Turkish khedivate, but from 1882 occupied by the British; a British protectorate 1914–22; from 1922 an independent kingdom. It became the Republic of Egypt on 18 July 1953, and on 1 February 1958 was united with Syria as the United Arab Republic (until September 1961). Since 2 September 1971, the name Arab Republic of Egypt has been used. Direct UPU membership from 1 July 1875.

Stamp issuing began in 1866. The names on the stamps are usually in two languages (though sometimes in Arabic only). From 1866 Turkish and Arabic; 1872–9, in Italian, 'PO-STE KHEDEVIE EGIZIANE' — and in Arabic (the Arabic inscription was afterwards used alongside the name in Latin script, even in subsequent years). From 1879 to 1914 the inscription was in French — 'POSTES ÉGYPTIENNES'; 1914–23, English 'EGYPT POSTAGE'; 1925–56, again French — 'ROYAUME D'ÉGYPTE', 'POSTES D'ÉGYPTE', 'ÉGYPTE', 'RÉPUBLIQUE D'ÉGYPTE'; 1957, English 'EGYPT'; from 1971 'A.R. EGYPT'; after 1976, just 'EGYPT' again.

Egypt had almost 40 post offices abroad (Turkey, Ethiopia, Greece, Sudan, for example), where only Egyptian stamps were used. The last was closed down in 1881. At the same time, there were British, French, Italian, Austrian, Russian and Greek post offices in Egyptian territory, particularly in Alexandria and Port Said, which used stamps that did not have the name Egypt on them. From 1932, British troops in Egypt used special stamps inscribed 'BRITISH FORCES IN EGYPT' or 'ARMY POST EGYPT': a total of 15 stamps. At first these were valid only for Great Britain, but later also for India, and from the spring of 1940 also for Australia and New Zealand.

Until 1958 a total of 528 + 115 stamps issued, most in reasonable quantities. In subject matter, they stressed chiefly Egypt's ancient architecture; during the period of the kingdom portraits of the ruler appeared and, later, other national propaganda subjects which, especially during the republic, reflected social changes, a typical example of using stamps for propaganda purposes. There have been a few limited printings of 1,500 sets to 3,750 sets, an example being the special printing of Farouk birthday stamps of 1929. Various influences from foreign designers and printers were at work in Egyptian production from the very beginning. From 1925 to 1963 all stamps were printed at the Typographical Institute in Cairo. Since 1963, practically all have been printed by the Postal Authority Press in Cairo. Both these printers almost exclusively used the photogravure process, giving Egyptian stamps their characteristic appearance.

From 1958 to 1971 the country was known as *United Arab Republic – Egypt*. Since 1971, when the country was renamed Arab Republic of Egypt, the name 'EGYPT' has appeared on stamps. Stamp-issuing activities continue with the production of about 30 stamps a year using many propaganda themes.

Philatelic bureau Philatelic Office, Post Organization, Cairo.

ELOBEY, ANNOBÓN AND CORISCO
Island group in the Gulf of Guinea (Elobey, 2.5 sq.km; Annobón, 17 sq.km; Corisco, 15 sq.km; **capital** Elobey-Chaco). Between 1778 and 1900 a Spanish colony; from 1900 part of Spanish Guinea. Today, the islands belong to Equatorial Guinea.

Before the islands' own stamps were issued, those of *Fernando Poo* were valid here from 1868. From 1903 definitives with the name 'ELOBEY, ANNOBON Y CORISCO' appeared in very small issues of the high values (around 2,000 complete sets). A total of 60 stamps of Spanish origin in Spanish colonial types, portraits and overprinted issues. From 1909 these territories were joined to Fernando Poo and Spanish mainland Guinea to form the postal region of the Spanish Territories of the Gulf of Guinea; in 1949–59, Spanish Guinea; then split up into Rio Muni (Elobey, Corisco) and Fernando Poo (Annobón).

EQUATORIAL GUINEA
Area 28,051 sq.km, **population** 304,000 (1983), **capital** Malabo.

A backward country with tropical agriculture. From 12 October 1968 an independent republic, which came into existence in place of the Spanish overseas territory of the same name (earlier Spanish Guinea). Indirect UPU membership from 1 May 1877 (Spanish colony); direct from 24 July 1970.

From 1964 to 1968, autonomous Equatorial Guinea was not a stamp-issuing territory, but continued to use the stamps of its two provinces, *Rio Muni* and *Fernando Poo*. The first definitive series was of Spanish origin and appeared shortly after the independence in 1968, bearing the inscription 'REPUBLICA DE GUINEA ECUATORIAL'. At first its stamp issuing was very reserved; until 1971 a total of only 16 stamps appeared. Then, under agency influence, a large number of issues designed specifically for the philatelic market appeared, including perforated and imperforate stamps, miniature sheets and large-size airmail stamps, with supplementary charges. The first issues had values ranging from 1 to 25 pesetas; later the face values were as high as 200 pesetas. For 1972 alone, 368 stamps were registered. Until mid-1973 more than 500 stamps appeared, and over 100 miniature sheets. World catalogues have not even recorded these 'stamps' in detail.

Philatelic bureau Oficina Filatélica, Malabo.

ERITREA
One-time Italian colony (1890–1941) in East Africa on the shores of the Red Sea (**area** 124,000 sq.km, **capital** Asmera), annexed by Italy in 1882. Its size varied — in 1894 it was provisionally increased by the addition of part of occupied Ethiopia; in 1936–41, when it became a part of Italian East Africa, it was 231,280 sq.km including the annexed section of Ethiopia. After Italy's defeat it was occupied by Great Britain; on 15 September 1952, it formed a federation with Ethiopia, with which it merged in 1962.

Before issuing its own stamps, joint issues of the Italian possessions ('Estero') were used. Stamp issuing began in 1893 when Italian stamps were brought out with the overprint 'CO-LONIA ERITREA'. Later came definitives with the same name and, still later, with only 'ERI-TREA': a total of 252 + 70 stamps of Italian origin chiefly overprinted provisionals (mainly on Italian stamps). Production in the 1930s was as high as 30 stamps annually. Relatively small quantities, with doubtful postal availability of a considerable number of them. In 1938–41 stamps of Italian East Africa were valid in Eritrea.

During the Second World War, Eritrea was occupied by British troops who, until 1948, used British issues overprinted 'M.E.F.' (Middle East Forces). In 1948, British stamps were issued with the overprint 'B.M.A. ERITREA' (British Military Administration); in 1950 the overprint 'B.A. ERITREA' on British stamps (British Administration), representing British civilian administration which replaced the military. In 1948–50 a total of 33 + 10 overprinted provisionals issued. Since 1952 stamps of *Ethiopia* have been valid here.

ETHIOPIA
Area 1,221,800 sq.km, **population** 33 m (1983), **capital** Addis Ababa.

An underdeveloped agricultural country, at one time known also as Abyssinia. One of the oldest independent states of Africa. The Ethiopian empire, established in 1853, was based on the one-time kingdom of Gojjam, Shoa, Jimma, Tigre, Amhara, Kafa and Wollo. From 1936 to 1941 occupied by Italy, which in 1936 incorporated it into Italian East Africa. In 1952 Eritrea was federated with Ethiopia, and since 1962 has been fully integrated. After the abolition of the empire (12 September 1974) the country was considered a kingdom, and by a government decree of 12 September 1975, it was given the new name of Socialist Ethiopia with a system of government close to that of a republic. Direct UPU membership from 1 November 1908 (empire); indirect from 1936–41 (Italian occupation); direct from 5 May 1941 (empire).

The first Ethiopian stamps appeared in 1894 with an Amharic text; from 1909 with the French inscription 'ETHIOPIE', 'POSTES ETHIOPIENNES'. From 1936 to 1938 an occupa-

231

tion set of 7 stamps of Italian origin with the inscription 'ETIOPIA, POSTE COLONIALI ITALIANE', and a text in Amharic and Somali was issued. In 1938–41 the stamps of *Italian East Africa* were valid. After liberation, the texts were in English ('ETHIOPIA') and Amharic, and this continued even after the empire was abolished.

Until 1908, when Ethiopia first entered the UPU, there were two kinds of postage. The first Ethiopian issue of 1894, authorized by Minister Ilgem (therefore called the ministerial issue), was valid only for internal use. The French post offices in Diredawa, Addis Ababa and Harar took care of most of Ethiopian foreign mailing until 31 October 1908. They used the stamps of Obock, Djibouti, French Somaliland, Port Said and the French Levant. In Harar there was an Egyptian post office between 1866 and 1880, which used Egyptian stamps; in Addis Ababa a British post office and in Harar a British consular post office which, at first, used stamps of British Somaliland, and later of India.

The stamps were printed in large numbers by various foreign printers, which explains the diversity of design styles. They chiefly depict national propaganda themes. During the imperial period this was reflected especially in glorification of the ruler. After the coup d'état of 1975, when his portrait disappeared from the stamps, the anniversary of the revolution has been recalled every year. At the present time, the annual output is about 40 to 50 stamps, among which one finds more general thematic subjects (women's hair-styles, fish, insects, domestic animals, etc.), likely to interest collectors.

Philatelic bureau Ethiopian Postal Service, Philatelic Section, Addis Ababa. **Trade sales** Inter-Governmental Philatelic Corporation.

FERNANDO POO

An island (**area** 2,017 sq.km, **capital** Santa Isabel) with profitable plantation agriculture; from 1964 an island province of autonomous Equatorial Guinea which, since 1968, has been an independent country. Together with the island Annobón it belonged to Spain from 1778, but between 1827 and 1845 it was temporarily occupied by the British. From 1900 to 1960 it was part of the colony of Spanish Guinea and then a Spanish overseas province.

Stamp issues began in 1868 when definitives appeared inscribed 'FERNANDO POO' (between 1869 and 1879 stamps of the Spanish overseas postal authorities). From 1879 Fernando Poo had its own issues, with some printings restricted to 500 complete sets. Fernando Poo stamps were used throughout Spanish Guinea between 1879 and 1902. Stamps of Spanish origin, mostly of basic Spanish colonial design, usually printed by letter-press process. Up to 1909 a total of 174 stamps were issued. Fernando Poo belonged to the postal region of the Spanish Territories of the Gulf of Guinea from 1909 to 1949, and used the stamps of that area. However, in 1929 Spanish stamps were issued with the overprint 'FERNANDO POO' for the Spanish exhibition in Seville, but these were not valid in Fernando Poo itself. In 1949–59 the name was Spanish Guinea.

From 1960 the island again had its own stamps with the name 'FERNANDO POO', which later had the additional inscription, 'ESPAÑA'. Typical Spanish production, printed usually by the photogravure process in the State Printing House in Madrid, in minimum printings of 225,000 stamps, most values being up to one million. Mainly standard pictorial stamps with many general themes largely designed to attract collectors. A total of 230 stamps, including the early period. From 1968 see *Equatorial Guinea*.

FEZZAN

The southern part of Libya occupied by the Free French; until 1948 a part of the French military region Fezzan-Ghadames. From 1951 a province of Libya. Capital, Sebha, then Marzuq.

The first stamps appeared in 1948 with the name 'TERRITOIRE MILITAIRE FEZZAN'; after the military administration was replaced by a civilian administration only the inscription became 'TERRITOIRE DU FEZZAN': a total of 29 + 6 stamps of French origin. Before 1948, the stamps of *Fezzan-Ghadames* were valid; after 1951, those of *Libya*.

FEZZAN-GHADAMES

The south-eastern area of Libya, occupied in 1942–3 by the Free French (**area** 550,000 sq.km, **capital** Sebha, then Marzuq). From 1948 divided into two territories (Fezzan and Ghadames); from 1951, a part of Libya.

In 1943 issues of the military administration for Fezzan-Ghadames, Italian and Libyan stamps with the overprint 'FEZZAN - Occupation Française/RF'. Printings were limited, the largest being 4,300; the lowest, 79, casting doubt on the postal status of the stamps. From 1946 definitives of French origin with the inscription 'RF FEZZAN - GHADAMÈS Territoire Militaire'. A total of 45 + 5 stamps. Before the French occupation, Libyan stamps were used, and after 1948 there were separate issues for *Fezzan* and *Ghadames*.

FRENCH CAMEROUN

After the defeat of the German troops in 1915–16, and following the occupation by French and British troops, a large part of the former German possession Kamerun was declared a mandate territory of the League of Nations in 1922 and placed under French administration. The area which France had given to German Kamerun in 1911 was annexed to French Equatorial Africa (**area** 3,432,000 sq.km, **capital** Yaoundé).

In 1915 Gabon stamps with the overprint 'Corps Expeditionaire Franco-Anglais CAMEROUN', later 'Occupation Française du Cameroun'. From 1921 French Congo stamps and then those of the Central Congo with the overprint 'CAMEROUN'; later, definitives with the same name: a total of 358 + 34 stamps, predominantly overprinted provisionals, otherwise standard French production of pictorial stamps including some designs common to the French colonies. The designs include remarkable work produced by the line-engraving process. From 1958 an autonomous government; from 1960 an independent republic *Cameroon*.

FRENCH CONGO

In 1880, France obtained, by treaty, the territory north of the River Congo, known as the Middle Congo, which — allied with Gabon — was known under the name French Congo from 1886 to 1904 (**area** 1,762,000 sq.km, **capital** Brazzaville). Parts of it — Gabon and Ubangi-Shari-Chad — then became separate colonies; the rest were again given the name Middle Congo and, in 1910, the whole territory of the French Congo was renamed French Equatorial Africa.

First issue appeared in 1891, being the French colonial general issue with the overprint 'Congo Français'. Then followed French colonial key-types (1892–1900) and, finally, definitives with the same name. A total of 50 stamps of French origin. These are overprinted provisionals, French key-types and pictorials.

FRENCH EQUATORIAL AFRICA

French territory in equatorial Africa, at first known as the French Congo; from 1910 renamed French Equatorial Africa, including the colonies of Gabon, Middle Congo and Ubangi-Shari. (Chad, a dependency of the colony of Ubangi-Shari until 1920, formed an independent colony from 17 March 1920 and became an autonomous republic in 1958.) Its borders kept changing until 1924, when it was 2,510,000 sq.km, with Brazzaville as capital.

Although the colony became established in 1910, stamps continued to be issued by its individual members and only in 1924 did the first overprints 'AFRIQUE ÉQUATORIALE FRANÇAISE' appear on stamps of the Middle Congo. From 1925 the stamps of all four colonies were valid anywhere on the territory of French Equatorial Africa. Nonetheless, issues of the individual colonies appeared until 1936, because each had its own postal administration. In 1936, there were again overprints on the stamps of Gabon and the Middle Congo with the same name as in 1924; in 1937 definitives appeared with the same inscription. A total of 312 + 21 stamps of standard French origin with a large representation of key-type designs. Pictorial stamps were printed by the more demanding engraving process. After 1958 came the stamps of the individual states, *Congo, Central African Republic, Gabon* and *Chad*.

FRENCH GUINEA

French territory in West Africa. A protectorate from 1860, a colony from 1893; from 1904 a part of French West Africa. From 1946 an overseas territory of France. Declared the Independent Republic of Guinea on 2 October 1958 (**area** 245,857 sq.km, **capital** Conakry).

In 1892 French colonial key-plate designs (with the text 'GUINÉE FRANÇAISE'; later, 'GUINÉE/AFRIQUE OCCIDENTALE FRANÇAISE': a total of 206 + 36 stamps of typical French origin. Standard pictorial stamps and many overprinted provisionals. From 1945 to 1958 the stamps of *French West Africa,* afterwards those of the Independent Republic of *Guinea.*

FRENCH SOMALILAND

French territory in north-eastern Africa. At first the port of Obock was captured (1862), then the whole territory by 1884, and in 1888 the port of Djibouti was built. A colony from 1896, between 1940 and 1942 occupied by Italy, then the French restored their colonial administration; in 1958 French Somaliland was proclaimed an overseas territory of France. In 1967 it acquired a higher degree of autonomy and a new name, the French Territory of the Afars and the Issas, and in 1977 it gained independence as Djibouti (**area** 23,000 sq.km, **capital** Djibouti).

The first issue in 1902 with the name 'CÔTE FRANÇAISE DES SOMALIS' (before this the stamps of Obock had been valid from 1892, those of Djibouti from 1894, which sometimes bear concurrently the name 'PROTECTORAT DE LA CÔTE DES SOMALIS'). A total of 325 + 53 stamps with general themes and a number of French colonial issues and typical French colonial designs by the more expensive line-engraving process. These also show some rather remarkable graphic designs. From 1967, see *French Territory of the Afars and Issas,* from 1977 see *Djibouti.*

FRENCH SUDAN

From 1893 a French colony in West Africa on the upper reaches of the Niger, joined to French West Africa in 1899; parts divided between neighbouring French colonies, and partially constituted into a new territory of Senegambia and Niger (1902); re-divided in 1904 and renamed Upper Senegal and Niger and Mauritania. In 1920 the colony was again renamed French Sudan (by excluding Niger and Upper Volta; the latter became a new colony in 1919). French Sudan was a member of French West Africa until 1958 when it was declared an autonomous republic, with which, on 17 January 1969, Senegal, Dahomey and Upper Volta formed an alliance as the Federation of Mali. In the event, however, Upper Volta and Dahomey did not join the Federation. At that time, French Sudan's area was 1,178,000 sq.km and its capital was Bamako.

The first stamps of French Sudan date from 1894 (stamps of the general issues of the French colonies) with the overprint 'SOUDAN FAIS', followed by the colonial key-plate issue inscribed 'SOUDAN FRANÇAIS'. In 1902–4 Senegambia and Niger stamps were valid here, and in 1904–21 those of Upper Senegal and Niger; later with the overprint 'SOUDAN FRANÇAIS'. The same inscription appears on definitives of 1931 onwards. In 1944–59 the stamps of *French West Africa* were valid in the territory of French Sudan. A total of 152 + 20 stamps, typical of French production.

FRENCH TERRITORY OF THE AFARS AND ISSAS

A backward territory on the shore of the Red Sea which in 1977 obtained independence as *Djibouti* (**area** 23,000 sq.km, **capital** Djibouti). Originally it had the status of an overseas territory of France, but from 1967 had a higher degree of autonomy than the former French Somaliland. The abbreviated name is Afars and Issas.

After being named *French Somaliland,* whose stamps were used, the first definitives appeared in 1967 with the name 'TERRITOIRE FRANÇAIS DES AFARS ET DES ISSAS'. Well-printed standard pictorial stamps of French origin. A total of 168 + 4 stamps with a considerable percentage of airmail stamps — almost one third. Design subjects relate not only to this African territory and to France, but also have common international themes.

FRENCH WEST AFRICA

French territory in West Africa, merged from 1895 to 1958 to form French territory West Africa, the largest colony in Africa (**area** 4,742,500 sq.km, **capital** Dakar).

The individual territories of French West Africa issued their own stamps independently. Only from 1944 (until 1959) did stamps appear with the inscription 'AFRIQUE OCCIDENTALE FRANÇAISE'. In 1958, French Guinea became independent. The other states — Dahomey, the Ivory Coast, French Sudan, Mauritania, Niger, Senegal and Upper Volta — were proclaimed autonomous republics and began gradually to issue their own stamps, although issues of French West Africa continued to be used until 1962. A total of 103 + 10 stamps were printed, of French origin, with many designs in common. Standard pictorial stamps of improved quality, due to the line-engraving process. Between 1944 and 1947 the stamps of *French Equatorial Africa* and *Togo* were used.

FUNCHAL

An administrative district of Portugal and major city of Madeira, off the north-western coast of Africa (**area** 707 sq.km, **capital** Funchal).

Funchal issued its own stamps in 1892 (definitives) in Portuguese colonial key-types inscribed 'FUNCHAL'. Prior to this, Madeira stamps were in circulation. A total of 34 stamps of Portuguese origin. Since 1910, Funchal has belonged to the postal territory of Portugal, whose stamps then became valid (as have those for *Madeira*).

GABON

Area 267,667 sq.km, **population** 1.29m (1983), **capital** Libreville.

A fairly developed state, predominantly engaged in forestry and mineral mining. A French colony from 1886 and until 1904 part of the French Congo. It then became a separate colony, but in 1910 was joined to French Equatorial Africa. In 1958 it won the status of an autonomous republic, and became an independent state in 1960. Indirect UPU membership from 1 July 1876 (as a French colony); direct from 17 July 1961.

Stamp-issuing activities as a French colony from 1886 when French colonial stamps were issued with the overprint 'GAB', later 'GABON'; and, in 1889, type-set definitives inscribed 'Gabon-Congo' and, finally, 'GABON' on colonial key-plate designs. From 1910 pictorials were inscribed, 'CONGO FRANÇAIS GABON' or 'AFRIQUE ÉQUATORIALE GABON'. This last (1910) issue was overprinted 'AFRIQUE ÉQUATORIALE FRANÇAISE' in 1922 before reverting to just 'GABON' in 1932. A total of 146 + 33 stamps, the overwhelming majority being overprinted provisionals, otherwise standard pictorial stamps of French origin. From 1936 until the declaration of the Republic of Gabon stamps of *French Equatorial Africa* were used.

Although the republic was established in 1958, the first republican stamps of Gabon did not appear until 1959, on the first anniversary of the republic. They are definitives with the name 'RÉPUBLIQUE GABONAISE', produced in France, first by line-engraving and later by photogravure. Apart from propaganda themes, the number of general subjects and omnibus issues showed an awareness of collector demand which was also reflected in the large production of airmail stamps (220 different stamps), miniature sheets (31), stamps on gold foil of high values (up to 1000 francs), etc. Annual output 40 to 50 stamps.

Philatelic bureau Service Philatélique, Office des PTT, Libreville. **Trade sales** Agence des Timbres-Poste d'Outre-Mer.

GAMBIA

Area 11,295 sq.km, **population** 695,886 (1983), **capital** Banjul (formerly Bathurst).

An underdeveloped country with plantation agriculture (peanuts). A British colony from 1843; in 1866–8 it became part of the West African settlements administered from Sierra Leone. Then, once again, it became a colony with a protectorate administrative system. Part of Gambia was incorporated into French Senegal in 1904. From 1963 it obtained internal autonomy, and in 1965 became an independent state within the British Commonwealth, and was declared a republic on 24 April 1970. Indirect UPU membership from 1 January 1879 (British colony); direct from 9 October 1974.

Definitive (first) issue of 1869 with the name 'GAMBIA'. From 1966 the inscription became 'THE GAMBIA'. Very conservative stamp-issuing policy. In its almost 100 years' existence only 185 stamps were issued until the declaration of independence in 1965. Then issuing increased somewhat, and at the present time The Gambia issues up to 35 stamps annually. Overall production represents the standard prints of British origin. The first issue of 1869, with the embossed head of Queen Victoria, is known philatelically as the 'Gambia Cameos'. After initial portrait issues (key-and-duty plate) came typical pictorial stamps and omnibus issues of the British Commonwealth, supplemented in recent times by Gambian propaganda themes. From 1972 the stamps have borne, as a supplement to the stamp picture, the portrait of the country's head of state.

Philatelic bureau Director of Posts, General Post Office, Banjul. **Trade sales** Crown Agents' Stamp Bureau.

GERMAN EAST AFRICA

The territory acquired from 1884 by the German East Africa Company for German colonization was officially declared a German colony in 1891 (**area** 826,325 sq.km, **capital** Dar es-Salaam). It included the island of Mafia. It was occupied by the Allies during the First World War (1916–17), and after the war the Versailles Treaty of 1919 gave the main part to Great Britain as a mandate (in 1920 it was given the name Tanganyika), Ruanda-Urundi became a Belgian mandate, and the triangle of Kionga became part of Portuguese Mozambique.

From 1890 the German post office used German stamps, from 1893 with a currency surcharge, later with the surcharge and a 'Deutsch-Ostafrika' overprint. In 1901 the German colonial key-and-duty designs were issued with the same inscription: a total of 39 stamps of German origin. The territory was gradually occupied, and by 1 November, 1917, it was in Allied hands.

From 1917 to 1922 stamps of British East Africa and Uganda with the overprint 'G.E.A.' (German East Africa): a total of 25 overprinted provisionals.

From 1916 stamps of the Belgian Congo with an overprint and then 'DUITSCH OOST AFRIKA/BELGISCHE BEZETTING — EST AFRICAIN ALLEMAND/OCCUPATION BELGE' and afterwards stamps of the Belgian Congo with the overprint 'A.O.' (Afrique Orientale): a total of 21 overprinted provisionals. For subsequent issues see *Tanganyika, Ruanda-Urundi* and *Kionga*.

GERMAN SOUTH-WEST AFRICA

In 1884 the area was declared a German colony (with the exception of the British Bay of Whales — Walvis Bay). During the First World War the territory was occupied by South African units (in 1915); in 1920, as a mandate of the League of Nations it came under the administration of the Union of South Africa (**area** 822,907 sq.km, **capital** Windhoek).

From 1888 German stamps were used, from 1897 German stamps with the overprint 'Deutsch-Südwestafrika'; later German colonial key-plate issues similarly inscribed: a total of 32 stamps of German origin. From 1915 stamps of the Union of South Africa were in use until those of South-West Africa first appeared in 1923.

GHADAMES

Territory in western Libya occupied in 1943 by troops of the Free French, and until 1948 a part of the French military territory Fezzan-Ghadames. From 1951 a part of Libya. The capital is Ghudamis.

Definitives appeared in 1949 with the inscription 'GHADAMÈS TERRITOIRE MILITAIRE': a total of 10 values. Before 1949 see *Fezzan-Ghadames*; after 1951 see *Libya*.

GHANA

Area 238,537 sq.km, **population** 12.83m (1983), **capital** Accra.

A developed agricultural country with important mineral mining. Formerly the Gold Coast, independent since 6 March 1957 as Ghana (including former British Togo); a republic (in the Commonwealth) from 1 July 1960. Indirect UPU membership as the Gold Coast from 1 January 1876 (British colony); indirect as Togo from 1 June 1888 (German protectorate); indirect from 10 July 1919 (British possession); direct as Ghana from 10 October 1957.

From 1957 definitives with the name 'GHANA' and overprints with the same name on Gold Coast stamps. Stamp designs are strongly propagandist: the independence of the state, the independence of Africa, African unity, the fight for peace, etc. However, many other themes are included to attract collectors, with a wide variety of designs by artists of many countries produced by many different printers. The collector's market also influences current production, represented by 30 to 40 stamps a year, with a large number of miniature sheets (over 80).

Philatelic bureau Principal Controller of Posts, Philatelic Bureau, General Post Office, Accra. **Trade sales** Inter-Governmental Philatelic Corporation.

GOLD COAST

The Gold Coast, given this name because of large deposits of the precious metal, was turned into a colony by the British in 1874. In 1901 it was joined by Ashanti as a protectorate and the so-called Northern Territories. After the First World War, in 1922, the western part of former German Togo — later the mandated territory of British Togo — was also joined to the Gold Coast. In 1954 the country gained self-government, and on 6 March 1957, its independence (together with integrated British Togo) in the British Commonwealth. It then adopted the name *Ghana,* and in 1960 became a republic.

In 1875 definitives with the inscription 'GOLD COAST': a total of 150 + 8 stamps of British origin. At first portrait issues (basically in colonial key-type designs); from the 1930s pictorial stamps and colonial omnibus types. On independence in 1957 the stamps of *Ghana* became valid.

GREAT COMORO (GRANDE COMORE)

The main island in the Comoros group (**area** 1,148 sq.km, **capital** Moroni). In 1886–1908 a French protectorate, then together with the islands Mayotte, Anjouan and Mohéli a part of Madagascar's Province de Mayotte et dépendances. Declared a colony in 1912. Today it is part of the *Comoros.*

From 1897 stamps of French colonial key-plate types with the inscription 'GRANDE CO-MORE': until 1911, 2 issues totalling 19 stamps of French origin. From 1911 to 1950 stamps of *Madagascar* were used here. The remainder of the Great Comoro stamps were given currency surcharges in 1912 and were used in Madagascar.

GRIQUALAND WEST

Cape Province district, earlier part of Orange River Colony, annexed by Great Britain in 1871; an independent colony until 1880, then joined to Cape Province (**area** 39,510 sq.km, **capital** Kimberley). Not to be confused with Griqualand East, between Basutoland and Natal which, from the postal viewpoint, was attached to Cape Province even earlier (annexed in 1869–1874).

In 1874–9, 20 overprinted provisionals appeared with the letters 'G.W.' and, later, 'G' on *Cape of Good Hope* stamps. After the merger, the Griqualand stamps were also used up in the Cape.

GUINEA

Area 245,857 sq.km, **population** 5.41m (1983), **capital** Conakry.

An underdeveloped country with plantation agriculture. A republic since 2 October 1958 (formerly a French colony, then the overseas territory French Guinea). On 21 November 1978, the name People's Revolutionary Republic of Guinea was introduced. Indirect UPU membership from 1 July 1876 (as a French colony); direct from 6 May 1959.

Stamp-issuing from 1958, when stamps of French West Africa appeared with the overprint 'RÉPUBLIQUE DE GUINÉE', then definitives with the same text. The official change of name is not reflected in the stamps. A large production showing a great diversity of design styles by designers from various countries and printed by several different foreign printing houses. This has resulted in marked differences in quality. The constant stream of new issues, on a wide variety of themes, is obviously aimed at the collector's market. There are overprinted provisionals in advance of the issues they 'advertise' and perforated and imperforate stamps of the same issue. Mostly general themes and joint common international issues, and only to a lesser extent national propaganda. More than 150 airmail stamps and 40 miniature sheets have already been issued. Annual output is between 30 and 70 stamps.

Philatelic bureau Agence Philatélique de la République de Guinea, Conakry.

GUINEA-BISSAU

Area 36,125 sq.km, **population** 826,000 (1983), **capital** Bissau.

A republic with very underdeveloped agriculture. A former overseas province of Portuguese Guinea, the first of the Portuguese possessions to be declared an independent state by the National Liberation Movement on 24 September 1973. (From 1973 to 1974 Modina da Boe was the headquarters of the National Liberation administration.) Portugal only recognized its independence a year later. Indirect UPU membership from 1 July 1877 (as a Portuguese possession); direct since 30 May 1974.

The first stamps of the independent republic appeared in 1973 with the name 'ESTADO DA GUINÉ-BISSAU'; later issues have the inscription 'REPUBLICA DA GUINÉ-BISSAU' or, only, 'GUINÉ-BISSAU'. Stamp production — currently with an annual output of 30 to 50 stamps — is strongly influenced by collector demand, as indicated by the choice of design themes of interest mainly to foreign customers. The output includes a large number of airmail stamps and miniature sheets, as well as stamps on gold and silver foil.

Philatelic bureau Director of PTT, Philatelic Service, Bissau.

HORTA

A district of the Portuguese island group of the Azores, consisting of Corvo, Flores, Faial and Pico islands (**area** 766 sq.km, **capital** Horta, on Faial).

From 1892 definitives with the inscription 'HORTA' (prior to this Azores stamps were used). A total of 34 stamps of Portuguese production in the appropriate colonial key-types. In 1905-31 Azores stamps were used, and then Portuguese.

IFNI

Barren territory of the Spanish enclave on the western coast of Africa (**area** 1,920 sq.km, **capital** Ifni).

From 1958 Ifni was administratively a Spanish province with district status. It had been declared a Spanish possession in 1860, but was only occupied in 1934. From 1946 to 1958 it was part of Spanish West Africa; in 1969 it was joined to Morocco.

In 1941 overprinted provisionals on Spanish stamps with the text 'TERRITORIO DE IFNI'; later, definitives with just the name, 'IFNI'. From 1960 these had the additional inscription 'ESPAÑA': a total of 237 stamps. Typical production of Spanish origin produced by the standard photogravure process in Madrid. Some older issues appeared in minimal printings of about 2,000 stamps, the last definitive printings ranging from half a million to about 1 million. Pictorial stamps, usually with general subjects (animals etc.) suggesting they were issued with the collector's market in mind. From 1969 Moroccan stamps have been in use in Ifni.

INHAMBANE

A district of the Portuguese province of Mozambique (**area** 54,600 sq.km, **capital** Inhambane).

The district had its own stamps in 1895–1920 with the name 'INHAMBANE' (prior to this the stamps of Lourenço Marques were valid and, earlier still, until 1895, Mozambique stamps). At first overprinted provisionals appeared on Mozambique stamps, then definitives with the same name. A total of 101 stamps of Portuguese origin (overprinted provisionals and Portuguese colonial key-types). From 1920, once again, Mozambique stamps.

ITALIAN COLONIES

Joint issues for all Italian colonies appeared from 1932 to 1934. At first these were Italian stamps with the overprint 'COLONIE ITALIANE' or 'POSTE COLONIALI ITALIANE' and, on definitives, 'R R POSTE COLONIALI ITALIANE': 87 stamps of Italian origin. The definitives include pictorials in very typically Italian designs. Printings were limited to between 10,000 and 30,000 with a view to encouraging philatelic investment.

ITALIAN EAST AFRICA

In 1936 the Italians created a colonial territory from Italian Somaliland, Eritrea and occupied Ethiopia, which was known as Italian East Africa (**area** 1,725,330 sq.km, **capital** Addis Ababa). The colony ceased to exist in 1941 after occupation by British troops.

In 1938–41 definitives inscribed 'AFRICA ORIENTALE ITALIANA': a total of 63 + 13 stamps characteristically Italian in style, with some designs common to Italy itself. Typical pictorial issues. From 1941 see *Somalia*.

ITALIAN SOMALILAND

Italian territory in East Africa, united into the colony of Italian Somaliland in 1908. From 1889 there was a colony here, originally known as Benadir, which, in 1905, was taken over by the Italian government; the territory was constantly expanded and in 1925 the region of Juba was added to it. Its area then became 513,550 sq.km, with the capital Mogadiscio. In 1936–41 Italian Somaliland was incorporated into Italian East Africa.

After stamp issuing by an Italian company administering this colonial territory under the name *Benadir*, it began to issue its own stamps in 1907. These were Italian stamps with the overprint 'SOMALIA ITALIANA' or 'SOMALIA' and, finally, definitives with the same names. Until 1936, 226 + 106 stamps of Italian origin appeared, chiefly overprinted provisionals and pictorial stamps. For subsequent issues see *Italian East Africa* and *Somalia*.

IVORY COAST

Area 322,464 sq.km, **population** 9.27m (1983), **capital** Yamoŭssoŭkroŭ.

An agricultural country with plantation agriculture and great forest wealth. Part of the coastline of the Gulf of Guinea, it was taken by the French in 1842; they then seized the inland territory in 1882, and in 1889 this was declared a French protectorate, then a colony in 1893. From 1895 it was a part of French West Africa. In 1958 it became autonomous, and on 7 August 1960, was declared independent. Indirect UPU membership from 1 July 1876 (as part of the French colonies); direct from 23 May 1961.

In 1892 French colonial stamps in the key-plate types with the inscription 'CÔTE D'IVOIRE'. From 1906 stamps carried the additional text, 'AFRIQUE OCCIDENTALE FRANÇAISE'. Up to 1944 a total of 203 stamps of French origin, many overprinted provisionals, pictorial stamps of the French stamp area and omnibus issues. Pétain issues during the war had no validity in the territory. Stamps of French West Africa were used from 1945 to 1959.

From 1959 definitives with the name 'RÉPUBLIQUE DE CÔTE D'IVOIRE', produced in France. Besides propaganda themes there are a number of issues with general subjects and stamp designs common to the French stamp-issuing areas, chiefly pictorial stamps. Annual output about 20 to 30 stamps.

Philatelic bureau Office des PTT, Service Philatélique, Abidjan. **Trade sales** Agence des Timbres-Poste d'Outre-Mer.

JUBA

In 1925 Great Britain gave Italy part of Kenya at the frontier river Juba (**area** 92,753 sq.km, **capital** Chisimaio) as payment for its participation in the First World War against Germany. In 1926 this territory was incorporated into Italian Somaliland.

In 1925 Italian stamps with the overprint 'OLTRE GIUBA': a total of 43 + 29 stamps of Italian origin, issued until 1926. Overprinted provisionals, then definitives with a map of the annexed territory. Postal use of the stamps was limited, the larger proportion of all printings being absorbed by collectors. On cover (original envelope), these stamps are rare. In 1926 these stamps were replaced by those of Italian Somaliland.

KAMERUN

The German occupation of Cameroun (Kamerun) culminated in the establishment of a colony in 1884. In 1911 it was enlarged by the inclusion of a large part (275,000 sq.km) of the French colony Ubangi-Shari-Chad in exchange for concessions in Morocco. After the defeat of the German colonial troops in 1915–16, the land was occupied by French and British units, and in 1922 the larger part of the territory was ceded to France and the smaller part to Great Britain, as mandate of the League of Nations (**area** 800,000 sq.km, **capital** Douala).

Before 1897 German stamps were valid. From 1897 German stamps with the overprint 'Kamerun'; later, definitives of the German colonial stamps in key-plate designs: a total of 24 stamps. The last Kamerun stamps were valid until February 1916 (some issues were sold only at the British philatelic counters and were even issued at a time — in 1919 — when the German occupation of Kamerun was long over, so that they cannot be regarded as postage stamps). From 1915 see *British Cameroons* and *French Cameroun*.

KATANGA

A province of the Congo which on 11 July 1960 unilaterally declared its independence (**area** 484,283 sq.km, **capital** Elisabethville). In 1963 Katanga once again came under the central Congo government.

From 1960 stamps of the Belgian Congo with the overprint 'KATANGA'; later, definitives also with the name 'ÉTAT DU KATANGA/INCHI YA KATANGA' (in Bantu). Up to 1962 a total of 86 + 7 stamps of fine quality (printed by Courvoisier in Switzerland). Stamps of *Congo (Kinshasa)* then followed.

KENYA

Area 582,646 sq.km, **population** 18.75m (1983), **capital** Nairobi.

A relatively developed agricultural country, independent since 1963 (prior to that the British colony and protectorate of Kenya from 1920, part of British East Africa); from 12 December 1964 a republic in the Commonwealth. Indirect UPU membership from 1 December 1895 (as a British colony of British East Africa); direct from 27 October 1964.

From 1963 definitives with the name 'KENYA' (but the issue celebrating independence in 1964 was inscribed 'REPUBLIC OF KENYA'). Stamp production of British origin with both national themes and general subjects. Restrained stamp issues supplemented by those brought out by joint postal services (*Kenya-Uganda-Tanganyika*, or *Tanzania*). In 1976–7 designs in common with Uganda and Tanzania, followed by a return to independent production, which, at the present time, is about 20 to 30 stamps a year.

Philatelic bureau Kenya Stamp Bureau, Nairobi. **Trade sales** Crown Agents' Stamp Bureau; Inter-Governmental Philatelic Corporation.

KENYA AND UGANDA

The territory of modern Kenya and Uganda was ruled by the British through the Imperial British East Africa Company from 1885 to 1895 (the German Protectorate of Witu or Swaziland was acquired in 1890). It then came under the administration of the British government as the British East African Protectorate (the coastline was given the name Protectorate of Kenya). In 1903 Uganda separated; the name Kenya was introduced for the whole colony (inland) only in 1920. From 1935 it became Kenya-Uganda-Tanganyika, with the last-named becoming Tanzania, from 1965. In 1925 Juba was ceded to Italian Somaliland.

From 1922 stamps were issued for the territory of British East Africa with the inscription 'KENYA AND UGANDA': a total of 28 + 6 portrait stamps of British origin. One issue has unusually high face values (£10, £20, £25, £50, £75 and £100), used for fiscal, rather than postal, purposes, such as wildgame licences for hunting elephants. These unusually high-face-value stamps are among the very expensive ones, which are included in postage stamp collections simply because they were available for postal purposes as well as fiscal ones. From 1935 see *Kenya-Uganda-Tanganyika* and also *Uganda*.

KENYA-UGANDA-TANGANYIKA (TANZANIA)
These three originally British territories concluded a joint postal agreement in 1930 to form the East African Postal Administration. In 1935 the first joint stamps were issued with the names of all three countries. Separate issues for Kenya and Uganda and for Tanganyika followed when the three countries obtained their independence (Tanganyika on 9 December 1961; Uganda on 9 October 1962; and Kenya on 12 December 1964), although joint commemorative stamps of the East African Postal Administration continued to appear with the requisite changes in names: first, Kenya-Uganda-Tanganyika; in 1964, Kenya-Uganda-Tanganyika-Zanzibar; from 1965, Kenya-Uganda-Tanzania. Separate definitive issues of the individual states continued for Kenya, Uganda, Tanganyika (Tanzania) and Zanzibar. The last state joined Tanganyika in 1964 to create Tanzania, and Zanzibar ceased to issue its own stamps.

Definitives from 1935 with the text KENYA, UGANDA, TANGANYIKA; in 1964, KENYA, UGANDA, TANGANYIKA, ZANZIBAR; from 1965, KENYA, UGANDA, TANZANIA (the order of the names alternates). Pictorial stamps of typical British colonial character. In the 1970s there was greater stress on propaganda subjects common to all three countries. In 1976–7 policy changed in that commemorative stamps of uniform design were issued for the individual countries (Kenya, Uganda and Tanzania), the stamps differing only in the name of the country. The East African Postal Union which justified these joint issues became moribund in 1977 and stamp-issuing co-operation ceased.

KIONGA
The southernmost part of German East Africa on the shores of the Indian Ocean (1,040 sq.km), occupied by the Portuguese from Mozambique in 1916 and then awarded to the latter in 1919 under the Treaty of Versailles.

In 1916 stamps of Lourenço Marques with the overprint 'KIONGA': a total of 4 stamps in a printing of about 20,000. In fact, these were used very rarely; only 5 examples are known of their use on letters.

LA AGÜERA
A Spanish possession in the western Sahara. From 1920 to 1924 it formed part of the southernmost tip of Rio de Oro colony. In 1924 it formed part of Western Sahara, whose stamps were valid here (see *Spanish Sahara*). From 1921 Rio de Oro stamps overprinted 'LA AGÜERA'; definitives with the inscription 'SAHARA OCCIDENTAL/LA AGÜERA'. A total of 2 issues, 26 stamps in small printings of 3,000 sets, few of which appeared to have been used postally.

LAGOS
The town of Lagos was placed under British administration in 1861. Its territory continued to be expanded, and in 1886 it formed the colony and protectorate of Lagos (189 sq.km as a colony; 8,995 sq.km as a protectorate) with Lagos as the capital. In 1906 it became part of Southern Nigeria.

In 1874 definitives with the name 'LAGOS'. Until 1904 a total of 52 stamps of characteristic British origin were issued, with the portrait of Queen Victoria and King Edward VII. In 1906 Lagos was merged with the protectorate of Southern Nigeria under a single administration, and Lagos stamps were also valid here. The united area was given the name *Southern Nigeria*. Subsequently (1914) it was joined to Northern Nigeria to form the colony and protectorate of *Nigeria*.

LESOTHO
Area 30,355 sq.km, **population** 1.7m (1983), **capital** Maseru.
A backward agricultural country with cattle breeding and some diamond mining. Until 1966

241

the British protectorate of Basutoland (from 1965 autonomous). It was declared independent on 4 October 1966, and its name has since been the Kingdom of Lesotho. Indirect UPU membership as from 28 October 1896; direct from 6 September 1967.

The first stamps were inscribed 'LESOTHO/BASUTOLAND' and appeared in 1965, when the country was made self-governing, although subsequent issues continued to use the inscription 'BASUTOLAND'. Only after independence in 1966 did stamps appear with the name 'LESOTHO'. Annual production about 25 stamps, virtually all of British origin, usually by the photogravure process. The designs are pictorial themes illustrating life and natural history in Lesotho. In 1974–6 every stamp picture also had the portrait of the ruler.

Philatelic bureau Philatelic Controller, Philatelic Bureau, Maseru. **Trade sales** Crown Agents' Stamp Bureau; Inter-Governmental Philatelic Corporation.

LIBERIA

Area 111,370 sq.km, **population** 1.9m (1981), **capital** Monrovia.

A developing agricultural country with mineral mining. An independent republic since 1847, Liberia was peopled by freed slaves from the USA, hence its name. Direct UPU membership from 1 April 1879.

In 1860 definitives with the name 'LIBERIA'. Stamp production was first British; in 1921–8 German; from 1928 mainly USA. Until the 1950s a conservative conception of stamp design prevailed, similar to older American issues. Production includes many miniature sheets (90 items), airmail stamps (more than 150), officials (156), as well as a number of overprinted provisionals. Annual output approximately 30 stamps. Primarily commemorating international events (such as Olympic Games), as well as using propaganda and general themes. Attention to collector demand has been more marked recently, manifested in attractive pictorial designs intended especially for foreign customers.

From 1893 to 1924, 8 stamps appeared for each of the Liberian towns of Robertsport, Monrovia, Buchanan, Greenville and Harper which were named on the stamps together with 'Liberia' — except for the first issue which had the town name only. The stamps were intended for paying registration fees on letters and are inscribed 'REGISTERED'.

Philatelic bureau Liberian Philatelic Agency, New York, USA.

LIBYA

Area 1,759,540 sq.km, **population** 3.5m (1982), **capital** Tarabulus (Tripoli).

A developing country with large oil deposits and nomadic tribes who live by stock raising. An independent republic from 1969; previously a kingdom created on 24 December 1951 out of the merger of Tripoli, Fezzan and Cyrenaica (a unitarian state from 1963). At one time occupied by the Turks — from 1556, Libya, as the province of Tripoli, was joined to the Ottoman Empire. In 1835 the country received the status of a Turkish vilayet. In 1901 an Italian post office was established in Benghazi, and in 1909 in Tripoli. During the Italian-Turkish war in 1911–12, Italian troops moved from these cities into the interior of the country, seizing the whole of Libya, and the country became an Italian colony. In 1938 the coast of Libya was declared an integral province of Italy, and the inland area formed the Libyan Sahara. In 1942–3 the country was occupied by the Allies (the British took Cyrenaica and Tripoli; the French Fezzan and Ghadamès). The Paris Peace Treaty of 1947 proclaimed Libya a United Nations mandate, but the country continued to be occupied. Its independence was announced in 1951. The Libyan Arab Republic was formed on 1 September 1969, and on 22 November 1976, the name was changed to the Libyan Arab People's Republic. On 3 March 1977, it became the Libyan Arab People's Socialist Jamahiriya. Indirect UPU membership from 1 July 1875 (Turkey); indirect from 1 October 1907 (Italian colony); indirect from 1 July 1940 to 1943 (under the name Italian overseas territory and Italian East Africa); indirect from 1943 to 3 June 1952 (British administration); direct from 4 June 1952.

The first Libyan stamps of 1912 are overprinted provisionals with the text 'LIBIA' on Italian issues, followed by definitives with the same name until 1941 (a total of 130 + 50 stamps of Italian origin appeared). At first they were more in the nature of overprints on Italian stamps, but from the 1930s they had their own stamp designs publicizing the country (from 1923

Cyrenaica and Tripoli had their own stamp issues running concurrently). During Allied occupation in the Second World War the stamps of Ghadamès, Fezzan, Tripoli and Cyrenaica were used on Libyan territory.

From 1951 the stamps of Cyrenaica (British occupation) with the overprint 'LIBYA' and with face values in Egypt's sterling currency (valid in Cyrenaica); in lira currency of the military MAL — Military Administration Lira (used in Tripoli); and, finally, in the franc currency of Algeria (issued for Fezzan). These overprinted provisionals indicate the complexity of the country's legal position. At the same time the printings are surprisingly small, 1,100 upwards. They were followed by definitives with the English inscriptions 'KINGDOM OF LIBYA', 'UNITED KINGDOM OF LIBYA'; later, only 'LIBYA', and the text in Arabic and sometimes, rarely, in French (1956 'LIBYE'). From 1970 'L.A.R.' (Libyan Arab Republic); later, the name only in Arabic script, and from 1977, after the change in the name of the country, there appeared alongside the Arabic also the name in English 'SOCIALIST PEOPLE'S LIBYAN ARAB JAMAHIRIYA'. Production as a whole characterized by a diversity of design (stamps were printed in various foreign printing houses). Current output is 30 to 50 stamps a year, with a decided preponderance of propaganda designs.

Philatelic bureau Post and Telecommunications Corp., Philatelic Service, Tarabulus.

LOURENÇO MARQUES
A district of the Portuguese colony of Mozambique near Delago Bay (**area** 72,480 sq.km, **capital** Lourenço Marques). From 1895 definitives with the name 'LOURENÇO MARQUES', also 'L. MARQUES', and, on some issues, the name Portugal. Until 1920 a total of 175 + 2 stamps of Portuguese origin with many overprinted provisionals, especially in the period when Portugal was proclaimed a republic (overprints, 'REPUBLICA'). Characteristic Portuguese production with similar designs. After 1920, Mozambique stamps were in use.

MADAGASCAR
The largest African island (**area** 587,041 sq.km, **capital** Tananarive, or Antananarive), proclaimed a French protectorate in 1885. After an uprising by the local population in 1896 it became a colony and, in 1905, the small nearby islands — Diégo Suarez, Sainte Marie and Nossi-Bé — were joined to it; in 1908 also the Comoros. In 1942 British-South-African units overcame the Pétain garrison and installed a governor of the Free French. In 1958, after a long struggle, Madagascar received the status of an autonomous republic (with the name Republic of Malgache), and in 1960 it achieved complete independence. The Comoros had separated from it in 1950. In 1975 it was renamed the *Malagasy Republic*.

Before the first Madagascan stamps appeared (1889), the British Consulate in Tananarive organized a postal service and issued stamps in 1884. In January 1895 there was a local British post office on Madagascar (whose stamps were inscribed 'BRITISH INLAND MAIL') which closed when the French entered Tananarive in September 1895. In 1889 a French post office was opened on Madagascar and stamps in the French colonial key-type were issued surcharged to meet local requirements; later with the overprint 'MADAGASCAR'. From 1896, when it was proclaimed a French colony, stamps appeared with the name 'MADAGASCAR ET DÉPENDANCES'. In 1898 the stamps of Diégo Suarez, Nossi-Bé and Sainte Marie were also used in Madagascar. After the archipelago of the Comoros was joined to Madagascar in 1908, the rest of the stamps of Great Comoro, Mohéli, Mayotte and Anjouan were used in Madagascar as well. Until 1958 a total of 348 + 40 stamps issued characteristic of French origin, with designs and subjects common to French stamp-issuing policy. Until 1921 they were principally overprinted provisionals; there were also pictorial stamp issues. During the Second World War, Free French issues. Madagascar stamps were also valid in the French Southern and Antarctic islands.

MADEIRA
Area 796 sq.km, **population** 257,822 (1981), **administrative centre** Funchal.

An archipelago near the north-western coast of Africa, which formed an administrative

243

district of Portugal under the name of Funchal and, since 1976, has been autonomous. UPU membership obtained explicitly as a part of Portugal, which received direct membership on 1 July 1875.

Since 1868 the overprint 'MADEIRA' on Portuguese stamps; later, definitives with the same name. Stamp production of Portuguese origin (overprinted provisionals and colonial key-types). Before issuing its own stamps, those of Portugal were used — and continued to be used in Madeira again from 1880. From 1892 to 1910 the stamps of *Funchal* were used, then the stamps of the *Azores* until 1931, then once again Portuguese stamps, with the exception of issues between 1925 and 1929, when compulsory surcharge stamps appeared bearing the name 'MADEIRA' (intended to raise money for a museum in Funchal). In 1980 stamp-issuing was revived, and stamps now bear the name 'MADEIRA/PORTUGAL' and are valid even in continental Portugal.

Philatelic bureau Servicios de Filatelia, Estaçao de Correio de Funchal, Madeira.

MAFIA
A small island south of Zanzibar (**area** 434 sq.km, **capital** Kilidini). In 1886–1915 a part of German East Africa, occupied by British-Indian units until 1920, then taken over by Tanganyika.

In 1915, the name 'MAFIA' and 'G.R. Mafia' overprinted on stamps seized from German East Africa; later, Indian stamps of the British-Indian field post used with similar overprints. A total of 32 overprinted provisionals. Tanganyikan stamps were used after 1920.

MALAGASY REPUBLIC
Area 587,041 sq.km, **population** 9.47m (1983), **capital** Antananarivo.

Previously the French colony of Madagascar. A developing country with plantation agriculture, cattle breeding and increasing mineral mining. An autonomous republic since 1958; independent from 26 June 1960. In 1975 the new name, the Malagasy Democratic Republic, was introduced. Indirect UPU membership from 1 July 1876 (French colony); direct from 2 November 1961.

From 1958 definitives with the name 'RÉPUBLIQUE MALGACHE'; after winning independence, stamps with the Malgache text, 'REPOBLIKA MALAGASY'; from 1976, 'REPOBLIKA DEMOKRATIKA MALAGASY'. Production of stamps characteristic of French origin, in some instances quite remarkable graphic work. Besides pictorial stamps, notably with general themes, there are issues for joint international projects. Current annual production around 35 stamps. Choice of subjects is influenced by the collector demand.

Philatelic bureau Service Philatélique, Office des PTT, Antananarivo. **Trade sales** Agence des Timbres-Poste d'Outre-Mer.

MALAWI
Area 118,484 sq.km, **population** 6.4m (1983), **capital** Lilongwe.

A developing agricultural country (originally Nyasaland). Until 1963 a member state of the Federation of Rhodesia and Nyasaland, from 6 July 1964 an independent country with the new name of Malawi; proclaimed a republic on 6 July 1966. Indirect UPU membership from 9 April 1925 as Nyasaland (British colony); directly from 25 October 1966. Its predecessor was British Central Africa.

Definitives from 1964 with the name 'MALAŴI', preceded (until 1963) by Nyasaland stamps; the designs of the last Nyasaland issue were used with the new name of Malawi. The name was altered to 'MALAWI' in 1973. In 1974 stamps were first printed in Holland. Stamp production — now in Britain — is going its own way from the standpoint of design and tends to be influenced by the collector demand for pictorial stamps on general themes and for miniature sheets (more than 50 to date). Annual output about 50 stamps.

Philatelic bureau Post Office Philatelic Bureau, Blantyre, Malawi. **Trade sales** Crown Agents' Stamp Bureau.

MALI
Area 1,239,710 sq.km, **population** 7.49m (1983), **capital** Bamako.

A developing agricultural country, formerly French Sudan, which on 24 November 1958 became an autonomous republic and on 17 January 1959 declared an alliance with Senegal, Upper Volta and Dahomey to form the Federation of Mali (in the event, however, Upper Volta and Dahomey withdrew from the federation). On 20 June 1960 the federation declared its Independence, but on 20 August 1960 Senegal withdrew; the remaining Sudan then adopted the name Republic of Mali. Indirect UPU membership from 1 July 1876 (French colony); direct from 21 April 1961.

From 1959 definitives with the name 'FÉDÉRATION DU MALI', valid also in Senegal; from 1960 the name 'RÉPUBLIQUE DU MALI'. Characteristic pictorial issues of French origin. Apart from several issues with propaganda intent, they show a rising trend towards general themes and participation in omnibus issues, reflecting the influence of the collector demand. This is underlined by the large production of airmail stamps, which outnumber the ordinary issues used for normal postage. Annual output about 50 stamps.

Philatelic bureau Office des PTT, Service Philatélique, Bamako. **Trade sales** Agence des Timbres-Poste d'Outre-Mer.

MAURITANIA
Area 1,030,700 sq.km, **population** 1.78m (1983), **capital** Nouakchott.

A backward country, mainly cattle breeding. The Mauritanian sultanate was recognized together with the sovereignty of Morocco, but the French seized the country and made it a protectorate in 1903, and in 1904 it was incorporated into French West Africa. This was confirmed after the southern part of Morocco had broken away in 1912. Mauritania became a colony in 1920, was declared an autonomous republic in 1958, and won its independence on 28 November 1960. Morocco laid claim to the territory of Mauritania until 1969, even at the United Nations. At the beginning of 1976 Mauritania occupied the southern part of Spanish Sahara (Tigri Gharbía), but on 16 August 1979 it withdrew from there. Indirect UPU membership from 1 July 1876 (as part of the French colonies); direct from 22 March 1967.

In 1906 definitives with the name 'MAURITANIE/AFRIQUE OCCIDENTALE FRANÇAISE'. Stamp-issuing continued until 1944, the stamps being of French origin and including the French colonial key-plate types of the period.

From 1944 to 1960 French West Africa stamps appeared. Afterwards, from 1960, definitives with the name 'RÉPUBLIQUE ISLAMIQUE DE MAURITANIE', printed in Arabic as well as in Latin script. Characteristic production of stamps of French origin. Propaganda themes alternate with a number of issues for the collector market (overprints to mark the appearance of thematic stamps, postage-due stamps with general themes of birds, triangular-shaped stamps, etc.), with many themes common to the French stamp region. A number of the stamps, designed by French artists, have a high graphic quality, better than average, and, in addition, printing is by excellent line engraving carried out in the French state printing house. At the present time about 30 stamps appear annually, a large proportion being airmails. The photogravure and offset-litho processes more frequently used now in printing. The effort to attract the collector's market is very evident.

Philatelic bureau Agence Philatélique, Nouakchott. **Trade sales** Agence des Timbres-Poste d'Outre-Mer.

MAURITIUS
Area 1,865 sq.km, **population** 994,000 (1982), **capital** Port Louis.

A substantially advanced country with agriculture. An island of the Mascarenes, Mauritius was a British colony from 1810 (until 1903 the Seychelles belonged to it); autonomous from 1966; declared an independent state on 12 March 1968 (a monarchy in the Commonwealth). Shortly before this, the more remote Chagos Islands, which had once belonged to Mauritius, were incorporated into a new colony known as British Indian Ocean Territory. Indirect UPU membership from 1 April 1877 (a British colony); direct from 29 August 1969.

Before issuing its own stamps, British stamps were used. In 1847 definitives with the name 'MAURITIUS'; one issue from 1873 has the name in French ('MAURICE') but this is an exception. The first issues, although produced by engraving, are primitives. The red (1d) and blue (2d) Mauritius stamps are among the most coveted and famous classical stamps in the world. At a Harmer auction in New York in 1968 a record of $380,000 was paid for an envelope with two 1d red Mauritius stamps. Following the first issue, which was produced locally, came stamps of British origin. Many portrait stamps characteristic of the British colonial issues in the key-and-duty designs of the British Commonwealth. Pictorial stamps from 1950, alternating with Commonwealth omnibus issues, most of them produced by photogravure. Annual production at the present time is about 15 to 30 stamps.

Philatelic bureau Postmaster General, P&T Department, Philatelic Service, Port Louis.
Trade sales Crown Agents' Stamp Bureau.

MAYOTTE
A French island, part of the Comoros archipelago (**area** 356 sq.km, **capital** Dzaoudzi).

A colony from 1843; together with the islands of Anjouan, Great Comoro and Mohéli, as the Province de Mayotte et dépendances. It was joined to Madagascar in 1908, in 1975 was separated from the Comoros, and on 5 May 1976 became the 102nd French overseas département. From 14 December 1976 had status of collectivité territoriale.

In 1892 French colonial stamps of key-plate design with the name 'MAYOTTE': a total of 20 stamps. After 1908 the remaining stamps were used up in Madagascar.

MIDDLE CONGO
In 1886–1904, when the separate colonies of Gabon and Ubangi-Shari-Chad were created out of the French Congo, the rest of the territory was again called Middle Congo. In 1910 it became a colony in the system of French Equatorial Africa, and remained in it until 1958, when it became an autonomous republic. Independence was proclaimed on 15 August 1960 (see *Congo Brazzaville*).

In 1907 definitives with the inscription 'MOYEN CONGO' and the additional text 'RÉPUBLIQUE FRANÇAISE'. These stamps appeared in 1924 with the overprint, 'AFRIQUE ÉQUATORIALE FRANÇAISE'. A total of 90 + 33 stamps of French origin. Pictorial stamps, typical of the French colonies, and overprinted provisionals. Superseded by stamps of *French Equatorial Africa* from 1936.

MOHÉLI
Island in the Comoros, in 1886–1908 a French protectorate. Together with Mayotte, Anjouan and Great Comoro, as the Province de Mayotte et dépendances, it was joined to Madagascar, and in 1912 was declared a colony (**area** 290 sq.km, **capital** Fomboni).

In 1906 French colonial stamps of key-plate design with the text 'MOHÉLI': 1 issue of 16 stamps. The rest of the stamps were used after 1908 on Madagascar. Since 1950 Mohéli has been part of the stamp-issuing country of the *Comoros*.

MOROCCO
Area 458,730 sq.km, **population** 21m (1983), **capital** Rabat.

An agricultural country with important mineral mining and developing industry. In the 19th century, the European powers endeavoured to gain a foothold in the country: in 1860, Spain seized Tetuan and in 1884 Río de Oro; France took Casablanca in 1907. In 1912 it was declared a French protectorate (399,050 sq.km) and a Spanish protectorate (20,800 sq.km), with Mauritania cut off from it. Only on 2 March 1956 was the French protectorate abolished and Morocco declared an independent country (a sultanate). On 7 April 1956, the Spanish protectorate was also abolished (the territory was ceded to Morocco on 10 April 1958), and on 29 October 1956 Tangier too came under Moroccan administration. On 15 August 1957 Morocco became a kingdom. Spain returned 'Southern Morocco' (26,000 sq.km) in 1958 and Ifni (1,920 sq.km) in 1969. On 11 December 1975, Morocco announced the annexation of the northern part of Spanish Sahara (the territory of Saquia al-Hamra), and on 16 August

1979, after the withdrawal of Mauritanian troops, it occupied the southern part of Spanish Sahara (Tigri Gharbia), thereby increasing its overall size by 266,000 sq.km and the number of inhabitants by 120,000. (However, the people of the Sahara are fighting for their independence.) Direct UPU membership from 1 October 1920 as Morocco (with the exception of the Spanish zone); and Morocco (Spanish zone); direct from 15 October 1956 as unified Morocco.

There were various post offices on Moroccan territory. The French post office used French stamps from 1863 to 1891. From 1891 it used French stamps with the surcharge in Spanish currency; from 1902 French stamps in the key-plate types with the inscription 'MAROC' (Spanish currency). A total of 38+16 stamps appeared until 1912. In 1914 French key-plate stamps with the name 'Maroc' and overprinted 'PROTECTORAT FRANÇAIS'; definitives from 1915 with the name 'MAROC'. Following stamps of a unified model and overprinted provisionals came definitives produced in France but with a strong Arabic influence in the designs. The designers (especially Josso) introduced new, personal elements into the stamps; chiefly engravings produced at the French state printers. Predominantly tourist publicity themes, especially in the depiction of monuments; artistically they are superior to most contemporary stamps. After the Second World War an annual Solidarity issue with a surcharge became common.

After winning independence in 1956, stamps with the name 'MAROC' were still in circulation, but new stamps with a new name now appeared: 'ROYAUME DU MAROC', stressing national themes. With contributions by different foreign designers and different printing houses (with diverse printing techniques) the resulting stamps vary greatly in appearance. In recent years there have been 30 stamps a year, frequently the work of local artists.

Under the name 'MARRUECOS', stamp-issuing continued after 7 April 1956, within the framework of an independent and united state in the northern (the one-time Spanish) zone, the larger part of independent Morocco; and from 1957 with joint stamp designs (but still in Spanish currency). Until 1958, when the two zones merged, 29 stamps of a national propaganda character were issued, at first still of Spanish origin, but then, gradually, based on joint stamp design with the rest of Morocco.

A German post office existed in Morocco from 1899, on French territory until 1914, and on Spanish territory until 1919. From 1899 German stamps were used with the overprint 'MAROCCO'; from 1911 with the name 'MAROKKO'. Virtually all are overprinted provisionals (a total of 57 stamps) on German stamps.

In 1898 stamps of Gibraltar with Spanish currency face values appeared with the overprint 'MOROCCO AGENCIES' with a surcharge in Spanish currency. These were valid throughout the territory of Morocco. Until 1906 the British Post Offices in Morocco were under the control of the Gibraltar Post Office, but from 1907, British stamps with the same overprint appeared (sterling currency). In 1912, when Morocco was divided between France, Spain and Tangier, stamps were adapted to this change. From 1914 there were British stamps with the overprint 'MOROCCO AGENCIES' (no surcharges, face value in British currency) and these continued to be valid in all three territories. A total of 68 stamps issued, nearly all overprinted provisionals. Their sale was halted in 1956. From 1912, British stamps with 'MOROCCO AGENCIES' and with Spanish currency surcharges were valid in Spanish Morocco. A total of 63 overprinted provisionals; their sale was stopped in 1956. From 1917 British stamps with the overprint 'MOROCCO AGENCIES' and with a surcharge in French currency, valid only in French Morocco. A total of 40 overprinted provisionals. Their sale ended in 1938.

The Spanish post office on Moroccan territory used Spanish stamps from 1867; and in 1902–14, Spanish stamps with the overprint 'MARRUECOS' (see *Spanish Morocco*). A total of 36 overprinted provisionals. Spanish post offices operated in the towns of Arzila, Casablanca, Larache, Mazagan, Mogador, Rabat, Safi, *Tangier* and *Tetuan*.

Besides the above-mentioned stamps which, of course, were also valid internationally, there were other post offices in the territory of Morocco — either of private firms or belonging to the sheiks ('sherifian posts') which also issued their own postage stamps and which, naturally, were not valid internationally.

Philatelic bureau Ministère des Postes, Services Financières, Section Timbres-Poste, Rabat.

MOZAMBIQUE

Area 799,380 sq.km, **population** 13.14m (1983), **capital** Maputo (formerly Lourenço Marques).

A backward agricultural country. It was Portuguese from the 16th century, but only in 1891 were its borders finally established, and it became a colony in 1907. In 1919, Kionga district — formerly part of German East Africa — was joined to it. Until 1941 the regions of Manica and Sofala were administered by the private *Mozambique Company* (Companhia de Moçambique). From 1951 Mozambique was considered an overseas province of Portugal (the term colony was withdrawn). It became an independent people's republic on 25 June 1975. Indirect UPU membership from 1 July 1877 (as a Portuguese possession); direct from 11 October 1978.

Definitives using the name 'MOÇAMBIQUE' from 1876 until the present. Stamp production of Portuguese origin. A great many overprinted provisionals until the 1920s (especially when Portugal became a republic). A number of subjects and designs in common with the other Portuguese colonies. Characteristic offset-litho process produced in various Portuguese printing houses. Primarily pictorial stamps, some with long series of as many as 20 values. Even after winning independence, the stamps still bear the name 'MOÇAMBIQUE'. Reasonable production employing chiefly national propaganda themes (for instance, an annual issue on the anniversary of the declaration of independence). Annual output about 20 stamps.

Mozambique consists of the following former stamp-issuing territories: Inhambane, Lourenço Marques, the Mozambique Company (Manica and Sofala), Zambezia, Quelimane, Tete, Mozambique, Nyassa and Kionga. In 1895–1920, stamps with the name of Moçambique were valid only for the Mozambique district (**area** 87,100 sq.km, **capital** Mocambique), today part of Nyassa district.

Philatelic bureau Servico Filatelico, Maputo.

MOZAMBIQUE COMPANY

The private Mozambique Company (Companhia de Moçambique) was established in 1891; for 50 years it administered the concession territory of Manica and Sofala (134,400 sq.km) in Mozambique. Its activities ended in 1941.

In 1892 stamps of Mozambique with the overprint 'COMPA. DE MOÇAMBIQUE'; later, definitives with the text 'COMPANHIA DE MOÇAMBIQUE: a total of 233 + 44 stamps. Many overprinted provisionals, superseded after 1918 by pictorial stamps printed in Great Britain by the recess-printing method. Towards the end of stamp issuing activity several Portuguese anniversaries were commemorated. In 1941 the company's concession ended and Mozambique stamps then became valid.

NAMIBIA see SOUTH WEST AFRICA

NATAL

After 1835, when Cape Province was occupied by the British, the Boers settled in Natal. Having defeated the Zulus at Bloody River in 1839, they set up the Republic of Natal with the capital at Pietermaritzburg. However, in 1843 the British occupied Natal and created a colony out of it, at first administered from the Cape, but from 1856 an independent Crown Colony which was enlarged by the addition of Tongaland, Zululand and the New Republic (Vrijheid, 1902). In 1910 the territory (91,382 sq.km) became a province of the Union of South Africa. In 1857 hand-embossed impressions on coloured papers featuring the name 'NATAL' and the Crown and 'V.R.' followed in 1859 by portrait issues of British origin similar to other contemporary colonial issues: a total of 92+15 stamps. Although, in 1910, Natal became part of the Union of South Africa (South Africa became a subsequent stamp-issuing territory), the stamps of Natal remained valid for use until 1937.

NEW REPUBLIC

A Boer republic from 1884 to 1889; in 1889–1902 a district of the Republic of South Africa called Vrijheid, in 1903 joined to Natal. Its territory was never precisely demarcated so that its size is not known (capital, Vrijheid).

In 1886 primitive hand-stamped issue with the inscription 'NIEUWE REPUBLIEK': a total of 62 primitives until 1888.

NIGER

Area 1,266,995 sq.km, **population** 6.04m (1983), **capital** Niamey.

A backward agricultural country chiefly living by livestock production. French from 1893, and from 1899 a part of French West Africa, though Niger as a colony was set up only in 1922 after being separated from the colony of Upper Senegal and Niger (previously a part of the colony of Senegambia and Niger). From 1912 it was a military, and from 1920 civilian, territory. As part of French West Africa, Niger became autonomous in 1958, and an independent republic on 3 August 1960. Indirect UPU membership from 1 July 1876 (as a unit of the French colonies); direct from 12 June 1961.

The first stamps of 1921 were overprinted 'TERRITOIRE DU NIGER' on stamps of Upper Senegal and Niger; definitives from 1926 inscribed 'NIGER': a total of 122+21 stamps of French origin (standard-type French colonial pictorial stamps; also some French colonial omnibus issues). Most of the Pétain issues during the Second World War had no postal validity in the territory. The stamps of *French West Africa* became valid in 1944 until 1959 when Niger's own stamps were resumed with the inscription 'RÉPUBLIQUE DU NIGER'. These are issues with a number of designs in common with other French-influenced areas of Africa. The stamps of the independent country include general themes, apart from specific propaganda designs and themes common to the French stamp region. The frequency, size and unusual printing bases (including metal foil) of Niger Republic stamps are designed to attract the collector. The annual output of about 50 stamps includes a large percentage of airmail stamps.

Philatelic bureau Office des P. et T. (Philatélie), Niamey. **Trade sales** Agence des Timbres-Poste d'Outre-Mer.

NIGER COAST

In 1885 the British protectorate of Oil Rivers (capital, Calabar) was set up in the south of today's Nigeria. In 1893 this became the protectorate of Niger Coast, which belonged to the Royal Niger Company. In 1900 the territory was taken over by the British government and incorporated into the protectorate of Southern Nigeria which, in 1906, was joined with Lagos into the colony and protectorate of Southern Nigeria.

In 1893 the overprint 'NIGER COAST' on un-issued stamps prepared for *Oil Rivers*. In 1894, portrait definitives inscribed 'NIGER COAST PROTECTORATE'. A total of 44 stamps of British origin. From 1900 the stamps of *Southern Nigeria*.

NIGERIA

Area 923,768 sq.km, **population** 82.39m (1983), **capital** Lagos.

A relatively advanced country with a developed mining industry. It was a British colony and protectorate created in 1914 out of Northern and Southern Nigeria; from 1922 the mandate of British Cameroons was part of it, and most of this territory was joined to Nigeria in 1961. Independence was proclaimed on 1 October 1960. From 1963 a republic under the name Federative Republic of Nigeria. In 1967 the eastern part of Nigeria proclaimed its unilateral independence under the name of *Biafra* until 1969. Indirect UPU membership from 1 January 1879 (British colony); indirect (as Southern Nigeria) from 1 October 1903 (British protectorate); indirect from 1 January 1929 (British colony and protectorate); direct from 10 July 1961.

In 1914 definitives inscribed 'NIGERIA'. Stamp production of British origin and, until 1936, in the standard colonial key-and-duty portrait types. Pictorial stamps from 1936 and other issues of international character. Since it became a republic there has been a preponderance of photogravure printing of stamps concerned with national propaganda but restricted to a small number of new issues (about 4 a year).

Philatelic bureau Nigerian Philatelic Service, Lagos. **Trade sales** Crown Agents' Stamp Bureau.

NORTHERN NIGERIA

At the end of the 19th century the Royal Niger Company was established. Its extensive inland possession was taken over in 1900 by the British government, which created the protectorate of Northern Nigeria (**area** 732,426 sq.km, **capital** Kaduna). In 1914 Northern Nigeria together with Southern Nigeria were merged into the colony and the protectorate of Nigeria.

In 1900 definitives with the text 'NORTHERN NIGERIA'. A total of 50 stamps of British origin, chiefly royal portrait colonial key-and-duty designs. From 1914 replaced by stamps of *Nigeria*.

NORTHERN RHODESIA

The protectorate of Northern Rhodesia came into existence in 1911. In 1923, when the charter of the British South Africa Company expired, the British government acquired the land by purchase. In 1953–63 Northern Rhodesia was part of the Federation of Rhodesia and Nyasaland, and after the dissolution of the Federation on 31 December 1963, it was granted internal self-government on 3 January 1964, and on 24 October 1964, it declared its independence as *Zambia*.

Definitives from 1925 with the text 'NORTHERN RHODESIA' in royal portrait designs; also British Commonwealth omnibus issues. Stamp issuing until 1953, then in 1954–63 the stamps of Rhodesia and Nyasaland were valid. In 1963 there was one issue of definitive heraldic stamps inscribed 'NORTHERN RHODESIA'. From 1964, superseded by the stamps of Zambia. A total of 88 + 4 stamps of British origin.

NOSSI-BÉ

Island off the north-western coast of Madagascar, French from 1841 (**area** together with the dependencies of Nossi-Cumba, Nossi Mitsin and Nossi Feli, 136 sq.km, **capital** Hell-Ville). Between 1885 and 1893 it was a dependency of the colony Diégo Suarez; in 1893–1906, a separate colony, then part of Madagascar.

At first stamps of the colony of Diégo Suarez et dépendances were used; from 1889 French colonial stamps with the currency overprinted and the letters 'NSB', later with the name 'NOSSI-BÉ'. A total of 38 + 13 stamps of French origin, mostly overprinted issues and French stamps of the colonial key-plate types. After incorporation into *Madagascar* the stamps of the latter became valid.

NYASALAND

From 1907, the name given to the territory of former British Central Africa (**area** 121,400 sq.km, **capital** Blantyre), modern Malawi. In 1953–63 a member country of the Federation of Rhodesia and Nyasaland; after the break-up of this Federation it gained autonomy and used the name Nyasaland until winning independence, when it changed its name to Malawi.

The name Nyasaland first appeared on definitives in 1908 with the text 'NYASALAND PROTECTORATE'; later,' NYASALAND' (until this time the stamps of British Central Africa were used). Stamp-issuing until 1953, a total of 113 stamps of British origin. In the earlier period royal portrait issues; later, pictorial stamps, typical of British colonial issue.

After the dissolution of the Federation of Rhodesia and Nyasaland, from 1963 Nyasaland again had its own stamps inscribed 'NYASALAND' and resumed its earlier pattern of stamp-issuing. A total of 25+5 stamps issued, overprinted provisionals and pictorial stamps of British origin, which continued until 1964. For subsequent issuing see *Malawi*.

NYASSA

The territory of northern Mozambique (**area** 189,000 sq.km, **capital** Vila Cabral), leased to the private Nyassa Company in 1897. The concession ended on 27 October 1929, and Portugal took over the administration of Nyassa.

In 1898, stamps of Mozambique with the overprint 'NYASSA'; later, definitives with the text 'COMPANHIA DO NYASSA': a total of 114 + 13 stamps. Pictorial colonial stamps printed in London by the firm of Waterlow, and overprinted provisionals. After 1929, superseded by *Mozambique* stamps.

OBOCK

A strip of land near the Bay of Obock which the French bought in 1862 from the Danakils and, through a number of agreements, acquired as a protectorate in 1884–7. At that time, in fact, they occupied this area with a port of the same name. In 1896, when the colony of French Somaliland was established, Obock became a part of it.

In 1892 stamps of the French Colonies general issue with the overprint 'OBOCK'; definitives with the same text later. Stamp-issuing activities continued until 1894; a total of 56 + 14 stamps of French origin. Earlier designs were the colonial key-plate types followed by pictorial stamps. In 1894 the post office was moved to Djibouti, which continued to use up the Obock stamps without an overprint.

OIL RIVERS

In the south of today's Nigeria, a British protectorate Oil Rivers (capital, Calabar) was established in 1885. The name is a reminder of the many palm-oil trees in the Niger delta. In 1893 the protectorate was changed to that of Niger Coast, which belonged to the Royal Niger Company.

In 1892 stamps of Great Britain with the overprint 'BRITISH PROTECTORATE OIL RIVERS'. Definitives were prepared but never put into circulation because the name was changed to Niger Coast. A total of 14 stamps, all overprinted provisionals. From 1894 superseded by *Niger Coast* stamps.

ORANGE FREE STATE AND ORANGE RIVER COLONY

The Boers, who abandoned Cape Province to the British in 1835, finally settled on the Orange River. In 1854 this territory declared itself independent, as the Orange Free State, although it had joined the Cape in 1846. After the discovery of diamond fields near Kimberley, the British occupied the whole area of Western Griqualand (in 1871). Following the outbreak of the Boer War (1899–1902), the Orange Free State was gradually occupied by the British, and through the Treaty of Vereeniging in 1902 it became a British colony (Orange River Colony). In 1910 it became a province of the Union of South Africa. The size of its territory varied: it is now 128,580 sq.km, with the capital at Bloemfontein.

In 1868, definitives with the name 'Oranje Vrij Staat', followed by provisionals with surcharges: a total of 22 values. Following the first definitives, of a symbolic character, there were only overprinted provisionals. Until the capitulation of the Orange Free State was confirmed (on 31 May 1902), its stamps were valid wherever there was no British garrison.

From 1900 occupation stamps of the Orange Free State appeared with the overprint 'V.R.I.' (Victoria Regina Imperatrix), then Cape stamps with the overprint 'ORANGE RIVER COLONY' followed by definitives with the same inscription. The overprint of 1902, after the death of Queen Victoria, was the initials 'E.R.I.' (Eduardus Rex Imperator) followed by royal portrait definitives inscribed 'ORANGE RIVER COLONY'. Until 1909 a total of 49 stamps issued, chiefly overprinted provisionals, the definitives are of British origin. From 1910, when the Union of South Africa was established, its stamps became valid, while the stamps of all the former colonies henceforth forming the Union were valid in all Union provinces until 1937.

OUBANGUI-CHARI (UBANGI-SHARI)

The territory of Ubangi-Shari (occupied by the French 1890–4) was at first part of the colony *Oubangi-Shari-Chad.* From 1920, however, it was set up as a separate colony (**area** 617,000 sq.km, **capital** Bangui), forming part of French Equatorial Africa. In 1946 it became an overseas territory of France; in 1958 an autonomous state (see *Central African Republic*) and as from 1960 it has been independent.

The 1922 stamps of Middle Congo with the overprint 'OUBANGUI– CHARI', sometimes with the additional overprint 'AFRIQUE ÉQUATORIALE FRANÇAISE': a total of 61 + 22 stamps of French origin, overprinted provisionals and pictorial stamps in typical French colonial designs. From 1935 the stamps of *French Equatorial Africa* were used.

OUBANGUI-CHARI-TCHAD (UBANGI-SHARI-CHAD)

After reorganization of the territorial division of the French Congo (which had existed from 1886) a separate colony, Ubangi-Shari-Chad (with the capital, Bangui), was set up in 1904 along with Gabon and the Middle Congo. Ubangi-Shari was French from 1894; Chad was occupied from 1897 to 1903 and became a dependency of this new colony (a territory in 1914; an independent colony in 1920). In 1911, a third of the colony Ubangi-Shari-Chad (about 275,000 sq.km) was ceded to German Kamerun with Germany's agreement on the setting up of a French protectorate in Morocco, but after the Versailles Treaty of 1919 it was returned to France again.

In 1915 stamps of Middle Congo with the overprint 'OUBANGUI-CHARI-TCHAD': a total of 24 provisionals. In 1922 the territory was divided postally (it had already been divided politically in 1920) into *Chad* and *Ubangi-Shari*.

OUTER SEYCHELLES
Area 150 sq.km, **population** 400 (1980).

The one-time island dependencies of Seychelles — Aldabra, Farquhar and Desroches — which from 1967 to 1976 were part of the British Indian Ocean Territory, but since 1980 have been known as the Zil Eloigne Sesel (Outer Seychelles). On 29 August 1980, a marine travelling post office was put into operation.

Part of the former British Indian Ocean Territory which became a dependency of the Seychelles, it has issued its own stamps from 1980 with the inscription in the local dialect, reading 'ZIL ELOIGNE SESEL', from 1982, 'ZIL ELWAGNE SESEL', from 1985 'ZIL ELWAN-NYEN SESEL', with the sub-title 'SEYCHELLES'. The postal need for these issues has not been confirmed, leading to the assumption that philatelic sales were anticipated.

Philatelic bureau Zil Elwannyen Sesel Philatelic Bureau, GPO, Victoria, Seychelles.

PONTA DELGADA
A district of the Portuguese Azores, including the islands of São Miguel and Santa Maria (**area** 844 sq.km, **capital** Ponta Delgada on São Miguel).

The district issued its own stamps from 1892 to 1905: a total of 34 stamps of Portuguese origin in designs common to Portuguese colonial issues. Before 1892 and after 1905 stamps of the Azores were valid.

PORT SAID
In Port Said (today in the Arab Republic of Egypt) a post office was opened in 1867 which at first used French stamps, then from 1899 French stamps with an overprint, then with the inscription 'PORT SAID'. By 1931 — when the post office was closed — a total of 86 + 12 stamps had appeared, French issues in the colonial key-plate designs and overprinted provisionals. Some of the stamps of the first issue, although they had the designation Port Said, were also valid in Alexandria, and vice versa.

Besides the French post office, there were British, Austrian and Russian post offices in Port Said at various times, but they used stamps which did not include the Port Said inscription.

PORTUGUESE AFRICA
Portuguese Africa was the designation for Angola, Cape Verde Islands, Mozambique, Portuguese Guinea and the islands of São Tomé and Principe. The first stamps for this territory, with the simple inscription 'AFRICA', appeared in 1898 on the 400th anniversary of its dis-

covery by Vasco de Gama (just as in Portugal) and were valid in all the above-mentioned African possessions. In 1918 a single 1c war tax postage stamp was created by overprinting a fiscal stamp 'TAXA DE GUERRA' for use as above except for Mozambique. A total of 8 + 3 stamps.

PORTUGUESE CONGO
North of Angola, the territory between the Rivers Ladje and Congo and the separate district Cabinda (capital, Cabinda). The Congo Conference in Berlin (1884–5), where Belgium laid claim to the delta of the River Congo, thwarted Portuguese plans to seize the mouth of this giant river.

Definitives in 1894 inscribed 'CONGO': a total of 133 stamps, largely overprinted provisionals, otherwise issues in the Portuguese colonial key-types. From 1920 the stamps of Angola, which had been valid here up to 1894, were re-introduced to the area.

PORTUGUESE GUINEA
A neglected agricultural region (**area** 36,125 sq.km, **capital** Bissau). The remainder of Portuguese rule in Upper Guinea, established in the 15th century, declared a colony in 1879. From 1951 it became an overseas province of Portugal, and was the first Portuguese possession to declare its independence, on 24 September 1973, under the name *Guinea-Bissau*. Indirect UPU membership from 1 July 1877 (as a Portuguese colony).

Before 1881 the stamps of Cape Verde Islands were used in Portuguese Guinea and, from that time, the stamps of Cape Verde Islands with the overprint 'GUINÉ', later also overprinted stamps of Macao, Portuguese Africa and Timor: a total of 344+58 stamps. At the outset a large number of overprinted provisionals, then definitives of Portuguese origin in the colonial key-plate types. In the subsequent period there was little stamp issuing (sometimes not a single stamp appeared in a whole year), as in other Portuguese colonies.

QUELIMANE
Mozambique district (**area** 103,680 sq.km, **capital** Quelimane), once administered by the Zambezia Company (it was a part of Zambezia whose capital also was Quelimane). Today this territory is called Zambezia.

A provisional issue of 1913 with the same design as Macao, Portuguese Africa and Timor and the overprint 'QUELIMANE'. Other issues inscribed 'QUELIMANE' were in the Portuguese colonial key-types. A total of 40 stamps which in 1920 were replaced by stamps of *Mozambique*.

RÉUNION
Island with sugar-cane agriculture (**area** 2,510 sq.km, **capital** Saint Denis). French from 1654 (occupied by the British 1810–14); from 1946 an overseas department of France. It received its present name in 1793; before that, from 1643, it used the name Bourbon. The islands of Europa, Bassas da India, Juan de Nova, Glorieuses and Tromelin, until 1960 administered from Madagascar, were joined to Réunion in 1968.

In 1852 primitives with the inscription 'Île de la Réunion' (among the most coveted classical stamps); then stamps of the French colonial general issue overprinted 'REUNION', followed by the colonial key-plate types inscribed 'RÉUNION'. A total of 324 + 40 stamps of French origin. From 1907 typical pictorials until the Second World War when Free French issues (as opposed to Pétain issues) were in use inscribed 'France Libre – RÉUNION'. Post-war stamp pictures have remarkable designs. Stamp-issuing ended in 1947, because Réunion became a French overseas department. In 1949–74 French stamps appeared with currency surcharges in 'CFA' francs.

RHODESIA
Present-day Zimbabwe. An advanced agricultural country (**area** 389,361 sq.km, **capital** Salisbury, now Harare) with a high-level mining industry. As Southern Rhodesia, the country

was a part of the Federation of Rhodesia and Nyasaland until 1963. This, on 11 November 1965, unilaterally declared its independence, adopting the name Rhodesia, and on 1 March 1970 declared itself a republic. On 12 December 1979 this independence was formally abolished, and on 18 April 1980, the country became the independent Republic of *Zimbabwe*.

After the break-up of the Federation, federal stamps continued to be valid until February 1964, when definitive issues inscribed 'SOUTHERN RHODESIA' appeared. After the declaration of independence, it issued its own stamps inscribed 'RHODESIA'. Annual output about 5 stamps.

From 1909 the name Rhodesia appeared on stamps of the *British South African Company* alongside the main name (indicating the territory of Northern and Southern Rhodesia, which had been introduced in 1895).

RHODESIA AND NYASALAND

From 1953 to 1963 the territories of Northern Rhodesia, Southern Rhodesia and Nyasaland were joined to form the Federation of Rhodesia and Nyasaland (**area** 1,268,630 sq.km, **capital** Salisbury). After the Federation was dissolved on 31 December 1963, there gradually came into existence the independent countries of *Zambia* (24 October 1964), *Malawi* (6 July 1964) and the self-governing British colony of *Rhodesia,* which unilaterally declared its independence on 11 November 1965.

In 1954, definitives inscribed 'RHODESIA AND NYASALAND'. Until 1963 a total of 51 + 4 stamps of British origin with a series of pictorial issues and designs common to British Commonwealth omnibus issues.

RÍO DE ORO

Spanish colonial territory on the West African coast from 1884, to which the territory of Saguia el-Hamra was joined in 1912 (**area** 226,000 sq.km, **capital** Villa Cisneros). Joined with the territories of La Agüera and Cape Juby in 1924 to form the Spanish possessions of Western Sahara (later called Spanish Sahara).

In 1905, definitives with the name 'COLONIA DE RIO DE ORO': a total of 144 stamps of Spanish origin, chiefly portraits in Spanish colonial key-types and overprinted provisionals. Most issues came out in very limited printings of less than 10,000 stamps. Stamps issued until 1921: from 1924 the stamps of *Spanish Sahara*.

RÍO MUNI

A backward agricultural area (**area** 26,017 sq.km, **capital** Bata), Spanish from 1843; in 1900 the Spanish occupation ended; 1900–60 a part of Spanish Guinea, then a Spanish overseas province (the status of colony was abolished). From 1964 the mainland province of *Equatorial Guinea* — which until 1968 was autonomous and since then has been an independent state with the islands of Corisco and Elobey belonging to it.

Following issues of *Spanish Guinea* the name 'RIO MUNI' first appeared in 1960 on definitives: a total of 59 stamps characteristic of Spanish production, printed in photogravure in Madrid, with the design emphasis on local features. The designs were planned to attract collectors, but the quantities printed (around 750,000 of each stamp) were sufficient to discourage speculation. From 1968 see *Equatorial Guinea*.

RUANDA

An African country (**area** 26,338 sq.km, **capital** Kigali), nominally part of German East Africa from 1894, but de facto only from 1899. In 1916 it was captured by Belgian units from the neighbouring Belgian Congo and in 1919, together with Urundi, it was placed under Belgian administration by the Treaty of Versailles as a mandate of the League of Nations.

In 1916 stamps of the Belgian Congo with the overprint 'RUANDA'. A total of 8 values, virtually all overprinted provisionals (see also *German East Africa*). For issues for the mandate from 1924 under the joint name see *Ruanda-Urundi*.

RUANDA-URUNDI

Originally part of German East Africa (nominally from 1894; de facto from 1899), it was seized during the First World War, in 1916, by Belgian units from the neighbouring Belgian Congo and in 1919 became a mandate of the League of Nations based on the Treaty of Versailles, to be administered by Belgium. From 1946 a UN trusteeship territory under Belgian administration (**area** 54,172 sq.km, **capital** Usumbura). Its trusteeship status was abolished on 1 July 1962, resulting in two independent states — Rwanda and Burundi.

From 1916 see *Ruanda, Urundi* and *German East Africa*. Stamps of the Belgian Congo appeared for the mandate in 1924 overprinted 'RUANDA – URUNDI'. Later, definitives with the same name. Until 1961 a total of 188+19 stamps of Belgian origin. Besides many overprinted provisionals, there were pictorial stamps, frequently with commemorative issues in designs common to other Belgian colonies. From the 1950s in particular there were designs in common with the Belgian Congo, differing only in the text. Ruanda-Urundi stamps, prior to 1916, were those of German East Africa; in 1962 superseded by the separate stamps of *Rwanda* and *Burundi*.

RWANDA

Area 26,338 sq.km, **population** 5.58m (1983), **capital** Kigali.

Developing agricultural country. Formerly part of the trusteeship territory Ruanda-Urundi, from 1961 it had a republican system and from the beginning of 1962 it was autonomous, gaining independence on 1 July 1962. Indirect UPU membership from 1 April 1891 as a German protectorate; indirect from 31 August 1923 as a Belgian territory; direct from 6 April 1963.

In 1962 stamps of Ruanda-Urundi with the overprint 'RÉPUBLIQUE RWANDAISE' and definitives with the same text. From 1976 the stamps only have the name 'RWANDA'. Stamp production is in Belgium. Usually designed by J. van Noten, the stamps were mostly printed in photogravure but also by line engraving at different printing houses abroad. Current production frequently relates to international issues, apart from reflecting many general themes of wider collector appeal, and including a great number of miniature sheets. At the present time an output of 50 to 80 stamps a year.

Philatelic bureau Direction Générale des PTT, Section Philatélique, Kigali. **Trade sales** Agence Philatélique Gouvernementale, Brussels, Belgium.

SAINT HELENA

Area 122 sq.km, **population** 5,268 (1981), **capital** Jamestown.

Volcanic island with agriculture, British since 1651, a Crown Colony from 1834. St Helena dependencies include the stamp-issuing islands of *Tristan da Cunha* and *Ascension.* Indirect UPU membership from 1 October 1879.

From 1856 definitives with the text 'ST. HELENA'. Stamps of British origin (with participation in British Commonwealth omnibus issues). First came portrait issues, then pictorials and omnibus issues. Chiefly line-engraving process at the outset; now photogravure and photolithography are more generally used. Current production irregular, seldom up to 3 issues a year.

Philatelic bureau c/o Postmaster, General Post Office, Jamestown. **Trade sales** Crown Agents' Stamp Bureau.

SAINTE MARIE DE MADAGASCAR

French island off the north-eastern shore of Madagascar (**area** 174 sq.km, **capital** Sainte-Marie). In 1885–93 it was a dependency within the colony of Diégo Suarez. In 1893–1906 it was a separate colony, and then became part of Madagascar.

At first the stamps of the colony Diégo Suarez et dépendances were used — and after it became an independent colony the French colonial key-type was issued inscribed 'STE MARIE DE MADAGASCAR' and were used in March and April 1894, until definitives with the same text (13 values) arrived on the island. From 1898 Madagascar stamps were valid, but local stamps were used until 1903.

SÃO TOMÉ E PRÍNCIPE (ST THOMAS AND PRINCE ISLANDS)
Area 964 sq.km, **population** 100,000 (1983), **capital** São Tomé.

Islands of volcanic origin. Portuguese from 1484; a province from 1522 (except during 1641–44); and from 1951 an overseas province of Portugal. On 12 July 1975 the islands were proclaimed an independent democratic republic. Indirect UPU membership from 1 July 1877 (Portuguese colony); direct from 22 August 1977.

In 1869 definitives with the inscription 'S.THOMÉ E PRINCIPE'; from 1914 a change in spelling to 'S. TOMÉ E PRINCIPE' (starting from 1938, issues had only the name as 'S. TOMÉ'). After establishment of the republic in 1975 the inscription became 'REPÚBLICA DEMOCRÁTICA DE S. TOMÉ E PRÍNCIPE'; later, 'SÃO TOMÉ E PRÍNCIPE'. Stamps of Portuguese origin with a large number of overprinted provisionals (especially when Portugal was declared a republic), and with designs of the Portuguese colonial key-plates. Issues since independence tend to nationalistic designs. In 1977 a programme of frequent issues started, going far beyond the postal requirements of the islands: up to 30 stamps a year, pictorials of large sizes, a multitude of overprinted provisionals and many issues of miniature sheets. This suggests an attempt to cater for collectors rather than the local people.

Philatelic bureau Directeur des PTT, Service Philatélique, São Tomé.

SENEGAL
Area 196,192 sq.km, **population** 6.18m (1983), **capital** Dakar.

Agricultural country with developing mineral mining. The oldest French territory in Africa, occupied in 1855; in 1895 it was declared a colony incorporated into French West Africa. In 1946 Senegal obtained the status of an overseas territory, in 1958 autonomy, and on 17 January 1959 it entered the Federation of Mali, which on 20 June 1960 declared its independence. On 20 August 1960, however, Senegal left the federation and proclaimed itself an independent republic. Indirect UPU membership from 1 July 1876 (as a French colony); direct from 14 June 1961.

In 1887 stamps in designs common to all French colonies; from 1892 with the overprint 'SÉNÉGAL', then issues with the name 'SÉNÉGAL ET DÉPENDANCES', to which was later added 'AFRIQUE OCCIDENTALE FRANÇAISE'. Issues of the colonial key-plate types, many overprinted provisionals and pictorial stamps of French origin. Pétain issues had no postal validity. From 1945 to 1959 the stamps of *French West Africa* were valid.

From 1960 issues of an independent republic, definitives with the text 'RÉPUBLIQUE DU SÉNÉGAL'; from 1976, only 'SENEGAL'. Typical French production. Besides propaganda subjects, there are especially joint issues for the French region with general themes. The considerable annual output of about 40 stamps has not affected the high-quality printing, first by recess and now photogravure, or the design excellence of the French designers involved. Many issues are directed at the philatelic demand rather than required by postal necessity.

Philatelic bureau Bureau Philatélique, Direction Office des Postes et Télécommunications, Dakar. **Trade sales** Agence des Timbres-Poste d'Outre-Mer.

SENEGAMBIA AND NIGER
A territory which was formed in 1902 because of a redivision of the northern French possessions in Africa, derived from the area of Upper Senegal and Middle Niger, which in turn had been created out of French Sudan. In 1904 Senegambia and Niger were incorporated into the territory of Upper Senegal and Niger (a part also went to Mauritania), and so it ceased to exist. (Capital, Bamako.) Today most of this territory has been incorporated into Senegal and the western part of Mali.

In 1903 French colonials of the colonial key-types with the text 'SÉNÉGAMBIE ET NIGER': I issue of 13 stamps. From 1906 superseded by stamps of *Upper Senegal and Niger*.

SEYCHELLES
Area 444 sq.km, **population** 64,314 (1983), **capital** Victoria on Mahé.

Group of islands in the Indian Ocean; an agricultural and fishing region. From 1794 the islands were British, a dependency of Mauritius in 1810–1903, a Crown Colony in 1903. In 1965 several islands of the archipelago (Aldabra, Farquhar, Desroches) were separated from it to form the new British Indian Ocean Territory. In 1976, however, they were returned. On 28 July 1976 the Seychelles became an independent republic within the British Commonwealth. Indirect UPU membership from 1 April 1877 (a British colony); direct from 7 October 1977.

At first the stamps of Great Britain were used on the islands and from 1861 those of Mauritius; came into circulation. Definitives were produced in 1890 with the name 'SEYCHELLES'. Until 1938 all stamps were in the appropriate British colonial key-and-duty royal portrait types. Pictorial stamps followed, always with the Queen's portrait until independence in 1976. Most stamps are now printed by photogravure or litho process, always in Great Britain. Approximately 30 stamps now appear annually. From 1980 see also *Outer Seychelles*.

Philatelic bureau General Post Office, Victoria.

SIERRA LEONE
Area 71,740 sq.km, **population** 3.67m (1982), **capital** Freetown.

A developing agricultural country. The British occupied it from 1787 and a Crown Colony was created in 1808 out of the area around Freetown. The rest of the territory was declared a protectorate in 1896. From 27 April 1961, Sierra Leone was an independent country and from 22 April 1971, a republic in the British Common wealth. Indirect UPU membership from 1 January 1879 (as a British colony); direct from 29 January 1962.

In 1859 definitives with the text 'SIERRA LEONE', from 1971 'REPUBLIC OF SIERRA LEONE'. Production of stamps very diverse in form and content. Following portrait issues in the British colonial key-and-duty types, pictorial stamps were issued and there were also British Commonwealth omnibus issues. Between 1932 and 1962 line-engraved printing was employed, although it was supplanted chiefly by photogravure towards the end of the period. In 1963 there was a change in producer and a new philatelic agency began the issue of an extremely large number of provisionals consisting of previous sterling-currency stamps surcharged in the new decimal currency. Many of the printings were small, even down to 540. Curious shapes (square, round or pear-like designs, an eagle with outspread wings, outline maps of the country, etc.) with self-adhesive backs and other unusual curiosities were intended to attract collectors — since they could only be sparingly used for postal purposes. From 1971, when the republic was established, a policy change brought about a more conventional stamp-issuing programme, using normal shapes and adhesives. Sometimes a year goes by without a new stamp appearing. In 1861–9 Sierra Leone stamps were valid in *Gambia*.

Philatelic bureau General Post Office, Freetown. **Trade sales** Crown Agents' Stamp Bureau.

SOMALIA
Area 637,661 sq.km, **population** 5.12m (1982), **capital** Mogadishu.

A developing agricultural country, once Italian Somaliland, it became part of Italian East Africa between 1936 and 1941. After Italy's defeat in 1941 it was occupied by British troops until 1950, and in 1950–60 became a trusteeship territory under Italian administration. On 1 July 1960, the Republic of Somalia came into existence through the fusion of this territory with British Somaliland — when both territories had already won their independence. It was declared the Democratic Republic of Somalia on 21 October 1969. Indirect UPU membership from 1 July 1904 (Italy); indirect from 1 October 1907 (Italian colony); indirect from 1 July 1940 to 1942 as Italian East Africa; indirect from 1942 to 31 March 1950 (British occupation); direct from 1 April 1959 as Somalia (under Italian administration), Somaliland (British); indirect from 1 June 1903 (British protectorate); direct UPU membership from 1 July 1960 (when it became a sovereign state consisting of former Italian Somaliland and British Somaliland).

257

At the time of the British occupation (1941–50) the overprint 'E.A.F' (East African Forces) appeared on British stamps: a total of 9 stamps between 1943 and 1946. Then British stamps with the overprint 'B.M.A. SOMALIA' (British Military Administration) and 'B. A. SOMALIA' (British Administration — by British troops and then by British civilian administration). A total of 22 overprinted provisionals (in 1948–50) in printings of about 20,000 each. Their validity ended on 31 March 1950.

From 1950, issues of the Italian administration of Somalia as a mandated territory. Definitives bearing the name 'SOMALIA'. Until 1960 a total of 132 + 15 stamps of Italian production in characteristic photogravure printing: propaganda and general themes. Some of these pictorial stamps have an interesting design approach, indicating an effort to achieve an original conception in production of stamps for what later became independent Somalia.

In 1960 stamps of Italian Somaliland with an overprint and definitives with the text 'SOMALIA' in Latin and Arabic. From 1970, in Latin characters with the inscription 'SOMALI DEMOCRATIC REPUBLIC'. Later other names were used with varied spelling: 'JUM. DIM. SOMALIYA', 'JAM. DIM. SOOMAALIYA', 'J. D. SOOMAALIYEED'. Stamp production of Italian origin (printed in Rome) with a fairly uniform graphic design (long represented by virtually one designer — Mancioli). A predominance of propaganda designs. Annual output is currently 10 to 15 stamps. For issues with the name 'SOMALIA' see also *Italian Somaliland*.

Philatelic bureau Somali Philatelic Service, Ministry of Post & Telecommunications, Mogadishu.

SOUTH AFRICA
Area 1,221,037 sq.km, **population** 26.12m (1983), **capital** Pretoria and Cape Town.

The most developed industrial and agricultural country of Africa. After defeating the Boers (1899–1902), the British joined their two colonies, Cape Province and Natal, and two one-time Boer republics, then the administrative colonies of Transvaal and Orange River Colony, into the Union of South Africa in 1910 (the constituent countries became its provinces), which received the status of a dominion. In 1961, the Union of South Africa was proclaimed a republic and in the same year it left the Commonwealth. Besides the above-mentioned four provinces, South-West Africa (Namibia) is considered the fifth province — but South Africa has a right to administer it only as a trusteeship territory. The Republic of South Africa also claims Walvis Bay, which from 1922 to 1977 was under the administration of South-West Africa; and, in the Antarctic region of the Indian Ocean, Marion, Prince Edward and Penguin Islands came under South African sovereignty. A measure of independence has been accorded to black Africans through the creation of 'independent' bantustans (known as homelands) (Transkei 1975, Bophuthatswana 1977, Venda 1979, Ciskei 1981). UPU membership (under the name of South Africa including also Walvis Bay and Prince Edward Island, Natal and Zululand) direct from 1 July 1892 (British colony); as the South African Republic direct from 1 January 1893; Orange Free State direct from 1 January 1898; as the British colonies and protectorates of South Africa direct from 1 January 1899; and direct from 1 June 1910 as the Union of South Africa, renamed on 31 May 1961 the Republic of South Africa.

When the Union was established in 1910, there were 46 postage stamps valid in the four above-mentioned provinces and 7 postage-due stamps of the Transvaal, which remained in circulation as the first stamps of the Union until 1913 in all four provinces. The use and validity of these stamps lasted probably until 31 December 1937. The Union of South Africa also provided postal services in Basutoland and Swaziland, which were under British administration; South African stamps were used there until 1933.

The country's own stamp-issuing activities began in 1910, when definitives appeared with the text 'UNION OF SOUTH AFRICA/UNIË VAN ZUID AFRIKA', then with the name 'SOUTH AFRICA/SUID-AFRIKA'. From 1961, 'REPUBLIEK VAN SUID-AFRIKA/REPUBLIC OF SOUTH AFRICA'; most recently, only 'RSA'. The stamps appeared either with bilingual inscriptions or using the same stamp design, they were printed alternately throughout the sheet with the name in either one or the other language. New issue output is moderate but is doubled due to the alternating languages, English and Afrikaans. Annual output at the present time is 15 to 20 stamps. At first, all stamps were of British origin. From 1930, printing was at Pretoria in photogravure. Designs emphasize aspects of South African history and current life. Also typical is production of official stamps (71) and postage-due stamps (70). Since the proclamation of bantustans, South African stamps have no longer been valid on their territories (see *Transkei, Bophuthatswana, Venda, Ciskei*).

Philatelic bureau Philatelic Services and Intersapa, GPO, Pretoria.

SOUTH AFRICAN REPUBLIC (TRANSVAAL)

After the Boers abandoned Cape Province to the British in 1835, they settled in Natal, and when the British annexed this territory as well in 1843, the Boers moved beyond the River Vaal, where they set up the republics of Potchefstroom, Lydenburg, Zoutpansberg and Utrecht. These joined together in 1849 into the Vereenigten Bond, out of which emerged the South African Republic (Zuid Afrikaansche Republiek) in 1856. From 1877 to 1880 it was occupied by the British, who renamed it Transvaal. The Boers revolted, and in 1881 the independence of the South African Republic was again recognized. In 1889 the new Republik (Vrijheid), and in 1893 Swaziland, became part of it. In 1899 the Boers attacked Cape Province, and the South African Republic temporarily occupied Vryburg but, from 1900, the British gradually occupied it and the Boer War ended in 1902 with the Peace of Vereeniging; the South African Republic under the names of Transvaal and Orange River Colony became British colonies. In 1910 Transvaal became a province of the Union of South Africa. The size of its territory has varied (today's Transvaal is 286,053 sq.km and its capital is Pretoria).

The stamp-issuing activities of the first period of the South African Republic is represented by a total of 6 stamps from 1869 to 1875. These are primitives, locally printed, heraldic in conception, bearing the name 'Z. AFR. REPUBLIEK'.

In the second period, stamps were issued from 1882 with the name 'Z. AFR. REPUBLIEK'; 'Z.A.R.' as an overprint or 'ZUID AFRIKAANSCHE REPUBLIEK'. These are overprinted provisionals, definitives and 1 commemorative. Until 1901 a total of 57 stamps were issued, of which the last was the final issue of the independent government of the South African Republic which then withdrew to the territory of Zoupansberg, where it organized the last resistance to the British. In 1899, when the South African Republic temporarily occupied Vryburg, provisionals appeared on *Cape of Good Hope* stamps with the overprint 'Z.A.R.' (Zuid Afrikaansche Republiek). From 1902 see *Transvaal*.

SOUTH KASAI

A province of the Congo which in 1960–62 declared itself an autonomous state. Its capital was Luluabourg.

Stamps of the Belgian Congo in 1961 with the overprint 'ÉTAT AUTONOME DU SUDKA-SAI'; also in the same year, definitives printed in Switzerland. Overall production 29 stamps (for the most part overprinted provisionals) including 1961, when stamp issuing ended on the return of South Kasai to central government rule.

SOUTHERN NIGERIA

In 1900 the British government took over the territory of the Royal Niger Company (a protectorate on the Niger Coast) and created the protectorate and colony of Southern Nigeria, which, in 1906, was joined by Lagos (**area** 236,328 sq.km, **capital** Enugu, later Lagos). In 1914 Southern Nigeria was merged with Northern Nigeria to form the colony and protectorate of Nigeria.

In 1901 definitives with the name 'SOUTHERN NIGERIA'. In 1906 Lagos and Southern Nigeria were united postally; the stamps of both territories were valid concurrently until their stock ran out. Until 1912 a total of 56 stamps of British origin (royal portrait issues).

SOUTHERN RHODESIA

A self-governing British colony in Central Africa, created by the British government after taking it over from the South African Company in 1923, when its charter ran out. In 1953–63 it was a member of the Federation of Rhodesia and Nyasaland; after the Federation was disbanded (31 December 1963) it adopted the name Rhodesia in October 1964, and on 11 November 1965, it unilaterally proclaimed its independence (**area** 389,361 sq.km, **capital** Salisbury).

From 1925, definitives with the name 'SOUTHERN RHODESIA'. A total of 107+7 stamps of British origin, very largely recess printing but with the last issue in photogravure. The annual output of new issues was very limited. In some years there were no new stamps. Chiefly pictorial and portrait stamps with many conservative traits. Stamp-issuing until 1953 (from 1954 to 1963 as *Rhodesia and Nyasaland*) and in 1964 a final issue with the name 'SOUTHERN RHODESIA'. For subsequent issuing see *Rhodesia*.

SOUTH WEST AFRICA (NAMIBIA)
Area 824,269 sq.km, **population** 1,039,800 (1981), **capital** Windhoek.

A backward, arid country with vanadium and diamond mining. Originally a German colony (from 1884), occupied by South African troops in 1915; in 1919 it became a mandate territory of the League of Nations and was placed under the administration of the Union of South Africa. In 1949 the country was annexed by the Union of South Africa, but this is not recognized internationally; in 1966 the United Nations declared an end to the South African mandate, and two years later gave the country the name Namibia. UPU membership under the name Namibia indirectly from 1 July 1888 (German protectorate); indirectly from 1920 (through the Union of South Africa); indirectly from 27 October 1966, in view of the declared responsibility for the territory's administration by the United Nations.

Before issuing its own stamps, the country used those of *South Africa* between 1915 and 1922. Furthermore, the stamps of all four provinces of the Union could be used here as well — i.e. Cape, Natal, Orange River Colony and Transvaal.

From 1923 South African stamps with the overprint 'SOUTH WEST AFRICA/ZUID-WEST AFRIKA'; then 'SOUTH WEST AFRICA/SUIDWES AFRIKA' and 'S.W.A.'. Later definitives with similar inscriptions. The stamps either had bilingual texts (English and Afrikaans) or were printed alternately in the sheet in the two languages. From 1968, only the initials 'SWA' have been used to express both English and German, the latter for the benefit of the remaining German colonists. Until 1977 South West African stamps were valid even on the territory of Walvis Bay, which was under its administration until 1 September 1977. Stamp production, both printing and design, is linked to that of South Africa except for many overprinted provisionals in the early years. In the last decade the designs have become more specific to South West Africa and output has grown to about 15 stamps per annum.

Philatelic bureau Philatelic Services and Intersapa, GPO, Pretoria, South Africa.

SPANISH GUINEA
A Spanish colony in Equatorial Africa (**area** 28,051 sq.km, **capital** Santa Isabel) with definitive borders established in 1900, but gradually occupied by the Spanish from the 19th century. It consisted of the mainland territory of Río Muni and the islands of Fernando Poo, Elobey, Annobón and Corisco. After the colonial régime was abolished in 1960, two overseas Spanish provinces were created — Río Muni (with the islands Elobey and Corisco) and Fernando Poo (with the island Annobón). In 1968 independent Equatorial Guinea came into existence.

Following stamps of the *Spanish Territories of the Gulf of Guinea*, from 1949 stamps were inscribed 'GUINEA ESPAÑOLA' (similar to those of 1902). A total of 112 stamps of Spanish origin: pictorial issues with a number of general themes in the photogravure technique characteristic of the State Printing House in Madrid. Issues in printings of around 1 million. Stamps-issuing until 1959. For earlier issues see *Fernando Poo* and *Río Muni*; from 1968 see *Equatorial Guinea*.

SPANISH MAINLAND GUINEA
The borders of the territory of so-called Río Muni, occupied by the Spanish in 1843 and called after the river of the same name, were established by the Treaty of Paris (26 June 1900) between Spain and France. The area was then 26,000 sq.km and the capital Bata. In 1909 the mainland territory was combined, for postal purposes, with the Spanish islands

Fernando Poo, Elobey, Annobón and Corisco, and the new entity was given the name Spanish Territory of the Gulf of Guinea. Today it is the independent state, *Equatorial Guinea*.

Following the stamps of *Fernando Poo*, valid here from 1879, in 1901 Fernando Poo stamps appeared with an unauthorized overprint 'BATA', then definitives with the text 'GUINEA ESPAÑOLA', 'GUINEA CONTIAL ESPAÑOLA' and overprints on stamps of *Elobey, Annobón and Corisco* reading 'GUINEA CONTINENTAL'. Until 1909 a total of 100 stamps of Spanish origin, some of which were in very small quantities of around 2,500 a set. For subsequent development see *Spanish Territories of the Gulf of Guinea* and then *Spanish Guinea*.

SPANISH MOROCCO

In 1912 Spain obtained a 50 km strip of the north Moroccan coastal area, which was given the name of Spanish Morocco (**area** 19,600 sq.km, **capital** Tetuan). Tangier was declared an international zone (from 1940 to1945 it was temporarily joined to Spanish Morocco). The Spanish protectorate was abolished only on 7 April 1956 (the territory was joined to Morocco on 10 April 1958) and on 29 October 1956 Tangier was also returned to Moroccan sovereignty. In 1956–8 this entire territory provisionally formed the so-called Northern (Spanish) Zone of the Kingdom of Morocco.

In 1914 Spanish stamps with the overprint 'MARRUECOS'. Later overprints were 'PROTECTORADO ESPAÑOL EN MARRUECOS' and 'ZONA DE PROTECTORADO ESPAÑOL': a total of 405 + 28 stamps of Spanish origin in a uniform style by their sole designer (M. Bertuchi) and produced by the Barcelona printers, Rieusset Heralmi. At the beginning a large variety of overprinted provisionals, then pictorial stamps, among which a good many airmails are intended for the collector's market. Stamp issuing until 1955. See also *Morocco* (Spanish post office).

SPANISH SAHARA

Desert country on the shore of western Africa (**area** 266,000 sq.km, **capital** El Aiun), Spanish from 1884, enlarged by the addition of so-called Southern Morocco (Cabe Juby) in 1912. The name Western Sahara is also frequently used. In 1924 it was joined with the Spanish territory Río de Oro, Cabe Juby and La Agüera to form the Spanish possession of Western Sahara, which in 1934 was given the name Spanish Sahara. In 1946–58 it was part of Spanish West Africa (that is, Spanish Sahara and Ifni). Politically, Spanish Sahara was regarded, until 1958, as an overseas province of Spain. Southern Morocco was returned to Morocco in 1958. On 11 December 1975 Morocco announced the annexation of the northern part of the Sahara (the territory of Saguia el-Hamra) and occupied El Aiun with troops, while Mauritania sent its forces into Agüera. In 1976 Spanish Sahara was divided between both countries and thus ceased to exist. The national liberation movement, Polisario, consequently declared it the Saharan Arab Republic.

In 1924 definitives with the inscription 'POSESIONES ESPAÑOLAS DEL SAHARA OCCIDENTAL'; in 1926 'SAHARA ESPAÑOL'; from 1960 'SAHARA', but with the main title 'ESPAÑA': a total of 320 stamps of Spanish origin. Following the early overprinted provisionals and stamps in the Spanish colonial key-types, that is, since the 1950s, there have been more purely pictorial stamps with general themes, many concerned with Spanish matters, printed by photogravure in Madrid in a characteristic fashion.

SPANISH TERRITORIES OF THE GULF OF GUINEA

After Spanish Mainland Guinea and the islands Fernando Poo, Elobey, Annobón and Corisco were joined for postal purposes, in 1909 a postal area came into existence known as the Spanish Territories of the Gulf of Guinea, identical to the political-administrative unit, Spanish Guinea (**area** 28,051 sq.km, **capital** Santa Isabel). In 1949 the name Spanish Guinea was also introduced on stamps. Today it is independent *Equatorial Guinea*.

Following issues of *Spanish Mainland Guinea*, came stamps in 1909 inscribed 'TERRITO-RIOS ESPAÑOLES DEL GOLFO DE GUINEA'. Afterwards came such names as 'GUINEA', 'GUINEA ESPAÑOLA' and 'GOLFO DE GUINEA' (often as overprints), suggesting governmental indecision. A total of 249 stamps of Spanish origin. Many overprinted provisionals, Spanish colonial key-types and pictorials. From 1949 see *Spanish Guinea*.

SPANISH WEST AFRICA

The territory of Spanish Sahara and Ifni, joined in 1946–58 to form Spanish West Africa (**area** 293,920 sq.km, **capital** Villa Cisneros).

In 1949 definitives with the inscription 'AFRICA OCCIDENTAL ESPAÑOLA': a total of 26 stamps of Spanish origin, which continued in use until 1951.

STELLALAND

In 1883–5 a Boer Republic in South Africa (**area** 13,000 sq.km, **capital** Vryburg), named after the 'Great comet of 1882'. After Great Britain protested against its establishment, Stellaland was occupied by the British on 27 February 1885, and then joined to British Bechuanaland. In 1898–1900 it was occupied by troops of the South African Republic (Transvaal), following whose defeat the territory of Stellaland became part of the Cape Province.

In 1884 primitive lithographs produced in Cape Town with the name 'REPUBLIEK STEL-LALAND': a total of 6 stamps.

SUDAN

Area 2,505,813 sq.km, **population** 18.9m (1981), **capital** Khartoum.

An agricultural country, from 1820 under the rule of the Egyptian khedives who founded Khartoum in 1823. From 1870 the British began to penetrate the territory in an attempt to stop the slave trade. In 1881 a revolt was led by the Mahdi, who scored great victories before being finally suppressed by Lord Kitchener's army. In 1899 a joint Anglo-Egyptian administration of the Sudan (condominium) was agreed upon, but in reality the British ruled. Self-government was granted in 1955; the Sudan acquired independence on 1 January 1956, when it became a republic. The Democratic Republic of Sudan emerged on 25 May 1969. Indirect UPU membership from 1 July 1875 (Egypt); direct from 27 July 1956.

Until the uprising of the Mahdi (1881) there were Egyptian post offices in several Sudanese towns. In 1897 Egyptian stamps with the overprint in Arabic and in Latin 'SOUDAN', later 'SUDAN'; from 1970 'THE DEMOCRATIC REPUBLIC OF THE SUDAN' or just 'D. R. SU-DAN'. Essentially low production, based only on postal requirements. A well-known series of postage stamps with a rider on a camel, which first appeared in 1898, was the first definitive issue. It was based on a design by E. A. Stanton and issued with minor alterations until 1954, that is, for 56 years. Apart from definitive issues, only a small number of thematic issues, usually on propaganda themes. Latterly, there has been participation in joint international themes. The origin of the stamps is dependent on political influence of the issue — British and Egyptian. Currently a uniform style of production designed by a single artist, Sayed Bastawi Baghdadi; photogravure-produced by the British printers, De la Rue. Sudan is one of the very few states in which stamps appear chiefly for postal and propaganda purposes. The relatively large number of service (official) stamps — more than 100 — is characteristic; some of these have perforations 'S. G.' (Sudan Government) through them. Current annual production about 10 stamps.

Philatelic bureau Director General, Post and Telegraphs Public Corporation, Philatelic Office, Khartoum.

SUEZ CANAL

In 1869 the Company established to build the Suez Canal issued 4 stamps with the text CANAL MARITIME DE SUEZ, valid from 8 July to 31 August 1868, for postal services between Port Said and Suez.

SWAZILAND
Area 17,363 sq.km, **population** 634,700 (1982), **capital** Mbabane.

Backward agricultural country. From 1889 it belonged to both the provisional government of Great Britain and the South African Republic (Transvaal). In 1893 it was annexed by Transvaal, then administered by Great Britain in 1899–1902; from 1903, subordinate to the Transvaal governor. From 1906 a British protectorate administered by the High Commissioner of the Union of South Africa. It became the self-governing State of Swaziland in 1967 and became independent on 6 September 1968. Indirect UPU membership from 20 March 1934 (British protectorate); direct from 7 November 1969.

In 1889 stamps of the South African Republic (Transvaal) with the overprint 'Swazieland' until 1892, a total of 9 overprinted provisionals. After incorporation into the South African Republic (Transvaal), which in 1903–13 became a stamp-issuing country, no definitives were issued until 1933. The new stamps were first inscribed 'SWAZILAND PROTECTORATE'; later, only 'SWAZILAND', all of British origin. Besides overprinted provisionals, a number of pictorial issues and general themes in addition to British Commonwealth omnibus designs before independence. In general, conservative output which in recent years has been expanded to 15 to 30 stamps per annum.

Philatelic bureau Swaziland Stamp Bureau, Mbabane. **Trade sales** Crown Agents' Stamp Bureau.

TANGANYIKA
Virtually the whole of German East Africa was declared a mandate of the League of Nations in 1919 under the Versailles Treaty. In 1920 it was administered by Great Britain under the name Tanganyika (**area** 934,629 sq.km, **capital** Dar es-Salaam). After the Second World War it became a United Nations trusteeship territory; from 9 December 1961, independent; and from 1962, a republic. After joining with the Republic of Zanzibar (26 April 1964) the new state adopted the name United Republic of Tanganyika and Zanzibar, and in October 1964 the name Tanzania (United Republic of Tanzania).

In 1922 definitives were issued inscribed 'TANGANYIKA'. A total of 35 stamps until 1935, of British origin. In 1935–61 superseded by stamps of *Kenya-Uganda-Tanganyika.*

In 1961 definitives again with the name 'TANGANYIKA': a total of 16 + 8 stamps of British origin (pictorial stamps with propaganda themes) until 1962. Common issues of the East African Postal Administration were produced simultaneously (see *Kenya-Uganda-Tanganyika*).

TANGIER
After the French-Spanish division of Morocco in 1912, the city Tangier and its environs (373 sq.km) were declared an international zone whose statute was drawn up in 1923 and revised in 1928. In June 1940, however, Spain occupied it and in November annexed it to its part of Morocco. The Paris Conference in August 1945 agreed to the provisional restoration of the pre-war state, and the Spanish withdrew from the zone in October. A new statute was drawn up in 1953, but by 29 October 1956, it was withdrawn and Tangier was returned to independent Morocco.

The Tangier international zone did not have its own postal authority, but there were British, French and Spanish post offices, and until 1914 also a German post office, which used the stamps of their own countries, the stamps of the post office in Morocco, and finally also issues overprinted for local use.

The British post office in 1927–57 used British stamps overprinted 'TANGIER': a total of 110 stamps issued, almost all overprinted provisionals. From 1950 all Tangier stamps could be used for postal purposes in Great Britain. Although Tangier was incorporated into Morocco in 1956, the British post continued to function until 30 April 1957, when the sale of stamps overprinted for Tangier was halted. This occurred only a few weeks after celebrations to mark the centenary of the British post office in Tangier with a 20-stamp set comprising British stamps overprinted '1857–1957 TANGIER'.

The French postal authorities used stamps (French and Moroccan) with the overprint 'TANGER' in 1918–24 (when they were superseded by stamps of French Morocco). Airmail stamps with the overprint 'TANGER' were issued, exceptionally, in 1929. A total of 38 overprinted provisionals.

The Spanish post office had Spanish stamps overprinted 'TANGER' from 1926 to 1939. From 1948 to 1951, the Spanish post office issued pictorial definitives of Spanish origin, printed by the line-engraving process in Madrid. During the Spanish Civil War, there were two different Spanish post offices in Tangier (July 1936–April 1939). One came under the Republican Government and issued 76 stamps of the Spanish Republican post office with the overprint chiefly 'TANGER'. The second belonged to the Nationalist Government and used the stamps of Spanish Morocco, frequently overprinted 'TANGER'. A total of 146 stamps.

The German post office in Tangier operated from 1912 to August 1914. It had no special stamps with the name Tangier but made use of those issued by the German post office in Morocco.

The French and Spanish post offices were closed down in 1956, while the British functioned until 1957.

TANZANIA
Area 945,087 sq.km, **population** 19.73m (1983), **capital** Dar es-Salaam.

Agricultural country with well-established mining. Formerly German East Africa, from 1920 a mandate territory of the League of Nations under the name Tanganyika, administered by Great Britain. After the Second World War a United Nations trusteeship territory, independent in 1961, from 1962 a republic. In 1964 it was joined with the Republic of Zanzibar and from October 1964 the name United Republic of Tanzania was introduced, reflecting the union of the two countries. Indirect UPU membership as Tanganyika from 1 April 1891 (German protectorate); indirect from 23 October 1922 (British possession); indirect for Zanzibar from 1 December 1895 (British colony); direct from 29 March 1963 as Tanganyika; direct from 26 April 1974 as the United Republic of Tanzania.

In 1964 a commemorative issue inscribed 'UNITED REPUBLIC OF TANGANYIKA & ZANZIBAR'. From 1965 definitives with the name 'TANZANIA'. Nearly all pictorial stamps of British origin valid on other territories of the East African Postal Administration (Kenya-Uganda-Tanzania). Although Tanzania represents the merger of Tanganyika and Zanzibar, its first issue was invalid on Zanzibar territory, and vice versa; the first issues on Zanzibar including the name Tanzania were valid only in Zanzibar. From 1968 Tanzanian stamps were valid throughout the entire territory, including Zanzibar (and, of course, the whole territory of the East African Postal Administration). Conservative stamp-issuing policy supplemented by issues of the joint postal administrations bringing out stamps for use throughout Kenya, Uganda and Tanzania. During 1976–7 all three states issued stamps in uniform designs which carried only the name of the issuing state. Individual stamp issuing was later resumed and the present output is about 20 to 30 a year.

Philatelic bureau The Regional Stamp Bureau, East African Posts and Telecommunications Corporation, Dar es-Salaam. **Trade sales** Crown Agents' Stamp Bureau; Inter-Governmental Philatelic Corporation.

TETE
Mozambique district (**area** 121,160 sq.km, **capital** Tete) formerly administered by the Zambezi Company as part of Zambezia. Today a part of the Manica-Sofala district.

In 1914 stamps of Portuguese Africa, Macao and Timor with the overprint 'TÉTE'. Later, the same text on definitives of Portuguese origin. A total of 40 stamps, overprinted issues and the Ceres Portuguese key-type. From 1920, Mozambique stamps were used once again.

TETUAN
A Moroccan city, capital of Spanish Morocco, which between 1956 and 1960 was under Spanish rule.

In 1908–9 a total of 15 stamps of the Spanish post office in Morocco and Spain with the hand-stamped overprint 'TETUAN'. See also *Morocco* and *Spanish Morocco*.

TOGO
Area 56,785 sq.km, **population** 2.96m (1983), **capital** Lomé.

A developing agricultural country. Originally part of German Togo; from 1922 a mandate under French administration (French Togo), from 1946 trusteeship status. On 24 April 1956, Togo was declared an autonomous republic; on 27 April 1958, a republic; and from 2 April 1960, an independent country. Indirect UPU membership from 1 June 1888 (German protectorate); indirect from 1919 (a French colony); direct from 21 March 1962.

Germany announced its protectorate over Togo on 5 July 1884, and in agreement with France in 1897 and with Great Britain in 1899 it defined the frontiers of its inland preserve (**area** 90,000 sq.km, **capital** Lomé). In 1914 French and British troops occupied German Togo; the Versailles Treaty of 1919 made it a mandate territory of the League of Nations and in 1922 it was divided between France (French Togo) and Great Britain (British Togo, which became a part of the Gold Coast and, later on, Ghana).

After the opening of the German post office in 1888, German stamps were used. In 1897 German stamps with the overprint 'Togo'; later, definitives with the same inscription: a total of 23 stamps, overprinted provisionals and in the German colonial key-types.

British occupation issues: stamps of German Togo issued in 1914 with the overprint, 'TOGO Anglo-French Occupation'. A total of 20 stamps each with a very small printing, few of which were used postally. In 1915 stamps of the Gold Coast appeared with the same overprint; a total of 24 overprinted provisionals.

French occupation issues: 1914 stamps of German Togo with the overprint 'TOGO Occupation Franco-Anglaise'. A total of 19 stamps in very limited printings allowing small opportunity for normal postal use; 1916 stamps of Dahomey with a similar overprint, a total of 17 provisionals.

In 1921, stamps of the French colony of Dahomey were issued with the overprint 'TOGO' followed by pictorial definitives similarly inscribed. The designs were characteristic of the French colonial issues of the period and included the French colonial omnibus issues. Pétain issues had no postal validity on Togo territory. During the war Free French stamps were issued. In 1944–7 stamps of French West Africa were used; from 1947, its own issues again. In 1957 a new inscription, 'RÉPUBLIQUE AUTONOME DU TOGO'; from 1958, 'RÉPUBLIQUE DU TOGO'; from 1962 'RÉPUBLIQUE TOGOLAISE'. Until 1960 stamps are of obvious French origin (with some interesting pictorial stamps). Production was then entrusted to a New York agency which substituted photogravure and offset litho printing for the excellent French line-engraving. French artists were replaced, in the main, by M. Shamir, a prominent Israeli graphic artist. Chiefly pictorial stamps and many issues for international omnibus projects. The many miniature sheets (over 130) and the large output of airmail stamps (400) are designed to attract the collector rather than be available for postal purposes. There are also pictorial postage-due stamps. Current annual output about 70 stamps.
Philatelic bureau Philatelic Service, Office des PTT, Lomé. **Trade sales** L'Agence des Timbres-Poste d'Outre-Mer; Inter-Governmental Philatelic Corporation.

TRANSKEI
Area 43,798 sq.km, **population** 2.5m (1983), **capital** Umtata.

The oldest South African bantustan, set up in 1963 as a reservation for the black inhabitants of Xhosa nationality, declared the Republic of Transkei by the South African government on 26 October 1976, but only recognized as such by South Africa. It is not recognized as a separate state by the UN or any other country. Economically speaking, it is an underdeveloped country with poor agriculture and livestock.

From 1976 definitives of South African origin with the name 'TRANSKEI' featuring publicity for the Transkeian way of life. Current production 10 to 29 stamps per annum.
Philatelic bureau Philatelic Services and Intersapa, GPO, Pretoria, South Africa.

TRANSVAAL

The name of the Boer South African Republic (beyond the River Vaal), which the British occupied in 1877–80. But the Boers revolted and the republic's independence was again recognized. From 1900 the British occupied the country for a second time during the Boer War, which ended in 1902 with the Peace of Vereeniging, as a result of which the country was declared a British colony under the name Transvaal. In 1910 it became a province of the Union of South Africa. The size of its territory has varied; today it is 286,053 sq.km with the capital at Pretoria.

In the initial period (1877–82) stamps of the South African Republic with the overprint 'V. R. TRANSVAAL', then definitives using the same text: a total of 21 stamps.

In the second period (1900–10) stamps of the South African Republic with the over-print 'VRI' (Victoria Regina Imperatrix). Following the death of Queen Victoria and the accession of King Edward VII to the British throne the overprint 'ERI' (Eduardus Rex Imperator) and 'TRANSVAAL' on definitives from 1902. Stamp issuing until 1909, a total of 48 + 2 stamps of British origin. From 1910 superseded by stamps of the Union of South Africa (see *South Africa*), on whose territory Transvaal stamps were valid until 1937.

TRIPOLI

A town in Tripolitania (today's Tarabulus in Libya) and its surroundings. During Turkish rule an Italian post office existed here in 1909–11 which, in 1909, issued 12 + 2 Italian stamps with the overprint 'Tripoli di Barberia' (Berber Tripolis). This was the predecessor of Italian Tripolitania. The name Tripoli continued to appear on Libyan stamps issued until 1938 on the occasion of the fairs held in that city.

TRIPOLITANIA

Until 1912 a part of Turkish vilayet; following the Italo-Turkish war, a part of the Italian colony of Libya from 1912. In 1942–51 occupied by British troops, then a province of the independent Kingdom of Libya (**area** 353,000 sq.km, **capital** Tripoli).

From 1923 Italian stamps with the overprint 'TRIPOLITANIA', followed by definitives with the same inscription : a total of 264+8 stamps, many issued specifically for the collector's market. (The stamps of Libya circulated in the territory for postal purposes.) Printings of many issues were quite small, some higher values being reported as only 750. Pictorial stamps of Italian origin. Stamp issuing continued until 1935 when Libyan stamps were used exclusively.

During the British occupation, first the stamps of Great Britain were used with the overprint 'M.E.F.' (Middle East Forces). From 1948 British stamps with the overprint 'B.M.A. TRIPO-LITANA' (British Military Administration); from 1950 issues of the civilian administration — British stamps with the overprint 'BA TRIPOLITANIA' (British Administration). A total of 34+ 10 stamps, nearly all overprinted provisionals. All occupation issues were replaced by Libyan stamps, from 1951 supplanted by Libyan stamps.

TRISTAN DA CUNHA

Area 98 sq.km, **population** 324 (1983), **main settlement** Edinburgh.

A group of volcanic islands (Tristan da Cunha, Inaccessible, Nightingale and Gough), British since 1816 and a dependency of St Helena from 1938. In 1961–3 the islands were abandoned because of a sudden volcanic eruption and the residents were removed to Great Britain, but in 1963 almost all returned home. Indirect UPU membership from 1 January 1952.

St Helena stamps were valid on the island from 1952 with the overprint 'TRISTAN DA CUNHA', then definitives with the same name. Stamp production of British origin. Pictorial stamps and British Commonwealth omnibus issues. Annual output 20 stamps.

Philatelic bureau The Postmaster, Edinburgh, Tristan da Cunha. **Trade sales** Crown Agents' Stamp Bureau.

TUNISIA

Area 164,150 sq.km, **population** 6.95m (1983), **capital** Tunis.

A relatively advanced agricultural and industrial country. Tunisia was dependent, but only formally so, on Turkey, but was then occupied by France in 1880 and declared a protectorate governed by a regent (bey) under French protection. After the Second World War, in 1946, France declared it an associated state of the French Union, and in 1955 Tunisia gained autonomy, becoming an independent monarchy on 20 March 1956. A republic was declared on 25 July 1957. Indirect UPU membership from 1 June 1878 (France); direct from 1 July 1888 (as the regency of Tunisia); direct from 1 November 1956 (as an independent state).

From 1888 definitives inscribed with the text 'RÉGENCE DE TUNIS'; later, 'TUNISIE'. From 1956 'TUNISIE AUTONOME' and, after the republic was established, the name became 'RÉPUBLIQUE TUNISIENNE'. At first, stamps of French origin and with characteristics of French colonial issues. After Tunisia gained independence, particularly, stamp production exhibited individual characteristics and showed an interesting graphic approach (artists Hatim El Mekki, Gorgi and other Tunisian designers). The stamps are now printed in French and other foreign printing houses. At first they were mainly by the line-engraved process, and later by photogravure and offset lithography. For years the designs were largely nationalistic, but greater attention is now being paid to wider themes. Annual production about 30 stamps.

Philatelic bureau Pr. Le Secretaire d'État aux PTT, Le Chef des Services, Bureau des Postes, Postaux, Tunis. **Trade sales** Agence des Timbres-Poste d'Outre-Mer.

UBANGI-SHARI and UBANGI-SHARI-CHAD see OUBANGI etc.

UGANDA

Area 236,860 sq.km, **population** 12.63m (1980), **capital** Kampala.

A developing agricultural country. On the basis of an agreement of 1890, the British seized the territory, and in 1894 declared Buganda a protectorate, followed in 1896 by Tore and Bunyor, thus creating the protectorate of Uganda. In 1900, Ankole was added, and more territory was acquired in 1920. In 1962 the country gained internal self-government, and the same year, on 9 October, independence as a member of the British Commonwealth of Nations. In 1966 its federal status was abolished and a republic created. Indirect UPU membership from 1 April 1901 (as a British colony); direct from 13 February 1964.

In 1895, primitives (produced on a typewriter by a missionary) and the text reading 'UG' or 'UGANDA'. From 1898, locally printed definitives inscribed 'UGANDA PROTECTORATE'. Stamp issuing continued until 1902: a total of 68 stamps — primitives and overprinted provisionals, and portrait definitives of British origin.

From 1903 to 1962 Uganda belonged to the postal territory of *British East Africa and Uganda* which, from 1920, was listed as Kenya and Uganda; from 1930 (but stamps from 1935) as *Kenya-Uganda-Tanganyika*.

In 1962 definitives with the name UGANDA, all stamps of British origin. Life in Uganda provides the theme of most designs. Stamps did not appear every year because commemorative issues of the common postal administration (Kenya-Uganda-Tanganyika or Tanzania) were then in circulation. In 1976–7 all three members of the common postal administration issued stamps identical except for the name of the country of issue. Then there was a return to independent stamp-issuing, the present output being about 20 stamps a year.

Philatelic bureau The Regional Stamp Bureau, Kampala. **Trade sales** Inter-Governmental Philatelic Corporation.

UNITED ARAB REPUBLIC—EGYPT

An agricultural country (**area** 1,001,449 sq.km, **capital** Cairo) with developing industry. From the inception of the UAR (an alliance of Egypt and Syria) on 1 February 1958, Egypt had the status of a province. When Syria withdrew from the UAR on 28 September 1961, Egypt kept the name United Arab Republic until 1971. From 3 September 1971, the name has been the Arab Republic of Egypt.

In 1958 definitives with the text 'UAR EGYPT', later only UAR. (See *United Arab Republic – Syria*.) A total of 517 + 40 stamps of Egyptian origin using typical Egyptian photogravure of a varying standard of design. Postage stamps were freely used for political and cultural propaganda, as is evident from the choice of subjects and size of the issues. Only in isolated instances was there a printing as low as 250,000, while issues showing the flags of African states in 41 values (in 1969) appeared in printings of 400,000. Various special items were issued for philatelists. From 1971 once again *Egypt*.

UPPER SENEGAL AND NIGER

A colony from 1904 to 1920 in the framework of French West Africa; prior to this a part of Senegambia and Niger (1902–4). Its capital is Bamako. In 1920 renamed the French Sudan, when Niger and Upper Volta were separated from it (Upper Volta in 1919). It covered about 1,750,000 sq.km.

In 1906 definitives with the inscription 'HT SÉNÉGAL-NIGER/AFRIQUE OCCIDENTALE FRANÇAISE'. Stamp issuing until 1915, a total of 35+15 stamps of French origin in French West Africa key-types.

UPPER VOLTA (BURKINA FASO)

Area 274,200 sq.km, **population** 7.29m (1982), **capital** Ouagadougou.

Agricultural country, predominantly livestock breeding. In 1897 the whole territory became a French protectorate and was incorporated into French West Africa. Out of the southern areas of what was then the colony of Upper Senegal and Niger, a new colony, Upper Volta, was formed in 1919. In 1933 Upper Volta colony was dissolved and divided among the Ivory Coast, French Sudan and Niger, only to be recreated in 1947. On 11 December 1958, it was declared an autonomous republic, and on 5 August 1960, an independent state. In 1984 it changed its name to Burkina Faso. Indirect UPU membership from 1 July 1876 (a French colony); direct from 29 March 1963 (Upper Volta).

Stamp-issuing activities as a French colony from 1920; stamps of Upper Senegal and Niger with the overprint 'HAUTE-VOLTA': a total of 69+20 stamps issued until 1931; the stamps are of French origin (chiefly overprinted provisionals).

The first stamps of the republic appeared only in 1959 — on the first anniversary of Upper Volta becoming an autonomous republic. Definitives with the name 'RÉPUBLIQUE DE HAUTE-VOLTA'. A rather large production of stamps of French origin, mainly pictorials. Besides national propaganda, general themes and omnibus issues, which, together with pictorial official stamps (something quite unusual in the French stamp region), are all aimed at the collector market. Definitive stamps from 1984 with the name 'BURKINA FASO'. Annual output ranges between 40 to 80 stamps. Typical at present time is the large production of airmail stamps.

Philatelic bureau Office des Postes et Télécommunications, Service Philatélique, Ouagadougou. **Trade sales** Agence des Timbres-Poste d'Outre-Mer.

URUNDI

African territory (**area** 27,834 sq.km, **capital** Usumbura), part of German East Africa, nominally from 1894, but actually from 1899. In 1916 it was seized by Belgian units operating from the neighbouring Belgian Congo, and in 1919 the Versailles Treaty placed it under Belgian administration as a mandate territory of the League of Nations, together with Ruanda.

In 1916 stamps of the Belgian Congo were issued with the overprint 'URUNDI': a total of 8 values. See also *German East Africa*. For stamps for the mandate territory from 1924, see *Ruanda-Urundi*.

VENDA

Area 6,500 sq.km, **population** 513,890 (1980), **capital** Thohoyandou.

Economically underdeveloped agricultural country of South Africa, on the border of Zimbabwe. A bantustan for the African inhabitants of Venda nationality, set up by the South African government in 1961; granted autonomy in 1973. Independence (recognized only by

South Africa and not by any other state) under the name of Republic of Venda, proclaimed on 13 September 1979.

From the time independence of this bantustan was declared, the validity of South African stamps ended on this territory, to be superseded by stamps of their own, inscribed 'VENDA'. They are of South African origin.

Philatelic bureau Philatelic Services and Intersapa, GPO, Pretoria, South Africa.

WITU (SWAHILILAND)
Coastal sultanate, a German protectorate (1885–90), then ceded to Great Britain and incorporated into British East Africa (**area** 3,120 sq.km, **capital** Witu).

In 1889 there appeared 60 + 36 stamps with a text in Swahili. The postal use of these stamps has never been established.

ZAÏRE
Area 2,345,885 sq.km, **population** 31.94m (1983), **capital** Kinshasa.

A republic, formerly the Congo Democratic Republic, abbreviated to Congo (Kinshasa). The new name was introduced on 27 September 1971. Direct UPU membership from 1 January 1886 (independent State of the Congo); direct from 1908 (Belgian colony); direct from 1 July 1960 (sovereign state).

New name 'RÉPUBLIQUE DU ZAIRE' appeared on definitives only in November 1971; later replaced by the abbreviated form 'ZAIRE' (or 'ZAÏRE'). Stamps are printed mostly by photogravure or the offset-litho process. Restrained stamp issuing, about 3 to 4 issues a year, which at first stressed national themes, but later also events which might interest the collectors' market abroad.

Philatelic bureau Directeur Général des Postes, Service Philatélique, Kinshasa, Zaire.
Trades sales Agence Philatélique Gouvernmentale, Brussels, Belgium.

ZAMBEZIA
A part of Mozambique at one time administered by the Zambezi Company (**area** 224,840 sq.km, **capital** Quelimane). It consisted of the territory of Tete and Quelimane districts. Today's Zambezia, however, corresponds only with the former Quelimane.

Before issuing its own stamps, those of Mozambique were used. Definitives with the name 'ZAMBEZIA' in 1893–1917 (in between, from 1914, issues for Quelimane and Tete, which were parts of Zambezia). A total of 101 stamps of Portuguese origin; many overprinted provisionals — especially when Portugal became a republic — and definitives in the Portuguese colonial key-types. After 1917, Mozambique stamps again.

ZAMBIA
Area 752,614 sq.km, **population** 6.24m (1982),**capital** Lusaka.

Country with an advanced mining and metallurgical industry. An independent republic since 24 October 1964; before that, the country was called Northern Rhodesia, which in 1953–63 was a member-state of the Federation of Rhodesia and Nyasaland. Indirect UPU membership from 1 July 1930 as Northern Rhodesia (British colony); direct from 22 March 1967.

In 1964, definitives with the inscription 'ZAMBIA'. Stamp production of British origin, subjects being drawn mainly from the life of the Zambian people and the country's natural beauties. Interesting designs by G. Ellison which are characteristic of the country; later production made greater use of photographic models. Modest stamp-issuing activity with annual output of, usually, 2 issues.

Philatelic bureau Nodla, Zambia. **Trade sales** Crown Agents' Stamp Bureau; Inter-Governmental Philatelic Corporation.

ZANZIBAR
Leading exporter of cloves, and once flourished as a slave-market. In 1832 the sultan of Oman transferred his capital here, and from 1856 the Zanzibar sultanate was independent

(**area** 2,642 sq.km, **capital** Zanzibar). in 1888–90 it came under de facto German protection, under the 1890 Heligoland-Zanzibar Treaty between Germany and Great Britain, then it became a British protectorate and, until 1925, belonged to Kenya. In 1963 it obtained internal autonomy (24 June) and independence within the British Commonwealth on 10 December 1963. On 12 January 1964 the sultanate was abolished and Zanzibar was declared a republic; on 26 April 1964 it entered into a union with Tanganyika under the name United Republic of Tanganyika and Zanzibar, and in October 1964 the name of the state was changed to United Republic of Tanzania.

There was a German post office on Zanzibar, using only German stamps; this was closed in 1891. A French post office used French stamps until 1894, and in 1894–1904 with the overprint 'ZANZIBAR': a total of 62 + 5 stamps, mostly overprinted and/or surcharged provisionals on basic French stamps. The French post office on Zanzibar was closed in 1904. An Indian post office functioned in 1868–9, and after being re-opened in 1875 it used the stamps of India until 1895.

At first, from 1895, the stamps of India with the overprint 'ZANZIBAR', and British East Africa issues with the same overprint, and then definitives from 1896. A total of 350+30 stamps of British origin, with the portrait of Zanzibar's ruler, as well as pictorial issues with his portrait and some British Commonwealth omnibus issues. After the republic was established in 1964, the first issues were the final sultan issues overprinted 'JAMHURI 1964'. These were followed by stamps of Zanzibar's own designing, with a preponderance of national propaganda themes.

Although Zanzibar was officially joined to Tanganyika in 1964 to form Tanzania, it retained its own postal sovereignty so that stamps bearing the inscription 'ZANZIBAR, JAMHURI ZANZIBAR – TANZANIA' continued to appear; however, they were valid only on Zanzibar: a total of 88 stamps. From 1 January 1968, these issues were halted, to be superseded by the stamps of *Tanzania*, valid for the entire territory, including Zanzibar.

ZIL ELWAGNE SESEL see OUTER SEYCHELLES

ZIMBABWE
Area 390,759 sq.km, **population** 7.53m (1982), **capital** Harare.

A developed agricultural country with advanced mining industry. The one-time British colony of Southern Rhodesia; from 1964, Rhodesia, which unilaterally declared itself an independent state on 11 November 1965, and a republic on 1 March 1970. This independence was formally abolished on 12 December 1979 so that Great Britain could, on 18 April 1980, grant its former colony independence under the name of the Republic of Zimbabwe. From 1980, stamps with the name 'ZIMBABWE'.   •

Philatelic bureau Post & Telecommunications Corporation, Harare.

ZULULAND
After the defeat of the South African Zulus, the British annexed the territory east of Natal in 1887 and created out of it a Crown Colony which, in 1897, was incorporated as a district or province (Province of Zululand) into the colony of Natal (**area** 27,108 sq.km, **capital** Eshowe).

In 1888 Natal and British stamps with the overprint 'ZULULAND', followed British colonial key-and-duty type stamps. Up to 1891 a total of 23 + 7 stamps of British origin. From 1898 superseded by *Natal* stamps.

270

THE AMERICAS

ANGUILLA
Area 96 sq.km, **population** 7,019 (1984), **capital** The Valley.

Caribbean island, British since 1650. In 1967 it left the associated state of St Kitts-Nevis-Anguilla, and on 17 June declared unilaterally its independence, proclaiming itself a republic. However, Great Britain did not recognize this and in 1969 sent troops to Anguilla for several months. On 28 July 1971 Anguilla became a British Crown Colony, and on 10 February 1976 was granted the status of an independent territory in the British Commonwealth.

Soon after the proclamation of independence, the Crown Colony stamps were issued with the overprint 'Independent Anguilla' and although not officially recognized, letters franked with the provisional stamps were accepted by the USA postal authorities for international transmission. Then came definitives with the text 'ANGUILLA' and, from 1971, with the words 'H. M. COMMISSIONER IN ANGUILLA', reflecting direct control by the Crown rather than the authorities of St Christopher-Nevis-Anguilla. Typical pictorial stamps of British origin and including either the royal portrait or the royal cypher E II R in the design. The frequent issues (up to 30 stamps plus miniature sheet each year) are blatantly produced to meet collector-demand, rather than postal needs, and provide a substantial revenue for the island.

Philatelic bureau General Post Office, The Valley.

ANTIGUA AND BARBUDA
Area 442 sq.km, **population** 78,241 (1983), **capital** St John's.

Antigua was a British colony in the Lesser Antilles from 1632 to 1871, then a presidency (one of four) of the colony of Leeward Islands, becoming a separate colony again from 1956. In 1958–62 a member of the West Indies Federation and from 1967 an autonomous associated state of Great Britain. The islands of Barbuda and Redonda are dependencies of Antigua, which gained independence on 1 November 1981. UPU membership since 1 July 1879.

Before Antigua had its own postal authority (established 1860), British stamps were used, and these remained valid until the postal authorities issued their own stamps. From 1862 definitives inscribed 'ANTIGUA' appeared. Antiguan stamps were also valid in Montserrat until 1876, marking the date of entry into the UPU. From 1890 until 1903 Leeward Islands issues only were in circulation, but from 1903 Antigua again also had its own issues. Except for the periods 1922–1924 and 1968–71, stamps from Antigua could also be used on *Barbuda*. In 1967, after an autonomous associated state was established, the first issue, exceptionally, carried the inscription 'STATE OF ANTIGUA'. The first stamps of the independent country appeared in 1981, bearing the name of 'ANTIGUA AND BARBUDA'. Barbuda, though a member state, continues to issue its own stamps.

The overall output of stamps is of British origin. Besides issues in the colonial key-types, Antigua has a number of pictorials characteristic of British Commonwealth stamps. Since 1967 the design themes have catered for collectors and the frequency of issues has accelerated to an annual output of about 50 stamps — together with miniature sheets. Since 1976, the portrait of the Queen or the royal cypher on stamps has been virtually abandoned.

Philatelic bureau General Post Office, St John's. **Trade sales** Inter-Governmental Philatelic Corporation.

ANTIOQUIA
A state of the Union of Colombia from 1868 to 1886; then a department of Colombia (**area** 70,000 sq.km, **capital** Medellín).

From 1868 definitives inscribed 'E. S. DE ANTIOQUIA', many with the supplementary text 'REPUBLICA (or 'U. U.') DE COLOMBIA'. By 1904, when stamp issuing ended, there had been a total of 158 stamps, most of them with heraldic devices or portraits. They were influenced by stamp production of North America, but were of Colombian origin, printed chiefly in Bogotá and Medellín. The stamps were valid until 26 July 1906.

AREQUIPA

A Peruvian town in the district of the same name. After Chile occupied Lima in 1881, the Peruvian government moved to Arequipa, which was the centre of resistance to the Chilean invasion. The Departments of Arequipa, Puno, Cuzco, Moquegua, Apurímac and Ayacucho formed the state of Southern Peru, with Arequipa as the capital. Chilean troops captured Arequipa in 1883, but following the peace treaty in October of that year, they withdrew from Arequipa and the other Peruvian towns. Civil war followed, and in 1884–5 stamps were issued in Arequipa by the forces opposed to the Peruvian government in Lima.

From 1881 emergency issues (fiscals of government departments) normally cancelled 'AREQUIPA' on use. A total of 29 provisionals was issued until 1885.

ARGENTINA

Area 2,776,889 sq.km, **population** 29.63m (1983), **capital** Buenos Aires.

Economically the most advanced country in South America, with immense production of cereals and important livestock breeding. An independent state from 1810 to 1816; from 1826 a confederation called Argentina, and a federated republic since 1853. Direct UPU membership since 1 April 1878.

There were foreign post offices on the territory of Argentina which normally used stamps of their own countries; the British postal authority in Buenos Aires (1860–73), the Italian postal authority in Buenos Aires (1856–73), which used stamps overprinted 'ESTERO' and French stamps with the Buenos Aires postmark. During the period of their temporary independence, the Argentine provinces used their own stamps (Buenos Aires — 1858–64; Córdoba — 1858–60; Corrientes — 1856–60).

In 1858 definitives with the text 'CONFEON ARGENTINA'; from 1862 'REPUBLICA ARGENTINA'; from the 1950s only 'ARGENTINA'; later, once again, 'REPUBLICA ARGENTINA' or only 'R. ARGENTINA'. Portraits of historic political leaders dominated the designs. Printing was carried out at first mainly in North America — and shows the influence in the designs — and later by the mint in Buenos Aires, when Argentinian influence became apparent. At the present time Argentina issues graphically interesting stamps designed by such artists as Héctor A. Viola, E. Miliavaca and Horaci El Alvares Boreo. The philatelic market is catered for in the low printings of miniature sheets and charity premium issues (70,000–200,000 stamps). Annual production is about 40 stamps. Typical of Argentine production is the large number of officials (more than 400).

Philatelic bureau Empresa Nacional de Correos y Telegrafos, Filatelia, Correo Central, Buenos Aires.

BAHAMAS

Area 13,939 sq.km, **population** 220,000 (1983), **capital** Nassau.

A chain of islands in the West Atlantic just off the US Florida coast. A British colony from 1719; obtained internal autonomy in 1964; from 10 July 1973 an independent country, but a monarchy in the British Commonwealth. Indirect UPU membership from 1 July 1880; direct membership since 24 April 1974.

Before issuing its own stamps, the Bahamas used those of Great Britain. Definitives since 1859 with the inscription 'BAHAMAS' (a printing of only 2,000 for the second issue). Until the Bahamas entered the UPU, the stamps were intended only for internal use and were inscribed 'Interinsular Postage'. Stamps of British origin (but sometimes also influenced by American production), at first only portraits; more recent issues are pictorial. British Commonwealth type portrait stamps and omnibus issues and also themes attractive to foreign customers. Annual output, at the present time, is about 20 stamps in addition to miniature sheets, issued largely to satisfy collector demand. Since 1975 the custom of adding the portrait of the Queen or the royal cypher to the stamps has lapsed.

Philatelic bureau General Post Office, Philatelic Bureau, Nassau. **Trade sales** Inter-Governmental Philatelic Corporation.

BARBADOS

Area 431 sq.km, **population** 250,500 (1981), **capital** Bridgetown.

Island autonomy from 1961. (From 1958 to 1962 Barbados was part of the West Indies Federation.) In 1966 Barbados became an independent country, a monarchy within the British Commonwealth. Indirect UPU membership from 1 September 1881; direct from 11 November 1967.

In 1852 definitive stamps appeared with the text 'BARBADOS' but no indication of face value (actually ½d, 1d, 2d and 4d) which was determined by the colour. The first issues were intended only for domestic needs. Production was in Britain. The figure of Britannia predominated until the Queen's portrait and pictorials or heraldic stamps and Commonwealth omnibus issues took over. Present-day annual output about 20 stamps, besides miniature sheets. Since 1971 the portrait of the Queen or royal cypher has been disappearing from the stamps.

Philatelic bureau General Post Office, Bridgetown. **Trade sales** Crown Agents' Stamp Bureau.

BARBUDA

Area 161 sq.km, **population** 1,300 (1982), **capital** Codrington.

Northernmost of the Leeward Islands, since 1860 a part (dependency) of Antigua.

One issue in 1922 of 11 stamps of the Leeward Islands with the overprint 'BARBUDA'. From 1924, Barbuda used Antigua stamps or those of the Leeward Islands (until 1956).

New issuing activities began in 1968, definitives with the inscription 'BARBUDA'. Pictorial stamps with general and social themes calculated to appeal to the collectors. There is little postal justification for issues separate from Antigua although the stamps are accepted internationally. One long series was a set of all the British monarchs from the 11th to 19th centuries (37 values). In 1971–3 the stamps of Antigua were used once again, and from 1973 were frequently overprinted 'BARBUDA' for use in the island which also continued to issue separate pictorials. Definitives with attractive, pictorial subjects (which since 1974 no longer feature the royal portrait or royal cypher). Annual output up to 80 stamps, besides miniature sheets. (See also *Antigua and Barbuda.*)

Philatelic bureau Post Office, Codrington.

BELIZE

Area 22,965 sq.km, **population** 157,700 (1983), **capital** Belmopan.

An independent country in the Commonwealth since 21 September 1981. The present name was introduced on 5 June 1973, replacing the former name, *British Honduras*. Indirect UPU membership since 1 January 1879.

In 1973, British Honduran issues were overprinted with the new name 'BELIZE', later followed by definitives with the same name. Pictorial stamps of British origin in designs catering for the collector. The portrait of the Queen or the royal cypher remain a part of the overall design. Annual output 10 to 20 stamps.

Philatelic bureau Philatelic Service, Belize Post Office.

BEQUIA see GRENADINES OF SAINT VINCENT

BERMUDA

Area 53 sq.km, **population** 54,670 (1980), **capital** Hamilton.

Strategically important island in the western Atlantic with naval and air bases. British colony from 1612; a self-governing Crown Colony from 1684. Indirect UPU membership from 1 April 1877.

In 1848 the local postmaster issued unauthorized hand-struck stamps, for local use, with the inscription 'HAMILTON-BERMUDA'. This issue includes some of the rarest and most valuable stamps in the world. This is true of similar issues until 1861.

Regular definitive portrait stamps first issued in 1865 inscribed 'BERMUDA'. They are of British origin. Later issues are mostly portraits and pictorials with local themes, together with several British Commonwealth omnibus issues. Annual output, at present, is about 15 stamps, all of which include in the design either the portrait of the Queen or the royal cypher.

Philatelic bureau G.P.O., Hamilton. **Trade sales** Crown Agents' Stamp Bureau.

BOGOTÁ

Capital of Colombia and also of the Colombian department of Cundinamarca. The local post office issued stamps in 1889 and 1903, for local use only, inscribed with the name 'BOGO-TÁ', in three values.

BOLIVAR

A state of the Union of Colombia from 1863–86; until 1904 a department of Colombia (**area** 63,000 sq.km, **capital** Cartagena).

In 1863 definitives with the text 'ESTADO (or CORREOS) DE BOLIVAR', mostly of North American origin or influence: a total of 73 stamps. From 1906, stamps of Colombia have been used in Bolivar. Bolivar's first issue, 1×1.3 cm, is among the world's smallest stamps.

BOLIVIA

Area 1,098,581 sq.km, **population** 6.08m (1983), **capital** Sucre, **seat of government** La Paz.

An agricultural and mining state, independent since 1825. In 1884, Chile seized the region of Antofagasta and in 1898 Argentina occupied adjacent territory. In 1903 Brazil seized Accre, and in 1932 and 1938 Paraguay occupied a large part of the Bolivian Chaco. UPU membership since 1 April 1886.

In 1866 definitives with the name 'BOLIVIA'. Production was both local and international. North American production, and others, substantially influenced the design of Bolivian stamps depending on where the stamps were printed. Chiefly, national publicity themes. As in other South American countries, airmail stamps are very well represented (over 300). A curiosity is the Solar Gateway Tiahuanacu issue with archaeological discoveries, which was printed and prepared for circulation in 1925 but, because of domestic political reasons, did not appear until 1961 when it was overprinted with new postage rates. Present-day production is, on the whole, sober, and annual output is 10 to 15 stamps.

Philatelic bureau Dirección Nacional de Bolivia, Sección Filatélica, La Paz.

BOYACÁ

A state of the Union of Colombia until 1886, then a department of Colombia (**area** 90,000 sq.km, **capital** Tunja) until 1904.

In 1899, definitives with the inscription 'DEPARTEMENTO DE BOYACA (REPUBLICA DE COLOMBIA): a total of 12 stamps of American origin. After the Boyacá department post office was abolished, Colombian stamps were used.

BRAZIL

Area 8,511,965 sq.km, **population** 129.66m (1983), **capital** Brasilia.

Country with plantation agriculture and mineral mining; an empire from 1822; from 1889 a republic. In 1903 Brazil annexed the Bolivian district Accre; in 1904 the eastern territory of Ecuador; and in 1907 part of Colombia. Direct UPU membership since 1 July 1877.

The third oldest stamp-issuing authority in the world after Great Britain and the Swiss canton of Zurich. Brazil has been issuing stamps since 1843, first without the name of the country, later with the name 'BRAZIL'; from 1918 to 1920 an orthographical change was made to 'BRASIL'. The first Brazilian issue, known as the 'Bull's Eye' (because of its oval design) includes some rare classical stamps. Brazilian production was influenced for a long time by North American stamp designers, but it gradually acquired its own characteristics which, especially in recent years, has produced many remarkable designs (among its designers, for instance, are A. Zaluar, W. Granado, Di Cavalcanti, and others). Printed at first in North America by line-engraving, though the Mint in Rio de Janeiro used other printing techniques later. The stamps have almost exclusively national publicity purposes, and their propaganda intent is responsible for the large printings (5 to 10 million of each). Even current production includes many issues of one stamp rather than a set; the annual output is as much as 50 to 80 stamps.

Catalogues also list the airmail stamps of private companies, like the syndicates Condor, Varig and Eta, from the beginning of air transport in the 1920s. Although not government-issued their use was obligatory on mail carried under contract by the companies.

Philatelic bureau Divisão Central Filatélica, Brasília.

BRITISH COLUMBIA AND VANCOUVER ISLAND

British Columbia (formerly New Caledonia), settled since 1846, became a Crown Colony in 1858 and in 1866 was joined with Vancouver Island which had been a colony since 1848. In 1871 the combined territories acquired the status of a Canadian province (**area** 948,600 sq.km, **capital** Victoria), which was joined to the Dominion of Canada, established in 1867.

To facilitate contact with the USA, the post offices in British Columbia also sold US stamps. Independent issuing began in 1860 — one definitive inscribed 'BRITISH COLUMBIA & VAN-COUVERS ISLAND' (despite its inscription it was mainly used in British Columbia). In 1865, 1 stamp with the text 'BRITISH COLUMBIA'. In 1868 these stamps of British Columbia had currency surcharges in cents and dollars, and were also valid on the territory of *Vancouver Island*, with which British Columbia was joined (6 stamps). Canadian stamps have been used since 1871.

BRITISH GUIANA

In 1831 the British possessions of Essequibo, Demarara and Berbice, which the British had seized in 1796, joined to form the colony of British Guiana (**area** 214,970 sq.km, **capital** Georgetown). Although the colony was due to be granted independence in 1962, in fact it came about four years later, in 1966, and the new country was called *Guyana*.

The first primitives from 1850, with the name 'BRITISH GUIANA', are among the world's most coveted stamps. Of these, the magenta one-cent stamp of 1856, known only in one single used copy, is the number-one world rarity and listed as the most precious stamp in the world. At the Siegel auction in New York in 1980 it sold for 850,000 US dollars. The first issues of stamps were valid only for domestic purposes; overseas mail had to have franked British stamps. Despite the long existence of this stamp-issuing country only 229+14 stamps of British origin appeared (with the exception of the first primitives of domestic production); pictorial stamps and British Commonwealth omnibus issues. The single motif of a ship persisted among the first issues for half a century.

BRITISH HONDURAS

British since 1786 (settled by the English from 1638); in 1862 declared a colony, subordinate to Jamaica; from 1884 a colony under direct administration; from 1954 a Crown Colony with internal self-government. The name Belize was introduced on 5 June 1973, and the country has been independent, under that name, since 21 September 1981. Indirect UPU membership since 1 January 1879.

In 1866 definitives with the inscription 'BRITISH HONDURAS': a total of 346+5 stamps of British origin. Very few commemorative stamps produced; for the most part only standard definitive stamps. Following colonial key-and-duty portrait issues came pictorial stamps and the occasional British Commonwealth omnibus issue. From 1973 see *Belize*.

BRITISH VIRGIN ISLANDS

Area 153 sq.km, **population** 12,034 (1980), **capital** Road Town.

A British island colony in the most eastern part of the Greater Antilles; discovered by Columbus in 1493 and given the name, 'St Ursula and her companions'; British from 1666; from 1876 to 1956 the presidential colony of the Leeward Islands, then a separate colony. Since it is closely linked economically with the neighbouring American Virgin Islands (which use normal USA stamps), it did not join the West Indies Federation in 1958 and, since 1962, United States currency has been used here. Indirect UPU membership from 1 July 1879.

Before issuing its own stamps, it used those of Great Britain; from 1866 to 1891, definitives inscribed 'VIRGIN ISLANDS'; in 1891 superseded by the stamps of the Leeward Islands. In 1891–9 Leeward Islands stamps alone were valid in the British Virgin Islands, but in 1899, once again, there were stamps of the British Virgin Islands (although the general issues of the Leeward Islands could be used here as well). From 1968, issued stamps even bear the name 'BRITISH (or BR.) VIRGIN ISLANDS'. The oldest issues depicted St Ursula, followed by colonial key-and-duty pictorial stamps, as well as the British Commonwealth omnibus issues. Stamps did not appear every year: at present, 15 to 20 stamps a year.

Philatelic bureau Post Office Department, Philatelic Bureau, Road Town. **Trade sales** Crown Agents' Stamp Bureau; Inter-Governmental Philatelic Corporation.

BUENOS AIRES

A province of Argentina; an independent republic from 1852 to 1859 (**area** 307,596 sq.km, **capital** Buenos Aires), then once again part of Argentina.

Overseas mail was transported by designated mail ships of Great Britain, France and Italy, and franked at the appropriate consulate with stamps of the given country.

Stamp issuing started in 1858 with the inscription 'BUENOS AIRES' (this was an independent state), and continued until 1862. A total of 13 definitives was produced by rotary letterpress in the mint in Buenos Aires. All are considered to be rare classical stamps. The stamps of Buenos Aires ceased to be valid in 1864.

CABO

Also known as Cabo Gracias or Cabo Gracias á Dios (14,300 sq.km), a cape, port and territory of Nicaragua.

Between 1904 and 1911 Nicaraguan stamps were used here with the overprint 'Cabo', 'CABO', 'COSTA ATLANTICA C' or simply 'C'. The overprints were necessary because here (as in Bluefields in *Zelaya*) silver coins were used as means of payment whereas elsewhere in Nicaragua paper money of half the value was in circulation. A total of 83+10 stamps appeared, almost all overprinted provisionals on Nicaraguan stamps. Since 1912 Nicaraguan stamps have been used.

CANADA

Area 9,976,139 sq.km, **population** 24.9m (1983), **capital** Ottawa.

Highly developed industrial and agricultural country. In 1791 the British created the colonies of Upper and Lower Canada; in 1836 there was an anti-British rebellion, but in 1840 the two Canadas were united as the Colony of Canada which, in the 1850s, obtained the right to its own government. In 1867 it became a self-governing federated dominion, and the Colony of Canada was transformed into Quebec Province (once Lower Canada) and Ontario Province (once Upper Canada) with the addition of the provinces of Nova Scotia and New Brunswick. In later years, Canada expanded by adding new territories, such as the stamp-issuing country of British Columbia (1871) and Prince Edward Island (1873). Newfoundland joined the confederation in 1949. Direct UPU membership from 1 July 1878.

From 1851 (while it was still Canada Province) definitive postage stamps with the inscription 'CANADA'. Stamp production first of American (US), then of Canadian, origin. A conservative policy of royal portrait definitives until 1925 (with a few exceptions for important commemorations). This persisted until the Second World War and it was not till the 1950s that Canada's own conception in stamps emerged (among the experienced stamp designers are H. Fitzgerald and P. Weiss). Canadian production is almost entirely on national themes. Large issues, around 30 million, only emphasize the postal and publicity value of stamps. Annual output is about 30 stamps.

The first Canadian issues are among the rare classical stamps. In 1908, Quebec stamps had both English and an extensive French text and from 1927 many Canadian stamps had both. When Newfoundland was absorbed by Canada in 1949, Newfoundland stamps became valid throughout the territory of Canada; this decision has not yet been rescinded, although the last Newfoundland stamp was issued in 1947.

Philatelic bureau Philatelic Service, Canada Post, Ottawa.

CARÚPANO

A Venezuelan port on the Caribbean coast which, in 1902–3, issued primitives with the text 'Correos de Venezuela' and 'CARÚPANO': a total of 13 stamps. They were emergency issues during the second Venezuelan conflict when Great Britain, Germany and Italy began a blockade, isolating the town.

CAUCA

A state of the Union of Colombia from 1882 to 1886 (**area** 135,000 sq.km, with a territory of 520,000 sq.km, **capital** Popayán). Until 1901, when a revolutionary government took power for a year, a department of Colombia.

Various primitives and emergency issues in 1879–1902, some with the name 'POPAYAN' or 'CAUCA': a total of 7 stamps. Postal purpose and function unclear.

CAYMAN ISLANDS

Area 260 sq.km, **population** 16,677 (1979), **capital** Georgetown.

British territory in the Caribbean from 1739. The islands became a British colony in 1962. Indirect UPU membership from 1 April 1877.

Until 1901 Jamaican stamps were in use, thereafter definitives with the words 'CAYMAN ISLANDS'. A total of 253 stamps of British origin, consisting of portrait series and pictorial stamps as well as stamps with themes and designs common to British colonial territories. Annual output is about 3 stamps.

Philatelic bureau Crown Agents' Stamp Bureau.

CHILE

Area 756,945 sq.km, **population** 11.7m (1983), **capital** Santiago.

A rather underdeveloped country with important mineral mining. Independent republic since 1818; increased its territory in wars with Bolivia (Antofagasta) and Peru (Arica and until 1919 Tacna) and by diplomatic negotiations (this war was reflected in the stamps of all the belligerents). Direct UPU membership since 1 April 1881.

From 1853 definitives with the name 'CHILE'. Early issues are among the rare classical stamps. The first issue was printed in Great Britain, then in Santiago from plates made in Great Britain. From 1877 production was influenced by North-American trends, with printing in the USA. From the thirties a new form of stamp production came into being, which tends to be uneven. Predominantly produced as publicity issues, the older issues were printed mainly by die stamping. However, offset began to dominate in the sixties. An unusual issue is a long series of stamps which appeared in 1948 on the natural history of Chile and which comprised 75 values. Unlike other Latin American countries, Chile has not issued any airmail stamps since 1973. Current output is between 10 and 30 stamps.

Philatelic bureau Departamento Filatélico, Santiago.

COLOMBIA

Area 1,138,914 sq.km, **population** 27.5m (1981), **capital** Bogotá.

Agricultural country with extensive cultivation and export of coffee. After the dissolution of Greater Colombia (New Granada, Ecuador, Venezuela), the Republic of New Granada emerged in 1831; in 1858, the Confederation of Granada; in 1861 the United States of New Granada and the United States of Colombia; then, from 1886, the Republic of Colombia. The Constitution of 1858 proclaimed a federation of eight states; in 1863, of nine states (from 1886 departments), which issued their own stamps whose validity ended for many only in 1906. These were *Antioquia, Bolivar, Boyacá, Cauca, Cundinamarca*, Magdalena, *Santan-*

277

der, Tolima and *Panama* (from 1903 an independent state). Furthermore, some catalogues list several towns which issued stamps (Baranquilla, Barbacoas, *Bogotá, Cúcuta,* Calí, Cartagena, Garzón, Honda, Manizales, Medellín, Popayán (see *Cauca*), Río Hacha, Tumaco) and the provinces of Cúcuta (see *Cúcuta*) and Choco. (Note: those areas whose names do not appear on stamps are not listed, nor are those whose issues at the time of appearance were not officially authorized or did not have universal postal validity.) In 1916, Colombia annexed the north-eastern territory of Ecuador, and in 1925 it shifted its frontiers southward at Ecuador's expense up to the River Putumayo. Direct UPU membership from 1 July 1881.

From 1862, definitives with the name 'E.U. DE COLOMBIA'(the United States of Colombia) and 'ESTADOS UNIDOS DE COLOMBIA'; from 1886, 'REPUBLICA DE COLOMBIA'; later, only 'COLOMBIA'. Stamp production until the 1950s was based on traditional North American style of design and printing. Then the overall conception changed and was modernized in favour of a more Latinized approach, as for other South American stamps. Besides propaganda issues, which predominate, several general themes and participation in international omnibus issues have appeared with an appeal designed to influence the collector. Colombia has a large number of airmail stamps produced at various printing houses. Annual production fluctuates between 10 and 15 stamps.

Philatelic bureau Oficina de Filatelia, Dirección de Correos, Bogotá.

CONFEDERATE STATES OF AMERICA

Eleven southern states of the USA — Alabama, Arkansas, North and South Carolina, Florida, Georgia, Louisiana, Mississippi, Texas, Tennessee and Virginia — seceded from the United States, and on 4 February 1861 set up the Confederate States of America with Richmond, Virginia, as its capital. In the American Civil War against the northern states, the Confederacy was defeated (the war began on 14 April 1861) and in 1865 its territory was again incorporated into the USA.

When the Civil War broke out, the Union (northern states) invalidated its existing stamps and issued new ones to prevent any manipulation in the issuing of stamps by the southern Confederation. As a result, individual postmasters in many large cities of the Confederacy issued provisionals. Many of these are rare philatelic items, some of them known only in a single specimen; their postal use, though limited, has in most cases been proved.

Postmasters' issues in individual towns (the names of which are always indicated on these issues) were, from 1861: Abingdon (Va.), Athens (Ga.), Baton Rouge (La.), Beaumont (Tex.), Bridgeville (Ala.), Chapel Hill (N.C.), Charleston (S.C.), Danville (Va.), Emory (Va.), Fredericksburg (Va.), Galatin (Tenn.), Galveston (Tex.), Goliad (Tex.), Gonzales (Tex.), Greenville (Ala.), Greenwood (Va.), Grove Hill (Ala.), Hallettsville (Tex.), Helena (Tex.), Hilsboro (N.C.), Independence (Tex.), Jetersville (Va.), Kingston (Ga.), Knoxville (Tenn.), Lenoir (N.C.), Liberty (Va.), Livingston (Ala.), Lynchburg (Va.), Macon (Ga.), Madison, Marion (Va.), Memphis (Tenn.), Mobile (Ala.), Mt. Lebanon (La.), Nashville (Tenn.), Newnan (Ga.), New Orleans (La.), New Smyrna (Fla.), Petersburg (Va.), Pittsylvania Court House (Va.), Pleasant Shade (La.), Port Lavaca (Tex.), Rheatown (Tenn.), Rutherfordton (N.C.), Salem (Va.), Spartanburg (S.C.), Talladega (Ala.), Tellico Plains (Tenn.), Uniontown (Ala.), Unionsville (S.C.), Victoria (Tex.).

Each of these postmasters issued one or several stamps, mostly primitives or just rubber-stamped direct on to the envelope. In that same year, 1861, regular issues of the Confederate States appeared.

In 1861, definitives with the presidents' portraits, and the name 'CONFEDERATE STATES OF AMERICA'. Issues continued until 1864.

CÓRDOBA

A province of Argentina, an independent republic from 1856 to 1860 (**area** 168,854 sq.km, **capital** Córdoba), then again part of Argentina.

It had its own stamps in 1858–60: 1 definitive issue of 2 stamps with the name 'CÓRDO-BA', valid only for internal mailing. Since 1860 Argentine stamps have been used.

CORRIENTES

A province of Argentina, an independent republic from 1856 to 1860 (**area** 89,355 sq.km, **capital** Corrientes), then again part of Argentina.

In 1856 definitives (based on the Ceres head design of French issues of 1849), produced in the state printing house in Corrientes with the inscription 'CORRIENTES'. A total of 6 values in 2 issues. In 1860 superseded by Argentine stamps.

COSTA ATLANTICA

The Atlantic coast of Nicaragua which from 1904 to 1911 had silver currency when the rest of Nicaraguan territory used paper currency. That is why overprinted provisionals were issued here with the designation 'Dpto Zelaya' (see *Zelaya*) and 'Dpto Cabo' (see *Cabo*). In 1907 and 1908 2 Nicaraguan issues appeared with the overprint 'COSTA ATLÁNTICA B' (i.e. for the Bluefields district of Zelaya departamento) and 'C' (Cabo Gracias a Dios): a total of 12 stamps each.

COSTA RICA

Area 50,700 sq.km, **population** 2.4m (1983), **capital** San José.

Central American agricultural country, independent since the dissolution of the United States of Central America in 1838. One of its provinces is *Guanacaste*, which had its own administration and stamps, and Coconut Island, in the Pacific, belongs to Costa Rica. Direct UPU membership since 1 January 1883.

In 1863 definitives with the name 'COSTA RICA'. Costa Rican stamps are printed by many different foreign printers and by several methods from line-engraving to lithography, thus militating against a regular standard of production. For decades, the stamp designs were influenced by those of North America, and even now, design is rather conservative. National politics and events predominate as themes. There are a very large number of overprinted provisionals and airmail issues, considerably outnumbering the other classes of stamps. Until the 1950s there was relatively little output, although the numbers fluctuated. After Costa Rica's attitude to pictorial stamps changed, it adopted modern ideas and now has an output of 15 to 50 stamps a year. Some of these stamps are issued in small quantities to attract the speculator (for instance, very small printings of 1,500 to 5,000).

Philatelic bureau Dirección General de Correos, Oficina Filatélica, San José.

CUBA

Area 110,922 sq.km, **population** 9.84m (1982), **capital** Havana.

Socialist republic. Large island in the Caribbean with sugar cane economy. Originally it belonged to Spain (until 1898); during the Spanish-American War, occupied by the Americans. According to the 1901 Constitution, an independent republic (the USA, however, retained the naval base of Guantanamo). In 1952, power seized by Batista; in 1953 an abortive revolt led by the revolutionary, Fidel Castro. From 1956, Castro and Che Guevara waged a guerilla war, Batista was overthrown in 1958 and Castro was soon in control of the nation. Indirect UPU membership from 15 June 1877 (Spanish colony); from 1899 as a US possession; direct since 4 October 1902.

Prior to 1873 Spanish stamps issued by the Spanish postal overseas authorities were used in Cuba, just as in Puerto Rico, at first without the name of the country. Only from 1877 (at the time of entry into UPU) did the name 'CUBA', and also 'ISLA DE CUBA', appear: a total of 131 stamps of Spanish origin, reflected in the stamp designs based on the Spanish colonial key-types. Some issues included the date of issue as part of the design, the Spanish custom at the time, in the fight against forgeries which reduced postal revenue.

From 1898, after the American occupation, American stamps were used with the overprint 'CUBA' and a surcharge in Spanish currency: a total of 23 + 4, all overprinted provisionals. Then again definitives with the inscription 'CUBA'. Most subsequent issues are inscribed 'REPUBLICA DE CUBA', more recent ones, again, just 'CUBA'. The production of stamps has been very varied. Until 1959 they were mainly recess-printed and conservative in style, mostly using propaganda themes, but also selecting rather unusual subjects, anniversaries and personalities to commemorate, such as the invention of stenography by J. R. Gregg. In 1959 production changed radically, switching from line-engraved printing to photogravure or lithography in Cuban printing houses. Output today is very diverse: there are some excellent graphic designs (for instance by G. Menendez, Quintana, Ruiz, Luccy), and besides propaganda themes, the number of issues with general subjects (butterflies, birds and animals) and others has increased to attract the collector. The basic stamps are printed in large numbers, but the numerous miniature sheets are in small printings of 3,000 to 15,000. Current annual output is 40 to 90 stamps.

Trade sales Coprefil, Habana.

CÚCUTA

A province of the Colombian state of Santander (today Santander Norte: **area** 20,490 sq.km, **capital** Cúcuta), where there was a rising in 1900 and a rebel government established in 1900.

In 1900 revolutionary issues of 12 stamps consisting of an overprint on Santander stamps, reading 'Gobierno Provisional' (without the name Cúcuta). In 1904 definitives with the name 'REPUBLICA DE COLOMBIA, Dep. DE SANTANDER, PROVINCIA CUCUTA', but these appear to have been an unauthorized issue. A total of 14 stamps. From 1906 the post office of the department was taken over by the postal authorities of the United States of Colombia.

CUNDINAMARCA

A state of the Union of Colombia from 1870 to 1886, then a department of Colombia until 1904 (**area** 25,000 sq.km, with a territory of 200,000 sq.km, **capital** Bogotá). The name means the land of the condors.

From 1870 a series of definitives of heraldic design showing the condor and the name 'ESTADO SOBERANO DE CUNDINAMARCA'; later, 'DEPARTAMENTO DE CUNDINA-MARCA': a total of 27 stamps. Since 1906 the stamps of Colombia have been used.

CURAÇAO

A Dutch colony consisting of the islands of Curaçao, Aruba, Bonaire, Saba, St Eustatius and, in part, St Maarten (**area** 988 sq.km, **capital** Willemstad); definitively Dutch from 1814. In 1948 it became an autonomous part of the Union of the Netherlands with the name Netherlands Antilles, which in 1954 acquired the status of an overseas member country of the Netherlands monarchy.

In 1873, definitives inscribed 'CURAÇAO': a total of 236 stamps mainly of Dutch origin. Stamp designs consist primarily of portraits and numerals, some issues in designs common to the Netherlands and colonies. During the Second World War the stamps were printed in the Dutch Indies and in British and American printing houses which also influenced the designs on the stamps. Some issues, especially those of high denomination, are in small printings (under 10,000). Although Curaçao became autonomous in 1948 and was renamed the Netherlands Antilles, stamps already printed with the name Curaçao continued to appear in 1949 and had postal validity until 1950, with a postage-due charge until 1953. Postage-due stamps with the text 'TE BETALEN/PORTO' were of uniform appearance with those of the Netherlands, differing only in colour – green.

DANISH WEST INDIES

The islands of St Thomas, St Croix and St John in the Antilles, Danish from 1671 to 1917, though briefly British around 1815 (**area** 345 sq.km, **capital** Charlotte Amalie, also known as St Thomas). When they became strategically important after the Panama Canal was opened, the United States bought them in 1917 for 25 million US dollars, and since then they have been known as the Virgin Islands of the United States. They are no longer a stamp-issuing country as they now use US stamps.

From 1855 definitives of Danish origin (without indication of country other than the currency which was in 'cents' instead of 'rigsbank skilling' — r.b.s. — and distinguished the stamps from the contemporary Danish issue). From 1873, with the inscription 'DANSK VESTINDIS-

KEØER'; later, 'DANSK VESTINDIEN'. A total of 56 + 8 stamps mainly heraldic and royal portrait, of Danish origin. Very small production with small printings of only about 20,000.

DOMINICA
Area 751 sq.km, **population** 74,069 (1981), **capital** Roseau.

Island in the Lesser Antilles, a British colony from 1783; from 1871 to 1940 part of the Leeward Islands; then under the administration of the Windward Islands until 1956, when it again became a separate colony. From 1958 to 1962 a member of the West Indies Federation; from 1967 an autonomous associated state of Great Britain; on 3 November 1978 it obtained its independence under the name of the Commonwealth of Dominica. Indirect UPU membership from 1 July 1879.

From 1874 definitives with the inscription 'DOMINICA'. From 1890 to 1903 Dominica used the stamps of the Leeward Islands then once again its own issues; until 1940 these were concurrently valid with the stamps of the Leeward islands. All issues of British origin. Issues up to 1966 include some British colonial key-types and British Commonwealth omnibus issues, typical portrait and pictorial stamps. At first little activity in terms of stamp issues — about 1 a year — but in recent years, under the pressure of keen marketing, this has grown to between 40 and 60 stamps. The stamps issued after the declaration of independence in 1978 bear the official name 'COMMONWEALTH OF DOMINICA'.

Philatelic bureau Postmaster General, GPO Roseau. **Trade sales** Inter-Governmental Philatelic Corporation.

DOMINICAN REPUBLIC
Area 48,442 sq.km, **population** 5.98m (1983), **capital** Santo Domingo.

Country in the eastern part of Hispaniola, with plantation agriculture. Independent since 1844, but from 1861 to 1865, although its sovereignty was recognized in Madrid, it came under the temporary rule of Spain. From 1916 to 1924 the country was occupied by the Americans. Direct UPU membership from 1 October 1880.

In Dominican ports there were British post offices using British stamps, and during the years of Spanish rule (1861–5) stamps of the Spanish overseas postal authorities were in use. Stamps began to be issued in 1865, when definitives appeared without indication of the country of origin. From 1880 (after entry into the UPU) stamps with the inscription 'REPUBLICA DOMINICANA' appeared. Stamp production of a varying standard and of diverse origins (some printed in the country, but others in Germany and the USA) which gave the issues a mixed appearance. The preponderance of stamps on national propaganda subjects has alternated since 1956 with stamps on common international subjects and general themes. Later, exploitation of the philatelic market was demonstrated by issuing identical stamps perforated and imperforate, multicolour overprints, small printings — sometimes as few as 1,500 — and so on. Current annual production fluctuates considerably; at times more than 50 stamps are produced (many of them airmail).

Philatelic bureau Dirección General de Correos, Sección Filatelia, Santo Domingo.

ECUADOR
Area 270,670 sq.km, **population** 9.25m (1983), **capital** Quito.

Underdeveloped agricultural country in the equatorial part of South America, independent since the break-up of the United States of Colombia (Greater Colombia) in 1830. Annexations by Brazil in 1904, Colombia in 1916 and Peru in 1942 considerably reduced the territory of the country. Direct UPU membership since 1 August 1880.

Definitives since 1865, which carried the name 'ECUADOR'. The stamps were produced in America, Great Britain and Germany, and were influenced especially by North American stamp production. After 1892 came the famous Seebeck issue: Seebeck, director of the Hamilton Bank Note Company in New York, where Ecuador's stamps were then being printed, concluded an agreement with Ecuador, Honduras, Nicaragua and El Salvador to supply stamps free of charge to be in circulation only one year and then all unsold remainders to be returned to Seebeck, the agent, for philatelic sale. Characteristic of present-day production are the large number of airmail stamps (the annual production sometimes consists almost exclusively of airmail stamps) and officials (and even miniature sheets of officials). Annual production is between 30 and 70 stamps, largely aimed at the collector's market. There is a predominance of propaganda themes with common international subjects, a number of overprinted provisionals. There is no reliable information regarding many issues.

Philatelic bureau Departamento Filatélico del Estado, Dirección General de Correos, Quito.

EL SALVADOR
Area 21,393 sq.km, **population** 5m (1982), **capital** San Salvador.

Central American country with plantation coffee cultivation. After the breakdown of the United States of Central America it became independent in 1838, and was formally declared an independent republic in 1841. From 1895 to 1898, together with Honduras and Nicaragua, it was part of the ephemeral Central American Republic. Direct UPU membership since 1 April 1879.

In 1867 definitives with the inscription 'SALVADOR'; later, 'REPUBLICA DE EL SALVADOR', 'EL SALVADOR' and similar wording. The stamps are mostly of characteristic North American origin with production by line engraving and the conservative pictorial style of American stamps. Also represented by the Seebeck printings (see *Ecuador*). In 1879 the text 'UNION POSTAL UNIVERSAL' was used to underline the UPU membership granted that year. Among the older issues are several with limited printings considered postally adequate. Stamps from 1897–8 had the heading 'REPUBLICA MAYOR DE CENTRO AMERICA'. Later, and up to the present, El Salvador's Central American location is stressed by 'AMERICA CENTRAL', 'CENTROAMERICA', 'C.A.' next to the name. National propaganda subjects predominate, although in recent times more general themes have been used. Current issues, especially, are aimed at the philatelic market through popular design themes and miniature sheets. A large number of overprinted provisionals. Since the 1950s the printing techniques have changed (and the printing houses as well) along with the concepts of stamp design. Current production is 25 to 40 stamps a year.

Philatelic bureau Departamento de Filatelia, Dirección General de Correos, San Salvador.

FALKLAND ISLANDS
Area 12,173 sq.km, **population** 1,900 (1984), **capital** Stanley.

British colony near the eastern shore of South America, claimed also by Argentina (under the name 'Malvinas') which briefly occupied the islands in 1982. The British occupied the islands in 1839 and in 1908 they added South Georgia, South Orkneys, South Shetlands, South Sandwich Islands and Graham's Land (Antarctic Sector) to form the Falkland Islands Dependencies. In 1962 Graham's Land, the South Orkneys and South Shetlands were made into the separate colony of the British Antarctic Territory, and South Georgia again became a stamp-issuing country. See also *Falkland Islands Dependencies, Graham Land, South Georgia, South Orkneys* and *South Shetlands*. UPU membership since 1 January 1879.

From 1869 to 1876, postage was paid for in cash and a 'frank' was struck on the letter. From 1878 definitives with the text 'FALKLAND ISLANDS'. Stamp production has always been British. Besides portrait issues, pictorial stamps and stamps with British Commonwealth omnibus themes. Contemporary production is about 2–3 issues annually.

Philatelic bureau Colonial Postmaster, GPO, Stanley. **Trade sales** Crown Agents' Stamp Bureau.

FRENCH GUIANA
Overseas department of France (from 1814 to 1946 a colony) with a very underdeveloped economy (**area** 91,000 sq.km, **capital** Cayenne). Part of the country is the inland Territory of Inini (with a special administration from 1930 to 1946).

Before issuing its own stamps, the country used the general issues of the French colonies. From 1886, stamps of French colonies with the overprint 'GUY. FRANÇ.'; later, 'GUYANE', then definitives with the inscription 'GUYANE FRANÇAISE'. A total of 252 + 31 stamps of French origin. Apart from overprinted provisionals, pictorial stamps and French colonial omnibus issues. During the Second World War, Pétain issues, which had no postal validity in the territory, and Free France issues. Stamp issuing continued until 1947, although from 1946 French stamps were valid in the territory. Because French Guiana is an overseas department of France, it now uses French stamps.

GRANADA CONFEDERATION
Present-day Colombia was known under this name from 1858 to 1861; in 1861 it was the United States of New Granada and the United States of Colombia.

In 1859–61 definitives inscribed 'CONFED. GRANADINA' or 'ESTADOS UNIDOS DE NUEVA GRANADA' (revolutionary issues for the south and the most southern part of Colombia): a total of 13 stamps in heraldic designs. From 1862, United States of Colombia issues.

GREENLAND
Area 2,175,600 sq.km, **population** 52,347 (1984), **capital** Godthåb.

The largest island in the world and a self-governing province of Denmark since 1979; it has been Danish since 1814. During the Second World War it was under US military control. Direct UPU membership from 1 July 1875 (Denmark, including Greenland).

Starting in 1938, definitives with the inscription 'GRØNLAND'; from 1969 the stamps also have, apart from the Danish name 'GRØNLAND', the island's name in Eskimo 'KALÁTDLIT NUNÁT'. From 1978 it was changed orthographically to 'KALAALLIT NUNAAT'. Stamp production predominantly of Danish origin. Chiefly touristic and historic subjects, primarily of a portrait and pictorial character, with some designs common to Danish stamps. Very moderate output, currently about 5 stamps annually. The most frequent designer is Rosing, and the engraver is the Swede Slania.

Postage fees for mail were introduced on 1 December 1938 — until that time it had been free of charge. From 1905 parcel stamps used for packages (with the designation 'PAKKE-PORTO' — without the name of the country), valid only for mailing packages from Greenland to Denmark and vice versa.

Philatelic bureau Greenland Post Office, Denmark.

GRENADA
Area 344 sq.km, **population** 113,000 (1982), **capital** St George's.

Island in the Lesser Antilles, British since 1762, definitively from 1783; part of the Windward Islands from 1871 to 1956, then a separate colony; between 1958 and 1962 a member of the West Indies Federation and from 1967 an autonomous associated state of Great Britain. Since 7 February 1974, an independent state, a monarchy in the British Commonwealth. Indirect UPU membership from 1 February 1881 (British colony, associated state); direct since 30 January 1978.

Before introducing its own stamps it used those of Great Britain. From 1861 definitives inscribed 'GRENADA', produced in Great Britain. Pictorial stamps from 1934 including British Commonwealth omnibus issues. Small output at first — new stamps appeared at intervals of several years — but then began to expand substantially after the island became autonomous. At the present time over 100 stamps a year. From 1969, 75 miniature sheets were produced, 27 airmail stamps during 1972, etc. Production decidedly directed at the collectors' market, as is that of *Grenadines of Grenada* and *St Vincent*.

Philatelic bureau Philatelic Service, GPO, St George's. **Trade sales** Inter-Governmental Philatelic Corporation.

GRENADINES OF GRENADA
Southern part of the Grenadines: islands of Carriacou, Ronde, Little Martinique, etc. (33 sq.km), under the administration of Grenada.

Until 1973 only Grenada stamps were used, but following the example of the *Grenadines of St Vincent* these islands also began to issue stamps locally. In 1973 the first Grenadine stamps came out with the overprint 'GRENADINES', followed by definitives inscribed 'GRE-NADA/GRENADINES' or 'GRENADINES OF GRENADA'. Large output, predominantly of pictorial stamps with common international themes, designed to attract the collector. Annual output is an unnecessarily large number — up to about 100 stamps — in addition to numerous miniature sheets. On the Grenadines of Grenada all stamps of Grenada are valid (and vice versa) thus demonstrating there is no need for both issues.

Philatelic bureau Philatelic Service, GPO, St George's, Grenada. **Trade sales** Inter-Governmental Philatelic Corporation.

GRENADINES OF SAINT VINCENT
The northern part of the Grenadines: the islands of Bequia, Canouan, Mayreau, Mustique, Union, Little St Vincent, etc. (43 sq.km), under the administration of St Vincent. UPU membership, listed under the complete name, Grenadines of St Vincent, indirect since 1 September 1881.

Although stamps of *St Vincent* are valid throughout the Grenadines of St Vincent, since 1973 definitives have been issued — unquestionably for sale to collectors — inscribed 'GRE-NADINES OF ST. VINCENT' and overprinted provisionals on St Vincent stamps with the supplementary text 'GRENADINES OF' ('St Vincent' is understood, being already in the stamp designs). Very lively issues of pictorial stamps of British origin, with omnibus issues of the Commonwealth, appear as an annual output of 25 to 50 stamps.

Philatelic bureau St Vincent Philatelic Services, General Post Office, Kingstown, St Vincent.

GUADELOUPE
Two islands in the Antilles under French administration since 1816 (but first occupied in 1635). From 1946 an overseas department of France (**area** 1,510 sq.km, with dependencies 1,780 sq.km, **capital** Basse-Terre). The dependencies are the islands of Marie Galante, Iles des Saintes, La Désirade, St Barthélemy (from 1784 to 1877 it belonged to Sweden) and the larger part of the island of St Martin.

From 1884 stamps of the French colonies with the overprint 'GPE.' or 'GUADELOUPE (et dépendances)'. A total of 233+50 stamps of French origin, overprinted provisionals and pictorial stamps, then issues and designs in common with other French overseas territories. During the Second World War, and under the Pétain government, there were issues that could have no postal validity. French stamps have been used since 1947 when Guadeloupe became an overseas department of France.

GUANACASTE
A province of Costa Rica (**area** 10,400 sq.km, **capital** Liberia) in the north-western part of the country.

From 1885 to 1889 the overprint 'GUANACASTE' on Costa Rican stamps: a total of 24 stamps, virtually all overprinted provisionals. The overprint was carried out for administrative reasons, because in view of its remoteness the province had its own laws. The stamps were valid only in the province.

GUATEMALA
Area 108,889 sq.km, **population** 7.7m (1982), **capital** Guatemala la Nueva (Guatemala City).

Underdeveloped agricultural country in Central America. After the dissolution of the United States of Central America in 1838, Guatemala became an independent republic. Direct UPU membership from 1 August 1881.

Definitives from 1871 with the inscription 'GUATEMALA'. Early stamp production chiefly of North American origin, but at present, also of European and Guatemalan origin, which has influenced the approach to stamp designing. A considerable number of overprinted and surcharged provisionals (even for thematic stamps) including international omnibus issues.

Production is uneven from the viewpoint of subject matter, designing and printing aspects, and is much influenced by collector demand. A large number of airmail stamps — some years only airmail stamps and no other kind are issued. Present-day annual production averages 15 to 30 stamps.

Philatelic bureau Oficina Filatelia, Dirección General de Correos, Guatemala City.

GUAYANA

A Venezuelan federal state (now called Bolívar) (**area** 238,000 sq.km, **capital** Ciudad Bolívar). It rebelled in 1902 and had its own revolutionary government until 1903.

In 1903 issues of the revolutionary government with the inscription 'VENEZUELA/ESTADO GUAYANA': a total of 22 stamps, mostly of inferior printing, produced in Trinidad.

GUYANA

Area 214,970 sq.km, **population** 900,000 (1983), **capital** Georgetown.

Agricultural country with bauxite mining. From 1831 a British colony, British Guiana, which declared its independence on 26 May 1966 under the name Guyana. Since 1970, a republic in the British Commonwealth. Indirect UPU membership from 1 April 1877; direct from 1967.

In 1966 definitives with the name 'GUYANA, SOUTH AMERICA'; later only 'GUYANA'. Stamp production of British origin with a preponderance of propaganda subjects. Annual output 15–20 stamps.

Philatelic bureau GPO, Georgetown. **Trade sales** Crown Agents' Stamp Bureau.

HAITI

Area 27,750 sq.km, **population** 6m (1982), **capital** Port-au-Prince.

Black republic in the western half of Hispaniola, with plantation agriculture. From 1617 its territory was under French rule; from 1804 it declared its independence as the first black republic in the world. The country was divided in 1807–20 into the northern and southern parts and in 1822–44 it was temporarily united with the eastern part of the island, out of which there later emerged the Dominican Republic. From 1915 to 1934 the country was occupied by US troops and became a protectorate. Direct UPU membership since 1 July 1881.

From 1881 definitives with the name 'RÉPUBLIQUE D'HAITI' or 'D'HAITI'. For a long time stamp production was restrained, under North American influence, but this changed in the 1950s under varied influences from European printing houses. A great many designs to attract collector sales (overprinted provisionals giving rise to thematic stamps, miniature editions, sometimes in printings of only 3,000); extensive output of airmail stamps. Overall output is without a design policy, but a number of features are common to American production. Erratic annual output of several dozen stamps.

The country also had foreign post offices (British and French).

Philatelic bureau Office du Timbre, Administration Générale des Contributions, Port-au-Prince.

HONDURAS

Area 112,088 sq.km, **population** 4.09m (1983), **capital** Tegucigalpa.

Central American republic with plantation agriculture, independent since the break-up of the United States of Central America in 1838. Together with Nicaragua and El Salvador it was a member of the ephemeral Central American Republic from 1895 to 1898. In 1914 it ceded to the United States Swan Island in the Caribbean (returned in 1971). Direct UPU membership since 1 April 1879.

From 1866 definitives with the name 'HONDURAS', 'REPUBLICA DE HONDURAS' or 'CORREOS DE HONDURAS', supplemented on some issues with the initials 'C.A.' (Central America). Production of stamps chiefly of North American origin with an unusually large number of overprinted provisionals and printings for sale to collectors, as with the Seebeck issues (see *Ecuador*). From 1945 virtually only airmail stamps, also a large quantity of officials and even miniature sheets of officials. Current production printed mainly in Europe, which influences the designs. A great many propaganda subjects (political and touristic) in traditional pictorial concept. Many issues with very low printings. Present-day production is extremely irregular: stamps do not appear every year, but some years, several dozen are issued.

Philatelic bureau Dirección General de Correos, Oficina Filatelica, Tegucigalpa.

ININI
An inland territory (since 1951 an arrondissement) of French Guiana (**area** 78,500 sq.km, **administrative centre** St Elie), under special administration between 1930 and 1946. Unexplored and primeval forests cover the territory.

In 1932 stamps of *French Guiana* with the overprint TERRITOIRE DE L'ININI: a total of 62+9 stamps, mostly overprinted provisionals, and issues with designs common to French colonial issues. After the Second World War separate issues were not revived and since 1947 French stamps have been used.

JAMAICA
Area 11,424 sq.km, **population** 2.23m (1982), **capital** Kingston.

Agricultural country with important bauxite mining. It became a British colony in 1655, obtained self-government in 1944, and from 1958 to 1962 was a member of the West Indies Federation. An independent dominion of the British Commonwealth since 6 August 1962. Pedro Cays and Morant Cays, two small guano island groups, are dependencies of Jamaica, as at one time were the *Turks and Caicos Islands* and the Cayman Islands. Indirect UPU membership from 1 July 1877 (British colony); direct from 29 August 1963.

From 1860 definitives with the name 'JAMAICA'. Until 1867 these were valid also on Turks Islands and, until 1901, on Cayman Islands. Stamp production of British origin. In addition to the usual royal portraits, pictorial stamps and issues with themes or designs common to the British Commonwealth. In recent years there has been an annual output of 10 to 15 stamps, mostly pictorials, and 1 to 2 miniature sheets.

Philatelic bureau Head Postmaster, General Post Office, Kingston. **Trade sales** Crown Agents' Stamp Bureau; Inter-Governmental Philatelic Corporation.

LEEWARD ISLANDS
A united British colony from 1871 to 1956, formed by the presidencies of Antigua, Montserrat, St Kitts-Nevis-Anguilla, the British Virgin Islands and, until 1940, Dominica, which then came under the administration of the Windward Islands.

Definitives with the name 'LEEWARD ISLANDS' in 1890 replaced issues of the individual presidencies. From 1903, issued concurrently with stamps of the individual presidencies. A total of 131 stamps issued until 1954, characteristic of British origin, royal portraits in the British colonial key-and-duty types and Commonwealth omnibus issues. Leeward Islands stamps became invalid in 1956, and the individual territories reverted to using only their own issues.

LIMA
The capital of Peru. Its name appears on stamps in various instances, but in many cases it is dubious to what extent the name expresses postal validity. In 1870 definitives, whose face value corresponded to the fee for mailing a letter along the Chorrillos-Lima-Callao route, appeared inscribed 'LIMA'. Another issue of 1873, also inscribed 'LIMA', was allegedly intended for local mailings in Lima. Other stamps with the word 'LIMA' can be found dated 1895, on provisionals during the Chilean occupation, and as provisionals issued by the government of Iglesios. A total of 55 stamps.

MARIÑO
A Venezuelan district with provisionals issued by the revolutionary government in 1903. Five stamps appeared with the inscription 'Venezuela Mariño'.

MARTINIQUE
French island in the Lesser Antilles (**area** 1,102 sq.km, **capital** Fort de France), colonized by the French in 1635–64; declared an overseas department of France in 1946.

In 1886 stamps of the French colonies with the overprint 'MARTINIQUE', then definitives with the same inscription. A total of 258+37 stamps until 1947, when stamp issuing ended. Pictorial stamps of characteristic French origin, including French colonial omnibus issues. A large number of overprinted and surcharged provisionals. Since Martinique is a French overseas department, French stamps have been used since 1947.

MATURIN
A Venezuelan federal state, known today as Monagas (**area** 28,900 sq.km, **capital** Maturín), which at the time of the rebellion in 1902–3 had its own revolutionary government.

In 1903, primitives inscribed 'ESTADO MATURIN': a total of 5 stamps.

MEXICO
Area 1,958,201 sq.km, **population** 75.39m (1983), **capital** Mexico City.

Republic with agriculture and an advanced mining industry. After liberation from Spanish rule an independent empire was created; the first republic was established in 1824. Texas declared its independence from Mexico in 1836, and in 1848 Mexico ceded two-fifths of its territory (1.3 million sq.km) to the USA. Since 1853 Mexico has existed within its present borders. In 1864 the empire was again restored, but with its fall in 1867 the second republic was born. In 1913–16 there was a civil war in Mexico. Direct UPU membership from 1 April 1879.

From 1856 definitives with the name 'MÉJICO' (using the old spelling); from 1864 the name was spelt 'MEXICO' and then, under the emperor in 1866, 'IMPERIO MEXICANO'; and then, again, 'MEXICO'. Stamp output until the 1930s was very much influenced by the conservative policy of American stamp issuing. The stamps were produced by diverse techniques, mostly in Mexican printing houses. In the 1920s to 1930s issues appeared which seemed to be aimed at collectors: some printings were of only 1,000; of a 1933 airmail issue only 200 copies in all were sold at the counter; and a number of printings were not issued officially. Current printings are around one million, and their propaganda subjects indicate that production is intended for just that purpose. What was once indifferent pictorial production gave way, at the end of the 1930s, to several artistically high-level issues with remarkable graphic designs. Large production of officials — by 1937, 226 official stamps had appeared (a 1929 issue came out in a very low printing of 128 sets). Annual output at present is 30 to 40 stamps, most of which are airmail (in conformity with Latin American custom).

World catalogues mention a number of local issues, especially during the war against Emperor Maximilian (1867) and from the period of the civil war (1913–16). Most of these provisionals do not even have the name of the territory for which they were issued, and they are mostly overprinted (or rubber hand-stamped) emergency primitives, whose postal validity and justification are not always reliably proven, if they are not, in fact, forgeries. Among them are the following: Campeche, a state in southern Mexico; Chiapas, a state in southern Mexico; Cuernavaca, capital of the state of Morelos; Guadalajara, capital of the state of Jalisco; Sonora, which in 1913 declared itself a free state; Acambaro, in the state of Guanajuato; Aguascalientes, capital Aguascalientes; Chihuahua, capital Chihuahua; Colima, capital Colima; Culiacan, capital Sinalca; Guaymas, capital Sonora; Juárez, capital Chihuahua; León, capital Guanajuato; Monterrey, capital Nuevo León; Salamanca, capital Guanajuato; San Luis Potosí, capital San Luis Potosí; Sinaloa, capital Sinaloa; Torreón, capital Coahuila; Yucatán; Zacatecas, capital Zacatecas.

Philatelic bureau Oficina Filatélica Mexicana, Palacio Postal, Mexico City.

MONTEVIDEO
Capital of Uruguay. From 1858 definitives with the name 'MONTEVIDEO', although they were valid throughout the whole of Uruguay. Other issues in 1859–62 with the same name,

while stamps from 1866 have the inscription 'REPUBLICA DEL URUGUAY', in addition to 'MONTEVIDEO'. A total of 24 stamps, printed in both Uruguay and Great Britain.

MONTSERRAT
Area 102 sq.km, **population** 11,733 (1983), **capital** Plymouth.

British colony in the Lesser Antilles, 1632–1871; then presidential colony of the Leeward Islands; from 1956 again a separate colony; from 1958 to 1962 part of the West Indies Federation. Indirect UPU membership from 1 July 1879.

Until 1876 Antiguan stamps were valid; from 1876 Antiguan stamps with the overprint 'MONTSERRAT'; later, definitives with the same text. From 1891 to 1902 Montserrat came under the postal authority of the Leeward Islands and did not issue its own stamps, but these appeared again in 1903 and were used concurrently with stamps of the Leeward Islands. Stamps of British origin: royal portraits, pictorial stamps, themes and designs common to the British colonial issues of the time. Current production is 15 to 35 stamps a year, besides miniature sheets.

Philatelic bureau Montserrat Philatelic Bureau Ltd, GPO, Plymouth.

MOSQUITO COAST
Also known as Mosquitia (from the name of an Indian tribe), capital Magdala. Today a part of Nicaragua's Zelaya province; yielded by the British to Nicaragua in 1860 (a part went to Honduras, which became the subject of disputes). A rising occurred here and a republic was declared during the years 1893–1900. During the fighting 5 Nicaraguan stamps overprinted 'MOSQUITO PROVISIONAL' were issued and used postally.

NETHERLANDS ANTILLES
Area 993 sq.km, **population** 260,000 (1981), **capital** Willemstad.

Until 1948, the Dutch colony of Curaçao in the Caribbean Sea; since 1954 an overseas member country of the Netherlands. It includes the southern group (Curaçao, Bonaire, Aruba) and the northern group of the Leeward Islands (Saba, St Eustatius and part of St Maarten). Indirect UPU membership from 1 May 1877 (Netherlands colony); direct from 1 January 1920 (Curaçao and Surinam); renamed the Netherlands Antilles and Suriname on 3 September 1948.

In 1949 definitives with the inscription 'NEDERLANDSE ANTILLEN'. Production of stamps was by Dutch printers. Besides Dutch artists, a number of local artists also designed stamps. Some of the issues are in designs common to other Dutch colonial issues. National propaganda themes predominate. Some of the most recent designs are of a remarkably high graphic level. Current annual production is from 10 to 20 stamps.

Philatelic bureau Postmaster, Willemstad. **Trade sales** International Philatelic Agencies, Netherlands.

NEVIS
One of the Leeward Islands of the Lesser Antilles (**area** 93 sq.km, **capital** Charlestown), British from 1628. Incorporated into the colony of the Leeward Islands in 1871, and from 1903 a part of the joint presidency of St Kitts-Nevis in the Leeward Islands (Anguilla was also part of it).

In 1861 definitives inscribed 'NEVIS'. Up to 1890 (when these were replaced by stamps of the Leeward Islands) 24 + 5 stamps were issued. From 1903 to 1952 see *St Kitts-Nevis*; stamps of the Leeward Islands were valid concurrently until 1956. Stamps are of British origin. In 1980 the island's own issues were revived — doubtless with a view to encouraging sales to collectors.

Philatelic bureau The Philatelic Bureau of Nevis, Head Post Office.

NEW BRUNSWICK
British colony in Canada from 1713; in 1867 it became one of the provinces of the present Federated Dominion of Canada (**area** 72,481 sq.km, **capital** Fredericton).

Definitives in 1851 with the inscription 'NEW BRUNSWICK'. Up to 1863 a total of 9 stamps of British origin were issued, most of which are coveted classical stamps. In 1868 replaced by Canadian stamps.

NEWFOUNDLAND

Island and province, with Labrador as a dependency (**area** 404,520 sq.km, **capital** St John's). From 1713 it was British (it had been occupied as far back as 1583), and became an independent colony in 1855, being declared a dominion in 1917. After the First World War the island's debts were so great that a British commission was set up in 1934 to administer its affairs, but gradually the economy improved, and in 1949 Newfoundland became the tenth province of Canada.

Definitives from 1857 with the inscription 'ST. JOHN'S NEWFOUNDLAND'; later, 'NEW-FOUNDLAND'. Stamp issuing until 1947, a total of 244 + 7 stamps. Several airmail stamps, issued to mark pioneering flights across the Atlantic, are coveted and expensive philatelic items; on the world market the rarest of these can reach a figure in excess of £20,000. Otherwise, the stamp designs reflect the influence of American, British and Canadian stamps, linked to the fact that they were produced by printers in these countries. Mostly heraldic and royal portrait designs with restrained pictorial stamps. The first pictorial stamps appeared in 1865. Natural history, scenery and life are widely used design themes. They were superseded by Canadian stamps in 1949, and from that year, Newfoundland stamps became valid throughout the whole of Canada (theoretically to the present day).

NICARAGUA

Area 148,000 sq.km, **population** 2.82m (1981), **capital** Managua.

Poorly developed Central American country, independent since 1838 (in 1860 it annexed the *Mosquito Coast*). From 1895 to 1898 it became part of a short-lived Central American Republic together with Honduras and El Salvador. From 1912 to 1933 the country was occupied by American units (in 1914 it leased the Corn Islands to the United States, which were returned only on 25 April 1971). Direct UPU membership from 1 May 1882.

In 1862 definitives with the name 'NICARAGUA'. For a number of decades stamps were printed by line-engraving in American printing houses, which influenced the stamp designs. Among these were the Seebeck issues (see *Ecuador*). A large number of overprinted and surcharged provisionals (especially in 1901–38) with small printings, often only a few hundred or thousand. In 1947, the conservative conception of older American stamps was replaced by new ideas. These involved triangular and rhomboidal stamps, large production of miniature sheets and airmail stamps, long series, printed in various printing houses using different techniques. These were produced to stimulate philatelic sales, hence the diversity of production — there are large numbers of official stamps, including airmail officials (a total of more than 400). Annual production about 500 stamps, besides miniature sheets.

From 1904 to 1911 there were overprinted issues in districts on the Atlantic Coast (Costa Atlantica). This was because this territory used silver coinage while the rest of the territory used paper currency. (See *Zelaya*, *Cabo* and *Costa Atlantica*.)

Philatelic bureau Oficina de Control de Especies Postales y Filatelia, Managua. **Trade sales** Inter-governmental Philatelic Corporation.

NOVA SCOTIA

British colony in Canada from 1713; in 1867 it became one of the provinces of the present Federated Dominion of Canada (**area** 54,566 sq.km, **capital** Halifax).

Definitives in 1851 with the name 'NOVA SCOTIA': until 1860 a total of 10 stamps, of which the first are among the most coveted classical issues. In 1868 Canadian stamps replaced them.

PANAMA

Area 77,082 sq.km, **population** 2.04m (1982), **capital** Panama City.

Agricultural country with extensive banana plantations. After liberation from Spanish rule the country was part of *Colombia* from 1821 to 1903, first as a state and then as a department. Colombia did not agree to the plan to build a canal through the Panama isthmus, and the US consequently sponsored a coup d'état in Panama and declared it an independent republic. The zone around the canal came under the US administration from 1903 to 1979, and used its own stamps (see *Panama Canal Zone*). Indirect UPU membership from 1 July 1881 (Colombia); direct from 11 June 1904.

In 1878 definitives with the name 'COLOMBIA' and subtitled 'E S DE PANAMA'. These were stamps for internal use in the territory of Panama. In 1887 issues show a map of Panamanian territory, but only with the name 'COLOMBIA' were they valid in all areas. Until 1903 Colombian stamps were valid in Panama concurrently with those mentioned above.

In 1903 stamps of previous issues and Colombian stamps with the overprint 'REPUBLICA DE PANAMA' on some; 'PANAMA', 'REPÚBLICA DE PANAMA' and 'R. DE PANAMA'. For many decades stamps were of North American and British origin with the restrained pictorial approach of American stamps. In the 1930s some issues had about 10,000 complete sets. Recent years' issues, printed in several countries by varying methods, reflect a variety of appearances. However, the frequency of issue suggests that many of the stamps were not necessary — some do not appear to have been on public sale in Panama at all — and the standard reference catalogues do not list them in detail.

Following extensive stamp-issuing activity in the 1960s, which had been encouraged by stamp agencies (in 1964 as many as 110 stamps were issued), current annual output is about 1 to 5 issues.

Philatelic bureau Dirección General de Correos y Telecomunicaciones, Sección Filatélica, Panama.

PANAMA CANAL ZONE

Territory 16 km wide along the Panama canal (**area** 1,676 sq.km) which from 1903 to 1979 was under US administration (for a fee). On 1 October 1979, the Republic of Panama took over the zone (including the postal administration). Indirect UPU membership from 1 July 1881 (Colombia); indirect from 1 August 1904 (USA); indirect from 1 July 1940 (US territory).

In 1904 stamps of Panama with the overprint 'CANAL ZONE', then US stamps with the overprint 'CANAL ZONE PANAMA'; also 'PANAMA CANAL'. From 1928, definitives with the inscription 'CANAL ZONE'. A total of 79 + 42 stamps of North American origin with designs similar to US stamps, in some instances even the same designs were used. The pictorials were in designs largely connected with canal scenes or with US stamp-issuing activities until stamp issuing ceased in 1979.

PARAGUAY

Area 406,752 sq.km, **population** 3.06 m (1982), **capital** Asunción.

Underdeveloped agricultural country in east South America, independent since 1811 (declared a republic in 1814). Between 1865 and 1870 it was at war with Argentina, Brazil and Uruguay, and lost a considerable amount of its territory. In 1932, and through a treaty of 1938, it obtained two-thirds of the Chaco. Direct UPU membership from 1 July 1881.

In 1870 definitives with the name 'REPUBLICA DEL PARAGUAY' or just 'PARAGUAY'. Overall production has varied widely, printing being by several techniques in various South American, North American and European printing houses. In a similar way, its stamp designs were first influenced by North America, then Latin America and, finally, Europe. The original predominance of national propaganda designs was replaced by more general themes, calculated to appeal to a wider range of collectors. A large number of overprinted provisionals, also many airmail stamps and miniature sheets. Commercial influences are evident in the small printings (10,000–30,000), some on tinfoil, perforated and imperforate and so on. Present-day annual production is more than 100 stamps, largely for the philatelic market.

Philatelic bureau Departamento Filatélico, Dirección General de Correos, Asunción.

PERU

Area 1,285,216 sq.km, **population** 18.3m (1982), **capital** Lima.

Agricultural country with mineral mining, until 1821 under Spanish rule. In 1879–84, in the 'nitrate' war with Chile, Peru lost Arica, Iquique, Pisagua and Tacna (until 1929) and a large part of the country was temporarily occupied (the capital Lima, and also Callao, Pisagua, Pisco, Icà etc.). In 1934 and 1942, Peru annexed half the territory of Ecuador. Direct UPU membership from 1 April 1879.

Issues first appeared in 1858 in heraldic design but without the name of the territory and distinguishable by the currency in 'dinero'. In 1866 definitives appeared with the inscription 'PERU' (also 'Lima'). From 1880 overprints reading 'UNION POSTAL UNIVERSAL PERU' appeared, stressing its entry into the UPU and also, therefore, the universal validity of its stamps abroad. In 1881–5 there were a number of local issues during the Chilean-Peruvian war and the civil war. Apart from those bearing the name *Arequipa* and *Lima*, these include, for example: Moquegua, Puno, Cuzco, Ayacucho, Ica, Pasco, Piura and Ancash. These are overprints on issues from Peruvian territory, but there are also Chilean stamps with overprints of the above-mentioned towns, very often only rubber-stamped. The postal validity and use of these stamps is confused on account of the war conditions prevailing during their issue.

Definitives, again, have the designation 'PERU' or 'PERÚ'. Stamp production was first carried out at Lima and then in North America by line-engraving. This influenced stamp design. From the 1930s the printing technique and printing houses were changed, which altered the design trend, although this remained conventional in common with most Latin American production. To a large extent the designs on Peruvian stamps fulfil national propaganda functions. Only some of the issues have a low edition from the collectors' viewpoint (15,000 to 30,000). Typical, and true of the Latin American area in general, is the high number of airmail stamps. At present, the country brings out 10 to 30 stamps a year, chiefly airmail.

Philatelic bureau Jefe del Museo Postal y Filatélico, Dirección General de Correos, Lima.

PRINCE EDWARD ISLAND

British colony from 1796 on the eastern coast of Canada in St Lawrence Bay. In 1873 it became a province of the Federated Dominion of Canada (**area** 5,656 sq.km, **capital** Charlottetown).

In 1861 definitives inscribed 'PRINCE EDWARD ISLAND': a total of 16 definitives of British origin, all of them with royal portraits. One stamp had face values expressed in dual currency: local currency and sterling, expressed as '3d stg: cy. 4½d'. In 1872, decimal currency (in cents) was introduced. From 1873 replaced by Canadian stamps.

PUERTO RICO

Island which until 1898 was part of the Spanish West Indies (**area** 8,860 sq.km, **capital** San Juan). Since that time it has belonged to the USA and is a self-governing federal state of the USA. In 1932 the official name of the country, then Porto Rico, became Puerto Rico. Since 1952 it has had the status of an associated state of the USA, confirmed by a plebiscite in 1967 (which rejected both full independence and integration by becoming the 51st state of the Union).

Prior to 1873 stamps of the Spanish overseas postal authorities were valid on the island; from 1873 these issues were with overprints in the form of signature flourishes (to distinguish them from the same issues valid in Cuba, which had silver currency, as compared to Puerto Rico, which had paper currency).

Only from 1877 were there definitives with the text 'PTO RICO', then 'PUERTO RICO', all being of Spanish origin and in designs common to all Spanish colonial issues of the period. From 1898, after the American occupation, American stamps with the overprint 'PORTO RICO' or 'PUERTO RICO'. A total of 174 + 11 stamps. US stamps have been used since 1900.

ST CHRISTOPHER

Island also known as *St Kitts*, British since 1623; incorporated into the Leeward Islands of the Lesser Antilles in 1871 (**area** 175 sq.km, **capital** Basseterre). Since 1903 a part of the presidency of St Kitts-Nevis in the Leeward Islands. *Anguilla* belonged to it before breaking away in 1967 to become a British colony.

In 1870 definitives with the inscription 'SAINT CHRISTOPHER'. Issues until 1890: a total of 19 + 6 stamps of British origin. In 1891 the stamps of the Leeward Islands became valid and were used concurrently from 1903 to 1952 with the stamps of *St Kitts-Nevis*, and then until 1956 with the issues of *St Kitts-Nevis-Anguilla*.

ST KITTS

Area 168 sq.km, **population** 35,104, **capital** Basseterre.

A British island in the Lesser Antilles, also known as *St Christopher*. From 1903 to 1952 it was part of the unified presidency of *St Kitts-Nevis* in the Leeward Islands (in 1952 there was a change of name to *St Kitts-Nevis-Anguilla*, but Anguilla broke away in 1967). From 1967 part of an autonomous associated state of Great Britain. Indirect UPU membership since 1 July 1979.

In 1980 it began to issue its own stamps with the release of overprints reading 'ST KITTS' on stamps of the associated state (Nevis did the same in 1980 and Anguilla had already done so from 1967). The definitives have the same designation.

Philatelic bureau General Post Office, St Kitts.

ST KITTS-NEVIS

The united presidency of the islands St Christopher (St Kitts) and Nevis (**area** 303 sq.km, **capital** Basseterre), which included, until 1967, the island of Anguilla, in the British colony of the Leeward Islands. From 1952 to 1967 the name was changed to St Kitts-Nevis-Anguilla. Since 1967 the islands have had the status of an associated state of Great Britain. Indirect UPU membership since 1 July 1879.

In 1903 definitives with the inscription 'ST KITTS-NEVIS': a total of 99 stamps of British origin issued; portrait and pictorial stamps and British Commonwealth omnibus issues. The stamps of the Leeward Islands were valid here concurrently (until 1956), although in 1952 they were replaced by new stamps of *St Kitts-Nevis-Anguilla*, following those of St Kitts-Nevis.

ST KITTS-NEVIS-ANGUILLA

British island territory in the Leeward Islands of the Lesser Antilles (St Kitts was British from 1623; Nevis from 1628; Anguilla from 1650), forming the presidency of the united British colony of the Leeward Islands until 1956 (**area** 414 sq.km, **capital** Basseterre). Used the name St Kitts-Nevis from 1903; from 1952 St Christopher, Nevis and Anguilla; in 1958–62 the islands were part of the West Indies Federation. In 1967 they became an autonomous associated state of Great Britain but Anguilla left this federation in the same year.

At first British stamps were in circulation. From 1861 Nevis had its own stamps, and from 1870 so did St Christopher. In 1890 both were replaced by a series of stamps issued by the Leeward Islands. From 1903 St Kitts-Nevis issues, while the Leeward Islands stamps were valid there until 1956.

In 1952 definitives with the inscription 'SAINT CHRISTOPHER NEVIS ANGUILLA', also the designation 'ST. KITTS NEVIS ANGUILLA', although Anguilla, at the time of this designation, was already issuing its own stamps. Since 1980 St Kitts and Nevis have also issued their own stamps. Production of stamps has been in Britain throughout. The designs, pictorial and symbolic, have been in the British colonial style.

ST LUCIA

Area 616 sq.km, **population** 122,000 (1981), **capital** Castries.

Island in the Lesser Antilles, a British colony since 1803, part of the Windward Islands from 1871 to 1956, then a separate colony, and from 1958 to 1962 a member of the West Indies

Federation. From 1967 an autonomous associated state in the British Commonwealth: from 22 February 1979 an independent state. Indirect UPU membership from 1 February 1881.

In 1860 definitives with the inscription 'ST. LUCIA' in a style characteristic of British origin. Royal portrait issues in key-plate types followed by stamps featuring social subjects and pictorials typical of British colonial issues. Latterly, the choice has been substantially influenced by anticipated sales to collectors. Output in recent years has been between 25 and 40 stamps with, in addition, miniature sheets.

Philatelic bureau Postmaster General, General Post Office, Castries. **Trade sales** Inter-Governmental Philatelic Corporation.

ST PIERRE AND MIQUELON

Area 242 sq.km, **population** 6,041 (1982), **capital** Saint-Pierre.

Islands near the eastern shore of Canada, all that is left of what was once a vast territory which belonged to France in North America. From 1946 a French overseas territory, and on 16 July 1976, a French overseas department.

In 1885 French colonial stamps with the overprint 'S P M' (St Pierre et Miquelon). Later, definitives with the full name 'SAINT PIERRE ET MIQUELON': a total of 509+86 stamps of French origin with a large number of overprinted and surcharged provisionals, designs typical of French colonial issues. During the Second World War, Pétain issues were prepared but were never issued. In 1941 provisional overprinted stamps of Free France were in use. Post-war pictorials in modern designs laid stress on life in the islands and the many technological advances of the period. Characteristic French line engravings have been supplemented by other techniques. Since 1976, after becoming an overseas department of France, only French stamps have been used.

ST VINCENT

Area 389 sq.km, **population** 123,000 (1984), **capital** Kingstown.

Island in the Lesser Antilles, a British colony from 1763, part of the Windward Islands from 1871 to 1956, then once again a separate colony; in 1958–62 a member of the West Indies Federation. The island's status as an autonomous associated state of Great Britain became valid on 27 October 1969. Independent from 27 October 1979. Indirect UPU membership from 1 September 1881 (listed under the joint name of St Vincent and the Grenadines).

At first British stamps were used, then from 1861 definitives with the inscription 'ST. VINCENT'. All production of stamps has been British. Until 1907, portrait stamps in key-and-duty plate types. Later, pictorials in typical British colonial designs and omnibus issues common to the British Commonwealth. Current annual output has increased to as much as 50 stamps, the design themes being planned to attract collectors.

Philatelic bureau St Vincent Philatelic Services, General Post Office, Kingstown. This centre is also in charge of the distribution of stamps for the *Grenadines of St Vincent*.

SANTANDER

State of the Union of Colombia, 1884–6; then until 1903 a department of Colombia (**area** 53,000 sq.km, **capital** Bucaramanga).

In 1884 definitives with the inscription 'ESTADOS UNIDOS DE COLOMBIA/ESTADO SOBERANO DE SANTANDER': a total of 33 stamps in heraldic designs, issued until 1905.

SURINAME

Area 163,265 sq.km, **population** 385,000 (1982), **capital** Paramaribo.

Republic with important bauxite mining. A Netherlands possession from 1667 (in the periods 1799–1802 and 1804–16 occupied by the British). Declared an independent republic on 25 November 1975; has held autonomous status since 1954 as an overseas member state of the Netherlands Union. Indirect UPU membership from 1 May 1877 (Netherlands colony); direct from 1 January 1922; renamed the Netherlands Antilles and Suriname on 3 September 1948.

In 1873 definitives with the name 'SURINAME' (production in the Netherlands). This and later portrait stamps were in designs common to all the Dutch colonies at the time. The same postage-due design as the Netherlands (with the text 'TE BETALEN/PORTO') differing from the Netherlands and the other colonies only in colour (violet). Following portrait and numeral types, pictorial stamps were gradually introduced as well as stamps for inclusion in international omnibus issues. Current annual output ranges between 40 and 60 stamps. The bid to attract collectors is reflected not only in the choice of pictorial subjects, but also in the considerable percentage of airmail stamps, as well as the introduction of miniature sheets.

Philatelic bureau Director of Posts, Filatelistische Dienst der Posterijen, Paramaribo. **Trade sales** International Philatelic Agencies, Netherlands.

TOBAGO

Island off the South American coast (**area** 297 sq.km, **capital** Scarborough), British 1794–1803; from 1814 a British colony. In 1889 it joined with nearby Trinidad and formed a colony under that name, which was renamed Trinidad and Tobago in 1913.

In 1879 definitives inscribed 'TOBAGO': a total of 30 stamps of British origin issued, including surcharged provisionals. Stamp issuing until 1896 when *Trinidad* stamps replaced them; from 1913 the new stamp issuing country of *Trinidad and Tobago*.

TOLIMA

A state of the Union of Colombia from 1870 to 1886, then a department of Colombia until 1903 (**area** 146,800 sq.km, **capital** Ibagué).

Primitives in 1870 inscribed 'EE. UU. DE C/E.S. DEL T', then definitives with the name 'TOLIMA' (with 'Estado' or 'Departamento' and the upper title 'Colombia'): a total of 64 stamps, heraldic in character and of conservative American conception. The post office of the department was incorporated into Colombia in 1906, whose stamps then became valid here.

TRINIDAD

Island off the South American coast (**area** 4,831 sq.km, **capital** Port of Spain); a British colony from 1797. From 1889 it joined with nearby Tobago as a colony, renamed Trinidad and Tobago in 1913.

In 1851 definitives with the name 'TRINIDAD': a total of 69 stamps of British origin, designs mainly based on the symbolical figure of Britannia. In 1896–1914 Trinidad stamps were used on *Tobago* ; from 1913 *Trinidad and Tobago* issues followed.

TRINIDAD AND TOBAGO

Area 5,128 sq.km, **population** 1.2m (1980), **capital** Port of Spain.

Republic in the British Commonwealth. Tobago Island was British from 1794, Trinidad from 1797; both islands joined in 1889 to form a colony under the name Trinidad (the name Trinidad and Tobago was introduced only in 1913). In 1958–62 they were part of the West Indies Federation; from 31 August 1962, an independent state; from 1 August 1976 a republic. UPU membership — indirect for Trinidad from 1 April 1877 (British colony); indirect for Tobago from 1 February 1881 (British colony); direct from 15 June 1963.

From 1913 the definitives of *Trinidad* with a new inscription, 'TRINIDAD & TOBAGO'. Production of British origin; from 1935, pictorial stamps and issues in designs used for British Commonwealth omnibus issues. Current annual output in the neighbourhood of 10 to 20 stamps. The choice of subjects nowadays is thematic so as to appeal to collectors who also show interest in miniature sheets.

Philatelic bureau Postmaster General, General Post Office, Port of Spain. **Trade sales** Crown Agents' Stamp Bureau.

TURKS AND CAICOS ISLANDS

Area 430 sq.km, **population** 7,436 (1980), **capital** Grand Turk.

British island colony in the south-eastern Bahamas from 1848. It was a Jamaican dependency from 1873, but separated from Jamaica in 1962 when the latter became independent. Indirect UPU membership from 1 February 1881.

The first stamps with the new designation Turks and Caicos appeared in 1900 (prior to this, from 1867, there were stamps with only the name 'Turks Islands'). There are definitives with the inscription 'TURKS & CAICOS ISLANDS'. Production of British origin and including all the British Commonwealth omnibus issues. Since 1957 a wide range of pictorial stamps. Current annual output is between 10 and 30 stamps, the designs being planned to appeal to collectors, as is production of miniature sheets.

Philatelic bureau Postmaster, Philatelic Bureau, Grand Turk. **Trade sales** Inter-Governmental Philatelic Corporation.

TURKS ISLANDS

Island group in the eastern Bahamas (**area** 25 sq.km, **capital** Grand Turk). A British colony together with Caicos Islands (405 sq.km) from 1848. In 1873 it became a dependency of Jamaica, but separated in 1962.

Stamps with the name 'TURKS ISLANDS' appeared starting in 1867 and continued even after it became a dependency of Jamaica. In 1900 these issues were replaced by one with the joint name 'TURKS & CAICOS ISLANDS'. A total of 33 stamps of British origin, mainly royal portrait issues typical of British colonial stamps with many surcharged provisionals. Prior to 1867 Jamaican stamps were used.

UNITED STATES OF AMERICA

Area 9,369,885 sq.km, **population** 232.06m (1982), **capital** Washington D.C.

Advanced industrial and agricultural country, independent since 1776. After the first stamps were issued in 1847, the country expanded by 1,300,000 sq.km through the annexation of California and northern Mexico (1848 and 1853). Later it acquired Alaska (1867); in 1898, Hawaii, Puerto Rico, the Philippines (until 1946), Cuba (until 1902) and Guam; in 1899, the eastern part of Samoa; in 1903, the Panama Canal Zone (until 1979); in 1917 the Danish Virgin Islands; in 1944, the Marshall Islands, the Carolines, the Marianas, the Bonin Islands (under American military administration from 1945 to 1968) and the Ryukyu Islands (until 1972). The USA includes such stamp-issuing territories as: from 1867 Alaska; from 1900 Hawaii, Puerto Rico, Guam; from 1914, Corn and Swan Islands (until 1971); from 1917 the former Danish Virgin Islands and from 1945 the Pacific Marianas, Carolines, the Marshall Islands. UPU membership from 1 July 1875.

After introduction of a unified postal tariff in 1845, postmasters' stamps were issued in several towns (mostly of 5-cent values for one zone and a unit of weight). Sometimes these are only a rubber stamp with the figure of value; at other times emergency issues with primitives, and in the case of New York an engraved adaptation of Washington's portrait taken from banknotes. Not all the designs included the name of the town that issued them. From the philatelic viewpoint these issues include some of the most rare and coveted items. They include, for example, such towns as: Alexandria (Va.), Annapolis (Md.), Baltimore (Md.), Boscawan (N.H.), Brattleboro (Vt.), Lockport (N.Y.), Millbury (Mass.), New Haven (Conn.), New York (N.Y.), Providence (R.I.), St. Louis (Mo.).

From 1847, nationwide definitives with the abbreviation 'U.S.' (which is used up to the present except for the abbreviation 'U.S.A.') or in the full-length version 'UNITED STATES' or 'UNITED STATES OF AMERICA'. After the outbreak of the Civil War in 1861, all the older issues became invalid to prevent smuggling and financial losses from stamps left on enemy territory.

American production created a characteristic style linked with line-engraving of North American printing houses, influencing a considerable number of other, especially South and Central American, states. Line-engraving is still used almost exclusively in the production of American stamps, and the choice of subjects tends to be broadly educational. Printings of many commemorative issues at the present time run to more than 100 million; and for Christmas stamps as many as about one thousand million. Typical of US production is that most commemorative issues are usually of only one stamp, whereas definitive stamp sets may include over 20 values. An exceptional set with the flags of the individual states of the Union (1976) has 50 values. There have been several stages in graphic conception; in recent years there have been some quite remarkable graphic designs based on modern artistic conceptions (Olden, McCloskey, Todhunter, and others). Annual production at the present time amounts to about 30 stamps, and there is a tendency towards thematic subjects of collector interest.

Philatelic bureau Philatelic Sales Branch,US Postal Service, Washington D.C.

URUGUAY
Area 176,215 sq.km, **population** 2.9m (1982), **capital** Montevideo.

An agricultural country with extensive livestock breeding for meat and wool. Independence proclaimed in 1825 and recognized by its neighbours in 1828. The official name 'Republica Oriental del Uruguay' indicates that the republic lies east of the River Uruguay. Direct UPU membership since 1 July 1880.

Postal services to overseas, prior to admission of the country to the UPU, were carried out by foreign post offices, which took care of foreign mailings. There was a British one from 1862 to 1872 in Montevideo, an Italian one, which used stamps with the overprint 'Estero', and a French one, though letters with French stamps are less common. Definitives for inland use appeared in 1856 with the inscription 'DILIGENCIA' (postal stage coach); along with others were the issues of Atanasio Lapida (postal services under government supervision). Issues appeared from 1858 with the name 'MONTEVIDEO' (although they were valid throughout the whole of Uruguay).

In 1864 came government definitives with the inscription 'REPUBLICA ORIENTAL', then 'REPUBLICA ORIENTAL DEL URUGUAY'; later, only 'URUGUAY'. Influenced for many decades by American stamp designing and by line-engraving in American and English printing houses. Gradually, various printing techniques and printing houses were used. At the present time, offset-lithography produced in the National Printing House in Montevideo is the normal process. Pictorial standard of design was not very high and was rather conventional until in the 1950s efforts were made to produce designs original to the country, and this is reflected in current production by several outstanding artists. Most issues have national publicity subjects (in printings of millions). In contrast, some issues with designs on general themes have been issued basically for sale to collectors and are printed in lower quantities of several thousand. A large number of officials. Current production annually is 20 to 30 stamps with a smaller number of airmail stamps. Because they are considered attractive, the stamps are very often of large size, and miniature sheet production has now been introduced.

Philatelic bureau Oficina Filatélica, Dirección Nacional de Correos, Montevideo.

VANCOUVER ISLAND
Island off the western coast of Canada (**area** 32,100 sq.km, **capital** Victoria); from 1849 a British colony; in 1866 joined to British Columbia and together with the latter became part of Canada in 1871.

It began to issue its own stamps in 1865; definitives inscribed 'VANCOUVER ISLAND', bearing the usual royal portrait. Philatelically, this first issue includes coveted collector's items. After incorporation into British Columbia, stamps with the joint name of British Columbia and Vancouver Island became valid in 1868. Stamps at 2½d face value were issued in 1860 with the inscription 'BRITISH COLUMBIA & VANCOUVERS ISLAND' but despite the name they were mainly used for inland postage in British Columbia (see *British Columbia and Vancouver Island*).

VENEZUELA
Area 912,050 sq.km, **population** 16.4m (1983), **capital** Caracas.

South American country with important oil deposits. After the dissolution of Greater Colombia (New Granada, Ecuador and Venezuela), an independent republic from 1831. It has claims on Guyanan territory, a claim which is reflected in some of its stamp designs. UPU membership from 1 January 1880.

In 1859 definitives with the name 'VENEZUELA' or 'EE UU DE VENEZUELA' (the United States of Venezuela); from 1954, 'REPUBLICA DE VENEZUELA'; later, only 'VENEZUELA'. Until 1937, that is, for almost 80 years, not quite 200 stamps were issued, whereas a far larger number has appeared during the past 30 years. Quite remarkable is the large number of airmail stamps which, although dated from 1930, represent roughly half the entire Venezuelan stamp production. The number of officials and fiscals is also high, and even airmail officials. Annual production in the 1950s reached a record high when, thanks to stamp sets depicting the individual Venezuelan states, they increased in 1951–3 to the level of over 100 stamps a year. In 1953 this number increased to as many as 214 stamps. At the present time production has decreased to about 20 to 40 stamps annually, the issue of airmail stamps having been halted in 1972. As for stamp designs, the period until the end of the 1940s was influenced by American ideas from American printing houses. Later, the use of other printers and printing techniques changed the style of design for pictorial stamps and, in the best cases, has attained a remarkably high graphic level. National propaganda themes predominate.

Philatelic bureau Oficina Filatélica Nacional, Caracas.

ZELAYA

Province of Nicaragua (**area** 55,985 sq.km, **capital** Bluefields) on the Atlantic coast. In 1904–1911 Nicaraguan stamps were used with the overprint 'B DPTO Zelaya' (B = Bluefields), because in Bluefields (just as in *Cabo*) only silver coins were used as currency, whereas in the rest of Nicaraguan territory paper money of half the value was in circulation. A total of 112 + 2 stamps were issued, almost all overprinted provisionals. In 1912 Nicaraguan stamps replaced these local provisionals.

AUSTRALASIA AND OCEANIA

AITUTAKI
Area 18 sq.km, **population** 2,335 (1981), **chief village** Arutanga.

A coral semi-atoll, one of the Cook Islands in Polynesia, since 1901 a dependency of New Zealand with others of the islands.

The first issues from 1903 to 1905 were New Zealand stamps bearing the overprint 'AITU-TAKI', on which the value was expressed in words in the native language of the Polynesian Maoris: 'Ava Pene' (half penny), 'Tai Pene' (one penny), 'Toru Pene' (three pence), 'Tai Tiringi' (one shilling), etc. *Niue, Penrhyn* and *Rarotonga* have similar texts. The stamp designs of these territories, between 1920 and 1927, are all alike. The pictorial definitive issues of 1920 were printed in London. During the first period, 31 stamps were issued. After 1932 *Cook Islands* stamps were introduced.

Stamp-issuing activities were revived in 1972 by an alleged treaty with the Cook Islands, through which Aitutaki remained a part of the group but assumed postal independence. Annual output is about 30 pictorial stamps bearing the name 'AITUTAKI' and the supplementary designation 'COOK ISLANDS'. That they are intended chiefly for the philatelic market is shown by the choice of subjects as well as by the introduction of miniature sheet production.

Philatelic bureau Post Office (Philatelic Service), Aitutaki.

AUSTRALIA
Area 7,682,300 sq.km, **population** 15.4m (1983), **capital** Canberra.

An advanced industrial and agricultural country rich in minerals and specializing in sheep breeding and wheat growing. A Dominion in the British Commonwealth since 1901, coming into existence by the merger of what had been the British colonies of New South Wales, Queensland, South Australia, Victoria, Western Australia and Tasmania. Indirect UPU membership from 1 October 1891 (as the British colony Australasia); direct from 1 October 1907 (listed as Australia, Coconut Islands and Lord Howe).

The first Australian stamps were postage-due stamps of 1902 (without the name of the country or state in which they were used), although their use in the individual states was not uniform. Apart from these postage-due issues, each former colony used its own stamps until 1913, when definitives were printed with the name 'AUSTRALIA'. Australian stamp production first called on British and American designers but it has since created its own school of stamp designers. From the end of the 1960s new artistic ideas appeared in a number of remarkable designs. Among the leading designers of Australian stamps are G. Hamori, W. Jardine and F. D. Manley. Stamp printing is carried out by various techniques which, from the beginning, were more often of Australian rather than British origin and are now entirely Australian. The postal function is linked with that of publicizing the country, shown by the subject matter and the large printings of up to ten million of most stamps. Annual output is in the region of 20 to 30 stamps.

Australian stamps were valid until 1947 on Norfolk Island; in 1945–52 on Nauru and Papua New Guinea; and from 15 February 1966 to 8 July 1969 on the Coconut Islands. The stamps of the *Australian Antarctic Territory* are also valid in Australian territory.

Philatelic bureau GPO, Melbourne. **Trade sales** Crown Agents' Stamp Bureau.

BRITISH NEW GUINEA
The south-eastern part of New Guinea (**area** 234,498 sq.km, **capital** Port Moresby), annexed in 1883 by the Australian state of Queensland. In 1884 it became a British protectorate and in 1888 a Crown Colony. In 1906 it was absorbed by Australia as a federal territory under the name of Papua, and in 1949 its administration merged with New Guinea to become Papua New Guinea. The islands of Trobriand, Woodlark, D'Entrecasteaux and Louisiada form part of it.

In 1898–1901 Queensland stamps were valid here. From 1901 to 1905 a total of 8 pictorial stamps of British origin were issued with the text 'BRITISH NEW GUINEA'. For later developments see *Papua* and *Papua New Guinea*.

BRITISH SOLOMON ISLANDS
A British protectorate consisting of six main islands: Choiseul, Santa Isabel, Malaita, New Georgia, Guadalcanal (called Tulagi until 1942) and San Cristobal, and a number of others (**area** 29,785 sq.km, **capital** Honiara on the island of Guadalcanal). In 1886, after joint German-British action, the northern part came under German influence. Great Britain then imposed its influence over the remaining part, which in 1893 was declared a protectorate. In 1899 part of the German area was ceded to Great Britain, the remaining German territories were occupied by Australian troops in 1914 and this part, together with New Guinea, was an Australian trust territory under UN administration. In 1942–3 the islands were occupied by the Japanese. In 1976 they gained internal self-government and changed their name to the *Solomon Islands*.

In 1907 definitives were issued with the inscription 'BRITISH SOLOMON ISLANDS PROTECTORATE'. Until September 1907 these stamps were valid only for internal use and for communication with Sydney. Mail going further was franked in Sydney with the stamps of New South Wales at the rate paid for island stamps. Since this extra rate was not collected, very often the stamps of New South Wales were simply pasted over the island stamps. Only with entry into the UPU did British Solomon Islands stamps acquire universal validity. From 1911 stamps were issued with the name 'BRITISH SOLOMON ISLANDS': a total of 261 + 8 stamps of British origin. Very restricted issues, including standard stamps of a pictorial character and issues with themes common to British Commonwealth issues. The line-engraving technique, carried out by British printers, later gave way to photogravure and offset-litho printing.

CAROLINE ISLANDS
A group of islands in Micronesia (**area** 1,046 sq.km, **capital** Ponape). At first Spanish, they were purchased by Germany in 1899 and remained German possessions until 1914. They were then occupied by Japanese troops in 1920 became a mandate territory of Japan (from 1947 a trust territory of the UN under US administration).

Before 1899 Philippine stamps were used. In 1899 German stamps with the overprint 'Karolinen'; later, German colonial key-type stamps with the same inscription: a total of 22 stamps of German origin. After the Carolines were occupied by Japan, Japanese stamps were used until 1944, and since then US stamps have been valid.

COOK ISLANDS
Area 241 sq.km, **population** 17,754 (1981), **capital** Avarua on Rarotonga.

Island group in the south Pacific, south east of Samoa, under British protection since 1888; formally affiliated to New Zealand in 1901 as one of its dependencies (island territory); acquired island autonomy as an associated state of New Zealand in 1965. They are divided into the southern group (including the Cook Islands themselves) and the northern group (Penrhyn, Manihiki) which geographically belongs to the Polynesian Sporades. Indirect UPU membership from 1 October 1891 (in the framework of Australasia); direct from 1 October 1907 (as New Zealand).

The Cook Islands first became a stamp-issuing country in 1892–1901. The first definitives came out in 1892 with the inscription 'COOK ISLANDS FEDERATION'; later, only 'COOK ISLANDS': a total of 15 stamps.

In 1919–31 the Cook Islands themselves had stamps under the name *Rarotonga*, the main island. Stamps were also issued, and continue to be issued, on adjacent islands: Aitutaki from 1903 to 1932 and again from 1972; Penrhyn from 1902 to 1932 and again from 1973. Niue has had its own administration and issues since 1901.

The year 1932 marked the beginning of another period of stamp-issuing activity in the Cook Islands: until 1965 a total of 178 stamps appeared. Most of them are pictorial stamps based on traditional designs of the British Commonwealth issues. Later, they were influenced by New Zealand designers and printers. Stamps were at first printed in Great Britain, then in New Zealand.

From 1966, after obtaining autonomy, issues expanded considerably, up to several dozen items a year, largely designed to attract collectors. Issues included long sets, miniature sheets and high face values up to $10 (NZ).

The name 'COOK ISLANDS' has appeared as a supplementary designation for *Niue* issues in 1938–45, and for *Aitutaki* issues in recent times. *Penrhyn* issues use the name 'NORTHERN COOK ISLANDS'.

Philatelic bureau Post Office, Rarotonga.

FIJI

Area 18,272 sq.km, **population** 663,485 (1982), **capital** Suva.

Melanesian island group in the south Pacific. From 1874 a British colony (prior to that a native kingdom), and with limited internal self-administration from 1965. Independence within the British Commonwealth was proclaimed on 10 November 1970. Indirect UPU membership from 1 October 1891 (British colony); direct since 18 June 1971.

The first issues in 1870 were primitive type-set stamps inscribed 'FIJI TIMES EXPRESS' and printed locally by *The Fiji Times* newspaper. In 1871 came stamps printed in Sydney inscribed 'FIJI' and on which, instead of the portrait underneath the royal crown, was the monogram 'CR' (Cakobau Rex — King Cakobau, the native ruler). After the abolition of the kingdom and the establishing of the Crown Colony, these stamps were overprinted with the monogram 'VR' (Victoria Regina). Definitives were later issued with this 'VR' monogram. From 1903 the first of the King Edward VII issues; the British colonial key-and-duty plate types were in use until the end of the King George V period. From 1938 pictorial stamps which, until 1974, usually incorporated the portrait or symbol of the British monarch. At the present time the annual output is 10 to 20 stamps.

Philatelic bureau Post Office, Suva. **Trade sales** Crown Agents' Stamp Bureau.

FRENCH OCEANIA

A French colony in Oceania (the Society Islands, Tubuai, Rapa, Morotiri, Tuamotu, the Gambiers, the Marquesas and Clipperton), occupied by France from 1841 to 1881 and declared an overseas territory of France in 1946. In 1957, after a change in name to French Polynesia, it obtained limited autonomy.

The first stamps were issued in 1892 (French colonial key-types) with the text 'ETABLIS-SEMENTS DE L'OCEANIE'; later, 'Ets FRANCs DE L'OCEANIE' (also Pétain issues and stamps of Free France during the Second World War). Besides pictorial stamps of French origin, there are a number of omnibus issues in designs common to similar issues throughout the French Empire, and also overprinted provisionals. A total of 242+27 stamps. Since 1958, replaced by stamps of *French Polynesia*.

FRENCH POLYNESIA

Area 3,941 sq.km, **population** 148,000 (1983), **capital** Papeete.

A French overseas territory consisting of the Society Islands, Tubuai, Rapa, Morotiri, Tuamotu, the Gambiers, the Marquesas and Clipperton. Formerly *French Oceania* which on 26 July 1957 obtained limited autonomy under the new name. Indirect UPU membership from 1 July 1876 (as a group of French colonies); direct since 23 December 1977 (France).

Definitives with the name 'POLYNESIE FRANÇAISE' first appeared in 1958. They were predominantly pictorial stamps along with omnibus issues common to French colonial issues. Some of the designs, by French artists, are of a remarkably high graphic level. Chiefly line-engraving of French origin but in recent times produced by other printing techniques. Consideration for the collector's market is reflected in the choice of subjects, the large size and the production of airmail stamps. Annual output from 10 to 20 stamps.

Philatelic bureau Recette Principale, Service Philatélique, Papeete.

GERMAN NEW GUINEA

The north-eastern part of New Guinea (Kaiser-Wilhelm-Land) together with the Bismarcks and other adjacent islands, occupied by Germany from 1883 (the Solomon Islands in 1886), becoming a German colony in 1885. In 1914 it was occupied by Australian troops and in 1920 became a mandate territory of the League of Nations under Australian administration. It was then given the name North-Eastern New Guinea and, after merging with the outlying islands, was called the Mandated Territory of New Guinea, or simply New Guinea (capital, Herbertshöhe).

At first, German stamps were issued; from 1898 German stamps with the overprint 'Deutsch-Neu-Guinea', then German colonial key-type yacht stamps with the same text and, finally, with the orthographical variant 'DEUTSCH-NEUGUINEA': a total of 24 stamps. Stamps issued in 1914–16 and sold only at philatelic counters in Berlin could not, of course, fulfil their postal function. From 1914 the key-plate yacht stamps were issued in very limited quantities, sometimes less than 100, with the overprint 'G R I' (Georgius Rex Imperator) and the value shown in British currency. Stamps of the *North Western Pacific Islands* followed from 1915 to 1925.

GILBERT AND ELLICE ISLANDS

Group of islands in central and south Pacific (**area** 1,037 sq.km, **capital** Bairiki). British since 1886, a protectorate from 1892, a colony from 1912. The group included the Gilbert Islands, Banaba Island (Ocean), the Ellice Islands, the Phoenix Islands and Line Islands (and also Christmas Island). The uninhabited islands of Starbuck, Malden, Flint, Vostock, Caroline, Fanning and Washington were never part of the colony but were administered by the High Commissioner for the Pacific. On 1 October 1975 (with validity from 1 January 1976) the colony was divided into the Gilbert Islands (now Kiribati) and Tuvalu (the one-time Ellice Islands). Indirect UPU membership from 1 October 1911.

From 1911 Fiji stamps with the overprint 'GILBERT & ELLICE PROTECTORATE' and definitives with the same inscription. Then (1912) British colonial key-and-duty type inscribed 'GILBERT & ELLICE ISLANDS'. British Commonwealth omnibus issues and from 1939 pictorial stamps. A total of 249+8 stamps of British origin. Christmas Island had private, local stamps from 1916 to 1938. After 1976 see the *Gilbert Islands* (later *Kiribati*) and Tuvalu.

GILBERT ISLANDS

Part of the British colony of the Gilbert and Ellice Islands which in 1975 was divided into the Gilbert Islands (**area** 934 sq.km, **main settlement** Bairiki on Tarawa Atoll) and the Ellice Islands. They consist of 16 small islands, of which the largest is Tarawa, followed by Banaba Island (Ocean), the Phoenix Islands (including Christmas Island) and the Line Islands. The first stamps bore the name 'THE GILBERT ISLANDS' and appeared on 2 January 1976; others have the designation 'GILBERT ISLANDS'. Until 1979 there were 79 stamps and 3 miniature sheets. Production is of British origin in the form of pictorial stamps including some British Commonwealth omnibus issues. After 1979 see *Kiribati*.

GUAM

The largest island in the Marianas (**area** 549 sq.km, **capital** Agana), an air and naval base of the USA to whom the island has belonged since 1898 when it was acquired from Spain.

In 1899 US stamps with the overprint 'GUAM': a total of 12 stamps, all overprinted provisionals. From 1901 to the present day US stamps have been used in Guam, and before 1899 Philippine stamps were used. In 1930 locals of dubious character appeared. These were 11 Philippine stamps with the overprint 'GUAM GUARD'. In 1941–4 Guam was occupied by Japan.

HAWAII

From the end of the 18th century an island kingdom, over which missionaries gained considerable influence in the second quarter of the 19th century. In January 1893 the queen was overthrown and a provisional republican government made up of local plantation owners was established, which on 4 July 1894 proclaimed the Republic of Hawaii and requested the United States to annex it. This came about on 7 July 1898, and on 14 June 1900 Hawaii was given the status of a US territory. Since 1959 it has been the 50th federated state of the Union (**area** 16,636 sq.km, **capital** Honolulu).

In 1851 primitive typeset issues with the text 'HAWAIIAN POSTAGE' or, sometimes, 'H.I. & U.S.', with face values expressed in US currency. Philatelically, these are among the classical and most highly coveted stamps in the world. They are called 'Missionaries' because they were used by American missionaries to frank their correspondence addressed to the United States. The first issues were invalid abroad. Some stamps had the direct inscription 'Inter-Island', limiting their postal validity to the islands. Other issues had the inscription 'HAWAII', 'HAWAIIAN ISLANDS' or 'REPUBLIC OF HAWAII'. A total of 65 + 6 stamps. Local typeset primitives were followed by stamps of American origin, influenced by American stamp production. On 14 June 1900 US stamps became valid here.

US stamps of 1928 with the overprint 'HAWAII' were an American commemorative issue to mark the 150th anniversary of the discovery of the islands; they were valid throughout the USA.

KIRIBATI
Area 684 sq.km, **population** 60,302 (1982), **main settlement** Bairiki on Tarawa Atoll.

The one-time British colony known as the *Gilbert Islands* which, since attaining independence on 12 July 1979, has been called the Kiribati Republic. Apart from Kiribati itself, it consists of the island of Banaba (formerly Ocean), the Phoenix Islands (including Christmas Island) and the Line Islands. Indirect UPU membership from 1 October 1911 (British colony of Gilbert Islands).

The first stamps were issued in 1979, on attaining independence, with the inscription 'KIRIBATI'.

Philatelic bureau Bairiki, Tarawa.

MARIANA ISLANDS
An archipelago in Micronesia (**area today** 466 sq.km, **capital** Garapan), at first Spanish, then sold to Germany in 1899 (with the exception of Guam which was taken over by the USA). In 1914 the islands were occupied by the Japanese, and in 1920 became their mandated territory. In 1944 they were occupied by the Americans. In 1947 they became a UN trust territory under US administration, and in 1978 they acquired the status of an associated state of the USA as Northern Marianas.

Until 1898 Philippine stamps were used; in 1898–9 Philippine stamps with the overprint 'MARIANAS ESPAÑOLAS': a total of 6 overprinted provisionals.

From 1899 German stamps with the overprint 'Marianen'; later, definitives in the German colonial key-type yacht stamps with the same inscription: a total of 21 stamps. In 1916–19 other German stamps were issued, sold only at philatelic counters in Berlin and, even then, they were unable to fulfil their postal purpose because from 1914 Japanese stamps were valid in the Marianas.

MARSHALL ISLANDS
Area 181 sq.km, **population** 31,041 (1980), **capital** Dalap-Ulliga-Darrit.

An archipelago in Micronesia. A German protectorate from 1885 to 1914, then occupied by New Zealand troops, but in 1915 ceded to the Japanese (with the exception of the island of *Nauru* which was occupied by the Australians). In 1920 the islands were declared a Japanese mandated territory. In 1944 they were occupied by the Americans, and since 1947 they have been a trust territory under US administration.

Although the Marshall Islands were a German possession from 1885, German post offices were opened only in October 1888 and, until 29 March 1889, had no stamps and postmarks of their own. The first issues in 1897–9 (before this date German stamps were valid) are German stamps with the overprint 'Marschall-Inseln'. Examples of bisected stamps on letters with fabricated addresses in Ponape in the Caroline Islands were made for the philatelic market. In 1899 these overprinted provisionals were issued with the corrected overprint reading 'Marshall-Inseln'; then German colonial key-type yacht stamps were issued bearing the same text. A total of 27 stamps of German origin. Stamps issued in 1916 and sold only at philatelic counters in Berlin could, of course, not fulfil their postal purpose. From 1915 to 1944 Japanese stamps were valid and were then replaced by United States stamps.

The government of the United States Trust Territory of the Pacific have now established the Republic of the Marshall Islands as an independent postal territory and first issued stamps inscribed 'MARSHALL ISLANDS' on 2 May 1984.

NAURU
Area 21 sq.km, **population** 8,421 (1983), **main settlement** Yaren.

An island state with phosphate deposits. From 1888 to 1914 it was part of the Marshall Islands, a German colony. Then it was occupied by Australian troops and from 1920 was a protectorate territory of the League of Nations under the joint administration of Australia, New Zealand and Great Britain. In 1942–5 the island was occupied by the Japanese, then again by Australia, and from 1947 it was a trust territory. In 1968 it was declared an independent republic within the British Commonwealth. Indirect UPU membership from 1 October 1888 (German protectorate); indirect from 1920 (Australia); direct from 17 April 1969.

At first, German stamps were valid, replaced in 1897 by German colonial stamps for the Marshall Islands. After the Australian occupation these had the overprint GRI (Georgius Rex Imperator); they were issued in very limited numbers of 50 or less of the high values and thus were evidently unable to fulfil their postal function. For a short time (1915–6) the stamps of the N W Pacific Islands were also valid here.

The first issue specifically for Nauru (1916) was of British stamps with the overprint 'NAURU'. In 1924 pictorial definitives, printed in Australia, were issued during the Australian mandate period. After the Second World War, Australian stamps were valid until 1954 when Nauru's own issues resumed. After the proclamation of independence in 1968, the stamps already in use came out with the overprint 'REPUBLIC OF NAURU'. From 1979 the inscription has, again, just been 'NAURU'. Stamp production is of considerable diversity. After the first overprinted issue of 1916, followed by definitives of Australian origin and a pictorial character, there were several omnibus issues with subjects common to the British Commonwealth or to Australian stamps. Very limited production; stamps were not issued every year but now there are 26 annually, designed to appeal to the collector's market.

Philatelic bureau Post Office, Republic of Nauru.

NETHERLANDS NEW GUINEA
The western part of New Guinea (area 412,781 sq.km, **capital** Hollandia), Dutch from 1886 (part of the Netherlands Indies), which remained under Dutch administration even after the emergence of independent Indonesia in 1949. From 1 October 1962 to 1 May 1963 the territory was temporarily under UN administration. From 1963 it came under Indonesia and was called *West Irian.* Until 1969 it remained under UN supervision.

Prior to 1950 stamps of the Netherlands Indies or the colony of Indonesia were used. Then stamps were issued with the text 'NIEUW GUINEA' (in designs similar to contemporary Netherlands stamps); later, with 'NEDERLANDS NIEUW GUINEA'. Until 1962 a total of 81+6 stamps of Dutch origin, mostly pictorials, printed by various techniques at the Dutch printers, J. Enschedé and Sons. Netherlands postage-due stamps were in use in Netherlands New Guinea but very few were actually used — from 2,980 down to 500 of individual values. From 1954 ordinary standard stamps were used to collect dues; Netherlands New Guinea postage-due stamps were not issued until 1957. From 1 October 1962 until 1 May 1963 stamps of Netherlands New Guinea were in circulation with the overprint 'UNTEA' (United Nations Temporary Executive Authority): a total of 19 values. See also *West Irian* and *New Guinea.*

NEW CALEDONIA
Area 19,103 sq.km, **population** 145,500 (1983), **capital** Nouméa.

A French overseas territory in Melanesia, a colony from 1853 to 1946. Its dependencies are the islands of Kunié (L'Ile des Pines), Belep, the Huons, the Chesterfields, Sand, Loyalty and Walpole, and, until 1959, also the Wallis and Futuna Islands. Direct UPU membership from 1 July 1876 (French colonies); indirect from 24 December 1977 (France).

First were primitives of 1860 (lithograph printing) which were valid only in the locality. From 1862 the standard General Issue for the French colonies was in use until 1881. Separate issues for the colony developed in 1881 after joining the UPU. Gradually, series of overprinted provisionals appeared on the basic stamps of the French colonies (overprinted 'NCE' = Nouvelle-Calédonie, or 'NLLE-CALÉDONIE'); then typical French colonial stamps with the inscription 'NLLE-CALÉDONIE ET DÉPENDANCES' or, more often, 'NOUVELLE-CALÉDONIE ET DÉPENDANCES'. A total of 558 + 60 stamps of French origin, generally in designs and subjects common to French colonial issues. During the Second World War, there were Pétain issues — these were sold only in France and were not valid on New Caledonia — and also Free France issues. At present, output is about 15 stamps a year, almost half of which are airmail, all in pictorial designs intended to appeal to collectors.

Philatelic bureau Office des PTT, Service Philatélique, Nouméa.

NEW GUINEA

The north-eastern part of New Guinea Island with the Bismarck Islands and the northern part of the Solomon Islands. It was German until the First World War, and in 1920 became an Australian mandated territory (240,870 sq.km). From 1949 it has been administratively linked to Papua and is called Papua New Guinea.

Before 1925 stamps of the North Western Pacific Islands. In 1925 definitives with the name 'TERRITORY OF NEW GUINEA'. New Guinea had its own issues until 1942 when the island was occupied by the Japanese. A total of 106 + 33 stamps, mostly pictorial and of Australian origin, but also many overprinted provisionals. After the liberation of the territory from Japanese occupation, Australian stamps became valid; then, from 1952, the stamps of *Papua New Guinea*.

NEW HEBRIDES

Island group in Melanesia (**area** 14,763 sq.km, **capital** Vila). The archipelago was under Franco-British administration from 1878. In 1906 it became a Franco-British condominium under joint dominion and included the islands of Espiritu Santo, Malekula, Banks and Torres. It was one of few countries in the world ruled simultaneously by two heads of state (the British monarch and the French president). According to the London Treaty of 1906, legal rights in this Franco-British condominium were such that in certain instances the representatives of both parties took joint decisions together, whereas in others, each of the participants acted separately. On 30 July 1980 the islands obtained their independence under the name of Vanuatu.

In 1908 (prior to this the stamps of New Caledonia and New South Wales were valid) Fiji issues with the overprint 'NEW HEBRIDES CONDOMINIUM' and the stamps of New Caledonia with the overprint 'NOUVELLES-HEBRIDES CONDOMINIUM'. As a rule, definitives came out with the same design in the French version (with the value in French currency) and in the British version (with the value in British currency), and the stamps usually bore, concurrently, symbols of French ('R.F.') and British (royal cypher) sovereignty. The 1925 issue showed the face values in British and in French currency (for instance, 2d–20c). After 1938 the stamps of both French and British origin showed the nominal value in obsolete gold francs, although Australian currency and local francs were in daily use. The country's own currency unit — the New Hebrides franc — was not introduced until 1977 when 47 surcharged provisionals appeared with the designated face value in the new currency unit, expressed as 'FNH'. A total of 555+45 stamps, printed in France and Great Britain, in designs showing both French and British influence without adopting any of the basic colonial designs of either country. From 1980 see *Vanuatu*.

NEW SOUTH WALES

A British colony from 1787 (originally established as a penal settlement), a Crown Colony from 1824 to 1901, self-governing after 1851, then a member of the Commonwealth of Australia (**area** 801,431 sq.km, **capital** Sydney). Van Diemen's Land became a separate colony in 1825, Victoria in 1850–51 and Queensland a self-governing colony in 1859. The Northern Territories came under the administration of South Australia in 1863.

In 1850 definitives (known as 'Sydney Views' but without any place name), followed by royal portrait issues inscribed 'NEW SOUTH WALES': until 1907 a total of 114 + 56 stamps, most of them line-engraved. The designs were mainly various portraits of the British monarch, but in 1888 an innovation was pictorial stamps to mark the centenary of the colony, considered to be the first commemorative stamps ever issued. A number of the Sydney Views are rare classical stamps coveted by collectors. Although from 1913 stamps of the Australian Commonwealth became valid in New South Wales (just as in all other member-states), officials of New South Wales with the perforated letters 'NSW' are dated as late as 1927.

The stamps were valid parallel with issues of *Victoria* on the latter's territory until 15 July 1851 and in *Queensland* until 1 November 1860.

NEW ZEALAND
Area 268,704 sq.km, **population** 3.23m (1983), **capital** Wellington.
. A country with mineral deposits and important agriculture comprising two main islands, North Island and South Island, as well as Stewart Island and the Chatham Islands. A Dominion in the British Commonwealth since 1907 (annexed by the British in 1814 and proclaimed a colony in 1840; it gained self-administration in 1852). Indirect UPU membership from 1 October 1891 (as Australasia); direct from 1 October 1907.

In 1855 definitives with the name 'NEW ZEALAND' (rare classical stamps known as Chalon Heads, the royal portrait being based on a picture of 1837 by Albert Chalon). Production of stamps was, at first, basically local but from dies prepared in Great Britain; later, it gradually took an original path, with the participation of New Zealand artists and printing houses and the introduction of Maori elements. In current production, national themes alternate with general subjects (birds, animals, etc.). Annual output is 25 to 30 stamps, most of which are of a pictorial character; a number of these issues are in miniature sheets as well. Exceptional to New Zealand since 1891 are officials issued for the Government Life Insurance Department bearing the picture of a lighthouse.

Philatelic bureau Post Office, Philatelic Bureau, Wanganui.

NIUE
Area 259 sq.km, **population** 3,296 (1981),**main settlement** Alofi.
From 1901 a dependency (island territory) of New Zealand; until 1946 associated with the Cook Islands whose stamps had been valid here from 1892. Since 1974 it has had the status of a New Zealand associated state. Indirect UPU membership from 1 October 1891 (as Australasia); direct from 1 October 1907 (as New Zealand including Niue).

From 1902 there were New Zealand stamps with the overprint 'NIUE' and in 1920 definitives with the same name. The issues of 1938 to 1945 have the supplementary designation 'COOK ISLANDS'. Most of the designs have been by New Zealand artists and the printing by British firms. Besides numerous overprinted provisionals, there are stamps of a pictorial character which show New Zealand influence in the designs. Several issues share designs in common with the Cook Islands. Stamps were not issued every year. At the present time, however, issues have increased to about 20 annually under the influence of philatelic agents more concerned with sales to collectors than with postal necessity. Since 1977 even miniature sheets have been issued — something quite atypical of the region.

On the first overprinted issues, the values are expressed in words in the native language: 'Taha' (1), 'Tolu' (3), 'Ono' (6). Contemporary stamps of *Aitutaki*, *Penrhyn* and *Rarotonga* have similar overprints. Pictorial stamps of these areas from 1920 to 1927 are in designs common to them all.

Philatelic bureau Niue Post Office, Alofi.

NORFOLK ISLAND
Area 35 sq.km, **population** 2,175 (1981), **capital** Kingston.

A Pacific island under Australian administration (an overseas territory) since 1914, with local self-government since 1960. Its main industry is tourism. Before 1914 it was part of New South Wales, annexed by the British in 1778. Direct UPU membership from 1 October 1907 (as Australia).

In 1947 definitives inscribed 'NORFOLK ISLAND' (previously Australian stamps were valid). Stamps of Australian origin (various printing techniques and designs characteristic of Australian production). Mostly pictorial stamps, also themes and designs common to the Australian stamp region. Annual production was very small but, at present, has increased to about 20 stamps, influenced by collector demand.

Philatelic bureau Senior Philatelic Officer, Philatelic Bureau, Kingston. **Trade sales** Crown Agents' Stamp Bureau.

NORTH WESTERN PACIFIC ISLANDS
Australian stamps with the overprint 'N. W. PACIFIC ISLANDS' were prepared for the Australian occupation of German possessions in the north-western part of the Pacific when the First World War broke out. However, the Japanese forestalled this Australian move by occupying the islands first, thereby obtaining them as a mandate after the war. The stamps of the North Western Pacific Islands were subsequently valid for postal services in the former German colony of New Guinea, occupied by Australia; they were used here until 1925 and were also valid on *Nauru* in 1915–16.

Between 1915 and 1925 a total of 37 Australian stamps overprinted 'N. W. PACIFIC ISLANDS'.

PALAU
Area 487 sq.km, **population** 12,177, **capital** Koror.

A group of islands in Micronesia, the Republic of Palau was established by the United States in January 1981. Originally a Spanish territory from 1686 to 1899, the islands concerned were sold to Germany in 1899 and became part of the *Caroline Islands*. A United States trusteeship operated from 1947 to 1981 and United States stamps alone were in use.

The U.S. Trusteeship continues to be responsible for administration, but the postal service was independently inaugurated on 1 November 1982. Stamps inscribed 'Republic of Palau' first appeared on 16 May 1983.

PAPUA
From 1906 an Australian federal territory in the south-eastern part of New Guinea (**area** 234,498 sq.km, **capital** Port Moresby), formerly a British colony called British New Guinea. From 1949 the administration merged with New Guinea and became *Papua New Guinea*.

In 1907 stamps of British New Guinea with the overprint 'Papua'. Later, definitives bearing the same text which, at first, had the same pictorial Lakatoi (native sailing craft) design as the previous issue of British New Guinea. In addition to many overprinted provisionals, there are pictorial issues specific to the country and issues with themes common to stamps of the Australian region. A total of 117+12 stamps. From 1942 Papua was occupied by Japan and Australian stamps were used from 1945 until 1952.

PAPUA NEW GUINEA
Area 462,840 sq.km, **population** 3.09m (1982), **capital** Port Moresby.

An independent member state of the British Commonwealth. From 1949 the jointly administered Australian territory of Papua (Australian federal territory) and North-Western New Guinea (a UN trust territory under Australian administration). Independence was granted on 15 September 1975. UPU membership as follows: Papua – indirect from 1 October 1891 (as Australasia); indirect from 1906 (as part of Australia). New Guinea – indirect from 1 January 1888 (German protectorate); indirect from 1920 (as part of Australia). Papua New Guinea – direct from 4 June 1976.

In 1952 definitives inscribed 'PAPUA AND NEW GUINEA' or 'PAPUA & NEW GUINEA'; later, 'PAPUA NEW GUINEA'. Chiefly pictorial stamps with general subjects and also publicity themes relating to the issuing territory, as well as issues with a common theme. Various printing techniques — line-engraving from the Australian government printing house and photogravure from the Swiss printers, Courvoisier. Chiefly Australian designers. Present annual output is about 20 stamps.

Philatelic bureau Port Moresby. **Trade sales** Crown Agents' Stamp Bureau.

PENRHYN

Area 7 sq.km, **population** 608 (1981), **main settlement** Omoka.

One of the northern Cook Islands in Polynesia, also known as Tongareva. From 1901 a dependency of New Zealand.

In 1902 New Zealand stamps with the overprint 'PENRHYN ISLAND' and definitives inscribed 'PENRHYN' (prior to 1902 stamps of the *Cook Islands*). A total of 28 stamps of New Zealand origin, mostly overprinted provisionals and pictorial stamps. From 1932 Cook Islands stamps were used again. The first overprinted issue (1902) had values expressed in the native tongue: 'Toru' (3), 'Ono' (6), 'Tahu Silingi' (1 shilling). Similar texts can be found in *Aitutaki, Niue* and *Rarotonga*. The stamp designs of these territories between 1920 and 1927 were common to all of them. In 1973 overprints on Cook Islands stamps appeared once again and, later, also definitives inscribed 'PENRHYN/NORTHERN COOK ISLANDS'; from 1976 only 'PENRHYN' once again. The production of pictorial stamps is aimed at the collector's market, as is evident from the annual increase of 10 to 20 stamps (besides miniature sheets) for a tiny population.

Philatelic bureau Post Office, Penrhyn.

PITCAIRN ISLANDS

Area 37 sq.km, **population** 59 (1983), **capital** Adamstown.

A British colony from 1839, consisting of Pitcairn Island and the uninhabited atolls of Henderson, Ducie and Oeno. Indirect UPU membership from 23 May 1939.

In 1940 definitives of British origin inscribed 'PITCAIRN ISLANDS'. Pictorial stamps and British Commonwealth omnibus issues. A number of subjects deal with the romantic history of the island's inhabitants (descendants of the mutineers of the *Bounty*). The stamps are printed by litho stamp processes in British printing houses. Present-day production is about 3 issues annually.

Philatelic bureau c/o Postmaster, Pitcairn Islands. **Trade sales** Crown Agents' Stamp Bureau.

QUEENSLAND

A British Crown Colony from 1859 to 1901 (prior to this, a part of New South Wales), then a member of the Commonwealth of Australia (**area** 1,727,529 sq.km, **capital** Brisbane).

In 1860 definitives inscribed 'QUEENSLAND' (formerly New South Wales stamps were valid). Until 1911 a total of 127+8 stamps of British origin, chiefly issues typical of the British colonial issues of the period. In 1913 these were replaced by Australian stamps.

RAROTONGA

The largest of the southern Cook Islands (**area** 67 sq.km, **capital** Avarua) in the Pacific, a dependency of New Zealand since 1901.

Cook Islands stamps were valid from 1892, replaced in 1919 by *New Zealand* stamps with the overprint 'RAROTONGA'. Then, until 1931, definitives totalling 27+9 stamps valid throughout the territory of the Cook Islands. They are overprinted provisionals and pictorial stamps of New Zealand. After 1931 Cook Islands stamps were used again. The first overprinted issues have values expressed in the native language: 'Apa' (half penny), 'Rua Pene' (two pence), 'Tai Tiringi' (1 shilling). *Aitutaki, Niue* and *Penrhyn* have similar overprints. These territories used stamp designs in common between 1920 and 1927.

SAMOA

Islands in Polynesia (**area** 3,124 sq.km), independent from 1860 but came under the trusteeship of German, British and American consuls. The islands' independence was formally confirmed in 1889, yet they remained under German-British-American administration. In 1899 Great Britain ceded its interests and in the following year Germany occupied the western part up to latitude 171°W (the islands of Savaii and Upolu, a total of 2,927 sq.km), and the United States the eastern part (Tutuila and Manua islands), called American Samoa (197 sq.km), thus ending Samoa's independence even in a formal sense. The western group was under German occupation until 1914 when it was occupied by New Zealand troops; in 1920 it became a New Zealand mandate territory. In 1935 it acquired the name Western Samoa and became an independent country in 1962.

Before 1900 German stamps were valid (from 1877 private post offices in Agara and Davis whose stamps did not, of course, have international validity). From 1900 German stamps with the overprint 'SAMOA'. Later, German colonial stamps in the yacht key-type. The last German issues during the First World War were sold only at philatelic counters in Berlin, having no postal validity because the territory was no longer under German administration. Until 1913 a total of 23 stamps of German origin were issued. After Allied occupation in 1914, German Samoan stamps were overprinted with the letters 'GRI' (Georgius Rex Imperator) and surcharged with values in sterling. In view of the very limited number of 126 sets (there were higher printings of some low values), there was considerable financial speculation associated with the issue, especially in alleged intentional 'errors' among the overprints. From 1914 New Zealand stamps with the overprint 'SAMOA', subsequently replaced by definitives with the same text. Until 1935, when the name was changed to *Western Samoa,* a total of 50 stamps of New Zealand origin were issued, however, chiefly overprinted provisionals.

Eastern (American) Samoa has used only US stamps since 1900.

SOLOMON ISLANDS

Area 29,785 sq.km, **population** 234,000 (1981), **capital** Honiara.

An independent country in the British Commonwealth since 7 July 1978; before this it was a British protectorate, with extensive internal autonomy granted on 1 January 1976. Until the end of 1975 it used the name *British Solomon Islands,* the word 'British' being omitted when autonomy was granted. Indirect UPU membership from 1 October 1911.

Starting in 1975 definitives were issued with the name 'SOLOMON ISLANDS' (preceded by provisionals on which the word 'British' was blacked out on the last British Solomon Islands issue). Production of pictorial stamps of British origin. Current annual output, 15 to 20 stamps.

Philatelic bureau Philatelic Bureau, General Post Office, Honiara. **Trade sales** Crown Agents' Stamp Bureau.

SOUTH AUSTRALIA

From 1836 to 1901 a British colony (self-governing from 1856), then a member of the Commonwealth of Australia (**area** 984,380 sq.km, **capital** Adelaide). In 1863 it took over the administration of the Northern Territories. No separate stamps were ever issued by the Northern Territories.

In 1855 definitives with the inscription 'SOUTH AUSTRALIA'. Stamps were issued until 1909 but had postal validity until 1913. A total of 119 + 45 stamps of British origin, based on various portraits of Queen Victoria.

TAHITI

A French colony in Oceania (**area** 1,647 sq.km, **capital** Papeete), a French protectorate from 1843 and a colony from 1880. It was incorporated into French Oceania in 1903.

From 1882 to 1893 overprinted provisionals with the name 'TAHITI' on French colonial stamps: a total of 29 + 26, all overprinted provisionals. From 1893 stamps of *French Oceania* were used; in two instances, in 1903 and 1915, these stamps were overprinted with the name 'Tahiti'.

TASMANIA
A British Crown Colony (from 1803 to 1825 a dependency of New South Wales), until 1855 known as *Van Diemen's Land* which, in 1901, became a member of the Commonwealth of Australia (**area** 69,978 sq.km, **capital** Hobart).

Definitives with the name 'TASMANIA' from 1857: a total of 88 + 13 stamps of British and Australian origin, predominantly portrait and pictorial stamps. Like all other member-states of the Australian Commonwealth, Tasmanian stamps were valid until 1913 when they were replaced by Australian issues. However, officials with the perforated letters 'OS' or 'T' were issued after this date, until 1938.

TOKELAU ISLANDS
Area 10 sq.km, **population** 1,572 (1981).

Three coral atolls – Afagu, Fakaofo and Nukunonu – British since 1877; until 1925 a part of the colony of the *Gilbert and Ellice Islands;* then under the administration of New Zealand. Direct UPU membership from 1 October 1907 (as New Zealand).

Definitives in 1948 with the inscription 'TOKELAU ISLANDS' (prior to this *Samoa* or *Western Samoa* stamps were in use). Production of stamps of New Zealand origin provided by the New Zealand postal authorities. Pictorial stamps (now only with the inscription 'TOKELAU') whose subject matter draws on life on the atolls. Annual output about 2 issues.

Philatelic bureau Post Office Philatelic Bureau, Wanganui, New Zealand.

TONGA
Area 784 sq.km, **population** 100,167 (1983), **capital** Nuku'alofa.

Originally an independent kingdom which, in 1900, became a British protectorate retaining some jurisdiction even in foreign affairs. The Fiji government represented the British Crown through its representative and consul. Tonga has been independent since 5 June 1970. UPU membership from 1 July 1930 (British protectorate); direct from 26 January 1972.

Before issuing its own stamps, Fiji stamps were valid. The spelling of the name of the archipelago has fluctuated: in 1886 definitives with the name 'TONGA'; from 1897 the name 'TOGA'; from 1949 again 'TONGA'. Altogether, 509+92 stamps of mixed origin, mostly New Zealand. Following portrait issues of the Tongan rulers, pictorial stamps in particular have appeared. In recent years, under a philatelic agency's influence, the collector's market has been catered for with curious shapes and materials. There are embossed issues with gold foil (made in Great Britain) of circular shape; stamps in the shape of a heart or the irregular outline of the map of Tongatabu island. These were the first stamps in the world to have such shapes and materials, which were then used by other philatelic agencies (for instance for Burundi) and among the earliest to be issued on backing paper from which they were peeled to allow the self-adhesive preparation on the back to adhere to the envelope. Annual production is about 50 stamps (half are airmails and officials), almost all of curious shapes. Since 1965 not a single standard-shaped stamp has been issued.

Philatelic bureau Stamp Section, Treasury Building, Nuku'alofa.

TUVALU
Area 26 sq.km, **population** 7,349 (1979), **main settlement** Funafuti.

Group of islands formerly known as the Ellice Islands which, until 1975, were part of the British colony of the Gilbert and Ellice Islands. Now they are a British Commonwealth territory (under the name Tuvalu), consisting of nine atolls, the largest of which is Funafuti. Indirect UPU membership from 1 October 1911 (British Colony).

In 1976 the first issues were provisionals on *Gilbert and Ellice Islands* stamps bearing the overprint 'TUVALU', followed by definitives with the new name. Pictorial stamps of British origin and incorporating the royal cypher of the British monarch. In 1978, after Tuvalu won independence, the stamps were overprinted 'INDEPENDENCE'. Current annual output is 20 to 40 stamps, largely directed towards the philatelic market.

In 1983 the Tuvalu government announced that eight individual islands within the Tuvalu group were to issue stamps of their own. These issues were only valid for international postage because the inscriptions included 'TUVALU' as well as the name of the particular island. These 'local' issues are not given full catalogue status by Stanley Gibbons but are listed, without any pricing, in the Appendix reserved for such issues. The islands concerned are: Funafuti, Nanumanga, Nanumea, Niutao, Nui, Nukufetau, Nukulaelae and Vaitupu.

Philatelic bureau GPO, Funafuti.

VAN DIEMEN'S LAND

A British colony (**area** 69,897 sq.km, **capital** Hobart) from 1825, self-governing from 1855 when it was given the name Tasmania.

In 1853 royal portrait definitives with the name 'VAN DIEMEN'S LAND': a total of 8 stamps of Australian and British origin, ranking among the rare classical stamps. Since 1857 see *Tasmania*.

VANUATU

Area 12,190 sq.km, **population** 128,000 (1982), **capital** Port Vila.

A Melanesian island state with plantation agriculture, comprising the islands of Espiritu Santo, Malekula, Banks and Torres. Until it became independent as the Republic of Vanuatu on 30 July 1980, it was the Franco-British condominium of the *New Hebrides*. Shortly after it became independent, an extensive separatist movement developed, centred on the islands of Espiritu Santo (Nagriamel Veramara) and Malekula (N'Makiaŭte), but this was not reflected in stamps.

Issues began in 1980 with definitives bearing the inscription 'VANUATU'.

Philatelic bureau Post Office, Port Vila. **Trade sales** Crown Agents' Stamp Bureau.

VICTORIA

A British Crown Colony from 1851 to 1901 (prior to that, a part of New South Wales), then a member of the Commonwealth of Australia (**area** 227,619 sq.km, **capital** Melbourne).

Definitives appeared in 1850 with the word 'VICTORIA' and until 15 July 1851, these were valid concurrently with New South Wales stamps. A total of 155+102 stamps of Australian and/or British origin, mostly royal portrait issues, with a number of officials which later had the perforated letters 'OS'. Stamps of Victoria were valid until 1913 (as were stamps of all the other states of the Australian Commonwealth) and were then replaced by Australian stamps.

WALLIS AND FUTUNA ISLANDS

Area 274 sq.km, **population** 12,391 (1983), **capital** Mata-Utu.

An island group of 12 small atolls, annexed by France in 1842 (Futuna and Alofi in 1887), until 1959 a dependency of New Caledonia and since then a French overseas territory. Direct UPU membership from 1 July 1876 (as a French colony); indirect since 23 December 1977 (France).

In 1920 stamps of New Caledonia with the overprint 'ILES WALLIS ET FUTUNA'. Later, definitives with the same wording, the stamps being of French origin. Apart from a large number of overprinted provisionals, themes (and even designs) common to the French colonial issues are characteristic. During the Second World War, there were Pétain government issues which had no postal validity here, and issues of Free France. Annual output is about 20 stamps, almost half of which are airmails.

Philatelic bureau Bureau des Postes, Service Philatélique, Mata-Utu.

WESTERN AUSTRALIA

A British Crown Colony in 1829-1901 (self-governing from 1851), then a member of the Commonwealth of Australia (**area** 2,527,631 sq.km, **capital** Perth).

From 1854 it had its own stamps with the name 'WESTERN AUSTRALIA' (some issues have the inscription 'WEST AUSTRALIA'): a total of 66 + 22 stamps of Australian and/or British origin. All stamps until 1901 bear the picture of a black swan — native to this part of Australia — since the old name of this colony was Swan River. The later issues included several royal portrait designs. These stamps were valid until 1913, as in the case of all member-states of the Australian Commonwealth, when they were replaced by Australian stamps. Characteristic features include a number of officials with the perforated letters 'WA' or 'OS'; these were issued until 1938.

WESTERN SAMOA
Area 2,842 sq.km, **population** 156,349 (1981), **capital** Apia.

Formerly German Samoa, from 1920 a New Zealand mandate territory, from 1935 with the name Western Samoa. Since 1962 a non-hereditary monarchy headed by one of the chiefs (the Samoan name for Western Samoa is 'Samoa I Sisifo'). Direct UPU membership from 1 October 1907 (New Zealand provided postal services even after 1962 when Western Samoa obtained its independence).

From 1935 stamps with the name 'WESTERN SAMOA'; from 1958 with the Samoan name 'SAMOA I SISIFO'. Some issues since autonomy bear the name of the country in English and Samoan; most recent use is simply 'SAMOA'. Stamps of New Zealand origin, influenced especially by New Zealand stamp design, printed in New Zealand but printing in Europe began in 1962, coinciding with independence. Current annual output is 20 to 30 stamps a year with designs planned to appeal to collectors. The production of miniature sheets was introduced for the same reason.

Philatelic bureau GPO, Apia. **Trade sales** Crown Agents' Stamp Bureau.

WEST IRIAN
The western part of New Guinea (**area** 421,951 sq.km, **capital** Sukarnapura) which, from 1963, became part of Indonesia but remained under UN supervision until 1969. Until 1962-3 *Netherlands New Guinea*.

In 1963 Indonesian stamps issued with the overprint 'IRIAN BARAT'; later, definitives which, apart from the main name of 'REPUBLIK INDONESIA', also have the inscription 'IRIAN BARAT' or just 'IB'. A total of 42 + 6 stamps.

ANTARCTICA

ADÉLIE LAND
Antarctic sector (400,000 sq.km) between longitudes 136° and 142° E, whose coastline was discovered by Dumont d'Urville in 1840. France claimed it as its own in 1893 together with Kerguelen, the Crozet Islands, Amsterdam and St Paul. This whole territory was made subordinate to the Madagascar governor in 1924; the border of the Adélie Land sector was officially announced in 1938, and in 1954 it was made an overseas territory under the name French Southern and Antarctic Territories.

In 1948 a French scientific expedition set up the Dumont d'Urville base and used a Madagascar airmail stamp with the overprint, 'TERRE ADÉLIE/DUMONT D'URVILLE. Since 1955 stamps of the French Southern and Antarctic Territories have been used.

AUSTRALIAN ANTARCTIC TERRITORY
Antarctic sector (about 6,120,000 sq.km) between longitudes 45° and 160° E (with the exception of the French sector, which is between longitudes 136° and 142°E). In 1933 it was annexed by Great Britain and given to Australia, which formally took it over as a union territory in 1936. In 1968–9 there were post offices at Casey, Davis and Mawson stations and on Macquarrie Island.

From 1957 definitives with the name 'AUSTRALIAN ANTARCTIC TERRITORY'. These are of Australian origin — issued by the Australian postal authorities — with designs relating to the Antarctic territory in which they were issued. Stamps are not issued every year but usually at intervals of several years. They are typical stamps issued to attract collectors, their actual postal function being minimal. In the 1964–5 season, a total of 3,365 philatelic mailings were stamped at all four post offices of this Antarctic region. The stamps are also valid on Australian territory.

Philatelic bureau GPO, Melbourne, Australia.

BRITISH ANTARCTIC TERRITORY
In 1962 all the British Antarctic Territory between longitudes 20° and 80° W and south of the 60th parallel (i.e. comprising Graham Land, the South Orkneys and South Shetlands) was associated into a new colonial unit known as the British Antarctic Territory (5,425,000 sq.km). Indirect UPU membership from 1 January 1879 (as Falkland Islands).

The first stamps appeared in 1963 with the name 'BRITISH ANTARCTIC TERRITORY'. Definitives are of British origin, with the designs relating to this Antarctic region. Appropriate omnibus issues of the British Commonwealth have also appeared. While the stamps were issued with the political intention of identifying the territory as a British colony, genuine postal sales are limited. The greater revenue comes from sales to collectors.

Philatelic bureau Colonial Postmaster, GPO, Stanley, Falkland Islands. **Trade sales** Crown Agents' Stamp Bureau.

FALKLAND ISLANDS DEPENDENCIES
Territories totalling 1,700,000 sq.km (Graham Land, South Georgia, the South Orkneys, South Shetlands, South Sandwich Islands) were proclaimed dependencies of the British colony of the Falklands in 1908 and given the name Falkland Islands Dependencies. Indirect UPU membership from 1 January 1879 (Falkland Islands — a colony and dependencies comprising South Georgia and the South Sandwich Islands).

Until 1944 stamps of the Falkland Islands were valid here. After overprinted provisionals for the individual dependencies appeared in 1944, stamps with the name 'FALKLAND ISLANDS DEPENDENCIES' were issued in 1946. A total of 37 stamps of British origin (pictorial issues and British Commonwealth omnibus issues). Stamps were not issued every year.

In 1962 a new colonial unit of the British Antarctic Territory was created out of Graham Land, the South Orkneys and the South Shetlands, which has had its own stamps since

1963: although South Georgia and the South Sandwich Islands remained a Falkland dependency, the Falkland Islands Dependencies ceased to exist as a stamp-issuing country. South Georgia had its own stamps from 1963, and in 1980 these were replaced once again by stamps of the Falkland Islands Dependencies, which in that year revived its own issues with a series of 15 definitive stamps.

Philatelic bureau Colonial Postmaster, GPO, Stanley, Falkland Islands.**Trade sales** Crown Agents' Stamp Bureau.

FRENCH SOUTHERN AND ANTARCTIC TERRITORIES

The overseas territory in the Antarctic — Adélie Land (400,000 sq.km), the Indian Ocean Kerguelen Islands (6,323 sq.km), the Crozet Islands (476 sq.km), St Paul (7 sq.km) and Amsterdam (50 sq.km) — were given the joint name of the French Southern and Antarctic Territories in 1955. Direct UPU membership from 1 July 1876 (as a group of French colonies); indirect from 23 December 1977 (France).

Before issuing its own stamps, stamps of *Madagascar* were used (for part of the territory there were *Adélie Land* issues).

The first stamps were issued in 1955 as overprinted provisionals on Madagascar stamps with the name 'TERRES AUSTRALES ET ANTARCTIQUES FRANÇAISES', then definitives with the same name. Characteristic production of French origin with design subjects mostly relating to this area, and with the collectors' market in mind. Current annual output 10–15 stamps, almost half of which are airmail.

Philatelic bureau Agence des Timbres Postes d'Outre-Mer.

GRAHAM LAND

A sector of the Antarctic continent between longitudes 20° and 80° E. 1,700,000 sq.km including the Antarctic peninsula (Graham Land itself). It was incorporated in 1908 into the British Falkland Islands Dependencies, and in 1962 became part of the British Antarctic Territory.

In 1944 a single issue of 8 stamps of the Falkland Islands appeared with the overprint 'GRAHAM LAND DEPENDENCY OF' (the Falkland Islands). From 1946 the stamps of the *Falkland Islands Dependencies* were valid here, and from 1963 stamps of the *British Antarctic Territory*.

KING EDWARD VII LAND

A territory on the shore of the Ross Sea (today called Edward VII Peninsula) in the New Zealand sector, discovered in 1902 by Capt. Robert Scott. It was the first of any to have Antarctic stamps. These were the New Zealand penny stamps of 1907 carrying the overprint 'KING EDWARD VII LAND' prepared for the Shackleton Antarctic Expedition on the ship Nimrod in 1908–9. Although 24,000 stamps were produced, and there were about 2000 stamped letters, they never reached their destination of King Edward VII Land, as ice prevented the Shackleton Expedition from reaching its goal.

ROSS DEPENDENCY

The New Zealand sector (about 900,000 sq.km) of the Antarctic continent between longitudes 160° E and 150° W. Great Britain laid claim to it in 1923, and then handed it over to New Zealand who proclaimed it an overseas territory. The post office is at Scott Base where several dozen people live in the summer season. Direct UPU membership since 1 October 1907 (New Zealand, including the Ross Dependency).

The first definitives with the name 'ROSS DEPENDENCY' were issued in 1957, and since that time new issues have appeared at infrequent intervals. The stamps are produced and issued by the postal authorities of New Zealand, the designs relating to the dependency. They are bought chiefly as collector's items, as they can only be sent from the post office at Scott Base which has a very limited mail service and then only in the Antarctic summer season.

Philatelic bureau Wanganui, New Zealand.

SOUTH GEORGIA

Since 1775 the island (**area** 4,144 sq.km, **capital** Grytviken) has been British and in 1908 it became part of the Falkland Islands Dependencies. After 1962 it remained a dependency of the Falkland Islands, although it had its own stamps.

The first stamps appeared in 1944 (stamps of the Falklands had been valid previously) as overprinted provisionals on Falkland Islands stamps with the text 'SOUTH GEORGIA/ DEPENDENCY OF' (the Falkland Islands). From 1946 stamps of the Falkland Islands Dependencies were valid. In 1963 definitives were issued bearing the name 'SOUTH GEOR-GIA'. Stamp production of British origin with designs whose subjects relate to this area or are omnibus issues of the British Commonwealth. Until 1979, 76 stamps and 1 miniature sheet were issued. From 1980 the *Falkland Islands Dependencies* stamps again became valid.

SOUTH ORKNEYS

An uninhabited island group in the sub-Antarctic region (662 sq.km) which Great Britain in 1908 declared a part of the Falkland Islands Dependencies. In 1962 it was incorporated into the British Antarctic Territory.

In 1944 a single 8-stamp issue of the Falkland Islands with the overprint 'SOUTH ORK-NEYS/DEPENDENCY OF' (the Falkland Islands). From 1946 stamps of the *Falkland Islands Dependencies* were valid; from 1963, stamps of the *British Antarctic Territory*.

SOUTH SHETLANDS

An uninhabited chain of islands off the coast of Graham Land (2,300 sq.km), incorporated in 1908 into the Falkland Islands Dependencies and in 1962 becoming part of the British Antarctic Territory.

In 1944 a single 8-stamp issue of the Falkland Islands with the overprint 'SOUTH SHET-LANDS/DEPENDENCY OF' (the Falkland Islands). From 1946 stamps of the *Falkland Islands Dependencies* were valid; from 1963, stamps of the *British Antarctic Territory*.

VICTORIA LAND

A territory on the shores of the Ross Sea in the New Zealand sector discovered and named after J. C. Ross in 1841. New Zealand stamps were issued for this territory with the overprint 'VICTORIA LAND', dedicated to the second Scott Antarctic expedition (1910–12). The stamps were used until 18 January 1913.

POSTAL REGIONS

Stamps with a common name valid in the territories of several stamp-issuing countries or territories.

FRENCH COLONIES

Stamps used throughout the French colonies, which between 1859 and 1886 (and even later) extended over an area of 3,112,110 sq.km, together with stamps bearing the name 'COLONIES DE L'EMPIRE FRANÇAISE', 'EMPIRE FRANÇ.', 'REPUB. FRANÇ.', 'REPUBLIQUE FRANÇAISE COLONIES': a total of 59 stamps of French origin, almost all definitives, using the basic definitive designs of France.

Not all French colonial stamps were valid in all the French colonial territories. In Algeria and Tunisia, French issues were used until the introduction of their own stamps. The general issues of the French colonies were gradually replaced by issues for the individual colonies and territories (from 1892 stamps were issued in a common design, the difference being only in the name of the territory). Postage-due stamps for the whole French colonial territory were in use until 1908.

In 1943–4 the government of Free France in Algeria issued a certain number of stamps for use in the French overseas regions and on Corsica. They bear the inscription 'FRANCE D'OUTRE-MER' or 'RÉPUBLIQUE FRANÇAISE', so that they tend to be mistaken for stamps of France itself. These are virtually all stamps carrying a high non-postal premium for charity (in one instance with the unbelievably unbalanced figures of 1.50 F for postage + 98.50 F for charity). The real postal function of such stamps is limited, sales being largely philatelic. In 1945–64 joint postage due stamps were again issued (the word 'TAXE' shows only the postage-due function without reference to any specific colony).

ITALIAN POST OFFICES ABROAD

From 1874 there were Italian stamps with the overprint 'ESTERO' ('Abroad'). A total of 17 stamps, almost all overprinted provisionals which became invalid on 1 January 1890, when they were replaced by Italian stamps.

Issues inscribed 'Estero' were used at Italian post offices abroad, especially on the African Mediterranean coast and in the Levant, as well as in South America (Buenos Aires, Montevideo).

LEVANT

The composite name for the Eastern Mediterranean and the coastal areas of what was the former Ottoman Empire, on whose territory Austria, France, Germany, Great Britain, Italy, Russia, Poland and Romania had their own post offices and used their own stamps, particularly in the second half of the 19th century. These issues have the composite name Levant, or the name of the place where the post office was situated (e.g. Jerusalem). There were issues consisting of stamps of the home country surcharged in Turkish currency. The last foreign post offices on Turkish territory were closed under the Lausanne Treaty of 1923 but the name Levant persisted. In 1931 the Levant was listed as a member state of the UPU (composite name for Syria and the Lebanon).

During the Second World War stamps were issued on Syrian territory with the inscription 'Free French Forces — Levant'. The following postal issues (listed as independent stamp-issuing countries elsewhere in this atlas) appeared in the territory of the Levant with their own names: Athos, Beirut, Bengazi, Cavalla, Constantinople, Dardanelles, Dedeagach, Jaffa, Janina, Jerusalem, Kérassunde, Mytilene, Port Lagos, Rizeh, Salonica, Smyrna, Trebizond and Vathy. There were other post offices on the territory of the Ottoman Empire which are included in the Levant region (e.g. the Balkans).

The following postal authorities issued stamps with the composite name of Levant for their post offices in the Levant:
British: From 1905 to 1921 overprints on British stamps with the name 'LEVANT': a total of

32 overprinted provisionals. An overprinted issue with the same name (but as 'Levant') appeared in 1916 for Thessalonica and was in circulation only 14 days.

French: In 1902–3 an issue of 15 stamps was released using the design of the French colonial issue of the time and inscribed with the name 'LEVANT', the currency being in piastres. In 1902 stamps of the same design and with the same name, 'LEVANT', but with the currency shown in francs, were used in Ethiopia. In 1942, Syrian stamps had the overprint of the Free French Army with the name 'LEVANT' prior to the issue of definitives: a total of 14 stamps.

Italian: In 1908–10 2 Italian stamps were overprinted with the name 'LEVANTE'.

Polish: In 1919–21 Polish stamps were issued with the overprint 'LEVANT', intended for Polish consular postal requirements in Constantinople from whence official new printings were made. The postal validity of this issue remains in doubt. Other, similar issues are regarded as fakes.

At different times, other countries also used their own stamps, frequently with currency surcharges, for their post offices in the Levant.

PORTUGUESE COLONIES

From 1945 issues of postage-due stamps with the inscription 'IMPERIO COLONIAL PORTUGUES' were valid mainly in Portuguese possessions in Africa: a total of 9 stamps of Portuguese origin.

SPANISH OVERSEAS POSTAL AUTHORITIES (ULTRAMAR)

Spanish possessions in the Caribbean (Cuba until 1898, Puerto Rico until 1898, and the Dominican Republic from 1861 to 1865) which had a joint postal authority until the 1870s.

From 1855 definitives of Spanish origin without the name of the state but with postal and currency indications were issued until the 1860s with the word 'ULTRAMAR' ('Overseas') and continued in use until 1876. In the meantime, *Puerto Rico* became an independent stamp-issuing country, *Cuba* issued its own stamps, and the *Dominican Republic,* too, began to issue its stamps independently. Some of these stamps were also valid in the Philippines, on Spanish islands in the Pacific and in Spanish Guinea.

THURN AND TAXIS POSTAL REGION

The Thurn and Taxis postal system was among the most significant in Europe. In 1625, for example, it had 20,000 couriers. In the middle of the 19th century the Thurn and Taxis family provided postal services in Germany, even to those states which had their own postal administration, with linking postal services throughout much of Europe. In accordance with provisions of the Vienna Congress, the German states within the Thurn and Taxis system were divided into two groups with different currencies:

North German district with Groschen currency: Hessen-Kassel, Saxony-Weimar-Eisenach, Gotha in the Saxe-Coburg-Gotha Dukedom, Lippe-Schaumburg and Lippe-Detmold, Reuss-Greiz and Reuss-Gera, Schwarzburg-Sondershausen, Camburg in the Saxe-Meiningen Dukedom and the postal authorities in the Hanseatic towns of Hamburg, Bremen and Lübeck.

South German district with Kreuzer currency: Hessen-Darmstadt, Nassau, Saxe-Meiningen, Coburg in the Saxe-Coburg-Gotha Dukedom, Hessen-Homburg, Schwarzburg-Rudolstadt, Hohenzollern and the free town of Frankfurt-am-Main.

The first stamps in 1852 were definitives with the name 'THURN UND TAXIS': a total of 54 stamps, virtually all definitives (made in Frankfurt), numeral designs, printed in either Groschen or Kreuzer currency. Prussia eventually purchased the entire Thurn and Taxis postal system whose stamps became invalid on 30 June 1867. They were replaced by Prussian stamps (Prussia then had to issue stamps in kreuzer currency for the newly acquired postal regions with kreuzer currency). From 1868 these were then replaced by the stamps of the North German Postal Confederation. The periods of validity of stamps of the former German states were as follows:

Territory	Period of Validity	Year of last issue
Baden	1 May 1851 — 31 December 1871	1868
Bavaria	1 November 1849 — 30 June 1920	1920
Bergedorf	1 November 1861 — 31 December 1867	1867
Bremen	10 April 1855 — 21 December 1867	1867
Brunswick	1 January 1852 — 23 December 1867	1865
Hamburg	1 January 1859 — 31 December 1867	1867
Hannover	1 December 1850 — 31 October 1866	1864
Heligoland	March 1867 — 9 August 1890	1890
Lübeck	1 January 1859 — 31 December 1867	1865
Mecklenburg-Strelitz	1 October 1864 — 31 December 1867	1867
Mecklenburg-Schwerin	1 July 1856 — 31 December 1867	1867
Oldenburg	5 January 1852 — 21 December 1867	1867
Prussia	15 November 1850 — 31 December 1867	1867
Saxony	29 June 1850 — 31 December 1867	1867
North German Postal District	1 January 1868 — 31 December 1871 (and/or 31 December 1874)	1869
Schleswig-Holstein	5 November 1850 — 31 December 1867	1866
Thurn and Taxis Postal System	1 January 1852 — 30 June 1867	1867
Württemberg	15 October 1851 — 31 March 1920	1920
Issues for Alsace-Lorraine and the occupied parts of France	10 September 1870 — 31 December 1871	1870

INTERNATIONAL ORGANIZATIONS

Certain international organizations have their own postage stamps issued on the basis of agreements with the postal authorities of the states on whose territory their headquarters are located. Strictly speaking, the stamps are to pay for the mailings of these international organizations, and they could actually be regarded as 'official' stamps. However, it has also become customary for the public to have access to these stamps for paying postage on letters sent from the premises of the particular international organization (usually in the main administrative building) where there is either a post office or, at least, a special mailing box. Mailings with these stamps can be addressed to anywhere within the framework of the world postal services. UPU membership is assumed as an extension of the membership of the postal administration within whose boundaries the international organization is situated. These postal services operate by agreement of the countries concerned with the international organization. The stamps of these institutions normally remain in circulation for several years. An exception is the United Nations Organization which issues stamps in the USA, Austria and Switzerland and which, by contrast to other institutions, publishes numerous stamps, largely for the collectors' market.

COUNCIL OF EUROPE
Stamps are issued for use at the headquarters of the Council of Europe in Strasbourg by agreement with the French postal authorities and bear the inscription 'CONSEIL DE L'EUROPE' as well as the words 'RÉPUBLIQUE FRANÇAISE '. In 1958 overprints on French stamps appeared as the first issue, followed by definitives (showing flags and the building of this institution), the latter having all the characteristics of French production. Stamps are issued only occasionally, always in French currency.The printing for the first issue was a million.

EUROPEAN OFFICE OF THE UNITED NATIONS ORGANIZATION
Issues of the European Office of the UN in Geneva appeared with the agreement of the Swiss postal authorities. From 1950 at first as an overprint on Swiss stamps, reading 'NATIONS UNIES OFFICE EUROPÉEN'. From 1955 definitives with the inscription 'NATIONS UNIES' and the country name 'HELVETIA'. A total of 39 stamps of Swiss origin with symbolic motifs and, in 1960, a stamp featuring the Palace of Nations in Geneva. All are in Swiss currency. Printings of the first issues ran from 26,000 to 274,000 pieces (the highest denomination being 10 Swiss francs). Later issues ranged from 60,000 to 200,000 of each stamp. From 1969 they were replaced by *United Nations* stamps but with the currency given in Swiss francs.

INTERNATIONAL COURT OF JUSTICE
From 1934, Netherlands stamps with the overprint 'COUR PERMANENTE DE JUSTICE INTERNATIONALE'. From 1950, definitives bearing the words 'COUR INTERNATIONALE DE JUSTICE' and 'NEDERLAND'. These were issued for use by the International Court of Justice in The Hague in agreement with the Netherlands postal authorities. The stamps have a numerical design or they depict the Palace of Peace in The Hague; later they carried the portrait of Queen Juliana. All are in Netherlands currency.

INTERNATIONAL EDUCATION OFFICE
In agreement with the Swiss postal authorities, Swiss stamps were issued in 1944 for the International Education Office with the overprint 'COURRIER DU BUREAU INTERNATIONAL D'ÉDUCATION'. In 1948 the overprint became 'BUREAU INTERNATIONAL D'ÉDUCATION'. In 1958 definitives of Swiss origin were printed with this same inscription and with the name 'HELVETIA': a total of 48 stamps, chiefly of overprinted provisionals alongside symbolic designs, all in Swiss currency. The printing of the first issue was 37,000 sets but among the definitives are sets totalling 170,000.

INTERNATIONAL LABOUR OFFICE
By agreement with the Swiss postal authorities, Swiss stamps were issued for the International Labour Office (ILO) between 1923 and 1950, variously overprinted 'S.d.N. BUREAU INTERNATIONAL DU TRAVAIL', 'SERVICE DU BUREAU INTERNATIONAL DU TRAVAIL' and 'COURRIER DU BUREAU INTERNATIONAL DU TRAVAIL'. In 1956, definitives appeared similarly inscribed and with the name 'HELVETIA'. The designs symbolised various forms of labour, as well as a view of the ILO building in Geneva: all in Swiss currency. Printings of the first issue ranged from 400,000 to 9,600 of each stamp with the highest value at 10 Swiss francs.

INTERNATIONAL REFUGEES ORGANIZATION
In 1950, Swiss stamps with the overprint 'ORGANISATION INTERNATIONALE POUR LES RÉFUGIÉS' were issued for the International Refugees Organization in Switzerland: a total of 8 stamps in Swiss currency. The printing comprised 24,000 sets.

INTERNATIONAL TELECOMMUNICATIONS UNION
By agreement with the Swiss postal authorities, since 1958, definitives of Swiss origin with the inscription 'UNION INTERNATIONALE DES TELECOMMUNICATIONS' and 'HELVETIA' have been appearing for use by the International Telecommunications Union (UIT) at its office in Switzerland. The designs depict various symbols of communications and the building of the institution itself in Geneva. All are in Swiss currency. For the first issue, the printing was 188,000 sets.

LEAGUE OF NATIONS
Between 1922 and 1947 Swiss stamps with the overprint 'SOCIÉTÉ DES NATIONS' and also 'SERVICE DE LA SOCIÉTÉ DES NATIONS' or 'COURRIER DE LA SOCIÉTÉ DES NATIONS' were used for the headquarters of the League of Nations in Geneva. A total of 90 overprinted provisionals. Until 1944 mint stamps could not be sold to the public or collectors.

UNESCO
By agreement with the French postal authorities, since 1961, definitives of French origin with the inscription 'UNESCO' and 'RÉPUBLIQUE FRANÇAISE' have appeared for use by the United Nations Educational, Scientific and Cultural Organization (UNESCO) headquarters in Paris. The activities and objectives of this institution are expressed symbolically in the designs. All are in French currency.

UNITED NATIONS ORGANIZATION
In 1951 the postal authority of the United Nations Organization (UNO), by agreement with the US postal authorities, began to issue its own postage stamps (in US currency). The stamps are valid on mail posted in the UN building in New York. Quite exceptionally, these stamps were also valid for use in the UN building in San Francisco as part of the celebrations to mark the 20th anniversary of the establishment of the United Nations and, by agreement with the Canadian postal authorities, they were valid for use in the UN pavilion at the World's Fair in Montreal in 1967, when they were inscribed, exceptionally, in Canadian currency. From 1969, by agreement with the Swiss postal authorities, UN stamps are also issued in Swiss currency and are valid on mail posted in the UN building in Geneva. The same happened in 1979, by agreement with the Austrian postal authorities, when UN stamps in Austrian currency were issued. These are valid for use in the UN buildings in Vienna. All are accepted internationally.

Although UN stamps are, in effect, 'officials' to pay for mailings of the organization, visitors to the United Nations premises can use these stamps for their mail if it is sent from the post offices within the buildings.

The 1951 definitives issued in New York are inscribed with the name United Nations in the official languages of the organization (English, French, Russian, Chinese and Spanish).

Most of the commemorative issues from New York have only 'UNITED NATIONS' and in Geneva 'NATIONS UNIES'. The issues from Vienna, which began in 1979, are inscribed 'VEREINTE NATIONEN'. Stamp output has three purposes: stamps for postal use; stamps to publicize the various agencies of the United Nations; and stamps for collectors. The design is expertly carried out, especially when dealing with stamps which emphasize the importance of the UN's individual institutions. They often stress the organization's worldwide efforts, as well as expressing important social and human themes symbolically. Many outstanding international stamp designers have contributed to its stamps including, for instance, Haman (Denmark), Perrot (France), El Mekki (Tunisia), Rashid ud Din (Pakistan), Plowitz (USA), Hamori (Australia), Medina Medina (Uruguay) and Helguera (Mexico). The best stamp printers in the individual member-states have contributed to producing the stamps. Annual output is about 30 stamps (now in three currencies). Although basically the stamps are in a common design for all three issues, this is not a hard and fast rule, and the UN postal authorities in New York, Geneva and Vienna at times issue stamps individually designed for specific occasions.

Philatelic bureaux United Nations Postal Administration, United Nations, New York; United Nations Postal Administration, Palais des Nations, Geneva; Postverwaltung der Vereinten Nationen, Vienna. In addition, UN stamps, according to agreements with individual postal authorities, are sold at the official rate of exchange in a large number of UN member-states (usually at philatelic windows of the main post offices).

UNIVERSAL POSTAL UNION
By agreement with the Swiss postal authorities, since 1957, definitives of Swiss origin with the inscription 'UNION POSTALE UNIVERSELLE' and the name 'HELVETIA' have been issued for the Universal Postal Union whose headquarters are in Berne, Switzerland. Symbolic designs interpret the international importance of this organization. All stamps are in Swiss currency.

WORLD HEALTH ORGANIZATION
By agreement with the Swiss postal authorities, Swiss stamps with the overprint 'ORGANISATION MONDIALE DE LA SANTÉ' first appeared in 1948 to be followed by definitives of Swiss origin with the same text and the name 'HELVETIA'. They were issued for use by the World Health Organization (WHO). The definitives bear the emblem of the World Health Organization, the staff of Aesculapius superimposed on the globe. All are in Swiss currency. The first issue was in a printing of 100,000.

WORLD METEOROLOGICAL ORGANIZATION
By agreement with the Swiss postal authorities, definitives of Swiss origin first appeared in 1956 bearing the name 'ORGANISATION METEOROLOGIQUE MONDIALE' and 'HELVETIA' and continue to be used by the World Meteorological Organization in Switzerland. The stamp designs are symbolic of the world's weather. The first issue was in a printing of 173,000 stamps. All are in Swiss currency.

LOCAL OR FAKE STAMP ISSUES

A number of stamps appear on the collectors' market which do not fulfil a postal function in the manner stipulated by the Universal Postal Union, the reason being that their publishers normally do not provide any postal services and have no postal sovereignty. True postal services do not accept mail franked with such stamps. Such fake stamps, with all the external features of postal stamps, are issued most often for the collectors' market. They are placed directly on this market and profits derive from the difference between the cost of producing the stamps and the nominal value given on them, for which no postal services are rendered. Fake stamps are often brought out by resistance movements, governments in exile, or separatist organizations, which have no postal sovereignty but use the stamps for political propaganda. The following list of publishers of such fake stamps could be further added to; a critical approach would include here a large number of individual stamps, issues and entire 'stamp producing countries' registered in world stamp catalogues. We have drawn attention to these in individual items of this atlas.

Abd El-Kuri
Ajman
Alderney (before 1983)
Ambergri
Atlantis
Azadind
Baldonie
Ile Barbre
Bardsey Is.
Isla de Bernera
Bokhara
Blukubade te Sarof
Brechou (Brecqhou)
Bretagne
Bulgarska carska pochta
Bumbunga Province
Caldey Is.
Calf of Man
Canna
Carn Iar
Celestia
Chan
Christmas Islands (in Kiribati)
Prov. de Cienfuegos
Clipperton
Counani
Crevichon
Cymru
Dahlak Islands
Commonwealth of Dalziel
Exilregierung der
   Freien Stadt Danzig
Davaar
Dhofar
Federation of Doutherty
   and Hesperies Is.
Drake's Is.
Eynhallow
Poste Eritrea liberta

Fauconnière
Feripäga
Freedomland
Free Territory
   of Freedom
Fryslan
Tierra del Fuego
Islas Galapagos
Great-Barrier Is.
Gugh Is.
Herm
Estado Hesperio
Hilbre
Government of Himriyya
Hutt River Province Principality
Isö
Jethou
Karema
Karen State
Kegelmugel
Khalistan
Kigoma
Rep. Koneuwe
Lihou
Rep. Lucconia
Lundy
Malakote
Republik Maluku Selatan
Marshall Islands (before 1984)
Republic of Mevu
Rep. Morac
Moresnet
Moschopolis
Island of Muck
Mustique Island
Nagaland
Republic of New Atlantis
Sultanate (of)
   Ocussi Ambeno

Oman Imamate State
State of Oman
Pabay
Pidgeon Is.
Queen Maud Land
Rainbow Creek
Rattlesnake Island
Redonda
Romania Posta
Insulo de la Rozoj
St. Kilda
St. Thomas – Porto Rico
Sanda
Sark
Sea Islands
Sealand
Sedang
Shuna

Skye
Pošta Slovenská
Soay
Sovrano Militare Ordine
  di Malta
Spitsbergen
Staffa
Stroma
Summer Islands
Principality of Thomond
Tabora
Tibet
Toga
Principauté de Trinidad
Vaikos
Vikingland
Waikoa Island
Zulia

INDEX

INDEX OF STAMP-ISSUING COUNTRIES AND STAMP INSCRIPTIONS

The index contains the names of all stamp-issuing countries found in the text and on the maps, as well as the actual wording – given in *italics* and with cross-references – of all stamp inscriptions quoted in the text. Figures in *italics* indicate page numbers and those in ordinary script map numbers. Thus, the country names, which reflect the titles of the text entries, are normally followed first by the page number in *italics* referring to the text and then by the map number (not page number) in ordinary script referring to the maps. Major maps are divided into horizontal sections, indicated by a letter, and vertical sections, indicated by a number, and sometimes, for reasons of space, a number (given in brackets in the index) is used to show the location of the country on the map instead of the name itself, which is given in a key by the side of the map. Thus, 'Brunei, *170*, 31B2, 37B2(8), 48B2' means that the textual description of Brunei is on page 170 and that the maps showing the country are numbers 31, 37 and 48, where in each instance the country's location is in horizontal section B and vertical section 2, but on map number 37 it is indicated on the map by a figure 8. '*Afghan Postage* see Afghanistan' means that Afghan Postage is the actual wording of a stamp inscription and that further details will be found under Afghanistan.

A

A&T see Annam and Tonkin
Abu Dhabi, *165*, 36
Abu Dhabi see Abu Dhabi
Acambaro, 76
Açores see Azores
Adélie Land, *312*, 97
Aden, *165*, 41
Aden see Aden; Kathiri; Qu'aiti
Administration of Western Thrace see
    Western Thrace
Afghani Post see
    Afghanistan
Afghanistan, *165*, 31 B1, 37 B1, 48 B1
Afghanistan see Afghanistan
Afghan Postage see Afghanistan
Africa see Portuguese Africa
Africa Occidental Española see
    Spanish West Africa
Africa Orientale Italiana see Italian East
    Africa
Afrique Équatoriale Française see
    Chad, French Equatorial Africa;
    Gabon; Middle Congo, Oubangi-Shari
Afrique Équatoriale Gabon see
    Gabon
Afrique Occidentale Française see
    Dahomey; French West Africa; Ivory
    Coast; Senegal
Aguascalientes, 76
Aitutaki, *298*, 88 B2, 95 B2
Aitutaki see Aitutaki
Ajman, *165*, 36 (1)
Ajman see Ajman
Ajman I and its dependencies see
    Ajman
Åland Islands, *108*, 2 A1
Åland see Åland Islands
Alaouites (Latakia), *166*, 45, 46
Alaouites see Alaouites
Albania, *108*, 2 B2, 13 B2, 16, 17 B2,
    22 B2, 23
Albania see Albania; Scutari
Alderney, *109*, 4
Alderney, Bailiwick of Guernsey see
    Alderney
Alexandretta (Hatay), *166*, 46
Alexandria, *219*, 55 A2, 60 A2
Alexandrie see Alexandria

Algeria, *219*, 50 A1, 55 A1
Algérie see Algeria
Allemagne Duitschland see Germany
Allenstein, *109*, 17 A2, 18
Allied Military Postage – Italy see Italy
Alsace, *109*, 13 B1
Alwar, 166, 49 (7)
America Central see El Salvador
AMG FTT see Trieste
AMG VG see Trieste, Venezia Giulia
*Amministrazione Militare A. J. Territorio
    Libero di Trieste* see Trieste
Am Post Deutschland see Germany
Amur Province, *166*, 47
*Amurskaya Oblastnaya Poshtovaya
    Marka* see Amur Province
Ancash, 85
Andorra, *110*, 2 B1 (4), 13 B1 (11),
    17 B1 (9)
Andorra see Andorra
Andorre/Andorra see Andorra
Andorre see Andorra
Angola, *219*, 50 B1-2, 55 B1-2, 60 B1-2
    73 B1
Angola see Angola
Angra, *220*, 54
Angra see Angra
Anguilla, *271*, 74a, 77
Anguilla see Anguilla
Anjouan, *220*, 52, 56
Annam, 48 B2
Annam and Tonkuin, *166*
Annobón, 60 B1, 61
Antigua, 77
Antigua see Antigua and Barbuda
Antigua and Barbuda, *271*, 74a, 77
Antioquia, *271*, 87
A.O. see German East Africa
Apa see Rarotonga
Arab Government of the East see
    Transjordan
Arabian Switzerland see Lebanon
Arabie Soudite see Saudi Arabia
Arbe (Rab), *110*, 20
Arbe see Arbe
Archipel des Comores see
    Comoro Islands
A.R. Egypt see Egypt
Arequipa, *272*, 84 A1, 85
Arequipa see Arequipa

Argentina, *272*, 83, 84
Argentina see Argentina
Armenia, *166*, 46, 47(2)
Army Post Egypt see Egypt
Ascension, *220*, 50B1, 55B1
Ascension see Ascension
Ascension Island see Ascension
Athos (Afon, Agion, Oros), *110*, 22B2, 23
Aunus (Olonetz), *110*, 17A2, 47
Aunus see Aunus
Australia, *298*, 88B1, 95B1
Australia see Australia
Australian Antarctic Territory, *312*, 101A-B2
Australian Antarctic Territory see Australian Antarctic Territory
Austria, *110*, 1(10), 2B1, 17B1, 22B1-2, 23, 27B1-2
Ava Pene see Aitutaki
Azerbaijan, *167*, 47(3)
Azores, *220*, 54

B

B see Bangkok
Bacska, 17B2
Baden, *112*, 11, 25, 27B1
Baden see Baden
B.A. Eritrea see Eritrea
Baghdad, *167*
Baghdad in British Occupation see Baghdad
Bahamas, *272*, 74, 78B2
Bahamas see Bahamas
Bahawalpur, *167*, 49
Bahawalpur see Bahawalpur
Bahrain, *167*, 31B1(6), 36, 37B1(9)
Bahrain see Bahrain
Bailiwick of Guernsey see Guernsey
Bakinskago GPTO see Baku
Bakinskoj Ok see Baku
Baku, *168*, 47
Bamra, *168*, 49(8)
Bamra see Bamra
Banat, 17B2
Banat-Bacska, *112*
Bánát Bácska see Banat-Bacska
Bangkok, *168*, 48B2
Bangladesh, *168*, 31B2

Bangla Desh see Bangladesh
Bangladesh Libertad see *Bangladesh*
Baranya, *112*, 17B1(11)
Baranya see Baranya
Barbados, *273*, 74, 77, 78B2, 87
Barbados see Barbados
Barbuda, *273*, 77
Barbuda see Barbuda
Barranquilla, 87
Barwani, *168*, 49(36)
Barwani State see Barwani
Basle (Bâle, Basel), *112*, 1(4)
Basle Dove see Basle
B.A. Somalia see Somalia
Basutoland, *220*, 55B2
Basutoland see Basutoland; Lesotho
Bata see Spanish Mainland Guinea
BA Tripolitania see Tripolitania
Batum, *168*, 47
Batumi Post see Batum
Batum. Ob. see Batum
Batum. Obl. see Batum
Bavaria (Bayern), *112*, 1(7), 17B1, 22B1, 25
Bayern see Bavaria
B.C.A. see British Central Africa
BDPTO Zelaya see Zelaya
Bechuanaland, *221*, 55B2, 59, 60B2
Bechuanaland Protectorate see Bechuanaland; British Bechuanaland
Began see Bhopal
Beirut, *168*, 45
Belgian-Congo, *221*, 55B2
Belgien see Belgium
Belgique see Belgium
Belgique België see Belgium
Belgium, *113*, 1(6), 2B1, 13B1, 17B1, 19, 22A1, 27A1
Belize, *273*, 74
Belize see Belize
Benadir, *221*, 60A2, 67
Benadir see Benadir
Bengasi, *221*, 60A2, 65
Bengasi see Bengasi
Benin, *222*, 50A1, 70
Bénin see Benin
Bergedorf, *113*, 25, 29
Bergedorf see Bergedorf
Berlin, *114*, 11, 15

328

331

East India, *175,* 48B1
East India see East India
East of Jordan see Transjordan
Eastern China, *175,* 43
Eastern Karelia, *122,* 13A2
Eastern Rumelia, *122,* 22B2
Eastern Saxony, *122,* 11
Eastern Silesia, *122,* 17B2(5), 18, 21
Eastern Szechwan, 42
Ecuador, *281,* 84A1, 85
Ecuador see Ecuador
E.E.F. see Palestine
Eesti see Estonia
Eesti Post see Estonia
Eesti Vabarik see Estonia
EE. UU. de CIE.S. del T see Tolima
EE UU de Venezuela see
   Venezuela
EFM see Algeria
Egeo see Rhodes and the Dodecanese
   Islands
Egypt, *230,* 45, 50A2, 55A2, 60A2, 73A2
Egypt see Egypt; United Arab Republic
   – Syria
Égypte see Egypt
Egypt Postage see Egypt
Eire see Ireland
Ell see Greece
Ellan Vannin see Isle of Man
Ellas see Crete; Greece
Ellice Islands, 95A2
Elobey, Annobón and Corisco, *230,*
   60B1(3), 61
Elobey, Annobon y Corisco see Elobey,
   Annobon and Corisco
El Salvador, *282,* 74, 78B2(6)
El Salvador see El Salvador
Elsass see Alsace
Empire Centrafricain see Central
   African Republic
Empire Franc see France
Empire Franç see French Colonies
Empire Francais see France
Emp. Ottoman see Ottoman Empire
Equatorial Guinea, *231,* 50A1
E.R.I. see Orange Free State and
   Orange River Colony
ERI see Transvaal
Eritrea, *231,* 55A2, 60A2, 67
Eritrea see Eritrea

E.S de Antioquia see Antioquia
ES de Panama see Panama
España see Fernando Poo; Ifni; Spain;
   Spanish Sahara
Estado see Tolima
Estado da Guiné-Bissau see
   Guinea-Bissau
Estado da India see Portuguese India
Estado Maturin see Maturin
Estado (or Correos) de Bolivar see
   Bolivar
Estados Unidos de Colombia see
   Colombia
*Estados Unidos de Colombia/Estado
   Soberano de Santander* see
   Santander
Estados Unidos de Nueva Granada
   see Granada Federation
Estero see Argentina; Eritrea; Italian
   Post Office Abroad; Uruguay
Estland-Eesti see Estonia
Estonia, *123,* 17A2, 18
Etablissements de l'Inde see
   French India
Etablissements de l'Oceanie see
   French Oceanic Settlements
Etablissements Français Dans l'Inde
   see French Indla
État Algérien see Algeria
État Autonome du Sudkasai see South
   Kasai
État Comorien see Comoro Islands
État du Cameroun see Cameroun
État du Katangallnchi Ya Katanga see
   Katanga
État Francais see France
État Indépendant du Congo see Congo
   (Kinshasa)
Ethiopia, *231,* 50A2, 55A2, 60A2, 67
Ethiopie see Ethiopia
Etiopia, Poste Coloniali Italiane see
   Ethiopia
Ets Francs de l'Oceanie see French
   Oceanic Settlements
E.U. de Colombia see Colombia
Eupen, *123,* 17B1, 19
Eupen see Eupen
Eupen and Malmédy, *123*
Eupen & Malmédy see Eupen and
   Malmédy

G

G. see Griqualand West
Gab see Gabon
Gabon, *235*, 50B1, 55B1, 60B1
Gabon see Gabon
Gabon-Congo see Gabon
Gambia, *235*, 50A1, 55A1, 60A1, 73A1
Gambia see Gambia
Gambia Cameos see Gambia
Garazon, 87
Gdańsk see Danzig
G.D. de Luxembourg see Luxembourg
G.E.A. see German East Africa
General Gouvernement (East) see
    Poland: General Gouvernement
General Gouvernement see Poland:
    General Gouvernement
Geneva, *126*, 1(3)
Genève see Geneva
Gen.-Gouv. Warschau see Poland:
    General Gouvernement Warschau
Georgia, *177*, 46, 47(1)
German Austria, *126*
German Democratic Republic, *126*,
    2A-B1
German East Africa, *236*, 60B2
German Military Command Areas, *127*
German New Guinea, *301*, 95A1
German South-West Africa, *236*, 59,
    60B1
Germany, *127*, 13B1-2, 16, 17A-B1,
    18, 19, 22A1-2, 27
Germany, French Occupation Zone,
    128, 11
Germany, Soviet Occupation Zone,
    128, 11
Gerskaya Soviet Socialist Republic see
    Mountain Republic
Gerusalemme see Jerusalem
Ghadamès, *236*, 65
Ghadamès Territoire Militaire see
    Ghadamès
Ghana, *236*, 50A1
Ghana see Ghana
Gibraltar, *128*, 2B1, 13B1, 17B1, 22B1
Gibraltar see Gibraltar
Gilbert and Ellice Islands, *301*
Gilbert & Ellice Islands see Gilbert and
    Ellice Islands

Gilbert & Ellice Protectorate see Gilbert
    and Ellice Islands
Gilbert Islands, *301*, 95A2
Gilbert Islands see Gilbert Islands
Gjirokastër, 22a
Gold Coast, *237*, 55A1, 60A1, 70, 73
Gold Coast see Gold Coast
Golfe de Bénin see Benin
Golfo de Guinea see Spanish Territory
    of the Gulf of Guinea
G.P.E. see Guadeloupe
Granada Federation, *283*, 87
Grand Duché de Luxembourg see
    Luxembourg
Grande Comore see Great Comoro
Grand Liban see Lebanon
Graham Land, *313*, 102, 103
Graham Land Dependency of see
    Graham Land
Great Britain and Northern Ireland,
    129, 1(1), 2A1, 13A1, 17A1
    22A1, 27A1
Great Comoro (Grande Comore), *237*
    52, 56
Greater Lebanon see Lebanon
Greece, *130*, 2B2, 13B2, 16, 17B2,
    22B2, 23, 27B2
Greece see Ionian Islands
Greek Administration see Greece;
    Icaria; Northern Epirus; Rhodes and
    the Dodecanese Islands
Greek Chimara see Northern Epirus
Greek Occupation of Mytilene see
    Mytilene
Greenland, *283*, 75A2, 78A2
Grenada, *283*, 74, 77, 77a, 87
Grenada see Grenada
Grenada/Grenadines see Grenadines of
    Grenada
Grenadines see Grenadines of Grenada
Grenadines of see Grenadines of Saint
    Vincent
Grenadines of Grenada, *283*, 77a
Grenadines of Grenada see Grenadines
    of Grenada
Grenadines of Saint Vincent, *284*, 77a
Grenadines of St. Vincent see
    Grenadines of Saint Vincent
GRI see German New Guinea;
    Samoa

335

Griqualand West, *237,* 59, 60 B2 (7), 73 B2 (1)
G.R.Mafia see Mafia
Grønland see Greenland
Grossdeutsches Reich see Bohemia and Moravia; Germany; Poland: General Gouvernement
G.S.S.R. see Montain Republic
Guadalajara, 76
Guadeloupe, *284,* 77, 78 B2
Guadeloupe (et dépendances) see Guadeloupe
Guam, *301,* 95 A1
Guam see Guam
Guam Guard see Guam
Guanacaste, *284,* 86
Guanacaste see Guanacaste
Guatemala, *284,* 74, 78 B2
Guatemala see Guatemala
Guayana, *285,* 87
Guaymas, 76
Guernsey, *130,* 2 B1, 4, 13 B1 (1)
Guernsey see Alderney; Guernsey
Guernsey Bailiwick see Guernsey
Guiné see Portuguese Guinea
Guiné-Bissau see Guinea-Bissau
Guinea, *237,* 50 A1
Guinea see Spanish Territory of the Guinea
Guinea-Bissau, *238,* 50 A1
Guinea Contial Española see Spanish Mainland Guinea
Guinea Continental see Spanish Mainland Guinea
Guinea Española see Spanish Guinea; Spanish Mainland Guinea; Spanish Territory of the Gulf of Guinea
Guinée/Afrique Occidentale Française see French Guinea
Guinée Française see French Guinea
Guyana, *285,* 83 A1-2, 87
Guyana see Guyana
Guyana, South America see Guyana
Guyane see French Guiana
Guyane Française see French Guiana
Guy. Franç. see French Guiana
G.W. see Griqualand West
Gwalior, *177,* 49
Gwalior see Gwalior

H

H see Schleswig-Holstein
Haiti, *285,* 74, 78 B2 (2)
Hamburg, *131,* 25, 29, 30
Hamburg see Hamburg
Hamilton-Bermuda see Bermuda
Hannover see Hanover
Hanover (Hannover), *131,* 1(14), 25
Hatay, *178*
Hatay Devleti see Hatay
Haute Volta see Upper Volta
Hawaii, *301,* 95 A2
Hawaii see Hawaii
Hawaiian Islands see Hawaii
Hawaiian Postage see Hawaii
Hedjaz Nedjde see Hejaz and Nejd
H.E.H. The Nizam's Govt. Postage see Hyderabad
Heilungkiang and Kirin, *178,* 42
Hejaz, *178,* 45, 48
Hejaz and Nejd, *178,* 48
Heligoland, *131,* 25, 27 A1
Heligoland see Heligoland
Hellas see Grece
Helvetia see European Office of the United Nations Organization; International Education Office; International Labour Office; International Telecommunications Union; Switzerland; Universal Postal Union; World Heath Organization; World Meterorological Organization
Helyi levél see Hungary
Herzegovina, 23
Herzogth. Holstein see Holstein
Herzogth. Schleswig see Schleswig
Hessen-Darmstadt, 25 (2)
Hessen-Hamburg, 25 (3)
Hessen-Kassel, 25 (1)
H.H. Nawab Shah Jahan Begam see Bhopal
H.I. & U.S. see Hawaii
Himara, 22a
HK Jordan see Jordan
H.M. Commissioner in Anguilla see Anguilla
Hohenzollern, 25 (14)
Hoi-Hao (Chai-Kcheu), *178,* 42
Hoi-Hao see Hoi-Hao

Holkar, *178,* 49(20)
Holkar State see Holkar
Holland see Netherlands
Holstein, *132*
Honda, 87
Honduras, *285,* 74, 78B2, 86
Honduras see Honduras
Hong Kong, *178,* 31B2, 37B2, 44, 48B2
Hongkong see Hong Kong
Hopeh (Hopei), *179,* 44
Horta, *238,* 54
Horta see Horta
Hrvatska see Croatia
Hrvatska SHS see Croatia
HRZGL Post FRM see Holstein
*HT Sénégal-Niger/Afrique Occidentale
    Française* see Upper Senegal and
    Niger
Hungary, *132,* 2B1-2, 13B1-2, 16,
    17B1-2, 18, 22B2, 23a, 27B2
Hyderabad, *179,* 49

I

IB see West Irian
Icaria, *133,* 23
Iceland, *133,* 2A1, 13A1, 17A1
Idar, *179,* 49(34)
Idar State Postage see Idar
Ierusalem see Jerusalem
Ifni, *238,* 55A1
Ifni see Ifni
Île de la Réunion see Réunion
Ile Rouad see Rouad Island
Iles Wallis et Futuna see Wallis and
    Futuna Islands
Imperial British East Africa Company
    see British East Africa
Imperial Chinese Post see China
Imperial Japanese Government
    see Sarawak
Imperial Japanese Post see Japan
Imperial Korean Post see Korea
Imperio Colonial Portugues see
    Portuguese Colonies
Imperio Colonial Portugues – Porteado
    see Portuguese Africa
Imperio Mexicano see Mexico
Independente see Tuvalu

Independent Anguilla see Anguilla
India, *179,* 31B1, 37B1-2, 48B1-2, 49
India see India
India Port. see Portuguese India
Indo-Chine see French Indochina
Indonesia, *180,* 31B2, 37B2, 88A1
Indonesia see Indonesia
Indore, *180,* 49
Indore State see Indore
Inhambane, *238,* 57, 60B2
Inhambane see Inhambane
Inini, *286,* 84A2
Interinsular Postage see Bahamas
International Court of Justice, *318*
International Education Office, *318*
International Labour Office, *319*
International Refugees Organization,
    319
International Telecommunications
    Union, *319*
Ionian Government see Ionian Island
Ionian Islands, *133,* 13B2, 16, 23
Ionikon Kratos see Ionian Islands
Ipeiros see Northern Epirus
Iraklion (Candia), *134,* 23
Iraklion see Iraklion
Iran, *181,* 31A-B1, 33, 37A-B1
Iraq, *181,* 31A-B1, 31b, 33,
    37A-B1, 46
Iraq see Iraq
Iraq in British Occupation see Iraq
Ireland (Eire), *134,* 1A1, 13A1, 17A1
Irian Barat see West Irian
Isla de Cuba see Cuba
Islamic Republic of Pakistan see
    Pakistan
Ísland see Iceland
Isle of Man, *134,* 2A1
Isle of Man see Isle of Man
Isole Italiane dell Egeo see Rhodes and
    Dodecanese Islands
Isole Jonie see Ionian Islands
Israel, *181,* 31A1(3), 31b, 37A1(3), 38
Israel see Israel
Istra see Istria and the Slovenian Coast
*Istra, Slovensko Primorje/Istria, Littorale
    Sloveno* see Istria and the Slovenian
    Coast
Istria and the Slovenian Coast, *134,* 10
Itä Karjala see Eastern Karelia

Kingdom of Libya see Libya
Kingdom of Saudi Arabia see Saudi
   Arabia
Kingdom of the Serbs, Croats and
   Slovenes, *136*, 17B2(16)
King Edward VII Land, *313*, 100
King Edward VII Land see
   King Edward VII Land
Kionga, *241*, 57(2)
Kionga see Kionga
Kiribati, *302*, 88A2
Kiribati see Kiribati
Kishangarh, *186*, 49(22)
Kishangarh State see Kishangarh
Kishengarh see Kishangarh
Kitaj see China
*K.K. Österr. Post im Fürstentum
   Liechtenstein* see Liechtenstein
K.K. Post Stempel see Austria
Klaipéda see Memel
Klaipéda (Memel) see Memel
Korcě see Korytza
Korçe Republika Shqipetare see Korytza
Korea, *186*, 48A-B2
Korea see Korea
Korean People's Democratic Republic,
   187, 31A2, 37A2
Korean People's Democratic Republic
   see Korean People's Democratic
   Republic
Korean Post see Korea
Korean Republic (South Korea), *187*
   31B2, 37A-B2
Koritza see Northern Epirus
Korytza (Korytzan Republic), *137*,
   17B2, 22a
Kotor, *137*, 13B1, 16
Kouang-Tchéou-Wan, *187*, 42, 48B2
Kouang-Tcheou see
   Kouang-Tchéou-Wan
Kouang-Tchéou see
   Kouang-Tchéou-Wan
Kouang-Tchéou-Wan see
   Kouang-Tchéou-Wan
Köztársaság see Hungary
Krajevina Srbija see Serbia
Kraljevina Jugoslavija see Yugoslavia
Kraljevstvo Srba, Hrvata i Slovenaca
   see Kingdom of the Serbs, Croats and
   Slovenes

K.S.A. see Saudi Arabia
K.S. Pošta see Serbia
K. Srbska Pošta see Serbia
K.U.K. Militärpost see Bosnia and
   Herzegovina
K.U.K. Milit. Verwaltung Montenegro
   see Montenegro
Kurland see Courland
Kuwait, *183*, 31B1(5), 33, 37B1(7)
Kuwait see Kuwait
Kvarner, *137*, 17B1(13), 20
Kwang-tung, *188*, 44
K. Wurtt. Post see Württemberg
Kypros see Cypros

L

La Agüera, *241*, 55A1
La Agüera see La Agüera
Labuan, *188*, 48B2
Labuan see Labuan
La Canea (Cania, Chania), *137*, 23
La Canea see La Canea
La Georgie see Georgia
Lagos, *241*, 60A1, 64, 73A1
Lagos see Lagos
Lajtabánság see Western Hungary
Laos, *188*, 31B2, 37B2, 37b
L.A.R. see Libya
Las Bela, *189*, 49
Las Bela see Las Bela
Latakia, *189*
Lattaquie see Latakia
Latvia, *137*, 17A2, 18
Latvija see Latvia
Latvijas PSR see Latvia
Latvija 1941.1.VII see Latvia
League of Nations, *319*
Lebanon, *189*, 31A1(2), 31b, 37,
   31A1(2), 39, 45
Leeward Islands, *286*, 77, 78B2
Leeward Islands see Leeward Islands
Lemnos, *138*, 23
Lemnos see Lemnos
León, 76
Lero (Leros), *138*, 23a
Lero see Lero
Leros see Lero
Lesotho, 51

Nigeria see Nigeria
Nikolayevsk na Amure/Priamurskoye
 Vremennoye Pravityelstve see
 Priamur District
Nippon see Japan
Nisiro (Nisiros), *144,* 23a
Nisiro see Nisiro
Nisiros see Nisiro
Niue, *305,* 88B2, 95B2, 98
Niue see Niue
Nlle-Calédonie see New Caledonia
Nlle-Calédonie et Dépendances see
 New Caledonia
Norddeutscher Postbezirk see North
 German Confederation
Noreg see Norway
Norfolk Island, *306,* 88B2, 91, 95B2
Norfolk Island see Norfolk Island
Norge see Norway
North Borneo, 196, 48B2
North Borneo see North Borneo
North-Eastern China, *196,* 43
North-Eastern Province of China, *196,*
 42
Northern China (Hwa-Pej,
 Pej-Chung-Kuo), *197,* 43,44
Northern Cook Islands see Cook Islands
Northern Epirus, *144,* 22a
Northern Nigeria, *250,* 60A1, 64
Northern Nigeria see Northern
 Nigeria
Northern Rhodesia, *250,* 55B2
Northern Rhodesia see Northern
 Rhodesia
North German Confederation, *145,* 25
North Ingermanland, *145,* 17A2(1),
 17a, 47(5)
North-Western China, *197,* 43
North Western Pacific Islands, *306,*
 95A1-2
Norway, *145,* 2A1-2, 13A1-2, 17A1,
 22A1, 27A1
Nossi-Bé, *250,* 56, 60B2
Nossi-Bé see Nossi-Bé
Nouvelle-Calédonie et Dépendances
 see New Caledonia
Nouvelles-Hébrides Condominium see
 New Hebrides
Nova Scotia, *289,* 78A2
Nova Scotia see Nova Scotia

N.R. Bulgaria see Bulgaria
N.R. Indonesia see Indonesia
NSB see Nossi-Bé
N. Sembilan see Negri Sembilan
NSW see New South Wales
N.W. Pacific Islands see North Western
 Pacific Islands
Nyasaland, *250,* 60B2
Nyasaland see Nyasaland
Nyasaland Protectorate see
 Nyasaland
Nyassa, *250,* 55B2, 57, 60B2
Nyassa see Nyassa
Nyugat-Magyarország see Western
 Hungary
N.Z. Hrvatska see Croatia

O

Oaxaca, 76
Obock, *251,* 60A2, 62
Obock see Obock
Occupation Française see
 France
Occupation Française du Cameroun
 see French Cameroun
Occupation Militaire Française Cilicie
 see Cilicia
OF Castelloriso see Castelrosso
Oil Rivers, *251,* 60A1(1), 64(1)
Oldenburg, *146,* 25
Oldenburg see Oldenburg
Oltre Giuba see Juba
Oman, *197,* 31B1, 36, 41
Oman Imamate State see Muscat and
 Oman
OMF see Syria
OMF Cilicie see Cilicia
One Anna see Jasdan
One Zone see Schleswig
ONF Castellorizo see Castelrosso
*Only for the Province of Heilungkiang
 and Kirin* see Heilungkiang and
 Kirin
Ono see Niue; Penrhyn
Orange Free State and Orange River
 Colony, *251,* 59, 60B2(5), 73B2(3)
Orange River Colony see Orange Free
 State and Orange River Colony

Republica Mayor de Centro America see El Salvador

Republica Oriental see Uruguay

Republica Oriental del Uruguay see Uruguay

Republica Populară Română see Romania

Republica Popular de Angola see Angola

Republica Portuguesa see Angola; Portugal

República Portuguesa see Timor

Repubblica Sociale Italiana see Italy

Republic of Biafra see Biafra

Republic of Botswana see Botswana

Republic of China see China; Taiwan

Republic of Colombia see Colombia

Republic of Hawaii see Hawaii

Republic of Iraq see Iraq

Republic of Kenya see Kenya

Republic of Korea see Korean Republic

Republic of Maldives see Maldive Islands

Republic of Nauru see Nauru

Republic of Palau see Palau (Belau)

Republic of Sierra Leone sèe Sierra Leone

Republic of Singapore see Singapore

Republic of the Maldive Islands see Maldive Islands

Republic of the Philippines see Philippines

Republiek Stellaland see Stellaland

Republiek Van Suid Afrika/Republic of South Africa see South Africa

Republika Bulgaria see Bulgaria

Republika NG Pilipinas see Philippines

Republika Popullore e Shqiperisë see Albania

Republika Popullore Socialiste e Shqiperisë see Albania

Republika Shqiptare see Albania

Republik Indonesia see Indonesia; West Irian

Republik Österreich see Austria

République Algérienne see Algeria

République Arabe Unie see United Arab Republic − Syria

République Autonome du Togo see Togo

République Centrafricaine see Central African Republic

République d'Azerbaidjan see Azerbaijan

République de Côte d'Ivoire see Ivory Coast

République de Djibouti see Djibouti

République de Guinée see Guinea

République d'Egypte see Egypte

République de Haute-Volta see Upper Volta

République Démocratique du Congo see Congo (Kinshasa)

République Démocratique Populaire Lao see Laos

République des Comores see Comoro Islands

République d'Haïti see Haiti

République du Cameroun see Cameroun

République du Congo see Congo (Brazzaville)

République du Congo see Congo (Kinshasa)

République du Burundi see Burundi

République du Mali see Mali

République du Niger see Niger

République du Sénégal see Senegal

République du Tchad see Chad

République du Togo see Togo

République du Zaire see Zaïre

République Fédérale see Cameroun

République Fédérale du Cameroun see Cameroun

République Fédérale Islamique des Comores see Comoro Islands

République Française see Algeria

République Française see Council of Europe; France; French Colonies; Middle Congo; Unesco

République Française Colonies see French Colonies

République Gabonaise see Gabon

République Georgienne see Georgia

République Islamique de l'Iran see Iran

République Islamique de Mauritanie see Mauritania

République Khmère see Khmer Republic

République Libanaise see Lebanon